The European Company – all over Europe

The European Company – all over Europe

A state-by-state account of the introduction of the European Company

Edited by

Krzysztof Oplustil
Christoph Teichmann

De Gruyter Recht · Berlin

♾ Printed on acid-free paper which falls within the guidelines of the ANSI
to ensure permanence and durability.

ISBN 3-89949-096-7

Bibliografische Information Der Deutschen Bibliothek

Die Deutsche Bibliothek verzeichnet diese Publikation in der Deutschen Nationalbibliografie; detaillierte bibliografische Daten sind im Internet über http://dnb.ddb.de abrufbar.

Data Conversion: Werksatz Schmidt & Schulz, Gräfenhainichen
Printing and Binding: Hubert & Co., Göttingen
Printed in Germany

Preface

On 8 October 2004, the Council Regulation (EC) No. 2157/2001 on the Statute for the European Company (SE) will enter into force. The final shape of the almost 50 years old idea of a „Societas Europaea" is very far from the first drafts of its statutes of 1970 and 1975, which provided for a complete code of the SE including the law of corporate groups and tax law provisions. The final Regulation and the Directive 2001/86/EC supplementing it with regard to the involvement of employees in the SE, are the result of a difficult compromise among Member States which each represent different views on the fundamental institutions of public company law such as company organs or the employee participation in these organs.

Although the Regulation, as such, is directly applicable in each Member State according to Art. 249 EC Treaty, it contains only scanty provisions for a genuine European company law. For the matters not covered by the Regulation, references are made to national public company law and to specific national regulations to be passed for the SEs by the national legislators in the execution of numerous instructions and options (see above all the general reference in Art. 9 para 1 lit. c of the Regulation). In order to make the SE a functional instrument for entrepreneurs and investors, as well as to ensure the effective application of European law, it is necessary to pass national implementation measures by 8 October 2004. National legislators have the opportunity as well as the challenge to shape, in some respect, a national model of the SE which would be attractive for investors and would influence their decision as to where the company be located. Thus, the coming into force of the SE-Regulation will also give "the starting shot" for the competition between national legislators with regard to the law of the European Company.

The aim of the present book is to provide the first indications in those national regulations specifically concerning the SE. Although no national law has so far been finally adopted, the first legislative steps have already been taken in many Member States and first drafts have been published. These drafts are presented in the book by the national experts. Moreover, the authors from Member States where no official drafts so far exist, express their personal reflections on how the specific regulations of national law would and should look. As the ultimate shape of the SE in each Member State will essentially be influenced by the national law of public companies, many reports contained in the book deal also with the provisions of this law. Given the fact that in 2004, when the SE-Regulation comes into force, the European Union will be enlarged by 10 new Member States, the reports cover also some of them, i.e. Poland, Hungary and the Czech Republic.

We express our thanks to all the contributors who proved great commitment to the idea of a European exchange of ideas. As time went by and further drafts or memorandums were published in one or another Member State, many of our authors had to update their contributions once or even twice. Nevertheless, this experience of establishing a working group all over Europe has been rewarding for all of us. Cooperation and even friendship grew and gave rise to other projects, such as the Moot Court at the French Senate in Paris, to a great extent prepared and organised by *Jacques-Louis Colombani* to whom we owe the acknowledgement that he has been the first of us all to extensively think about the European Company – long before the historic breakthrough of Nice came into sight.

Prof. Dr. Dr. h.c. *Peter Hommelhoff*, currently rector of the University of Heidelberg, was the „spiritus rector" of all our efforts and gave us ernormous support – academically and, via the Max-Planck-Preis granted by the Alexander von Humboldt-Foundation, financially, too. The *Alexander von Humboldt-Foundation* is to be mentioned twice, since the Sofja-Kovalevskaja-Award, granted to K. Oplustil filled all the gaps young researchers usually have to face when it comes to budgeting conferences or collections of articles like this one.

Last but not least, our special thanks go to *Austin Dunne*, Solicitor, Munich, who helped us to forge a consistent English style throughout the book and showed endless patience in correcting and commenting on the various styles of the 21 non-native speakers in our team of authors. Responsibility for any possible mistakes in content and language remains, of course, with the editors and the authors.

To publish a book on the implementation of the European Company nine months before the European Regulation comes into force in october 2004 is like shooting on a moving target. We will help our readers not to loose sight of the target: The table survey on national implementation measures at the end of the book (Annex IV) should facilitate the use of this collection; follow-up information will be provided on our website www.se-network.org. Any comments about the book and/or the further development of the law on the European Company are welcome.

Heidelberg/Kraków, December 2003

Dr. Krzysztof Oplustil
(koplustil@wp.pl)
Dr. Christoph Teichmann
(christoph.teichmann@urz.uni-heidelberg.de)

Table of Content

List of Contributors

Austria	Mag. Marie-Agnes Arlt / Mag. Kristoffel Grechenig / Prof. Dr. Susanne Kalss *Wirtschaftsuniversität Wien*
Belgium	Prof. Christoph van der Elst *Universiteit Ghent*
Czech Republic	Prof. JUDr. Irena Pelikánová, DrSc. / Mgr. Petr Čech, LL.M. *Univerzita Karlova – právnická fakulta, Prague*
Denmark	Prof. lic. iur. Søren Friis Hansen *Syddansk Universitet*
France	Dr. Jacques-Louis Colombani *CIMIC Officer (R), Coordinator of expert group on implementation of the SE chaired by Senators Branger and Hyest, Paris*
Germany	Dr. Christoph Teichmann *Institut für deutsches und europäisches Gesellschafts- und Wirtschaftsrecht, Ruprecht-Karls-Universität Heidelberg*
Greece	Prof. Evanghelos Perakis *University of Athens*
Hungary	Gabor Kozma *Solicitor, Budapest*
Ireland	Mr. Rossa Fanning BCL LL.M (NUI) LL.M (Michigan) *Barrister-at-Law, Lecturer, Faculty of Law, University College Dublin*
Italy	Prof. Dr. Federico Pernazza *University of Rome II "Tor Vergata"* Dr. Valentina Allotti *Associazione fra le società italiane per azioni (Assonime)*

The Netherlands Michiel Huizinga, LL.M.
Ruprecht-Karls-Universität Heidelberg
Dr. Martha Meinema
Ministry of Economic Affairs, The Hague

Poland Dr. Krzysztof Oplustil / Dr. Anna Rachwał / Jacek Sokołowski
Uniwersytet Jagiellonski Kraków

Portugal Prof. Rui Pinto Duarte
Faculdade de Direito da Universidade Nova de Lisboa

Spain Prof. Dr. José Maria Muñoz-Paredes
Universidad de Oviedo

Sweden Dr. Paulina Dejmek (LLM.)
Officer, EFTA Surveillance Authority, Brussels

United Kingdom Mike Edbury
Department of Trade and Industry

Austria

Marie-Agnes Arlt/Kristoffel Grechenig/Susanne Kalss

Literature published on the SE in Austria: *Arlt/Bervoets/Grechenig/Kalss* The Societas Europaea in Relation to the Public Corporation of Five Member States (France, Italy, Netherlands, Spain, Austria), European Business Organization Law Review (EBOR) 2002, 737; *Artmann* Die Organisationsverfassung der Europäischen Aktiengesellschaft, Wirtschaftliche Blätter (wbl) 2002, 190f; *Doralt* Die Europäische Aktiengesellschaft Societas Europaea, lecture on Walther Kastner Gedenksymposion on June 28, 2002 (http://recht.wu-wien.ac.at); *Kalss* Der Minderheitenschutz bei Gründung und Sitzverlegung der SE im Diskussionsentwurf, in Zentrum für Europäisches Wirtschaftsrecht, Europäische AG und der Disskussionsentwurf zum deutschen Begleitgesetz, Volume 135, (2003) 5,29ff; (also published in Zeitschrift für Gesellschafts- und Unternehmensrecht [ZGR] 5–6/2003); *Schindler* Die Europäische Aktiengesellschaft, Wien 2002; *Schindler* Vor einem Ausführungsgesetz zur Europäischen Aktiengesellschaft, ecolex 2003, Heft 06, Script 26, 1; *Torggler* Zur Europäischen Gesellschaft (SE), ecolex 2001, 442 and 533.

I. Introduction

Discussion of the opportunities offered by the SE to the Austrian economy commenced soon after the Nice summit in December 2000. While the discussion was led by academics, some law-firms considering the SE an opportunity to develop their international practice participated.

In summer 2002, the Austrian Ministry of Justice established a working group to draft an Austrian law to complement the Regulation of the European Council of October 2001. The Ministry also set up a second group which deals with the more "political issues", i.e. the corporate structure (two-tier and one-tier system; relation of day-to-day-management and management in general of the administrative organ; the question of making use of the option in Art. 43 par. 4; design of the structure of the day-to-day managing organ consisting only of members of the board etc.) and employees' co-determination, in particular on the one-tier board. The second group consists of representatives of various pressure groups (chamber of commerce, chamber of employees, association of entrepreneurs, lawyers, notaries, judges of the commercial court of Vienna and some outstanding academics). The smaller working group consists of civil servants of the Ministry, a judge of the commercial court (commercial register) and some academics (commercial and corporate law). They discuss in detail, general and also more technical questions about the foundation of the SE and the transfer of seat. At the end of August 2003 the Ministry of Justice distributed the first working-draft to the members of the larger working group. By beginning of 2004 the draft was finished after drastic amentments.

In the Ministry of Labour and Economic Affairs, another group is working on the co-determination aspects; the two working groups of the different ministries meet regularly and continuously consult on appropriate solutions for the co-determination on the board.

II. Basic considerations

The implementation of the Regulation and – from the point of view of European law – the Austrian rules required to supplement the Regulation are the main focus. The Ministry has already decided to confine reform generally to the matters required by the Regulation, while also developing the Austrian Stock Corporation law in substance (option for one tier system) and availing of some of the options provided by the Regulation and dealing with some small legislative deficiencies which have become apparent. Finally, the extent of reforms depends on the pressure of interest groups and the current political climate.

The Regulation is based on the theory of the real seat (Art. 7). The famous *Centros*[1] *judgement* of the European Court of Justice has been developed further by the Austrian Supreme Court; the Court has held that section 10 of the Austrian National Private Law Act will be overruled by the freedom of establishment within the European Union and the European Economic Area.[2] In addition, the *Überseering BV* judgement of the ECJ[3] guarantees freedom of establishment fully not only to natural persons but also to companies.[4] Although the Austrian legislator is aware of the European and national court decisions, the real seat theory laid down in Art. 7 of the Regulation will not be contested and the supplementary national rules will be shaped according to the concept of the Regulation. The Austrian law will not extend the scope of application of the Regulation to companies outside of the EU (Art 2 section 5 of the Regulation).

[1] ECJ I-1459.

[2] Austrian Supreme Court, Der Gesellschafter 1999, 248, s *Bachner/Winner* Das österreichische internationale Gesellschaftsrecht nach Centros, Der Gesellschafter 2000, 73 et seq.

[3] ECJ C-208/00.

[4] See also the most recent case General Attorney, 30.1.2003 C-167/01 Kamer van Koophandel en Fabrieken voor Amsterdam/Inspire Art Ltd.

The Austrian legislator should make available the one-tier-system not only for an Austrian SE but also for national stock corporations; every company should be entitled to opt for the one-tier-system in the articles. However, the final draft distributed in January 2004 abstains from introducing that option for the national stock corporation and thereby passes up the opportunity to accelerate national corporate law development.

To same extend the Act deals with aspects arising only indirectly from the SE-Regulation but which will then apply not only to national companies but also to the SE. According to the on-going discussion, the legislator avails of the opportunity to progress the development of corporate law in small steps[5]: foundation of a public company by one person (until now only a private limited company can be founded by one person, with one exception: if all shareholders but one leave the company, a public company can continue to exist and need not be wound up); a minor amendment of the special procedure to assess the adequacy of the exchange ratio (merger) and the appraisal right, a clear-cut rule on the winding-up of a company by decision of the court (*Amtslöschung*); regulation of the use of information technology for board-meetings and finally, the possibility that a company can transfer its assets and liabilities to another company in exchange for the allocation of shares of the recipient company to the transferring company (not to the shareholders) directly (*Ausgliederung durch Gesamtrechtsnachfolge*).[6]

The working committee focused on corporate law issues notwithstanding the fact that other fields of law have to be kept in mind: in particular, the take-over code and other regulations of securities law (disclosure of major shareholdings, directors' dealings, insider-dealing, compliance etc.). As Art. 10 of the Regulation states that an SE shall be treated as a public limited liability company, it is not necessary to draft special regulations applicable to the SE, but to explore the implications of the application of securities and take-over law to the SE.

The question of co-determination in general and the role of representatives of the employees on the supervisory board or on the administrative organ is only to a certain extent an issue of the working group, because another group set up by the Ministry of Labour and Economic affairs is dealing in detail with the whole field of co-determination (negotiating process etc); nevertheless, the two groups must find a common position about the relationship between the representatives of the shareholders and the employees on the board, in the final

[5] The "policy of small steps" is a quite typical Austrian technique to shape corporate law; cf. only *Kalss/Burger/Eckert* Die Entwicklung des österreichischen Aktienrechts (Linde Verlag Wien 2003) 42.

[6] See below IV.6.

draft. From the point of view of corporate law, the crucial point lies in the question of how to shape the competencies of the administrative organ, the relationship between the board of directors and the day-to-day management and the weight of voting rights of the single members (see under III Organisation).

The working group does not deal with general questions of the raising and maintenance of capital; again Art. 5 of the Regulation will be the key for application of the relevant rules for national public companies to the SE. Further steps to rethink the current concept of capital-maintenance should and must be taken together on the European level.[7]

III. Organisational structure of the SE

1. Implementation of the Regulation

As the choice between the one-tier and the two-tier system is mandatorily[8] offered by Art. 38 of the Council Regulation, the Austrian legislator has to offer both models and will make use of the possibility to concretise the different organisational structures. Since 1938 the Austrian legal model is the dualistic system.[9] Austria must, therefore, provide statutory rules, within the framework of the Regulation, integrating the monistic model into existing law. The so-called precept of equal treatment in the fifth recital has to be taken into account, any differences in the treatment of the national stock corporation and the European Company has to be justified by serious factual reasons.[10] The Austrian legislator, therefore, will introduce the monistic system which will be on a par with the dualistic system. As the organisational structure of the na-

[7] See only the recommendations of the final report of the High Level Group of Company law experts of Nov 4, 2002; www.europa.eu.int/comm/internal_market/de/company/company/modern/index.htm; printed in parts also in Neue Zeitschrift für Gesellschaftsrecht 2003, 22; or the proposals put forward by the SLIM-group; *Maul* Vorschläge der Expertengruppe zur Reform des Gesellschaftsrechts, Der Betrieb 2003, 27.

[8] *Artmann*, wbl 2002, 190f; *Hommelhoff* Einige Bemerkungen zur Organisationsverfassung der Europäischen Aktiengesellschaft, AG 2001, 282; *Teichmann* Die Einführung der Europäischen Aktiengesellschaft. Grundlagen der Ergänzung des europäischen Statuts durch den deutschen Gesetzgeber, ZGR 2002, 383, 400, 442; *Hopt* Europäsiche Aktiengesellschaft – per aspera ad astra?, EuZW 01/2002, editorial; *Arlt/Bervoets/Grechenig/Kalss*, EBOR 2002, 737.

[9] Until 1938 the Austrian corporation law has known the option of an alternative between the two organisational structures. In practice the monistic system was preferred: *Kalss/Burger/Eckert* (see note 5), 264 et seq, 317, 328; *Kastner* Zu den legistischen Aufgaben auf dem Gebiet des österreichischen Gesellschaftsrechts, Juristische Blätter 1990, 547.

[10] See also *Teichmann*, ZGR 2002, 401.

tional stock corporation could be freely chosen up to 1938,[11] the Austrian legislator will take into account its historical background and experiences. However, as the SE is a European company, it is very important to take into account comparative work and to analyse foreign legal systems, i.e. the Spanish and Swiss system that already know the one-tier board system as well as the French and Italian systems that are characterised by the choice between different organisational structures.[12]

2. National aspects

The main national factors to be taken into account in the legislation implementing the SE in Austria are (i) the legal concept of the national stock corporation and (ii) the economic situation of the Austrian capital market, (iii) competition between jurisdictions and (iv) the possibility and probability of circumventing Austrian Corporate law.

(i) The political question is whether the Austrian legislator will modernise the organisational structure of the Austrian stock corporation or not. The answer to this question requires a differentiated analysis of Austrian stock corporation law.

The Stock Corporation Act[13] considers the stock corporation as a publicly owned company – a legal entity that brings together many small shareholders to contribute the necessary share capital (*Kapitalsammelbecken*).[14] Although the Austrian Stock Corporation Act applies in generall equally to listed and non-listed companies, the stock corporation is de facto divided into listed and non-listed stock corporations with different rules (single regulations of Stock corpo-

[11] *Kalss/Burger/Eckert* (see note 5), 264 et seq, 317, 328.

[12] *Leyens* Deutscher Aufsichtsrat und U.S.-Board: ein- oder zweistufiges Verwaltungssystem? Zum Stand der rechtsvergleichenden Corporate Governance-Debatte, RabelsZ 67 (2003), 57 (59) gloss 1.

[13] BGBl 1965/98 idF BGBl 2001/98.

[14] See *Kalss* Anlegerinteressen. Der Anleger im Handlungsdreieck von Vertrag, Verband und Markt, Wien, New York: Springer 2001, 63; *Kalss/Burger/Eckert* (see note 5), 315 et seq, 347 et seq; *Lutter* Anteilseigner und Unternehmen in *Lutter/Semler*, Rechtsgrundlagen freiheitlicher Unternehmenswirtschaft 1990, 16, 25; *Roth* GmbH und AG: Versuch einer Neuorientierung in Roth, Das System der Kapitalgesellschaften im Umbruch – ein internationaler Vergleich. GmbH, AG und entsprechende Gesellschaftsformen in Deutschland, Frankreich, Grossbritannien, Italien, Japan, Kanada, Österreich, der Schweiz, den USA und im Recht der EG, Köln: Otto Schmidt 1990, 1.
Bär looks upon the major shareholder as *untypical*; *Bär* Grundprobleme des Minderheitenschutzes in der Aktiengesellschaft, ZBJV 1959, 405 cited after *Nobel* Börsengesellschaftsrecht?, Bär-FS 1998, 302.

ration law and securities law).[15] The importance of this distinction lies in the different purposes of the protection intended by the norms.

As the legal archetype of the Austrian Stock Corporation is the publicly held stock corporation, the Stock Corporation Act is characterised by *ius cogens* (*gesetzliche Satzungsstrenge*) that is considered as an important element for the functioning of the stock corporation and the prerequisite for creating tradable securities.[16]

Notwithstanding that listed and non-listed stock corporations are regulated by the same law, the addressee (ie different types of shareholders) and the function (protection of the interests of the shareholders) are totally different. The mandatory character of the Stock Corporation Act, therefore, and its mandatory organisational structure applicable to non-listed companies, should be reconsidered.

(ii) The legal stock corporation model can more or less not be found in the Austrian reality. Instead the "closed" stock corporation, held by one or two major shareholders, is rather the typical ownership structure. In December 2001, about 110 companies out of totally 1400 were listed at the Vienna Stock Exchange;[17] the majority of Austrian stock corporations do not obtain capital on the capital market. At the same time, the stock corporations are almost always held by one or two major shareholders (group, family) that dominate the company's strategy.[18] Compared to the European average the concentration of shares and voting rights in the hand of one shareholder is highest in Austria.[19] The introduction of the one-tier-system which entails a stronger influence of the shareholder will therefore approximate the legal rules to the requirements of practice and reality.

[15] *Kalss* Special duties and responsibilities of companies with public securities, International and comparative corporate Law Journal, 2000, 385 cont; for the European tendency see *Wymeersch* Gesellschaftsrecht im Wandel: Ursachen und Entwicklungslinien, ZGR 2001, 304 et seq; *Roth* (see note 14), 9 et seq.

[16] *Kalss* Anlegerintressen (see note 14), 46 cont; *Hirte* Die aktienrechtliche Satzungsstrenge: Kapitalmarkt und sonstige Legitimationen versus Gestaltungsfreiheit in Lutter/Wiedemann, Gestaltungsfreiheit im Gesellschaftsrecht, ZGR-Sonderheft 1998, 61 cont, *Roth* (see note 14), 14 et seq; *Beier* Der Regelungsauftrag als Gesetzgebungsinstrument im Gesellschaftsrecht, Köln, Berlin, Bonn, München: Heymanns 2002, 43.

[17] For monthly statistics of the Vienna Stock Exchange see www.wienerboerse.at/cms/1/18, for annual statistics see www.wiederboerse.at/cmy/1/19.

[18] *Gugler/Kalss/Stomper/Zechner* The Separation of Ownership and Control in Austria in Barca/Becht, The Control of Corporate Europe, New York: Oxford University Press 2001, 49.

[19] *Gugler/Kalss/Stomper/Zechner* The Separation of Ownership and Control in Austria in Barca/Becht, The Control of Corporate Europe, New York: Oxford University Press 2001, 58.

(iii) However, the modernisation of the Austrian Stock Corporation Act is also required because of the fact that the Societas Europaea will probably increase competition between jurisdictions[20] and economic locations, because of its "artificial pyramids of legal layers".[21] The mixture of legal sources has as the consequence that the national Stock Corporation Acts of the different Member States will characterise the different European companies because each will be subject to the law of the Member State in which its registered office is located.[22] Other reasons for the future competition are the *Centros*, *Überseering* and *Inspire Art*[23] judgements of the ECJ which have (indirectly) postulated the free choice between legal systems.[24]

[20] The competition of lawmakers will not obligatorily cause the so-called Delaware effect or a race to the bottom (see i.e. *Bebchuk/Hamdani* Vigorous Race or Leisurely Walk: Reconsidering the Debate in State Competition over Corporate Charters, Disscussion Paper No. 376, 2002, www.law.harvard.edu/programs/olin_center, 12; *Bebchuk/Cohen* Incorporation Choices and the Market for Corporate Law, 2001, http://kuznets.fas.harvard.edu/~acohen/Incorporation.Nov29.pdf, 6 et seq; *Forstinger* Delawares komparative Vorteile. Warum Delaware auch in Zukunft der führende In- und Reinkorporationsstaat der USA bleiben wird, ZfRV 2002, 42; *Merkt* Das Europäische Gesellschaftsrecht und die Idee des "Wettbewerbs der Gesetzgeber", RabelsZ 1995, 539 et seq); but also a race to the top is possible (*Merkt* Das Europäische Gesellschaftsrecht und die Idee des "Wettbewerbs der Gesetzgeber", RabelsZ 1995, 547; *Hopt* Europäisches Gesellschaftsrecht – Krise und neue Anläufe, ZIP 1998, 98 (gloss 44), 99). As the initial situation (different languages, harmonisation within the European Union ...) and because of the so-called path dependency (see i.e. *Bebchuck/Roe* A theory of path dependence in corporate ownership and governance, Discussion Paper No. 266 10/99, www.law.harvard.edu/programs/ olin_center; *Heine/Kerber* European Corporate Laws, Regulatory Competition and Path Dependence, European Journal of Law and Economics 13/2002, 47 et seq) the impact of the competition will evidently not be the same; see also *Arlt/Bervoets/Grechenig/Kalss*, EBOR 2002, 550 et seq.

[21] *Hommelhoff* Einige Bemerkungen zur Organisationsverfassung der Europäischen Aktiengesellschaft, AG 2002, 284 et seq.

[22] In this regard *Doralt* compares the SE with a centaur with a national (law) body and with the head of the European harmonised law; *Doralt* Die Europäische Aktiengesellschaft Societas Europaea, lecture on Walther Kastner Gedenksymposion on June 28, 2002 (http://recht.wu-wien.ac.at); *Teichmann* Die Einführung der Europäischen Aktiengesellschaft. Grundlagen und Ergänzung des europäischen Statuts durch den deutschen Gesetzgeber, ZGR 2002, 364 et seq; *Brandt/Schleifele* Die Europäische Aktiengesellschaft und das anwendbare Recht, DStR 2002, 547; *Artmann*, wbl 2002, 197.

[23] ECJ from 30.3.2003 C-167/01, Kamer van Koophandel en Fabrieken voor Amsterdam/Inspire Art Ltd, Slg 2003; see i.e. *Adensamer/Bervoets*, Nationaler Gläubigerschutz auf dem Prüfstand. Die Entscheidung des EuGH in der Rs. "Inspire Art", RdW 2003, 617 et seq.

[24] Because of the real seat theory and the impossibility of corporation's free movement *Merkt* considered the competition of lawmakers within the European Union as implau-

Although competition must not be the (only) benchmark for legislation,[25] the legislators will, and must, react.

(iv) Art. 35, in conjunction with Art. 2 para. 4 of the Council Regulation, offers the formation of an SE as a subsidiary of every legal entity. The modernisation is therefore important to prevent SE-subsidiaries being incorporated only to avoid the mandatory norms of national corporate law; that requires regulation of the organisational structure.

For these reasons, the Austrian legislator will be well advised to introduce an option between the one-tier board and the two-tier board system.

3. Probable legislative measures concerning the organisational structure

As the two-tier system is already well established for the national stock corporation, the Austrian legislator will avail only of the option, provided by the Regulation, of limiting the number of members of the supervisory board and the enumeration in the statutes of transactions that require the authorisation of the supervisory board.

In order to shape the one-tier system Austria will make use of the option and – at the same time obligation – offered by Art. 43 para. 4 of the Council Regulation.

First of all, the Austrian administrative organ (*Verwaltungsrat*) will consist of at least three members. Additionally, Austria will probably make use of the possibility of providing a day-to-day management offered by Art. 43 para. 4 of the Council Regulation. The administrative organ generally will be entitled to appoint either executive directors (*Geschäftsführer*) or keep the day-to-day management within the board. Listed companies will not only be entitled but obliged to appoint executive directors. While the board will, at the same time, be the strategic organ that determines long-term strategy and business policy, the executive directors will take over the day-to-day management.[26] Executive directors may be chosen from among administrative organ or, alternatively,

sible (*Merkt* Das Europäische Gesellschaftsrecht und die Idee des "Wettbewerbs der Gesetzgeber", RabelsZ 1995, 567), these obstacles seem to be eliminated.
By the way, the incorporation theory supports the competition; *Wymeersch* Gesellschaftsrecht im Wandel: Ursachen und Entwicklungslinien, ZGR 2001, 308.

[25] *Wiedemann* Gesellschaftsrecht I, München: Beck 1980, 783; *Ebke* Ein Gesellschaftsrecht für Europa? in 75 Jahre Max Planck Institut-FS, (2001), 204 et seq.; *Kalss/Burger/Eckert* (see note 5), 27et seq., 375.

[26] In this context one has to mention § 95 para. 2 no. 8 Austrian Stock Corporation Act which determines a comparative power for the supervisory board.

external executive directors can be appointed. However, executive directors cannot form the majority on the board, nor can the chairman of the board be an executive director.

In addition, committees should be established by the administrative organ. A similar regulation is also provided by § 92 para. 4 of the Austrian Stock Corporation Act, under which specialised committees are established. While specific matters of the day-to-day management may be fulfilled by single members or even a committee, the business management as such cannot be determined by an individual committee. As the employees' participation is located in the board (in the dualistic system on the supervisory board), there will not be any participation in the day-to-day management if external executive directors are established. Co-determination is foreseen at the board at large and in the specialised committees of the board.

Other subject areas that have to be discussed concerning the implementation of the one-tier system in general and with regard to the Austrian stock corporation has to be brought in line with the general principles of the Stock Corporation Act and should differ from the already existing dualistic system only if the monistic system does require separate regulations. Apart from the drafting of the monistic system for the SE, there is the intention by the legislator for the introduction of this model also as an option for the national stock corporation.[27] Apart from the discussion of employees' participation, several unsolved questions arise, although a general tendency towards a solution can already be identified.

Due to the lack of a separate supervisory board (*Aufsichtsrat*) in the monistic system, the powers of this board have to be executed by another organ. The powers of the general meeting of the shareholders could be strengthened while the establishment of different committees and of independent or executive directors could be envisaged. Austria makes use of the authorisation in Art. 48 para. 2 of the Council Regulation and enumerates transactions which must at least be indicated in the statutes of the SEs. Austria already provides a catalogue of matters which require a resolution by the supervisory board.[28] The same question arises if the administrative organ also will have such mandatory powers.

[27] The SE would then fit completely into the system for national corporations.

[28] § 95 para. 2 Austrian Stock Corporation Act.

4. Employee participation

As already mentioned above, a special working group set up by the Ministry of Labour and Economic Affairs is dealing with the implementation of the Directive concerning worker-participation in the SE. A draft of the Austrian regulations has already been presented, regulating the negotiating process, the nomination of representatives and the influence of the promoting companies and the representative bodies of the employees in the different companies. However, the two drafts have been coordinated at a very late stage only.

The influence and the power of the employees depend not only on the implementation of the Directive but to the same extent on the decision of the national legislator (of corporate law) to shape the one-tier structure; the weight of influence of the worker-representatives depends therefore on whether Austrian law offers more alternatives to set-up a one-tier system and not only the system with the board and extern executive directors according to Art. 43 of the Regulation. The two-tier system probably will not be changed.

IV. Some details on the formation and transfer of the SE

1. General considerations

The Regulation is based on the concept of a *numerus clausus* of techniques by which the SE may be formed;[29] although the Regulation does not only enumerate the different ways of formation, but regulates different aspects quite in detail, the national legislators have to complement the Regulation to make the formation process operable. The different forms have therefore to be analysed in detail and embedded into the national law. The scope of additional national rules depends on the formation method chosen:

- Merger SE created from at least 2 national public companies of at least two different states;
- Holding SE created from at least 2 national public companies or companies with limited liability of at least two different states;
- Subsidiary-SE created from at least 2 national companies according to Art. 48 of the Treaty or other public or private legal bodies of of at least two different states;
- Transformation SE from one national public company;
- Subsidiary SE, created by separation from a parent SE.

[29] See only *Hommelhoff*, AG 2001, 279.

Two main peculiarities – at least for some of the different ways of formation – have to be kept in mind:

The cross-border aspect, and therefore, the clear-cut separation of national competence to regulate the rights and duties of the transferring company and the recipient company.

Whereas a national merger or creating a holding falls within the competence of one jurisdiction, so that the material rules and the provisions of enforcement fit well together, in many cases the SE-formation procedure takes place in at least two different Member States. Therefore (i) the substantial law must be harmonised – at least to a certain extent – and (ii) it must be guaranteed that the responsible authorities are working closely together to avoid any gap in the controlling- and registration procedure. Because of the cross-border character of the individual formation procedures[30] one has – at least intellectually – to separate the transferring (and leaving) aspect of a merger or similar transaction and the receiving (and arriving) aspect. The Member State cannot regulate the merger (or creation of a holding) as a whole, from the first disclosure of information to the last steps of registration and disclosure of the final act, but the national legislator has to regulate only "one side" of the whole transaction – either the transferring or the receiving company and the affected shareholders and creditors. Only one part of the whole procedure takes place in the territory of one Member State. The national rules must then be so co-ordinated with other national rules that the transnational aspect can be realised. The foundation of the SE is therefore enriched with the aspect of the cross-border transfer of the seat, so that the regulations dealing with national measures must be complemented by rules arising out of the need for creditor-protection and shareholder protection in this very special situation. Art. 8 of the Regulation (transfer of seat) and all its detailed rules must therefore be kept in mind for the different formation forms.

2. Transfer of the registered office

a) Basis for the formation of an SE

The transfer of the registered office functions as a basis for the formation of an SE by companies located in a different Member State than the future SE. Issues of shareholder and creditor protection should be regulated homogeneously.

The international transfer of the registered office of a national company is not regulated under current Austrian company law. Austrian private inter-

[30] *Hommelhoff*, AG 2001, 279.

national law basically follows the *Sitztheorie* (real seat theory) and prohibits the international transfer. Within the European Union, however, the freedom of movement allows (national) companies to transfer their seats within EU borders.[31]

b) Protection of minority shareholders – Appraisal right

Apart from a well-established regime of minority shareholder protection consisting of information in advance and participation in the decision,[32] the Regulation leaves to the Member States the option to establish further minority rights. Although the intention of the European legislature is rather concealed (in Art. 25 p. 3), by citing the judicial review of the appraisal, it is quite clear that the Regulation offers the possibility to the Member States of regulating an appraisal right for the minority shareholders who oppose the transfer of seat.[33]

Due to possible disadvantages for the shareholders (language problems, distance, different applicable law), the Austrian legislator will make use of the option to provide for an appraisal right, i.e. the shareholders can exit the company and get the real value of their shares refunded. Austria might provide for an unconditional appraisal right, i.e. without additional requirements apart from the international transfer of the registered office, or an appraisal right for just cause.[34] In the second case, the legislator would have to provide this majority right explicitly only for specific causes (language problems, distance, loss of shareholder rights, etc). It seems to us, that an unconditional appraisal right is a

[31] See "Centros" European Court of Justice, C-212/97, Der Gesellschafter (GesRZ) 1999, 248; "Überseering" European Court of Justice C-208/00; for Austria see the judgements of the Supreme Court: OGH 15. 7. 1999, 6 Ob 124/99z (wbl 2000/60) and OGH 11. 11. 1999, 6 Ob 122/99f (ecolex 2000/288). *Lutter* in *Lutter*, $UmwG^2$ 138–139; *Kalss* Anlegerinteressen (see note 14), 497; *Behrens* Die Umstrukturierung von Unternehmen durch Sitzverlegung oder Fusion über die Grenze im Licht der Niederlassungsfreiheit im Europäischen Binnenmarkt (Art. 52 und 58 EWGV), Zeitschrift für Gesellschafts- und Unternehmensrecht (ZGR) 1994, 15–21. See above II (b).

[32] Look *Hommelhoff/Riesenhuber* Strukturmaßnahmen, insbesondere Verschmelzung und Spaltung im Europäischen und deutschen Gesellschaftsrecht in Grundmann, Systembildung und Systemlücken in Kerngebieten des Europäischen Privatrechts (2000), 272 et seq.

[33] *Kalss* Anlegerinteressen (see note 14), 498; see also *Lutter* in *Lutter*, $UmwG^2$ 141–142; *Wiedemann* Das Abfindungsrecht – ein gesellschaftsrechtlicher Interessenausgleich, ZGR 1978, 489.

[34] *Kalss* Der Minderheitenschutz bei Gründung und Sitzverlegung der SE im Diskussionsentwurf, in Zentrum für Europäisches Wirtschaftsrecht, Europäische AG und der Disskussionsentwurf zum deutschen Begleitgesetz, Volume 135, (2003) 5,29ff; (also published in ZGR 5–6/2003 p. 593).

better guarantee of a secure legal position, specifically with regard to its practical use. In most cases, the formation of an SE will trigger sufficient justification to exit the company.

However, in specific situations an unconditional appraisal right could contradict the European freedom of movement, i.e. when a considerable number of shareholders intends to exit a company which cannot afford their claims. Due to the obligation of the company to pay the shareholders the real value of their shares, the appraisal right could make it practically impossible for the company to transfer its registered office. Consequently, the company has the right to urge that the withdrawal of a considerable number of shareholders would be a hardship for the company and apply that the exit be disallowed, if shareholders do not suffer significant disadvantages (language, distance, shareholder rights and the whole legal framework). The Austrian legislator could explicitly provide for such an exception to the unconditional appraisal right. Due to European requirements and their direct effects, however, this does not seem to be necessary.

The Austrian legislator will not distinguish between listed and non-listed companies concerning the issue of appraisal rights. Shareholders of listed companies could, in principle, exit the company by selling their shares and withdrawing from the company via the capital market. However, this concept requires a fully functioning capital market with sufficient free float in all companies. Although European law requires a certain dispersion of the company's ownership,[35] Austrian companies hardly ever meet such requirements – most Austrian companies have very little free float.[36] A limitation of the appraisal right to non-listed companies would not, therefore, be an adequate response to the current economic situation.[37]

c) *Protection of creditors*

The SE-Regulation regulates creditor protection prior to the registration of the company. Art. 8 paragraph 7 requires from the companies that the interests of creditors are adequately protected before the certificate is issued by the authorities.[38] This refers to all liabilities that have arisen before the publication of the

[35] See *Kalss/Zollner* Stück- und Namensaktien aus börsenrechtlicher Sicht, ÖBA 2002, 597 et seq. with regard to the Directive 34/2001, May 28, 2001.

[36] See above III (Organization).

[37] Besides, the possibility to sell the shares would not fully replace the right to be paid the value of the shares, because shareholders who sell their shares will only receive the value of their shares after the company's intentions have become known; see *Ruffner* Die ökonomischen Grundlagen eines Rechts der Publikumsgesellschaft (2000), 198.

[38] With regard to national mergers, current Austrian company law provides for protec-

transfer proposal. As provided for in the Regulation, Austria could extend this point of time to the time of registration of the transfer as is the case for (national) mergers,[39] so that all creditors, whose claims have arisen before the registration of the transfer, are protected. Austria will probably choose a different point of time, e.g. one that covers all liabilities that have arisen up to one month after the resolution of the general meeting (this point of time will probably be before the registration). However, one decisive difference between national and international mergers has to be kept in mind – the protection of creditors will be applicable before the registration only with regard to the international merger, whereas, in the case of national mergers, the creditors enjoy this protection only after the registration.

Under Austrian company law, creditors of merging companies must provide credible evidence that their claims are prejudiced in order to obtain security for their claims from the company. As Art. 8 par. 16 SE Reg. broadly protects creditors interests, the required evidence will be harder to bring forward with regard to the international transfer of an SE.

d) *Qualified majority*

As for (national) mergers, the transfer of the registered office requires a qualified majority of three fourths of the shares present (or represented) in the general meeting, as an Austrian company generally requires this majority for modifications of the statutes.[40] This requirement prevents a withdrawal of more than 25% of the shareholders, as shareholders may only exit the company if they have opposed the transfer and therefore must have participated in the general meeting. Consequently, the requirement of a qualified majority also protects the creditors' interests, as it limits the maximum loss of capital. Another vehicle to avoid the outflow of capital will be the possibility that not only the company itself but also a third person (parent company) can take over the shares and pay the compensation to the withdrawing shareholders.

tion (through securities) subsequent to the registration (§ 226 AktG); see *Kalss* Verschmelzung – Spaltung – Umwandlung (1997), § 226 No. 6 and 11.

[39] § 226 AktG. See *Kalss* (see note 38), § 226 No. 4.

[40] Art. 8 par. 6 refers to Art. 59 of the SE-Regulation. Consequently the national norms apply, if the legislators do not make use of the option given by Art. 59 par. 2 SE-Regulation. Art. 146 Austrian Stock Corporation Act requires a majority of 3/4 of the present (or represented) shareholders.

3. Conversion

The discussion of the smaller working group mainly concentrated on the formation of an SE by merger as well as the transfer of seat within the European Union. Nevertheless the conversion of and into an SE triggers several questions.

As a matter of fact, one has to differentiate between the conversion of an existing public limited-liability company into an SE (Art. 37 of the Council Regulation) and the (re-)conversion of an SE into a public limited-liability company (Art. 66 of the Council Regulation).[41] Both lead to the change of the legal form of the company. As a consequence, the applicable law will change from national law to the mixture of national and European law. The difference between these two types of companies is rather slight, therefore the Regulation does not offer additional minority rights, in particular an exit right (in contrast to the transfer of seat, merger and creation of a holding).

A conversion may, therefore, take place after the fulfilment of the information duties and the shareholder's general meeting has approved the conversion. The Austrian legislator shaped some regulations dealing with the preparation of the conversion.

The (financial) audit of the conversion by an independent expert regulated by Art. 37 para. 6 of the Council Regulation, is already required by the Austrian Stock Corporation Act.[42]

4. Formation by merger

a) *Elements of the merger*

The formation by merger consists of three elements to be considered when analysing devices for shareholder and creditor protection and when adopting provisions concerning procedural issues. The formation by merger consists of a transfer of the registered office of the acquired company, a conversion of the merging companies from a national stock corporation to a European Company and the transfer of assets of the acquired companies into one SE (actual merger). However, these three elements do not apply to all of the merging companies. The acquiring company does not transfer its registered office, thus its creditors and shareholders are not affected to the same extent. Consequently, protection devices as well as procedural problems need to be discussed and

[41] See *Oplustil/Schneider* Zur Stellung der Europäischen Aktiengesellschaft im Umwandlungsrecht, Neue Zeitschrift für Gesellschaftsrecht (NZG) 2003, 13 cont.

[42] *Jabornegg* in Schiemer/Jabornegg/Strasser, AktG^3 (1993) § 247 number 9.

regulated separately for each of the companies, depending on their role as an acquiring company or company that is being acquired.[43]

b) Technical problems in the procedure

Several problems arise when it comes to practical issues in the procedure. The Council Regulation requires that the Member States determine a court, notary or other authority that issues a certificate conclusively confirming the completion of the pre-merger acts and formalities (Art. 68 and 25). Under Austrian law, only the court of the acquiring company is competent. With regard to the SE, the courts of the other involved companies have to provide this certificate. The Austrian legislator should concentrate this competence at the commercial register that administers the registration of the relevant company. A further concentration of competences at only one register in Austria (for example, Vienna) does not seem to be necessary.

To register the SE, national authorities must examine a foreign certificate – different languages may cause difficulties. The Austrian legislator should require that the company submit the certificate translated by a certified translator when applying for registration.

Austrian company law provides for a concentrated procedure concerning national mergers, which applies to the SE as far as two of the merging companies are located within national borders. The competent court of the acquired company stays proceedings and sends the documents to the competent court of the acquiring company, which examines the lawfulness of the procedure with regard to both companies.[44]

c) Shareholder protection

(1) Obstacles for the shareholders as a consequence of the formation by merger

Two different issues are involved in shareholder protection on the formation of an SE by merger. Firstly, the protection of shareholders of the acquiring company and secondly, the protection of shareholders of the acquired company which does not have its registered office in the Member State of the future SE.[45] With regard to the second issue, shareholders have to face the same disadvan-

[43] For a more precise distinction see below.

[44] § 225 AktG (Austrian Stock Corporation Act), see *Kalss* (see note 38), § 225 No. 20.

[45] Acquired companies that have their registered offices in the same country as the future SE, have to be equally treated as the acquiring company, concerning international aspects of protection devices.

tages that result from an international transfer of the registered office. Consequently, these issues have to be regulated homogeneously.[46] Austrian company law provides for a regime of prior information, rules for decision-making and additional shareholder rights, such as the right to initiate a procedure to review the share-exchange ratio[47], subsequent to the merger. The information requirements and the rules for decision-making are determined by the third directive and the SE-Regulation.

(2) *Report requirements*

The information of shareholders will be regulated as in the case of national mergers. Austrian company law provides for a report by the management board, by the supervisory board and by an independent expert. The report of the supervisory organ is a specific requirement of the Austrian legal system, as the organisational structure follows a two-tier system.[48] It is also intended to protect the interests of employees;[49] consequently, the shareholders cannot waive this requirement.[50] The supervisory board reports on the legality and the economic purpose of the merger.

(3) *Resolution of the general meeting and corporate groups*

The formation of an SE by merger requires a resolution by the general meetings of *all* of the merging companies.[51] Current Austrian company law requires a majority of 75% of the shareholders present at the general meeting.[52] With regard to corporate groups, Austrian company law excludes the competence of the general meeting of the acquiring company.[53] The Austrian legislator cannot apply this legal provision to the formation of an SE, as the Regulation refers to

46 See for more details: *Kalss* Der Minderheitenschutz bei Gründung und Sitzverlegung der SE im Diskussionsentwurf.

47 See below (4).

48 See the exception mentioned in § 220c par. 1 second sentence; *Kalss* (see note 38), § 220c, No. 7.

49 *Kalss* (see note 38), § 220c, No. 1 and No. 7.

50 For possible exceptions in corporate groups, see below.

51 Explicitly Art. 23 paragraph. 1 Council Regulation.

52 This requirement meets with the Arts. 57 and 59 of the Council Regulation. See above transfer.

53 *Kalss* (see note 38), § 231, No. 5 et seq. Art. 231 Austrian Stock Corporation Act mentions two cases: (1) if the acquiring company holds 90% or more of the acquired company, (2) if the transferred shares do not exceed 10% of the share capital of the acquiring company.

Art. 24 of the third directive but not to Art. 27. Consequently, the general meeting has to decide on the merger; the management board cannot pass a merger resolution on its own, without the consent of the general meeting. The reason is that the acquiring company converts from a national stock corporation to a European company and the formation by conversion is subject to a resolution of the general meeting. If the executive directors could decide on the merger, the principle that the shareholders decide on important changes in the company's structure would be breached.[54]

(4) Share-exchange ratio

Art. 25 paragraph 3 of the Regulation refers to a procedure for reviewing and amending the share-exchange ratio and the compensation of minority shareholders, without delaying the registration of the merger. Austrian stock corporation law provides a special procedure, according to § 225c of the Austrian Stock Corporation Act, by which the shareholders of the merging companies (acquired and acquiring) have the right to demand compensation if the share-exchange ratio does not fairly reflect the value of their shares. As a counterbalance, they cannot contest the general meeting's resolution on the basis of an inadequate share-exchange ratio or the non-compliance with information obligations in the preparatory documents. Consequently, the merger can proceed and be registered, because the claim of the shareholders does not suspend the registration process. This special shareholder right, together with the lack of a right to contest the merger resolution, is intended to accelerate the procedure, as it prevents the delay which would otherwise be caused by a number of objections by small shareholders. Shareholders who demand compensation must have a minimum holding of 1% or € 70, 000. This limit ensures that the costly procedure takes place only when it is sufficiently supported by the shareholders[55]. The requirements for the availability of the (review) procedure will probably not be changed for the SE-merger.

The Council Regulation allows this compensation procedure for the European Company only when the other merging companies – registered in Member States, which do not provide for such procedure – agree. The vote of the shareholders of the other Member State will be required because the special procedure can lead to a significant outflow of capital after the merger, to the detriment of the shareholders of the other companies.

[54] The possibility of calling the General Meeting with a stock of 5% – provided for in Art. 25 and 8 of the third directive and Art. 231 of the Austrian AktG – cannot replace such competence.

[55] *Bachner* in Kalss, Verschmelzung – Spaltung – Umwandlung § 225c No. 13 et seq.

If the companies do not agree to the review procedure, the shareholders can make use of their right to contest the resolution under Austrian company law.[56] This would result from a teleological interpretation of §§ 225b and 225c of the Austrian Stock Corporation Act. If the shareholders are deprived of the right to initiate a compensation procedure, there would no longer be any justification for depriving them of the right to contest the merger resolution. The Austrian legislator does not have to regulate this issue; it could include it in its legislation for clarification. The Austrian legislator is well advised to find a way of participation of the shareholders of the foreign companies[57] in order to establish a level playing field for all shareholders involved in the merger, in particular to reduce the danger of the powerful weapon of objectors' actions. Therefore the Austrian law will offer the special procedure to Austrian Companies as far as possible and will offer an option even for shareholders of foreign companies.

(5) Appraisal right

Due to language problems and changes in applicable legal norms, especially with regard to shareholder rights, there is a need for special protection of the shareholders of the acquired company. The Austrian SE Act will distinguish between shareholders of (acquiring and acquired) companies that stay within national borders and such acquired by a foreign company.[58] Only the latter are granted the right to leave the company since without the cross-border element of the transaction the shareholders position is not sufficiently effected. The appraisal right will not require additional justification, as indicated above for the transfer of seat.[59] With regard to other companies, shareholders of the acquiring company will not have to face the same difficulties or disadvantages as the shareholders of the acquired company. It seems to us that the mere conversion of the national stock corporation into a European company does not lead to major changes, as national company law widely applies to the European company. In accordance with the formation by conversion, shareholders need not be given additional protection.

[56] See only *Teichmann* Ausführungsgesetz in Deutschland in Theisen/Wenz (editors), Die Europäische Aktiengesellschaft, 573 (587).

[57] See the German draft, Section 2 (§ 6); www.bmj.de (Diskussionsentwurf).

[58] See the different approach of the German draft, section 2 (§ 7); www.bmj.de.

[59] See above transfer of the registered office for the distinction between listed and non-listed companies.

(6) Approval right

New applicable law may affect basic mandatory rights of the shareholders of the acquired company Legal rules concerning the relation to third parties have been unified in many cases by the European directives; however, the internal governance and organisation of the company has not yet been unified. Due to differences in mandatory company law, the acquiring company may be subject to shareholders' rights differing from those applicable to the acquired company. Under Austrian company law, shareholders cannot be deprived of their right to participate in the general meeting, whereas for example, Spanish company law allows the companies to deny shareholders participation in the general meeting if their stock is not higher than 1/1000 of the total shares (Art. 105.1 Spanish Stock Corporation Act).[60] With regard to such situations, shareholder interests seem to be sufficiently protected by the appraisal right. National Austrian company law as well as European law does not provide for special shareholder protection if the participation of a shareholder decreases and the shareholder consequently cannot initiate a special audit procedure to examine the accounts or demand the convocation of a General Meeting.[61]

Shareholders require that approval is reserved to them if a resolution would deprive them of statutory privileges, such as the right to appoint a member of the supervisory organ.[62] Under current Austrian law, the shareholder has to be given the same privilege in the new company, otherwise the right to approve the resolution must remain.[63] Due to differences among European company laws, a shareholder cannot always be given such statutory privileges. Consequently, the shareholder may – in addition to his appraisal right – prevent the completion of the merger (or transfer of the registered office).

d) Protection of creditors

Protection of the creditor's of the acquired company (that has its registered office in a different Member State than the registered office of the future SE) must be regulated as in the case of the transfer of the registered office. In addition, the Austrian legislator can apply the merger's regime. It should adopt –

[60] *Andrés Recalde* in Arroyo/Embid, Comentarios a la ley de sociedades anónimas II, 1024–1026.

[61] For further examples see *Kalss* (see note 38), § 99 GmbHG No. 6; *Hommelhoff/Riesenhuber* (see note 32), 274 et seq.

[62] § 88 AktG; see *Strasser* in *Jabornegg/Strasser*, AktG^4 II (2001), 218–220 (Nr. 63–71).

[63] § 10 Austrian Divisions Act and § 99 Austrian Limited Liability Company Act; see *Kalss* (see note 38), § 221 No. 7 with regard to mergers.

analogously to the provisions on the transfer of seat – a protection prior to the issue of the certificate. Under current Austrian company law the creditor's right to demand security is subsequent to the registration and creditors could lose their rights.[64]

5. Holding SE

The provisions on forming a holding SE will be the first special regulation of the formation of a holding company under Austrian law.[65] Under current law, some regulations applicable to mergers have to be applied by analogy.[66] The Austrian legislator has, therefore, to face the challenge of shaping regulations for this kind of formation.[67] Apart from the fact that the Regulation deals quite briefly with the holding, the legislator has to draft the technical procedure (timing and scope of disclosure of draft terms; majority at General Meeting, contribution of shares in the promoting companies and allotment of shares in the SE) which must be embedded into the Austrian Law on public corporations, and to decide whether minority shareholders or creditors should be granted special protective rights (for example, appraisal right for shareholders). It must be kept in mind that neither shareholders nor creditors are affected in the same manner as by a merger or other restructuring procedure. Minority shareholders who do not opt for membership in the future SE, will remain in the – then subsidiary – company. The change of control could be recognised as a reason justifying an appraisal right of the opposing shareholders (Art. 34).[68] Owing to the different situation on the final draft the Austrian legislator decided not to provide for any measures that grant shareholders or creditors the same level of protection as in the case of a transnational merger or transfer of the seat.

[64] They could especially lose their rights if an Austrian company is acquired by a foreign company and foreign company law provides for prior protection. For the contrary situation, i.e. an Austrian company acquires a foreign company; creditors might reap the benefits of a double right to be secured. This needs to be regulated by the legislator.

[65] *Torggler*, ecolex 2001, 442.

[66] *Rüffler* Lücken im Umgründungsrecht (Vienna 2003) 333 et seq.

[67] Because of the similarity of Austrian and German Stock Corporation Law the article of *Oplustil* Selected problems concerning formation of a holding SE (Societas europaea), German Law Journal Vol 4, Nr 2-1, is very instructive and helpful.

[68] *Kalss* Der Minderheitenschutz bei Gründung und Sitzverlegung der SE im Diskussionsentwurf.

6. Division of the Societas Europaea

The Regulation mentions only the merger as a form to found an SE, but not the parallel measure "division". Due to this restriction of the European legislator various questions about the division emerge: (i) can an SE be founded by other companies via a division?; (ii) is an already founded and existing SE entitled to take part in a division?; (iii) is the division restricted to the involvement of SEs?

(i) As already mentioned the Regulation follows the concept of a *numerus clausus* of formation forms. The division is not enumerated; although it could be argued that a division is quite similar to a merger, that it is in essence a "part-merger" and that the regulation only takes account of the voluntary character of the sixth directive (division directive) and therefore the division may be added to the explicitly regulated forms of formation, the wording, the legislative system and finally the intention of the legislator show quite clear that a European Company cannot be created by division of a public company or a private company with limited liability.[69]

(ii) If a national legislator has made use of the option of the sixth directive on company law (so called division-directive) to regulate the division of public companies as a measure to transfer assets and to reorganise companies, Art. 9 of the Regulation can be applied, so that the SE will be entitled to take part in a division either as dividing (transferring) company or as recipient company.[70] In Austria, the division of public companies is regulated in a single act on divisions (Spaltungsgesetz 1996).[71] Therefore an already existing SE may found another SE by means of a division; different variants of divisions are available: Division by formation of a new company and by acquisition (of an already existing company).

Under current Austrian law, the possibility that a company can transfer its assets and liabilities to another company in exchange for the allocation of shares of the recipient company to the transferring company (not to the shareholders) directly is not regulated in the Act on Divisions. Interpreting the Act on Divisions and the law on mergers in a broad sense, practitioners have found a way to transfer assets from the parent company to the (100%) subsidiary company with the effect of a *ipso iure* transfer without being obliged to grant shares of the recipient subsidiary company in exchange to the shareholders of the transferring parent company. Neither the transferring company nor its shareholders receive shares. The practitioners and the courts applied a special rule

[69] *Oplustil/Schneider* (see note 41), 13, 17.

[70] *Oplustil/Schneider* (see note 41), 13, 17.

[71] Federal Gazette (Bundesgesetzblatt) 1996/304; s only *Kalss* (see note 38).

dealing with mergers (Art. 224 of the Stock Corporation Act) also for divisions with already existing recipient companies within a group of companies. The preparing committee is discussing a proposal for a clear-cut rule that enlarges the different types of division. A company should be entitled to transfer its assets and liabilities to another company in exchange for the allocation of shares of the recipient company to the transferring company (not to the shareholders) directly, regardless of an already existing holding of the transferring company in the recipient company.

(iii) Under current Austrian law, only public and private companies with limited liability are entitled to participate in a division. Both types of companies may be involved in one single division. Art. 9 of the Regulation makes national provisions on public companies applicable to the SE. The SE will, therefore, be treated like a national public company. There are no restrictions which prohibit an SE from taking part in a national division; however, if the division takes place between an SE and a private company with limited liability or vice-verse, an appraisal right of the objecting shareholders must be observed according to section 9 of the Act on Divisions. Due to the restrictive rule of Art. 34 of the Regulation, a division between a public company and a SE would not trigger that minority right.

V. Final remarks

The work on drafting a bill to implement and complement the Regulation of the European Company is in progress; at the latest in spring 2004 the final draft should be presented by the Ministry of Justice and the consultation procedure should be commenced. The parliament should adopt the law in summer 2004.

Apart from the first regulation of the transfer of seat of a company without winding-up and the regulation of the founding of a holding, the most important aspect of the law will be the introduction of the one tier system; for the time being that option right is granted only to the SE whereas the national stock corporation remains restricted to the traditional two-tier systems.

Belgium

Christoph van der Elst

Literature on SE published in Belgium: *F. Blanquet* La société européenne n'est plus un mythe, Rev. Dr. Intern. Comp. 2001, 139–170; *F. Blanquet* Enfin la société européenne «la SE», Revue du Droit de l'Union Européenne 2001, 65–109; *F. Bouckaert* Eerste kennismaking met de Societas Europaea naar aanleiding van een recente studiedag aan de K. U. Leuven, Tijdschrift voor Notarissen (T. Not.) 2002, 75–83; *P. P. De Châtelet* La société européenne, Tijschrijft voor Belgische Handelsrecht (T.B.H.) 2002, 167–184; *J. De Leenheer* De Europese vennootschap is er!, Praktijkgids voor de vennootschap, 2002/7, 5–8 and 2002/8, 3–8; *K. Geens* Zetelverplaatsing van de Europese Vennootschap in Liber Amicorum Lucien Simont, Brussel, Bruylant, 2002, 1025–1039; *J. L. Joris* Will the European Company Work?, International Financial Law Review 2002, 19–23; *P. Nicaise* La société européenne: une société de type européen!, Journal des Tribunaux (J.T.) 2002, 481–490; *M. Olislaegers and B. Peeters* De Europese Naamloze Vennootschap (SE): Een nieuwe vennootschapsvorm met een Europees en nationaal karakter, Tijdschrift Fiscaal Recht 2003, 151–167; *D. Szafran* Chronique de législation: Société européenne, J. T. 2002, 249–250; *K. Vorlat, J. Swinnen and C. Michiels* De Europese vennootschap, DAOR actualiteit 2001–2002, 3–6.

I. Introduction

The discussions about a legal framework for the European company had continued for more than 30 years before the Council Regulation No 2157/2001 (the "Regulation" or "RE-SE") was finally adopted in October 2001. The choice of a regulation as legal instrument presents the advantage that no further implementation in national law is needed. The European Company (SE) will exist by virtue of the Regulation. However, Article 9 of the Regulation states that the "Societas Europaea" will be governed not only by the Regulation (RE-SE), but also by its statutes, specific laws, and the company law of the Mem-ber State where the SE will be incorporated.* Hence, the advantage of the choice of a regulation is in part neutralised by the numerous references to national law.

The national law of the Member States may not be inconsistent with the RE-SE, must offer the necessary legal framework to establish an SE, and must

* Parliament has given the King the authority to take the necessary measures to implement the regulation, but not for the directive. These measures must receive the assent before the and of 2005 (Article 388 and 389 Law of December 22, 2003; Official Gazette 31. December 2003, p. 62240).

allow for an optimal functioning of the SE. However, so far, no specific Belgian legislation has been drafted. Due to the general elections that have taken place on May 18, 2003, the Belgian parliament did not yet start discussions on this subject. Hence, this paper will focus on the Belgian company law in force and indicate where new rules need to be established before October 2004.

It remains unclear whether the Belgian government will opt for the approach of the High Level Group of Company Law Experts, whose report states "listed and open companies should have the choice between the two systems" (of management).[1] However, Belgian company law was amended in August 2002 and a new management structure introduced, after the publication of the RE-SE. Contrary to the new Italian Act, the Belgian approach has offered companies only the option of a one tier or a modified one-tier structure. Hence, in all probability Belgium will not offer all open and public companies a free choice between a one-tier or a two-tier management structure.

This paper starts with the basic rules for the establishment of an SE in Belgium. It continues with the rules on the management structure. Section C will then highlight the possibilities of a transfer of seat. The involvement of employees is discussed in section D. Finally, section E will draw conclusions on the abovementioned subjects.

II. Formation of the European Company

The Regulation offers four basic possible ways in which an SE may be formed: a merger of at least two companies, a holding SE, a subsidiary SE and the transformation of a "national" company. A detailed analysis of the legal procedures to establish an SE goes beyond the scope of this paper. This paper will focus on the general rules for establishing a Belgian SE and will provide some additional information on the rules that govern the merger SE, the holding SE, the subsidiary SE and the conversion of a Belgian public limited liability company into an SE.

1. General rules

The Societas Europaea must be set up in the form of a public limited liability company.[2] In Belgium, the SE will take the form of a "société anonyme"/

[1] The High Level Group of Company Law Experts, Brussels, November 4, 2002, Recommendation III.9, p. 59. The report may be downloaded at: www.europa.eu.int/comm/internal_market/en/company/company/modern/index.htm.

[2] Article 1, § 1 RE-SE.

"naamloze vennootschap" (SA/NV). The incorporation of this company type is subject to a number of conditions.

Firstly, the involvement of a notary is mandatory. The document of incorporation of an SA/NV must be enacted in the form of a deed drawn up by a notary. Depending on the area within Belgium in which the company will have its seat, the deed of incorporation must be enacted in Dutch, French or German.

Secondly, the company has to be incorporated by a minimum of two founders. These founders can be natural or legal persons, and Belgian citizens or foreigners. This rule is consistent with Article 2 RE-SE. Once incorporated, one shareholder can acquire all the shares. This will not result in the dissolution of the company. However, if this situation persists for a year without the entry of a new shareholder, the sole shareholder is deemed to guarantee all the obligations of the company arising from the time when the shareholder became a sole shareholder until the time of the entry of a new shareholder.[3]

Article 3, section 2 RE-SE has introduced an exception on the number of founders for the subsidiary SE of an SE. One shareholder, the parent SE, may set up a subsidiary SE. In that case the provisions of the Belgian law on the implementation of the Twelfth Company Law Directive will be applicable. Under Belgian law, the limited liability of the shareholder of the limited liability company ceases to exist: if a legal person sets up a private limited liability company (BVBA/SPRL), this shareholder is deemed to guarantee all the obligations of the subsidiary (SE).[4] This regime is consistent with the exception provided in Article 2 (2) of the Twelfth Company Law Directive,[5] which allows Member States to lay down special provisions if a single member company or another legal person is the sole member of the company.

By obliging an SE to have a legal capital of minimum 120.000 Euro, the European Union has judged the advantages of the preservation of the legal capital higher than the disadvantages.[6] All the other legal requirements concerning the capital, its preservation, changes, shares, bonds and other similar securities of an SE, are, for the Belgian SE, governed by the Belgian company law.[7] Since the latter has implemented the Second Company Law Directive, the RE-SE refers to other European rules for a significant number of requirements.

[3] Article 646 Belgian Companies Act (CA).

[4] Article 213 Belgian CA.

[5] Twelfth Council Company Law Directive (89/667/EEC) of 21 December 1989 on single member private limited-liability companies, *OJ L* No 395, 30 December 1989, p. 40.

[6] The number of disadvantages is however large. For a brief overview see *C. Van der Elst* Economic Analysis of Law, A. Hatzis (ed.), Cheltenham, Edward Elgar, 2004.

[7] Article 5 RE-SE.

At least one fourth of a Belgian SE shares' nominal value or accountable par has to be paid up in full.[8] In any event a minimum of 61,500 Euro must always be paid up in full.[9] The funds should be deposited into a bank account, which must be opened for this purpose at a bank, under the name of the company in formation. If an SE sets up a Belgian subsidiary, the Belgian rules on a single member private limited liability company forces the parent SE to pay up in full each share to at least 20% of its value.[10] Hence it is sufficient that a single member subsidiary SE has a paid up capital of only 24,000 Euro. It has already been argued that 120,000 Euro only prevents founders from making a "frivolous use of this form".[11] If only 24,000 Euro is needed to establish a subsidiary SE, even this argument cannot be sustained.

Contributions in kind must be paid up in full within five years after the incorporation of the company.[12] The founders must appoint an auditor to report on the contribution in kind. The auditor's report must contain a description of the asset and the methods of valuation. Further, the report must contain information on the value of the asset and whether it corresponds with the number and nominal value or accountable par of the shares to be issued.[13]

The founding parties have to prepare a budget forecast in which they account for the amount of capital of the Belgian SE, which is about to be incorporated. The draft budget must be submitted to and kept by the notary.

The founders of the Belgian SE can be held liable for the obligations of the company if the company becomes insolvent within *three* years of incorporation, if it is found that the starting capital was obviously inadequate to sustain the normal course of its business over a period of at least *two* years. The notary will hand over the draft budget to the court if the company goes bankrupt within a period of three years.

For certain types of activities, the subscribed capital has to be substantially higher. Banks, for example, must have a subscribed capital of at least 6,200,000 Euro.[14]

[8] Article 448, 1° Belgian CA.

[9] Article 439 Belgian CA. See also Article 9, section 1 Second company law Directive.

[10] Article 223, 1° Belgian CA.

[11] *R. Drury and A. Hicks*, Journal of Business Law, 1999, p. 440.

[12] Article 448, 2° Belgian CA. See also Article 9, section 2 Second company law Directive.

[13] Article 444 Belgian CA. See also Article 10, section 2 Second company Law Directive.

[14] See Article 16 Law of March 22, 1993 op het statuut van en het toezicht op de kredietinstellingen, Offical Gazette April 19, 1993, regularly modified.

The shares of a Belgian SE must be in bearer or in registered form. The shares always have to be in registered form until they are paid up in full, even if the statutes of the SE require shares to be in bearer form. A shareholder of bearer shares may always request the conversion of the shares to registered shares at his cost. It is allowed under Belgian law to prohibit the conversion of registered shares to bearer shares. In 1995, the Belgian legislator introduced a third kind of shares, the incorporated shares ("gedematerialiseerde effecten" / "titres dématérialisés"). The rights attached to the latter kind of shares are "incorporated" by way of entering the shares in an account with an authorised account holder under the name of the owner.[15]

A Belgian SE can issue several other financial instruments: shares without voting rights for a maximum of 1/3rd of the subscribed capital,[16] founders' shares, bonus shares, bonds, convertible bonds, warrants or instruments for which no contribution is made. The statutes describe the rights attached to these instruments.

2. Formation by merger

The Belgian legislator has already developed detailed rules on the merger by acquisition as well as on the merger by formation of a new company.[17] A Belgian limited liability company must prepare draft terms of the merger in a public deed or in a private instrument and deposit the terms at the clerk's office of the commercial court at least six weeks prior to the general meeting convened to decide on the merger. The information to be included in the draft terms is comparable with the particulars in Article 20 of the RE-SE. However, two differences must be mentioned. Firstly, the Belgian merger rules oblige the board of directors to mention the purpose of the merged company.[18] Under the RE-SE, not only the purpose of the SE, but also the statutes, which contain the purpose, must be included in the draft terms.[19] Secondly, information on the procedures of arrangements for employee involvement must be part of the draft terms to form an SE by means of a merger. Belgian company law contains no rules on employee participation.[20] It should be noted that, in the one-tier

[15] Article 468 Belgian CA.

[16] Article 480 Belgian CA.

[17] See Article 671 and 672 Belgian CA.

[18] Article 693, 1° Belgian CA.

[19] Article 20, section 1, (h) RE-SE.

[20] Cf. infra part D.

structure, the board of directors is the organ to decide on the rules concerning employee involvement. It is unclear whether the same applies if a company has opted for the modified one-tier structure.[21]

Under Belgian law, the experts to examine the draft terms are the statutory auditor, the certified auditor or the registered accountant. The notary must review the legality of the operations.[22]

Belgian company law does not contain an exception to draft reports for a merger by acquisition, if the company already holds at least 90% of the shares. Only if a company holds all the shares, a specific procedure is available.[23]

The SE must be registered. Until recently, the registration was filed at the commercial register. The law of January 16, 2003 has changed this registration procedure.[24] From mid-2003, the SE has to register with the "Kruispuntbank van Ondernemingen" / "Banque-Carrefour des Entreprises". Intermediaries, the "ondernemingsloketten" / "guichets-entreprises", make the necessary filings. This electronic system simplifies the registration procedures. Companies only need to file once and one registration number will identify the company. This number is used as a VAT number, social security number, trade registry number etc. Public services must contact the "Kruispuntbank" to ascertain the information they need.

After the procedure of the merger has been completed, the instruments can be invoked against third parties as soon as an extract or a notice is published in the Annexes of the Belgian Official Gazette.[25] The deeds establishing the merger must be filed for deposit. Belgian law imposes special formalities on the SE for the transfer of rights related to real estate, intellectual and industrial property rights.[26]

For minority shareholders who oppose a merger, Member States may adopt appropriate protection provisions.[27] The Belgian law requires a decision to be taken by three quarters of the votes cast and at least half of the subscribed capital to be represented at the first general meeting of the public limited liability companies involved in the merger. If a second general meeting is convened, there is no requirement of the subscribed capital to be represented.[28] Hence,

[21] Cf. infra part B.II.

[22] Article 700 and 713 of the Belgian CA.

[23] Article 676 Belgian CA.

[24] Law of January 16, 2003; Official Gazette 5 February 2003, p. 4478.

[25] Article 683 Belgian CA.

[26] Article 683 Belgian CA.

[27] Article 24 section 2 RE-SE.

[28] Article 558 Belgian CA.

minority shareholders have less than 25% of the votes. Up till now Belgian company law offers no protection for this group of shareholders. The right to leave the company is not open to these minority shareholders as case law shows that a merger is not a well-founded reason to leave the company. This reason is only present if there is continuous and severe disagreement between the shareholders of the company. It is not expected that the Belgian Parliament will adopt provisions designed to ensure appropriate protection for minority shareholders.

3. Formation of a holding SE or a subsidiary SE

As for the formation by merger, the same procedure applies for the formation of a holding SE. Under Belgian law, at least 50% of the shareholders – i.e. 50% of the permanent voting rights – of each company must agree to the formation. A higher threshold can be set in the draft terms. Belgium company law does not impose additional requirements on, nor contains any inconsistencies with the rules in the Regulation to set up a holding company.

The rules on the formation of a Belgian public limited liability company will govern the procedure to set up a subsidiary SE.[29]

4. Conversion of a public limited liability company to an SE

As for the other mechanisms to establish an SE, draft terms must be drawn up on the conversion of a Belgian public limited liability company into an SE.

Belgian company law is not (yet) in line with section 6 of Article 37 RE-SE. The latter states that the experts must certify that the company has net assets at least equivalent to its capital, plus those reserves, which must not be distributed under the law or the statutes. The former requires that the certified auditor or the registered accountant reports on the statement of the assets and liabilities and indicates whether it gives a full, true and correct view of the condition of the company. If the net assets of the company are less than the capital shown on the aforementioned statement, the difference must be stated in the conclusion of the report. In that case, the report cannot certify that the net assets are at least equivalent to the capital and the reserves.[30]

Under the Regulation, Member States can require that the conversion of a public limited liability company into an SE must be voted on in the organ

[29] Cf. supra A.I.

[30] See Article 776 and 777 Belgian CA.

within which employee participation is organised. However, since the Belgian works council cannot be qualified as such an organ,[31] no such condition can exist in Belgium.

Under Belgian company law, the conversion has to be decided on by a general meeting that can deliberate and pass a valid resolution only if the shareholders and other persons in attendance represent not only one half of the company's capital, but also one half of the number of such securities that do not represent the capital, if there are such securities. If these conditions are not met, a new convening notice is required. The second general meeting can deliberate and resolve if any part of the capital is represented. The decision is adopted only if it has obtained no less than four-fifths of the votes.[32] A unanimous consent of the shareholders is required if the company has not existed for at least two years or the articles provide that another legal form may not be adopted.

III. Management Systems

The Belgian Parliament has changed the management system of the public limited liability company in 2002.[33] Until September 1, 2002 the only model a public limited liability company could opt for was the one-tier board model. In this regime, the board of directors has the most extensive power to manage the company. The new Act introduced an optional system to make it possible to choose between the classic one-tier model and a modified one-tier structure.

1. One-tier structure

According to Article 522 Belgian company law, the board of directors has the most extensive powers to manage the company and perform all acts which are necessary or useful for the accomplishment of the company's objects, except those reserved to the general meeting by the Companies' Code. This is in line with Article 43, section 1 RE-SE. Within the board of directors, the management functions can be distributed, this distribution of responsibilities cannot be invoked against third parties. This rule does not seem to be in conflict with the RE-SE.

The Belgian Companies' Code does not impose an obligation to list in the statutes the categories of transactions that need an express decision of the

[31] *M. Olislaegers and B. Peeters*, Tijdschrift Fiscaal Recht 2003, 156.

[32] Article 781 Belgian CA.

[33] Law of August 2, 2002, Official Gazette 22 August 2002, p. 36555.

board.[34] However, there is no reason why a list of such transactions requiring consent, should not be included in the statutes.

The board has a compulsory duty to draft minutes of its meetings.[35] If a board member has a conflict of interest, the minutes must include a justification of the decision.[36] If the company is listed, for each important decision – except intra group decisions at arm's length – a committee of *independent directors* has to be consulted and the board has to deliberate and explicitly mention in the minutes of the meeting that the compulsory procedure has been followed.[37] Foreign companies, which would otherwise consider transferring their seat to Belgium, may see this burdensome procedure as a crucial disincentive.

Article 525 Companies' Code provides that the day-to-day management can be the responsibility of one or more managing directors. It is not required that a member of the board of directors be elected as managing director, nor does the managing director need to be a shareholder of the company. Day-to-day management has not been defined in the Companies' Code, but the Belgian High Court has decided that day-to-day management is the power to manage the daily necessities of the company, which, due to their minor importance and the necessity to act quickly, do not reasonably require a board's decision.[38] This interpretation is not contrary to Article 43 RE-SE, as it allows the establishment of a management committee or managing director under the same conditions as for public limited liability companies. It might be expected that a new Belgian legislation will allow this option for an SE.

The board of directors of a Belgian public limited liability company must be composed of at least three members, in line with Article 43 RE-SE. The Belgian Companies' Code allows a two member board, if the company has been founded by two members or if it is resolved at a general meeting that the company shall not have more than two shareholders. Although not forbidden, Belgian companies have no employee representatives.

Since September 1, 2002, it is mandatory to designate a natural person to represent a legal entity which is elected as a member of the board. This natural person is liable as if he himself were the board member. Notwithstanding the

[34] See Article 48 RE-SE.

[35] *Tilleman, B.* Bestuut van vennootschappen, Kalmthout, Biblo, 1996, p. 480.

[36] Article 523 CA.

[37] Article 524 CA.

[38] Cass. 17 September 1968, Pasicrisie belge (Pas.) 1969, I, p. 61, Revue pratique des sociétés (R.P.S.) 1970, nr. 5578, p. 197 and Cass. 21 February 2000, Tijdschrift voor Rechtspersoon en Vennootschap (T.R.V.) 2000, p. 283.

important number of difficulties inherent in the implementation of this new rule,[39] Article 61 Belgian Companies' Code is consistent with section 1, Article 47 RE-SE. However, one question remains unsolved. In Belgium, a natural person who represents a legal entity must be an employee, board member or shareholder of the entity he represents. Article 47 RE-SE does not contain additional requirements. On the other hand, the Member State can provide that legal entities may not be members of the board. Hence, one can argue that it must be possible to require that the legal entity is represented by the aforementioned classes of individuals.

Board members are not subject to professional secrecy under Belgian law, but there is the general duty not to divulge any information, which might be prejudicial to the company's interests. This is in line with Article 49 RE-SE.

As provided in section 3, Article 43 RE-SE, the Belgian members are appointed by the general meeting. There are no specific rights for minority shareholders to appoint one or more members of the board. However, the statutes frequently stipulate that an important minority shareholder or holder of a class of shares can select a number or even the majority of the board members to be appointed by the general meeting. These rules do not conflict with section 4 Article 43 and 47 RE-SE.

Belgium board members are appointed for a renewable period of a maximum of six years, but the general meeting may terminate their appointment at any time without giving notice or stating reasons ("ad nutum").[40] This is a rule of public order.

Belgian company law contains no rules relating to quorums or decision taking by the management organs of the company. Section 1, Article 50 RE-SE is applicable. However, to avoid uncertainty, the Belgian SE might opt to indicate in the statutes that the decision will be taken if a majority of *all* members is present or represented, since it is generally accepted in Belgium that the majority of votes cast decides. In Belgium, if the statutes do not contain such provision, it is a general rule that the abstentions are not taken into account.

The SE's administrative organ has to meet at least four times a year. Under Belgian law it is sufficient to meet only once a year to draft the board's report.[41] Boards of listed companies have to meet twice, since listed companies must

[39] *E. Wymeersch*, T.B.H. 2002, p. 604, noot 21; *F. Hellemans en M. Wauters*, T.R.V. 2002, nr. 7, p. 478.

[40] Cass. 22 january 1981, Revue critique de jurisprudence belge (R.C.J.B.) 1981, p. 495; *Pas.* 1981, I, p. 543, Arresten van het Hof van Cassatie (Arr. Cass.) 1980–81, p. 559, R.P.S.1981, nr. 6165, p. 285.

[41] Article 95 Belgian CA.

publish half-yearly reports. This rule forces these boards to meet at least twice a year. As soon as quarterly reporting becomes compulsory, four meetings will be the minimum.[42] Research has shown that the boards of Belgian public limited liability companies meet on average 7 times a year.[43] The only new element concerns the necessity to "discuss the progress and foreseeable development of the SE's business".[44] Under the Belgian regime, it is only compulsory to discuss these items once a year. The board's report must disclose information on the circumstances that significantly influence the development of the corporation and important facts that have occurred after the end of the accounting period.[45] The Belgian Companies' Code does not need to be adapted. However, the minutes of at least four board meetings must contain information on the discussion of the SE's business. The statutes of the SE must disclose the intervals of the meetings at which these items must be discussed by the board.

The RE-SE does not contain any rules on the representation of the SE. The board of directors or, within its powers, the day-to-day management represent the Belgian public company and hence the Belgian SE. However, the statutes may provide that one or more board members will represent the company.[46] Frequently used statutory clauses requiring the signature of usually two directors are valid and effective against third parties, if published in the Annexes to the Official Gazette. Limitations of the power to represent the company, including *ultra vires* limitations, cannot be invoked against third parties. This is in line with section 3, Article 9 of the First Company Law Directive.[47]

Belgian company law does not contain specific rules to guarantee that board members have access to all information of the company. It is generally acknowl-

[42] See article 6 of the proposal for a Directive of the European Parliament and of the Council on the harmonisation of transparency requirements with regard to information about issuers whose securities are admitted to trading on a regulated market and amending Directive 2001/34/EC, March 2003.

[43] *C. Van der Elst* voordracht studiedag 17 april 2002, Institute for International Research (IIR, Antwerpen.

[44] Article 44, section 1 RE-SE.

[45] Article 96 Belgian CA.

[46] The Belgian Cour de Cassation has decided that the representation of the company can be delegated to one board member and one third party (employee), acting jointly. Cass. 22 December 1977, Arr. Cass. 1978, p. 498; Rechtskundig Weekblad (R.W. 1977–78, p. 2199–2208, noot *P. Crab*; R.P.S. 1978, nr. 5978.

[47] First Council Directive 68/151/EEC of 9 March 1968 on co-ordination of safeguards which, for the protection of the interests of members and others, are required by Member States of companies within the meaning of the second paragraph of Article 58 of the Treaty, with a view to making such safeguards equivalent throughout the Community, O. J. nr. 65, March 14, 1968, p. 8–12.

edged that board members have a right and a duty to be informed.[48] The Regulation explicitly recognises the right to examine information. However, two important features limit this right. Firstly, only information submitted to the administrative organ is included. Secondly, only an examination right has been established. Thus, Belgian law does not conflict with the RE-SE. However, neither the Regulation nor the Belgian Companies' Code resolves the question as to what information should be submitted to the board, to whom the demand should be addressed, etc.

Under Belgian company law, the election of a chairman is not compulsory. However, the statutes frequently stipulate that the board of directors elects a chairman from among its members. To be consistent with the RE-SE, a statutory provision on the casting vote of the chairman is recommended. Belgian company law explicitly mentions that the statutory provision concerning the casting vote of the chairman is not valid if the company has only two board members.[49] Hence, in the absence of a statutory provision, the chairman does not have the casting vote under Belgian law, contrary to section 2, Article 50 RE-SE.

2. Modified one-tier structure

The Act of August 2, 2002 has significantly modified the organisational structure of the public limited liability company. Companies can opt for a modified one-tier board structure with a board of directors ("raad van bestuur" – "conseil d'administration") and a management board ("directiecomité" – "comité de direction"). The management board must be composed of at least two members. The board of directors appoints and dismisses the management board. It is also possible to provide for the appointment and the dismissal of the management board members in the statutes. This rule seems to be consistent with Article 39, section 2 RE-SE.

The powers vested in the management board are determined in Article 524 Belgian Companies' Code. All powers of the board of directors are included with the exception of deciding on the general policy of the company and those powers explicitly vested in the board of directors. The board of directors has the duty to supervise the management board.

The Belgian Companies' Code has imposed a significant number of duties upon the board of directors. The board is responsible for drafting the annual

[48] *L. Simont*, R.P.S. 1963, nr. 5148, p. 195; *P. Colle*, Liber Amicorum Yvette Merchiers, Brugge, Die Keure, 2001, p. 451.

[49] Section 1, Article 518 *in fine* Belgian CA.

accounts,[50] calling the general meeting of shareholders,[51] drafting the report on the basis of which the general meeting decides on a capital increase,[52] deciding to distribute an interim dividend,[53] etc.

The law does not indicate what "general policy" is. It might be clear that the decision by a real estate company to acquire a company with industrial activities is a major turnaround. It is up to the board of directors to decide upon this new development.[54] However, it can be questioned whether one can state that the management board of a real estate company specialising in commercial property contracted unlawfully when it acquired an industrial real estate property.

The introduction of the Act was the start of a vigorous debate between legal scholars.[55] Indeed, it is unclear whether the board of directors still has the power to manage the company once a management board has been installed. The discussion results from the difference between the Dutch and the French translations of the Act. The Act mentions, in Dutch, "overdragen" or "allocate" whereas in French it mentions "déléguer" or "delegate". It seems that only a new bill or a decision of the highest court can solve this question.[56]

The Belgian modified one-tier regime needs to be modified to serve as a two-tier SE system. Firstly, in the Belgian system, board members are allowed to be members of the management board at the same time. This rule is inconsistent with section 3, Article 39 RE-SE. However, the Belgian rules do not forbid a statutory provision with special conditions of eligibility. Hence, this provision can contain the prohibition of being, at the same time, a member of the management board and a member of the board of directors.

Secondly, the division of powers between the board of directors and the management board is not in line with the RE-SE. Belgian law is deficient in several respects. First, the power to "manage" the company has not completely shifted to the management board. The board of directors still has a significant number of reserved powers. Second, the board of directors is empowered with the general policy. It can be argued that "general policy" is part of management as it includes the strategic decisions of the company.

[50] Article 92 Belgian CA.

[51] Article 532 Belgian CA.

[52] Article 582 Belgian CA.

[53] Article 618 Belgian CA.

[54] If this possibility is included in the objects of the company.

[55] For an overview of the discussion see *P. Ernst en L. Van Den Eynden*, T.R.V. 2002, p. 567.

[56] *C. Van der Elst*, Ondernemingsrecht, 2003, to be published.

Third, if the arguments of the concurring powers of the board of directors and the management board stands up to scrutiny, the Belgian law conflicts with section 1 of Article 39 and 40 RE-SE.

The rule on the number of meetings and the duties to report to the supervisory board,[57] do not conflict with Belgian law but must be stipulated in the statutes. Belgian company law allows additional particulars, not contrary to article 41 RE-SE to be established in the statutes of the SE.

The modified one-tier board structure also conflicts with the one-tier system of the SE. Too many powers have been delegated to the "directiecomité".

3. The general meeting of shareholders

The organisation and conduct of the general meeting of an SE is to be governed by the national laws of the member states.[58] The Regulation itself requires that one or more shareholders, who hold at least 10% of the subscribed capital, may request the calling of a general meeting[59] and/or put additional items on the agenda of a general meeting.[60] The Belgian Companies' Code provides that the board of directors or the statutory auditors have to convene the general meeting, if it has been requested by the shareholders that represent a sufficient amount of the subscribed capital.[61] These shareholders must hold at least 20% of the subscribed capital. The reduction of the threshold to 10% must be supported: Economic scholars have proved that this "anti-director right" can enhance the capital market.[62] A Belgian general meeting must be convened by three weeks notice.[63] The RE-SE adds that the period within which the general meeting shall be convened cannot be longer than 2 months.

[57] Article 41 RE-SE.

[58] Article 53 RE-SE.

[59] Article 55, section 1 RE-SE.

[60] Article 55, section 1 and Article 56 RE-SE.

[61] Article 532 Belgian CA.

[62] *R. La Porta, F. Lopez-de-Silanes, A. Shleifer and R. Vishny*, The Journal of Finance 1997, p. 1134 and p. 1141.

[63] The board of directors and the statutory auditors can be punished with a fine of up to 250 Euro (multiplied by 200) if they fail to convene the general meeting (Article 647, 1° Belgian CA).

IV. Transfer of Seat

1. The Belgian real seat theory

An important innovation of the Regulation concerns the transfer of seat of an SE. The seat of a company is similar to the nationality of a natural person.[64] Until now, a cross-border transfer of the seat of a public limited liability company was, if it was at all possible, extremely burdensome. The RE-SE allows a transfer of seat of an SE to another Member State, if the conditions of only one Article – although with sixteen sections – have been met. The transfer will not affect the continuity of its legal personality.

Belgium adheres to the real seat theory. A company the real seat of which is in Belgium is subject to Belgian law, even if it has been incorporated abroad.[65] The real seat theory connects a company to the jurisdiction where the company has its headquarters. The headquarters is the place where the important decisions are taken, the board of directors meets, the general meeting is convened and the offices are located. If the said meeting places are located in different areas, the place where the board meets is preferred.[66] The company must have a link with the state the legal system of which it claims to apply.[67] In some older decisions, the place of the general meeting was preferred,[68] although in 1973, all the residual powers shifted to the board of directors. Hence the meeting of the latter is the starting point to determine the headquarters.[69]

Article 56 Belgian Companies' Code refers only to the application of Belgian law. However, the courts have given this article a multinational application. Not only do the courts decide whether a company is foreign or Belgian, they

[64] *V. Edwards* EC Company Law, Oxford, Clarendon press, 1999, p. 362.

[65] Article 56 Belgian CA.

[66] Kh. Hasselt 22 April 1998, T.B.H. 1998, p. 404; *J.-P. Blumberg*, Tijdschrift voor Privaatrecht (T.P.R.) 1992, p. 815; *G. Van Boxsom* Rechtsvergelijkende studie over de nationaliteit der vennootschappen, Brussel, Larcier, 1964, p. 185.

[67] *E. Wymeersch*, Financial Law Institute, working paper, April 2003, p. 7.

[68] See Brussel 23 March 1903, R.P.S. 1903, p. 175, note.

[69] In older case law, the nationality or residence of the board members or shareholders have been taken into account (Brussel 25 June 1962, Receuil general de l'enregistrement et du notariat 1966, p. 138, note *M. Donnay*; Brussels 27 March 1912, R.P.S. 1912, p. 311 note; Rb. Brussel, 26 February 1923, R.P.S. 1923, p. 185, note F. Paridant) but legal scholars deny these criteria (*L. Fredericq* Traité de Droit Commercial belge (IV), Gent, Editions Fecheyr, 1950, p. 168, *G. Schrans and H. Van Houtte* Internationaal handels- en financieel recht, Leuven, Acco, 1991, p. 77).

also decide the "nationality" of the company.[70] Once its nationality has been decided, the law of the (foreign) jurisdiction is the "*lex societatis*".

Finally, it is important to point out that the real seat of a company will be decided by the "Belgian" rules, i.e. the *legi fori*. From this rule it is clear that under Belgian law the registered office can be different from the real seat. When this rule was enacted it was the purpose of the Belgian legislator to avoid the use of "letterbox companies". However, these rules are not always consistently applied. So far, no Belgian court has decided that, when a subsidiary of a foreign company goes bankrupt due to the behaviour of the foreign parent company, the parent company will also be declared bankrupt. The decision can be different if the parent company has its seat in Belgium.[71]

It is possible that the "*lex societatis*" applied by the Belgian court, refers to a third law regime. Legal scholars generally accept that this referral to the third law regime will be applied.[72] However, no Belgian case law can be found.[73] In France, it has been decided that a Turkish bank with its headquarters in the United Kingdom was nevertheless a Turkish company, as the United Kingdom applies the incorporation theory.[74]

2. The competent Authorities in Article 8 RE-SE

The transfer of the SE's seat is determined in Article 8 RE-SE. However, the RE-SE has left part of the procedure to transfer the seat to be decided by the Member States. Firstly, the Member States have to define the competent authority to issue a certificate attesting the completion of the acts and formalities before the transfer of the seat.[75] As the notary has already been appointed in the Dutch "ambtelijk Voorontwerp"[76] as the competent authority, it can be

[70] Cass. 12 April 1888, *Pas.*, I, 1888, p. 186, concl. Proc.-Gen. Mesdach de ter Kiele and Cass. 12 November 1965, *R. W.* 1965–66, p. 911, concl. Adv.-Gen. F. Dumon.

[71] *J. Meeusen*, Artikel 56, Commentaar W. Venn., Mechelen, Kluwer, 2000, p. 35.

[72] It is recognised that there are not many theoretical arguments to support this thesis. There are however a number of practical elements: preventing the nullity of the company and supporting the possibility of a cross border transfer.

[73] *J. Meeusen*, Artikel 56, Commentaar W. Venn., Mechelen, Kluwer, 2000, p. 11.

[74] Paris 19 maart 1965, Journal du Droit International 1966, p. 117, note *B. Goldman*.

[75] Article 8, section 8 RE-SE.

[76] Ambtelijk Voorontwerp – Wet houdende uitvoering van Verordening (EG) Nr. 2157/2001 van de Raad van de Europese Unie van 8 oktober 2001 betreffende het statuut van de Europese vennootschap (SE) (Uitvoeringswet verordening Europese Vennootschap).

expected that the Belgian legislator will also appoint the notary as the competent authority.

Secondly, on grounds of public interest, a Member State can appoint the competent authority to oppose the transfer of the seat. The Dutch "ambtelijk Voorontwerp" has appointed the Minister of Justice as the competent authority to oppose the transfer. It is not yet clear whether the Belgian parliament will appoint a competent authority, though it is not unlikely that a minister, such as the Minister of Finance or the Minister of Justice, will be given this competence. The Minister of Finance could use this authority in order to prevent companies transferring their seats without paying taxes on the surplus value of their assets.[77]

3. The procedure to transfer the seat

Belgian does not prohibit a transfer of the seat of a company. In the *Lamot* case, the Belgian highest court, the Court de Cassation, decided that a transfer of the seat from the United Kingdom to Belgium will not force the winding-up of the company.[78] The company maintains its corporate personality if both legal systems accept the transfer. In Belgium, there are no legal rules that prevent or prohibit the transfer of the seat of a foreign company to Belgium. The new legal rules, i.e. the Belgian law, will apply, as soon as the seat has been transferred.[79]

Looking at the corrollary, legal scholars argue that the transfer of the seat from Belgium to another country is possible, if both national legal systems accept the continuity of the corporate personality. This view is based upon a decision of the highest administrative court, the Conseil d'Etat.[80] The court decided that the Belgian company, *Vanneste,* remained a Belgian company as long as the general meeting of the company did not decide to transfer the seat. However, if one applies the real seat theory, an analysis of the exact location of the headquarters decides whether the seat has been transferred. No decision of the general meeting needs to be taken. Due to this specific case law, the question may be asked as to how and under what conditions the Belgian company

[77] Cf. infra III.

[78] Cass. 12 november 1965, *R. W.* 1965–66, p. 911, concl. Adv.-Gen. F. Dumon.

[79] In this case, the Lamot company had two "nationalities": the British and the Belgian. The United Kingdom supports the incorporation theory. Hence the transfer of the seat does not deprive the company of its British "nationality".

[80] R.v.St. 29 June 1987, T.R.V. 1988, p. 110 note *K. Lenaerts*.

can decide to move its seat and what sanction there is available under Belgian law if the decision process has been violated.[81]

The procedure for an authorised transfer of the seat of an SE can be compared with that for a merger of two public limited liability companies. First, a proposal to transfer the seat has to be drafted, together with a report explaining and justifying the legal and economic aspects for shareholders, creditors and employees.[82]

The SE should satisfy the interests of creditors and holders of other rights. This duty concerns the liabilities of the SE arising prior to the publication of the transfer proposal. Under Belgian law the creditors of a company that decides to reduce its capital[83] or to merge, have the possibility, within a period of two months after the publication of the decision to reduce the capital or to merge, to demand security for the claims that have not become due by the date of that publication. The company can avoid such a demand if it pays the claim at the nominal value, minus the rate of discount. Article 8, section 7 RE-SE is worded somewhat differently than Article 32 of the Second or Article 13 of the Third Company Law Directive. However, it might be expected that the Belgian legislator will copy the protective measures for creditors in the case of a capital reduction or a merger.

The general meeting has to decide upon the transfer of the seat of an SE. It requires a decision taken by a majority of at least two thirds of the votes' cast.[84] The Belgian Parliament must resolve two problems. Firstly, the parliament must specify the majority required to decide on the transfer of the seat. To change the statutes of the company, Belgian law requires a decision to be taken by three quarters of the votes' cast and at least half of the subscribed capital represented at the first general meeting. If a second general meeting is convened, there is no requirement as to how much of the subscribed capital has to be represented.[85] The seat of the company must be mentioned in the statutes of the company.[86]

However, a Belgian legal scholar[87] has already proposed an 80% majority to approve the transfer of the seat. He refers to the majority required to change

[81] *J. Meeusen*, Artikel 56, Commentaar W. Venn., Mechelen, Kluwer, 2000, p. 18.

[82] Article 8, section 3 RE-SE.

[83] Article 618 Belgian CA. See also Article 32 Second Company Law Directive.

[84] Article 8, section 6 RE-SE.

[85] Article 558 Belgian CA.

[86] An accurate description – street, number and community – of the seat of a Belgian company must be disclosed in the annexes of the official journal (Article 69).

[87] *K. Geens*, Liber Amicorum Lucien Simont, Brussel, Bruylant, 2002, p. 1034–1035.

the objects of the company[88] and the transformation of the company to another company type.[89] This approach can be supported, as for both decisions, the transformation and the transfer, the same requirements must be applied. The only limitation is the prohibition on deciding to transform and to transfer at the same time.[90]

Secondly, for minority shareholders who oppose a transfer, appropriate protective provisions can be adopted by the Member States. In Belgium, it will be difficult to agree upon the appropriate measures and preserve the harmonious entirety of company rules. Every shareholder in a public limited liability company has the right to leave if well-founded reasons are present. Since the introduction of this rule in 1995, a significant number of court decisions have been published. These decisions refine the interpretation of well-founded reasons. It concerns continuous and severe disagreement between the shareholders of the company.[91] Neither a merger nor a transformation, nor a decision to change the purpose of the company have been accepted in case law or by the legislator as well-founded reasons to leave the company. If the transfer of seat by an SE were approved as a reason for leaving the company, this would imply that the legislator viewed the transfer of the seat as more important than other decisions. If no resignation is allowed, it remains unclear what measures the Belgian legislator might develop to protect the minority shareholders who oppose the transfer of the company seat.

After the proposal has been published, the SE has to wait for at least two months to decide upon the transfer.[92] After this period, the SE must be registered and the registration authority shall notify the register of the Member State where the SE previously had its registered seat.

The registered office can be transferred if the head office is in the Member State to which it is intended to transfer the registered office. If the head office has been transferred "de facto" to another Member State, the Member State where the SE has its head office must immediately inform the Member State where the SE's registered office is situated.[93] The latter Member State must take the measures necessary to ensure the regularisation of the division of the two seats. If the Member State fails, the SE will be liquidated.

[88] Article 558 Belgian CA.

[89] Article 781, section 1, 2° Belgian CA.

[90] Article 37, 3° RE-SE.

[91] See an overview of a number of court decisions in *K. Geens, M. Denef, F. Hellemans, R. Tas and J. Vananroye*, T.P.R. 2000, p. 447–448.

[92] Article 8, 7° RE-SE.

[93] Article 64, section 4 RE-SE.

Not all problems have been resolved. For the first time, a cumbersome but clear legal company law procedure is offered for a cross-border transfer of seat. However, no tax solution has been offered. Article 210, section, 4° of the Belgian Code of Revenue Taxes, explicitly indicates that in the case of a cross-border transfer of the registered seat or the real seat of a Belgian company, the taxable profits of the company include the surplus value of the assets of the company.[94] "De facto" this rule prohibits a cross-border transfer.

V. Involvement of employees

Under Belgian law two distinct legal frameworks enable employees to influence corporate decision making. Firstly, the works council has a number of powers. Secondly, different specific rules for the acquisition of shares by employees have been introduced since the beginning of the last decade.

The works council is composed of representatives of the employer and the employees[95] and has powers in relation to economic and financial affairs on the one hand, and social matters on the other.[96] The works council receives information concerning the operations of the company[97] and it acts as a consultative body.[98] A (statutory) auditor is required to submit its report concerning the annual accounts and reports and to certify the accuracy and comprehensiveness of economic and financial data of the company.[99] The works council has to be consulted before the election of a (statutory) auditor.

The council must be established in every company that employs at least 100 employees. Under certain conditions companies with less than 100 employees also have to establish such a council.

The Belgian system does not have rules that ensure that employees are represented on the board of directors or at the general meeting of shareholders. Part 3 of the Standard Rules for participation of employees in the annex of the Council Directive 2001/86/EC states that the SE is not required to establish pro-

[94] Article 210 refers to Article 208 and 209 of the same Code.

[95] The number of representatives of the employees must be higher or equal to the number of representatives of the employer.

[96] For more information see the Law of September 20, 1948, houdende organisatie van het bedrijfsleven, Official Gazette September 27, 1948, regularly modified.

[97] Information on general performance, financial results, etc.

[98] Advice on specific economic matters, to confer on the social impact of the introduction of new technologies, etc.

[99] Article 184 to 191 Royal Decree of January 30, 2001 to execute Belgian company law (Official Gazette February 6, 2001).

visions for employee participation, if the participating companies are not governed by participation rules before registration. Until now, it is unclear and too early to evaluate whether and how Belgium will introduce a system of employee participation.

However, it must be mentioned that the collective bargaining agreement 32[100] applies to every change of employer which is the result of a transfer by virtue of an agreement of a company. The application of this collective bargaining agreement implies the automatic transfer of all employment contracts, the prohibition on dismissing employees except in case of serious fault or economic or technical reasons, the automatic transfer of all terms and conditions of all employment contracts and the joint and several liability of the former and the new employer, for all debts that existed at the time of the transfer.

VI. Conclusion

The Regulation on the European Company has required an enormous amount of effort for more than thirty years. The co-determination issue was a stumbling block for the adoption of the rules on the SE.[101] It was only at the Nice summit in December 2000 that an agreement could be reached.

The Regulation refers to the rules on "national" public limited liability companies. for a large number of issues on the formation and the governance of an SE. Nevertheless, the Belgian Companies' Code conflicts with the Regulation. In that case, the Belgian SE must apply the Regulation. Hence, due to the reference of the Regulation, it is a necessity to adapt the Belgian legislation by October 2004. A well-developed two-tier board structure must be offered by the Belgian Companies' Code. Furthermore, the Belgian rules that govern the general meeting and the transfer of the seat need to be modified. The involvement of employees must be studied.

The SE constitutes a number of major advantages. It allows the establishment of a company with which all in the European Union can easily become familiar. It settles rules on the cross-border merger and the transfer of seat. Hence, it can be the engine for a new competitive economic environment. However, some disadvantages must be mentioned. Except for the subsidiaries of an SE, there is no direct access to the SE regime. At least fifteen (twenty-five) kinds of European companies will be established. The Regulation does not cover the tax rules. This is a missed opportunity. If we refer to the Belgium

[100] See Royal Decree of 25 July 1985, Official Gazette August 9, 1985.

[101] *E. Wymeersch in:* First European Jurist Forum – Nürnberg 2001, Nomos, 2001, p. 144.

situation, the tax rules concerning the transfer of seat or an international merger will, de facto, almost prohibit these operations. But let us end with a positive note: the SE is an important step forward in the development of a harmonised European company law.

Czech Republic

Irena Pelikánová/Petr Čech

Literature on the SE published in the Czech Republic: *Kanda, A.* Evropská akciová společnost (Societas Europaea) – věčná vize nebo blízká realita?, in Právník, 8/1993, p. 629 to 653; *Pelikánová, I.* Evropská akciová společnost a její význam pro české právo, in XIII. Karlovarské právnické dny, Linde Praha, 2003, p. 180 to 193.

I. Introduction

The adoption of the Council Regulation No. 2157/2001 on the Statute for a European company (further referred to as „SE-Regulation") and of the Council Directive 2001/86/EC supplementing the Statute for a European company with regard to the involvement of employees (further referred to as „SE-Directive") has so far attracted only limited attention of the Czech public, whether professional or general. Despite the forthcoming accession of the country to the European Union, the advantages of the new corporate form are neither widely analysed nor discussed. The size of the list of all professional articles recently published on the matter in Czech is self-explanatory.

Yet, amongst insiders, a suspicion prevails that the SE, once brought to the attention of Czech businessmen and legal professionals, shall produce a massive echo and capture the interest of many. Recent changes to the Czech corporate law have made this field of law quite unstable and unfriendly to its users and their legitimate demands. From the mid nineties the Czech legislator felt it necessary to respond to a series of unfortunate developments and, as it happens, overreacted. The opinion prevailed that the letter of the law can solve every real life problem and prevent any kind of mischief. Lack of professional know-how and little willingness to follow advice from the academic world and the market contributed to the sometimes poor outcome of the parliamentary work. Two major amendments to the Commercial Code were passed since its adoption in 1991: in 1996 and 2000, supplemented by a large number of minor amendments. Their aim was to reflect e.g. relations to the bankruptcy proceedings or, which is worse, to correct legislative errors of the previous enactments.[1]

[1] So the fundamental amendment Nr. 370/2000 Coll. (the so-called "Harmonisation Amendment" for its objective to streamline the Czech legislation with that of the EU)

The disputable quality of the Czech judicial system in the field of company law (mainly the sometimes disastrous situation at the commercial registers) made life of the companies incorporated under Czech law no easier.

Under such circumstances it would be of no surprise to see the SE being used as an instrument for some most unhappy Czech corporations to move to other jurisdictions. It must be borne in mind that the upcoming EU-enlargement shall add countries, with which Czech entrepreneurs are quite familiar, to the list of possible target jurisdictions. In Slovakia, for instance, Czech companies keep good contacts from times when both countries formed part of one federation. There is no language barrier in existence. Observing the newest reform attempts of the Slovak government in the field of business regulation and mainly taxation (lowering the corporate tax to nearly half of the current rates in the Czech Republic), one could suspect this to be one of the directions for the possible corporate migration. In fact, it has been communicated to us by a participant during one public lecture on the SE, that some clients are considering the use of the SE as an instrument to merge Czech and Slovak public limited-liability companies, the future seat of the SE being possibly Bratislava. The fact that the participant works for a major tax advising firm speaks for itself.[2]

Some positive effects of the SE on the Czech company law doctrine are becoming apparent even now. The fact that the SE-Regulation requires the introduction of the one-tier model of corporate governance into Czech law seems to be opening some academic minds. First signals are being broadcast that once the one-tier model is designed for the SE, no reason can justify why the same freedom of choice should not be allowed to purely domestic public limited-liability companies. Some proposals go as far as suggesting simply copying the provisions created for the SE into the Commercial Code. An idea impossible to table only some years ago, when no-one was prepared to take the time and courage to draft the whole one-tier system provisions, might be near realisation. An excellent opportunity is being offered: the new Commercial

contained so many shortcomings, that only one year later yet another needed to be passed, Act Nr. 501/2001 Coll., known as the "Technical Amendment". However, for procedural mistakes, Act Nr. 501/2001 Coll. was few months later repealed by the Constitutional Court. The Parliament adopted its text anew as Act Nr. 308/2003 Coll.

2 It must nevertheless be noted, that although the Slovak Parliament seems to be capturing some of the latest trends in development in a more successful manner, in the field of company law it mostly copies from the Czech law. However, this is done in a selective way, the resulting legislation coming far from being sufficiently exact and complete. Thus, e.g. the protection of minority shareholders and creditors under Czech law is much more complex than under Slovak law. The question therefore arises, to what extent Czech law will be able to compete in the end. The speed of companies registrations or tax incentives alone may prove to be an indicator of insufficient reliability.

Code is being drafted. On the other hand, academic opinions have clearly lost much respect in recent politics. Further decrease in the quality of commercial law legislation is feared, should the power of various lobbyist groups become its sole determinant.

None of the above alters the conclusion that a notable lack of academic interest and discussion has accompanied the formation of the draft Act, which implements necessary rules on SE into Czech law, where the national legislator is authorised to do so by the relevant provisions of the SE-Regulation. In the light of the described situation, some of the views and ideas presented in this article are to be understood as preliminary and certainly not representing the final or majority standpoint of the Czech corporate doctrine.

The Czech Ministry of Justice, aware of the obligations of the Czech Republic as a future Member State, took the first steps towards the implementation of the SE-Regulation into Czech law, soon after its adoption. An external expert working group, including both authors of this article, was established in the course of 2002 and entrusted with the task of formulating the draft bill. The implementation of the SE-Directive has fallen within the competence of the Ministry of Labour and Social Affairs. Both ministries soon reached a rational agreement to implement both the SE-Regulation and the SE-Directive in one Act. The mandate and the composition of the expert group were broadened accordingly.

The group presented its first proposal to both authorities by mid February 2003. Taking into account the scope of the matter, as well as the lack of know-how in other national jurisdictions, the group members would have wished a rather more generous timeframe for their work. Despite such calls, the proposal was sent out to central government authorities for comments. The deadline for the dispatch of the comments was set for the middle of May. The processing of the comments received, many of which were based on a misunderstanding of the limited space for implementation in case of the SE-Regulation, was also used as an opportunity to correct some shortcomings of the previous version, which the group discovered during further studies and negotiations.

Having responded to all comments, both ministries submitted the draft bill to the cabinet by the end of June. Before the cabinet debates it, an official standpoint must be delivered by its legislative council and sub-committees. These professional advisory bodies have the capacity to propose legislative changes, if necessary. In the absence of a final text of the future Act, where analysing particular provisions the authors refer to the wording of the draft as presented to the cabinet. Later alterations, including perhaps of a fundamental nature, cannot be excluded.

Some comments on the general framework of the proposed Act may be appropriate. The Czech commercial law is codified in the Commercial Code of

1991. The codification was affected by the historic circumstances prevailing at the time of its adoption. Forty years of experience with a totalitarian regime resulted in a situation where company law had been practically forgotten. The company law part of the Commercial Code therefore was among the weakest parts of its text.

Business companies legislation is to be found in the second of the four parts of the Commercial Code. It contains general provisions followed by stipulations on the particular company types, namely the general commercial partnership (veřejná obchodní společnost), the limited partnership (komanditní společnost), private limited-liability company (společnost s ručením omezeným) and the public limited-liability (joint stock) company (akciová společnost), as well as stipulations on co-operatives. The limited-liability partnership by shares (akciová komandita) was abolished in 1991. As mentioned above, the SE is to be governed by a special Act, it will nevertheless be entered on the list of business companies in the Commercial Code.

II. The formation of the SE in the Czech Republic

1. Participation of companies with head offices outside the EC

Article 2 para. 5 of the SE-Regulation authorises Member States to provide that a company, the head office of which is not in the Community, may participate in the formation of an SE as long as that company is formed under the law of a Member State, has its registered office in that Member State and has a continuous link with a Member State's economy. Although recent amendments to the Commercial Code have brought Czech corporate law closer to the real-seat doctrine, Section 3 of the draft bill proposes to make use of this option.

The aim is to encourage companies established in the various incorporation doctrine Member States, whose head offices are situated outside the EC or EEA, to participate in the formation of an SE, should the participating companies choose to register the SE in the Czech Republic. Such companies, although enjoying the status of duly formed entities under the law of a Member State, would otherwise be excluded from this process on the basis of Art. 2 para. 1 to 4 of the SE-Regulation. The draft endeavours to avoid a situation where certain companies are granted different treatment and are thus subjected to discrimination. By allowing such companies to form an SE, a clearly positive result might be reached. Since the head office of the SE must be established within the Member State where the registered office is located (Art. 7 of the SE-Regulation), the real seat of the participating company will, in many cases, have to be transferred to this State, i.e. to the Community. It remains to be seen, whether there will be any use made for the provision, the question mainly being if the described effect will not dissuade such companies from taking part in the formation of the SE.

2. The location of the seat of the SE within the Czech Republic

In addition to the general requirement of Art. 7 of the SE-Regulation it is proposed to impose an obligation upon the SEs registered in the Czech Republic to locate their head office (the place of their main administration) in the same place as the registered office (section 5 para. 1 of the draft bill). The local unity of both offices must be preserved throughout the existence of the SE, unless the SE transfers its registered office to a different Member State. In case of discrepancies, the court of registration shall demand regularisation of the situation within a given period. Should the company fail to comply, the court will be entitled, upon its own initiative, to declare the dissolution of the company and appoint a liquidator, as is the case in Art. 64 of the SE-Regulation.

In such a way, the SEs with registered offices in the Czech Republic would be under obligations comparable to local companies established under Czech law. According to Section 2 para. 3 of the Czech Commercial Code, each entrepreneur – a natural person must have the real place of his business as his statutory office registered. A similar requirement is imposed on legal persons. Section 19c para. 2 of the Czech Civil Code demands that the registered office be located in the place where the entity is effectively situated, i.e. the place of its main administration provided that the general public can actually contact the entity there (the place must be publicly accessible). The provisions were inserted in both codes only recently as a response to past developments resulting in serious damages to creditors or other third parties when seeking to contact the entrepreneur in question. Unlike the SE-Regulation, which provides for dissolution of an SE in breach of provisions on the territorial unity of its offices, the Czech Civil Code stipulates that anybody can rely upon the real seat of the legal person, if different from the registered one. The law does not contain the second part of the rule, which appeared in the draft amendment to the Commercial Code and proposed to prohibit any legal person from using its registered seat against third parties, if it is different from its real seat. These instruments aim at protecting good faith of third parties and preventing the legal persons in question from abusive misconduct.

The general Czech law, which earlier made no distinction between the registered (statutory) and the real office, continues to use the term "seat" on its own as an expression of the registered (statutory) office. The draft bill proposes to adhere to the terminology of the SE-Regulation: "registered office", translated as "statutární sídlo". However, the innovative nature of the term has given rise to numerous objections to such an enrichment of legal terminology.

3. Protection of minority shareholders and creditors in the formation of the SE

Minority shareholders protection under Czech law is (in relative terms) very intense since the adoption of the Harmonisation Amendment to the Commercial Code in 2000[3]. The amendment extended the circle of shareholders with special protection rights (Section 181 – see also below) and supplemented a number of protective provisions regarding transformations of companies, general meeting resolutions, groups of companies, takeover bids and other matters. It appears that, due to the limitations contained in the SE-Regulation, the applicability of these provisions to the SE will lead to a decrease of the level of such protection for shareholders of the SE, compared to domestic public limited-liability companies. Parts of the problem will be analysed below.

4. Formation by merger

In accordance with Art. 24 para. 2 of the SE-Regulation, which allows Member States to adopt provisions designed to ensure appropriate protection for minority shareholders in the companies participating in the merger and which are subject to its law, Section 16 of the draft bill refers to national rules applicable to domestic mergers. The relevant provisions are found in Sections 220k and 220m of the Commercial Code.

a) Cash compensation for inappropriate share-exchange ratio

Section 220k of the Commercial Code provides for cash compensation for minority shareholders in case of inappropriate share-exchange ratios. The proceedings must be brought before the commercial court, unless the draft terms of the merger establish the competence of an arbiter or a court of arbitration. They represent the only way to challenge the share-exchange ratio or the amount of the compensation to be paid to shareholders in the merger. The registration of the merger itself cannot be successfully prevented for such reasons (Section 220h para. 2 of the Commercial Code). The right to proceed against the acquiring or the successor companies is generally given a) to any

[3] See under 1 above.

shareholder of the participating company registered in the Czech Republic on the day of the resolution of the general meeting on the merger provided that b) the shareholder has remained in the possession of the shares and c) has not waived this right. The preconditions sub a) and b) above need not be met, if the claimant holds shares representing at least one per cent of the registered capital of the company or the face value of these shares exceeds CZK 100,000 (approx. EUR 3,000). The right must be exercised within one year from the publication of the registration of the merger. If one shareholder succeeds, the court ruling becomes binding upon the successor company vis-á-vis all other shareholders, even if they have not filed their actions within the given period.

The application of such provisions to the SE, however, implies questions which yet remain to be answered. The main source of difficulty is the limited scope of authority allowed to Member States when creating such protective procedures. While Czech law entitles each shareholder fulfilling the cited preconditions to demand compensation, whether or not he/she voted in favour or against the merger or even whether he/she voted at all, Art. 24 para. 2 of the SE-Regulation makes it possible for Member States to protect only minority shareholders "*who have opposed the merger*"! Hence, while the original version of the proposal referred to Section 220k of the Commercial Code in its full width, it was realised later that its scope of application must be modified by narrowing the circle of shareholders entitled to proceed against the SE to those who have actively (i.e. with a negative vote in the general meeting) opposed the merger. The same limitation must be applied to the circle of other beneficiaries of a positive ruling of the court on any similar claim brought before it. A consultation with the European Commission confirmed that such is truly the only and intended scope of the relevant provision of the SE-Regulation.

However, under these circumstances a fundamental question arises, namely, to what extent such regulation respects the principle of equality. The mere fact that somebody voted in favour of the merger, abstained from the voting or has not attended the meeting for whatever reasons, appears to be a weak ground for excluding such a person from the circle of shareholders who can demand a remedy in case of an inappropriate share-exchange ratio or cash compensation. At least under Czech national company law standards, such a provision would and will be perceived as discriminatory. This is even a greater problem in a situation where the shareholders in question have neither the right to demand higher compensation, nor to challenge the merger itself (it must be noted that in Czech company law the right to challenge a general meeting resolution is not made subject to a negative vote or any kind of protest of the entitled person raised in the meeting or even to his/her attendance to the meeting).

Even shareholders who have opposed the merger might be confronted with the same "double" exclusion. Such problem will arise if the merging companies from other jurisdictions, which do not provide for such procedure, refuse to accept the possibility of the shareholders of the Czech merging companies having recourse to such procedure, when approving the draft terms of the merger (Art. 25 para. 3 of the SE-Regulation).

For the reasons described, whether or not to depart from the generally applicable rule on the impossibility of challenging the merger on grounds of an inappropriate share-exchange ratio or insufficient cash compensation in situations where the merger is to result in the formation of an SE, is still under consideration. The fact that such modification has not yet been introduced in the draft bill is due only to the perceived fear that the change might create a serious obstacle to the process of establishing the SE on the side of the Czech participation companies. It is clear that until all proceedings on such challenges would have been finalised, the relevant authority would not be able to issue the certificate necessary for the creation of the SE. If, on the other hand, the proceedings were only commenced after the issuance of the certificate, their result could not prevent the SE from being established, even if the court declared the general meeting resolution void.

The proposed wording of Section 16 of the draft bill contains no special rules concerning the transnational character of the merger. As provided in Art. 24 para. 2 of the SE-Regulation, the protection offered by the Commercial Code covers only specified minority shareholders of participating companies registered in the Czech Republic. Ways to make the proceedings more acceptable for the shareholders of foreign participation companies within the meaning of Art. 25 para. 3 of the SE-Regulation (e.g. allowing them to send a representative before the Czech court to have their voice heard in the proceedings) have not been suggested. The general conviction is that merely allowing a representative of such shareholders to participate in the proceedings cannot achieve this objective, while the procedural complications would be immense. Besides, the Czech court could not reflect the interests of the shareholders of the foreign companies participating in the merger.

b) Offer to buy out shares

Section 220m of the Commercial Code, to which reference is also made in Section 16 of the draft, requires that the project of the merger imposes an obligation on the successor company to buy out its shares issued in exchange for the shares of the merging companies. The offer is to be addressed to shareholders who held the shares of the merging companies on the day when the general meeting approved the merger, provided that these shareholders also took part in the general meeting either personally or through a proxy and did not vote in favour of the merger. However, the obligation only arises, where the shares exchanged for those of the merging companies are of different class or not freely transferable, where they incorporate different rights or are not listed compared to the shares of the merging companies. The protection under Section 220m of the Commercial Code hence applies only where a merger results in the specified decrease in the quality of the shares exchanged for the shares of the merging companies.

The buy-out offer must be published within two weeks from the publication of the registration of the merger. The price offered is to reflect true value of the shares in question as demonstrated by an independent expert valuation and must be discharged no later than one month after the shares have been transferred to the offeror. Similarly, as in the case of a reference to Section 220k of the Commercial Code, also the scope of application of Section 220m was reduced to reflect the limitation of Art. 24 para. 2 of the SE-Regulation. While in case of a domestic merger the public offer must be made also to shareholders who abstained from the vote, the SE-Regulation explicitly allows only for protection of dissenting shareholders.

The orderly discharge of the obligations of the offeror, i.e. of the SE, under Section 220m of the Commercial Code is subject to supervisory and enforcement competence of the Czech Securities Commission. Penalties for non-compliance can, depending on the degree of the breach, rise to an amount of CZK 100 million (approx. EUR 3 million). The question nevertheless arises as to how such supervision and/or administrative sanctioning shall be carried out in cases where the future SE, despite being subject to the provisions of the Commercial Code, is not registered in the Czech Republic.

c) Creditor protection

As regards protection of creditors of the merging companies, Article 24 para. 1 of the SE-Regulation refers directly to national laws governing each merging company, which apply in the case of a merger of public limited-liability companies. In Czech law the reference is aimed at Section 220j of the Commercial Code. Under this provision the creditors of the participating companies who register their claims within six months after the registration of the merger is published and who cannot obtain immediate satisfaction of these claims, can demand additional security, provided that the merger will affect the enforceability of the claims. If the creditor is capable of demonstrating that the merger will result in substantial deterioration of the enforceability of his claims, he can demand security even before the merger is registered. The provisions do not apply to claims which would be treated as preferential or secured in bankruptcy proceedings, to claims established after the registration of the merger or incorporated in bonds if the bond-holder meeting approved the merger.

According to Art. 24 para. 1 of the SE-Regulation, the application of these national provisions should take into account the cross-border nature of the merger. However, there remains no room for Member States to specify how such account is to be taken, especially in cases where the SE is to be registered in a different Member State than that in which one or all of the merging companies were. With regard to the fact that such merger will enable the merging company to escape its creditors by transferring to a different jurisdiction (posing some difficulty on the enforcement of their claims), one can expect that creditors will be often tempted to make use of their right to demand security even before the merger is registered. In case of a seat transfer of the SE, Art. 8 para. 16 of the SE-Regulation stipulates that in respect of any cause of action arising prior to the transfer, the SE which has transferred its registered office to another Member State shall be considered as having its registered office in the Member State where the SE was registered prior to the transfer, even if the SE is sued after the transfer. The creditors will continue to be entitled to bring their actions against the SE before the courts of the Member State of the original registration. Although the effects of a transnational merger combined with an effective seat transfer are equal, no similar rule was adopted. Once the merger is registered, the creditors will loose their right to sue in the original Member State.

5. Formation of a holding SE

a) Protection of minority shareholders

National rules on protection of minority shareholders of the participating (i.e. future subsidiary, "promoting") companies in case of establishing a holding SE correspond to those applicable in a merger. However, there remains some uncertainty concerning how to apply these rules, given the specific nature of the operation. As in the case of a merger, Art. 34 of the SE-Regulation authorises Member States to protect only shareholders *who have opposed the operation.* Yet, it is not very clear in what forms the dissenting shareholder is to manifest his opposition in order to qualify for the protection. He may certainly do so by voting against the project in the general meeting of the promoting companies within the meaning of Art. 32 para. 6 of the SE-Regulation. However, if the project is adopted despite his vote, the shareholder remains free to decide whether or not to assign the shares of the holding SE in exchange for his shares in the promoting company. Logically, the protective provisions of Section 220k and 220m of the Commercial Code, to which reference is made in Section 20 of the draft bill, can only apply if the shareholder chose to assign the shares of the holding SE, i.e. upon his own initiative and with an implied will to support the project of establishing the SE, no matter how he previously voted. It seems doubtful if the assigning shareholder can still be considered as having opposed the operation. Apparently, the protective rules must be based on different principles. The situation seems to require protection of shareholders who decide not to assign shares in the holding SE and remain left in a solitary minority in the shareholding of the promoting companies controlled by the SE. This protection could take the form of a mandatory bid by the SE or similar. The expert group has nevertheless delivered no final answer for the implementation law. The issue is being analysed, considered and consulted. It remains to be seen what solutions are adopted in the other Member States.

b) Creditor protection

Unlike in a merger, Art. 34 of the SE-Regulation makes it possible for Member States to formulate special rules to protect creditors of the promoting companies. Section 20 of the draft bill makes use of this authorisation merely by referring to national provisions applicable to mergers, i.e. again to Section 220j of the Commercial Code. With regard to the specific situation in establishing the holding SE and especially to the fact that the promoting debtor companies remain in existence, only the controlling body changes, it appears that the protection under the described provisions will usually not be necessary. The creation of the holding SE will rarely qualify as justifying a conclusion that the creditors' claims against the promoting companies shall be affected or even substantially affected. Perhaps with the exception of cases when the change in the governing entity might also result in the change in control mechanisms (the new entity will demand profit transfers etc.). The rules on creditor protection in case of groups of companies might thus come into play.

c) Employee protection

Section 20 of the draft bill foresees no provisions on employee protection. This part of Art. 34 of the SE-Regulation remains uncovered. The expert group believes that transposing the SE-Directive results in sufficient protection. Such is also the opinion of the relevant employees of DG Employment of the European Commission, who have been surveyed on the issue. The special reference to employee protection in Art. 34 of the SE-Regulation seems to constitute a pre-SE-Directive relict of older versions of the text, which managed to escape the attention of future revisors and was by omission not deleted.

6. Other questions arising in connection to the establishment of an SE

One of the key instruments of the SE-Regulation in the process of establishing an SE by a merger (as well as of its seat transfer to a different jurisdiction) is *the certificate* issued to confirm the legality of the steps conducted on the territory of the issuing Member State. The identification of the authority competent to issue the certificate (Art. 25 para. 2 of the SE-Regulation) is left with the Member States.

a) Competence to issue the certificate confirming the legality of the procedure

The Czech draft proposes to entrust this competence to the notaries, despite the fact that the standard company registration agenda is processed by the courts. The inefficiency and unreliability of the performance of the registration courts in the Czech Republic has produced much dissatisfaction. Other solutions are being discussed, including one to delegate the agenda to private entrepreneurs, as in the French model. Allegedly out of fear of high costs associated with the privatization model, the cabinet appears more likely to create a central government body with branches all over the country (the public administration model). Whatever the outcome of the discussions, the expert group wished to limit the exposure of the founders of the SE, and the SE itself, to the Czech registration courts.

The draft bill further endeavours to speed up the whole process by authorising the Ministry of Justice to issue a piece of subordinate legislation (a decree) providing a complete list of documents, which the notaries would be entitled to demand from the applicants. It is believed that this measure could significantly strengthen legal certainty and expedite the acquisition of the certificate. On the other hand, it remains clear that drafting such a list in order to make it complete and correct will not be free from all difficulty. And yet, any delay in the issue of the decree could prevent the applicability of the whole national legislation on the SE.

For each participating company a separate certificate will be issued, even if two or more of them come from the territory of the same Member State. After the notary issues the certificate, the participating company will have six months to submit it to the competent authority in the Member State of the proposed registered office of the SE. The competent authority of this Member State shall scrutinise the legality of the merger, though only regarding the part of the procedure concerning the completion of the merger. As to the part concerning each merging company, the competent authority shall be entitled (and obliged) to rely on the work performed by the authority of the Member State where the merging companies are registered, i.e. the notary in the Czech Republic, and the outcome of this work as expressed in the certificate.

b) Challenges to the general meeting's resolution

The significance attached to the certificate in the process of creating the SE by way of merger is therefore huge. Any negligence of the notary will incur immense liability. Any procedures pending against the general meeting resolution on the approval of the draft terms of the merger will surely create the main obstacle to the issue of the certificate. According to Section 131 para. 1 of the Czech Commercial Code, a petition to declare the resolution void must be filed within three months from the day on which the general meeting was held or on which the entitled person learned of the general meeting which was improperly convened. Even in the latter case, no person can challenge the resolution after one year from the general meeting. Hence, whatever the judgement of the notary concerning the legality of the resolution, he/she will most probably be careful enough to postpone the issue of the certificate for at least three months from the general meeting. In case of any doubts as to the manner in which the meeting was convened, the notary might be advised to let the one-year-period elapse. Only in doing so, he/she can avoid that the resolution will be challenged after the issue of the certificate. As mentioned, Czech company law does not subject the right to challenge a general meeting resolution to any kind of formal protest raised during the meeting. The mere fact that no protest was recorded in the minutes cannot establish expectations concerning future actions against the resolution.

If no petition against the resolution is filed within the specified period, the resolution is considered valid despite its shortcomings, however serious. Such is at least the opinion of many influential representatives of the Czech corporate law science, though it is by far not shared by all. The court may (and must) nevertheless conduct a new scrutiny of the legality of the resolution when deciding upon the entry of the matter in question in the commercial register. It goes without saying that the notary requested to issue the certificate cannot wait for the outcome of this scrutiny. However, after the certificate is issued, the SE can be registered in the Member State of its proposed registered office. No further scrutiny of the legality of the acts conducted in the Member States of the participating companies will take place. Conversely, once the SE is registered, the Member State where the merging companies are registered must respect the registration. Art. 30 of the SE-Regulation makes it absolutely clear that a merger may not be declared null and void once the SE has been registered. This seems to imply for the merging companies and their shareholders that once the certificate has been issued, the resolution on the merger cannot be successfully challenged. The second subparagraph of Art. 30 of the SE-Regulation provides that the absence of scrutiny of the legality of the merger pursuant to Articles 25 and 26 may be included among the grounds for the winding-up of the SE. This construction corresponds to the provisions on nullity of a company as contained in Directive 68/151/EEC. If the merger cannot be declared void, the SE might be *ex nunc* dissolved and wound-up for reasons expressly provided in law. The winding-up will prevent the further existence of an SE established in most serious contravention of the relevant regulations. However, one may ask if such construction is sufficient. Similar questions were raised in connection with the current provisions on nullity of mergers according to Section 220h of the Czech Commercial Code. It seems that the amendment of 2000 introduced a more logical solution to this problem. After the merger has been registered, the pending court proceedings on the validity of the general meeting resolution or of the contract on the merger may resume only if the applicant changes the subject of the petition to a claim for compensation for damage suffered.

c) Legal nature of the certificate confirming the legality of the procedure

Another problem which may arise, concerns the question of what form to assign to the certificate (especially if it is issued by a notary) and whether to allow judicial review thereof. The SE-Regulation gives no answer, yet it seems to treat the certificate as a valid and final deed which can be relied upon by the competent authorities of the Member State to register the SE without any reservations, whatever the circumstances. We might, however, see situations where it will be appropriate or even necessary to question the certificate before it is used by the competent authority as a basis for the registration of the SE. Or will the competent authority be entitled (or even compelled) to ignore that the certificate is being subject to judicial review in the Member State where it was issued? Or worse, that the reviewing court has issued a preliminary ruling depriving the certificate of any legal effect?

Owing to the uncertainty as to the correct implementation of the SE-Regulation, the expert group proposed no special provisions on the nature of the certificate and its judicial review. Section 15 of the draft bill merely responds to the option given to the Member States in Art. 19 of the SE-Regulation. The certificate shall be denied if a competent public authority raises an objection against the participation of the applicant in the merger. The objection must be recorded in writing, based on grounds of public interest, orderly reasoned and delivered to the participating company and to the commercial register for entry and publication. The participating company may challenge the objection in court within two months from delivery. The notary issues the certificate only if it is demonstrated that the company has reached an agreement with the objecting authority, that the court has repealed the objection, or that it has imposed conditions under which the certificate may be issued and these conditions were met. It must be added, though, that some fundamental objections have been raised against such a provision. It is feared that exercising the option might in practice lead to unnecessary obstacles being imposed on the corporate migration from the territory of the Czech Republic. It therefore remains open whether the option will be exercised in the end.

III. Transfer of the seat of the SE from the Czech Republic

The implementation provisions of the draft bill concerning the transfer of the seat of the SE registered in the Czech Republic into a different Member State cover mainly three subjects: protection of minority shareholders, protection of the creditors of the SE, and the issue of the certificate demonstrating the validity of the steps preceding the transfer.

Protection of minority shareholders who have opposed the transfer by a negative vote in the general meeting (Art. 8 para. 5 of the SE-Regulation) is provided by reference to the relevant provisions of the Commercial Code on the buy-out obligation of the successor company in case of a merger, i.e. to Section 220m. Similarly the draft bill refers to the relevant provisions on creditor protection (i.e. to Section 220j). Stipulations on the certificate are structured identically to those concerning the creation of the SE by way of merger, including the disputed right of a public authority to prevent the issue of the certificate.

IV. Corporate governance of the SE

The implementation of the SE-Regulation will not bring any fundamental changes to the Czech law on corporate governance, with the exception of the need to introduce the one-tier system (see below).

One problem, however, remains open in the draft bill. It will probably need to be solved in the general provisions of the Commercial Code on business companies. It concerns corporate directors. After the adoption of the Commercial Code in 1991, the doctrine seemingly took the view admitting only natural persons as members of company bodies. The Harmonisation Amendment of 2000, however, drew from the fact that corporate directors are allowed in partnerships. As legal persons can become partners, they also automatically enjoy the status of directors.

As recent amendments to the provisions on relations between companies and their directors in Section 66 of the Commercial Code, which were pushed through by the Members of the Deputy (lower) Chamber of the Czech Parliament, show, the law *de facto* takes account of the general possibility of corporate directors. The newly inserted paragraphs namely relieve particular members of company bodies, who represent certain public law corporations on such bodies, of accountability. If this is admitted in the case of specified corporations being shareholders, one can hardly reject the idea of corporate directors in general. However, the current situation is not free from contradictions. The law provides that if a member of the board is e.g. an employee of the National Property Fund, the Fund carries responsibility for his actions on the board. However, this contravenes the concept of a natural person's membership in the body. The solution should be the opposite: the membership should be the legal person's, yet the natural person sent to represent the legal person would be treated, as though this natural person were him/herself the member. The draft law on the SE nevertheless introduces no special provisions on corporate directors of the SE – the solution must be discussed and found in the general provisions of the Commercial Code.

1. The two-tier system

The two-tier system is the regular and so far exclusive corporate governance model of a public limited-liability company established under Czech law. Only a few adjustments of this system to the SE were needed.

It was felt necessary to make use of the authorisation of Art. 39 para. 2 of the SE-Regulation. According to Section 23 para. 1 of the draft bill, the statutes of the Czech SE might entrust the competence to appoint and dismiss members of the board of directors to the general meeting. Such is the regular way of creating and dissolving the board of directors under Czech law and such is also the common practice in the vast majority of the public limited-liability companies in the Czech Republic. The Czech law allows for this right to be exercised by the supervisory board, if authorised in the statutes (the Czech doctrine refers to this governance scheme as to the "German model"). However, only a few Czech companies have adopted this structure (mostly companies with large German shareholdings).

Section 26 of the draft bill authorises each individual member of the supervisory board to require information of any kind, as foreseen in Art. 41 para. 3 of the SE-Regulation. The expert group believed that this measure might increase the efficiency of the work of the supervisory board, sometimes thought to be rather low. The conviction is based on practical experience. Czech law denies a single supervisory board member such individual right, unless authorised by a resolution of the supervisory board. Such authorisation is sometimes difficult to acquire, especially if the composition of both boards reflects the same interests. On the other hand, the same practical experience teaches that the individual right of inquiry into the matters of the company can be misused for purposes of espionage in the interest of a minority shareholder or even the trade unions. Section 26 of the draft bill therefore imposes some limits on the individual exercise of such right. The information must be necessary for the individual member's activity in the supervisory board and the use of the right must be justified by a significant interest of the company. Should a dispute arise over what is to be considered a significant interest of the company, a court decision must be sought either by the individual member of the supervisory board or by the board of directors.

2. The one-tier system

The Czech Commercial Code contains no provisions on the one-tier system. Large parts of the draft bill therefore include provisions introducing this system into Czech law. Inspiration was mainly sought in the French amendment to the Commercial Code of May 2001 (so called NRE – Nouvelle regulation économique), which brought elements of the corporate governance principles into French public limited liability company law.

The core provisions are those on the administrative board. It is proposed that this be composed of between three and eighteen natural persons (no legal members admissible), the highest number to be specified in the statutes. Such solution is rather unusual in Czech law as it enables a certain variability of the exact number of the administrative board members. Equally unusual is the variability of the particular model of control (the chairman of the administrative body with various scope of powers). Completely new to Czech law is a solution admitting wide decision-making and general representation powers to several bodies in parallel. The present Czech law has so far been based on the principle that there is only one "statutory body" (whose main characteristic is the general power of representation) in each legal person. The principle has been adhered to for many decades despite the practical difficulties it created. The draft bill endeavours to break this tradition, but the outcome of the initiative still remains uncertain.

The management functions (business leadership) are entrusted to the chairman of the administrative board, provided he is simultaneously the general manager of the company (PDG after the French model). If this is not the case, the managerial functions are performed exclusively by the general manager. Such is also the allocation of the power of representation. If the chairman is concurrently the general manager, the power to conclude all acts in the name of the company is his. Otherwise it is the general manager who possesses the authority to perform legal acts for the company. The personal unity vis-á-vis the separation of functions of the chairman and the general manager must be resolved by the administrative body itself. However, the preconditions for such a resolution must be specified in the SE statutes. Once the resolution is taken, it is to be entered into the commercial register and published in the printed form of the national gazette (Obchodní věstník). There are no specific rules on later changes to this resolution, yet it is generally presumed that such changes are possible.

The chairman is elected by the administrative body from among its members, as stipulated in Art. 45 of the SE-Regulation. The draft bill adds that only the administrative body can replace him. However, having regard to the possible employee participation in the board, provisions are made that the chairman can only be dismissed if a majority of the votes in favour of such dismissal are cast by members representing the shareholders. It is foreseen in Art. 45 of the SE-Regulation that if half of the members of the administrative board are appointed by employees, only a member appointed by the general meeting of shareholders may be elected chairman. Theoretically, a question may arise as to whether it would be permissible to elect a chairman from among the employee representatives in an SE where the employees appoint fewer than half of the board members. Practically, however, this question will hardly need to be answered. As regards the powers of the chairman, whether or not he acts as the general manager, he represents the administrative board, organises and chairs its meetings and reports to the general meeting on the board' work. The chairman is further obliged to review the work of other bodies of the SE and to make sure that other members of the board are qualified to perform their functions.

The draft bill further introduces the function of a delegate general manager. Upon the initiative and the proposal of the general manager, the administrative board may appoint one to five natural persons to assist the general manager; the exact number to be specified in the SE statutes. If appointed, the powers of the delegate general manager equal those of the general manager (including power of representation in its full and externally unlimited scope).

For matters not specifically covered by the draft bill, Section 28 includes a general competence clause. It stipulates that the provisions on the powers of the board of directors and the supervisory board in a two-tier public limited-liability company, as provided for in the Commercial Code, are to be applied on the one-tier SE in such a way that such distribution of powers between the administrative board, its chairman, the general manager and the delegate general managers is reached, which in substance reflects to the greatest extent possible the nature and the competence of the respective bodies in the one-tier SE. The expert group wished to avoid long lists of provisions on the allocation of each single power in the SE amongst the various bodies. It was believed that no matter how detailed the list, it would still leave space for future disputes. Instead, the door was open for a just doctrinal or judicial judgement based on particulars of each specific case.

It is foreseen that members of the administrative board may not take up similar functions (i.e. ones of members of an administrative board or a board of directors) in more than four other SEs or public limited-liability companies. This precondition is only ascertained at the moment of the election or appointment. A later infringement of the rule is not penalised by the member's removal from office.

The Czech draft law endeavours to reflect the general principles of good corporate governance also by allowing the board in Section 42 para. 4 to create committees and entrust them with various specialised functions. The French inspiration has been used also in drafting provisions on the performance of legal acts with potential conflict of interest. The currently drafted minor amendment to the Czech Commercial Code might even copy these provisions proposed for the SE to become the general rules on public limited-liability companies.

As regards rules concerning the general meeting of the SE, the draft bill lowers the threshold necessary for the existence of a right to request that a general meeting be convened and for drawing-up the agenda thereof, to 5 per cent, where the total amount of legal capital of the SE does not exceed 100 million CZK (approx. 3.2 million EUR), and 3 per cent in all other cases. Those are the proportions for comparable rights in national public limited-liability companies. The expert group thought it advisable to treat SEs similarly, given that such right has been provided to the Member States in Art. 55 para. 1 of the SE-Regulation.

V. Employee involvement in the SE

1. General

Rules on employee involvement in the SE were amongst the most complex to create. Since the first version was produced, it was altered a few times. Even up to the present day and despite an enormous amount of technical assistance provided by experts from DG Employment of the European Commission, uncertainty remains as to whether all details of the SE-Directive have been properly understood and duly implemented. No matter what progress has been made since the adoption of the Directive, selected matters only wait to be resolved by the Commission and the Member States. The relevant department of DG Employment so far finalised 21 out of 33 Working Papers on the interpretation and implementation of the SE-Directive. Some of the Working Papers already produced have even had to be reviewed, other revisions are likely to follow. It appears that the wider the understanding of the SE-Directive, the more problems are being discovered.

The great amount of resources invested in the coordination of the implementation process by the European Commission only illustrates the complexity of the matter. And of course its significance. The main idea behind such efforts is clear: if the European Commission did not take the initiative, the outcome of the national implementation procedures would be certain to be chaotic, and the result could undermine the whole success of the SE. The question of how many SEs we shall see established in practice, will, in fact, to a large extent depend on how properly each Member States implements the SE-Directive. According to Art. 12 para. 2 of the SE-Regulation, an SE may not be registered unless an agreement on arrangements for employee involvement pursuant to the SE-Directive has been taken or has not been taken within the specified six – (or possibly twelve –, if prolonged) month period. Since the transnational element must be present in the establishment of every SE, the pre-condition of a duly carried out compulsory negotiation procedure as stipulated in the SE-Directive will not be met, unless all involved jurisdictions transposed the SE-Directive in time and correctly. The main legislation applicable to the negotiation procedure may be that of the Member State in which the registered office of the SE is to be situated (Art. 6 of the SE-Directive), however these "principal" provisions of the Member State of the proposed place of registration of the SE cannot function without the support from the "accessory" provisions adopted in the other Member States, where e.g. the participating companies or the concerned subsidiaries and establishments of the future SE are situated. Failure of one Member State to transpose the SE-Directive in a compatible form might make future establishments of SEs involving companies or establishments from this Member State virtually impossible. In fact, one of the working papers of the European Commission (No. 5) has been devoted to the problem of insufficient transposition of the SE-Directive by one or more Member States.

2. Creation of the special negotiating body

a) Allocation of seats

The necessary interplay between the principal and accessory provisions of the various legislations can be best demonstrated on the creation of the special negotiating body (SNB), perhaps the most crucial issue of the whole directive. The seats in the SNB are allocated according to the law of the Member State where the SE is to be registered (a principal provision). How the seats allocated to the employee representatives from one Member State are to be distributed and taken is a matter of the Member State, where the representatives are to be appointed or elected (accessory provision). If the SE is to be created by way of merger, additional seats may need to be allocated to some Member States to make sure that the SNB includes at least one member directly representing employees from each participating company which is registered and has employees in that Member State and which it is proposed will cease to exist as a separate legal entity following the registration of the SE. This rule makes part of the principal provisions. Nevertheless, the necessity to allocate additional seats can only be ascertained on the basis of the accessory provisions, i.e. the laws of the Member States, where the original distribution took place. It might well be that the accessory provisions allocate the original number of seats in such a way as provides that direct representatives from such companies are satisfied in the first round, so no additional seats need to be allocated to the employee representatives from the given Member State. The distribution of the additional seats in a Member State is once again a matter of the law of the Member State in which the distribution is to take place. Should one of the Member States fail to implement the SE-Directive or to implement it correctly, the whole system collapses: the SNB cannot be created as required by the SE-Directive, no negotiating procedure might commence and the SE cannot be registered.

The Czech draft bill endeavours to take due regard of the described relations between principal and accessory provisions of the bill itself and of other Member States with which it will have to be combined. Somewhat unusual formulations to the legal system were therefore inevitable, such as that expressing the above mentioned additional seats rule, which reads: "If the SE is established by merger and the seats in the special negotiating body will not *according to this law or that of the relevant Member State* be distributed in such a way as secures that the employees of the participating companies, which are proposed to cease to exist as result of the merger, are represented by at least one member from amongst such employees or by one directly or indirectly elected or appointed by such employees (further referred to only as "direct representative") ..." (Section 51 para. 3 of the draft bill). It should be stressed that as accessory rule, Section 51 para. 6 of the draft bill provides that in a situation where the Czech law is to govern the occupation of the seats allocated by a different legislation and some Czech companies participating in a merger are proposed to cease to exist, the employees of such companies are to be directly represented from the very beginning. In such a way, the expert group tried to avoid the need for additional seats to be allocated to representatives of the employees from the Czech Republic. Some Member States might be tempted to opt for the very opposite: the fewer of such participating companies are directly represented after the "first round" of distribution, the higher the chances for additional seats to be allocated to employee representatives from this Member State. Yet, no advantage was seen in the fact that the SNB will grow in number of members. The more members on the SNB, the higher only the transactional cost, and perhaps the chance of no reasonable agreement to be reached. The voting procedures stipulated by the SE-Directive make it rather irrelevant how many persons have taken the vote. What counts is the number of employees that the voters represent.

The described attitude predetermines the wording of further accessory rules governing the manner in which seats are to be distributed to representatives of the Czech employees (meaning persons employed in the Czech Republic or more precisely employed under Czech labour law, regardless of nationality). A general rule applies that where possible, employees of each company or establishment should be represented by at least one direct representative. If this is not possible, the above mentioned priority rule for workers of companies disappearing in the merger must be used. If workers from all disappearing Czech companies cannot be directly represented (i.e. there are more such companies than the number of seats allocated to the representatives of Czech employees, even after additional seats have been allocated), only the largest ones in number of employees will be satisfied. The same holds for the remaining companies or establishments. However, if employees from any company or establishment cannot be represented by a direct representative, it is expressly required that the direct representatives of workers from other companies and establishments must serve as indirect representatives of the former ones. Each of them will represent an equal number of the other workers. In this way the fundamental rule, which demands that every employee must be represented in the SNB, will be adhered to.

Thus, if Czech companies A (3,000 employees), B (2,000 employees) and C (1,000 employees) participating in the merger are to cease to exist on the day of registry of the SE, but only two seats on the SNB were allocated to representatives of workers employed in the Czech Republic, all of the workers employed in the Czech Republic will be represented by a person appointed or elected by employees of companies A and B. Workers in company C will have no right to appoint or elect their direct representative. Their interests will nevertheless be represented by both of the SNB members. One of them will therefore represent 3,500 workers, the other 2,500.

Rules on selecting the direct representative within each company or establishment, have been incorporated by way of reference to the provisions of Section 25e of the Labour Code, which basically provides that the person to represent the workers on the SNB will be nominated by trade unions of the company or establishment. If there are competing trade union organisations within one company or establishment, they shall sit together and elect the representative in a proportionate vote. If there are no trade unions in the relevant company or establishment, direct elections will be held among the employees.

b) Commencement of the negotiation procedure

The establishment of the SNB is a precondition for the commencement of the negotiation procedure. The six-month period relevant for its outcome may only start upon the creation of the SNB. The problem of the exact determination of this day is therefore of the essence. Should we count the period from the day on which the SNB first assembled in its full composition? What if a few members are missing, though duly summoned? Should the day then not be the one, on which the last member of the SNB was appointed or elected? What if some employees or their representatives remain inactive and do not elect or appoint a representative to the SNB despite conditions having been created by the participating companies for them to do so? Having regard to some uncertainty among Member States as to what is to be considered the exact day of the establishment of the SNB, no legislative measures were proposed for the draft bill, although the problem seems to be a practical one. Although the solution tabled by Sweden within the EU working group appears inspirational, the members of the expert group nevertheless decided to wait for it to be finalised, and to see what other solutions will be adopted by the Member States, if any. The Swedish delegation proposed that, unless both parties to the negotiations agreed otherwise, a day a few months (the figure to be inserted) after the employees in all participating companies and concerned subsidiaries and establishments have received all prescribed data necessary to enable negotiations to be initiated, should be deemed to be the day of the establishment of the SNB.

c) Transnational character of SE formation

There are other unresolved questions concerning the establishment of the SNB and its voting. It is no secret that some practitioners think of using the SE as a vehicle for company migration. The requirement for transnational character of its establishment, i.e. by way of merger, can be easily evaded, given that no provision of the SE-Regulation demands either of the merging companies to engage in any activities.[4] An active German company could thus merge with its letter-box subsidiary created in the Czech Republic especially for this purpose only few days before the merger is to be approved. We might even see SEs

[4] Enriques, L.: Silence is Golden: The European Company Statute As a Catalyst for Company Law Arbitrage, Working paper Nr. 7/2003 published on the website of the European Corporate Governance Institute.

established on a just-in-case basis by law firms by merging two utterly inactive companies from different jurisdictions. In the field of company formation that at least is common practice in the Czech Republic. Applying the rules on the establishment and the voting of the SNB might under such circumstances prove really difficult. Then how to apply the rules if on one out of two sides there are no employees to send their representatives to the SNB? And what if there are no employees on either side? At least according to Czech law, statutory bodies of the company as well as their members are not considered employees. Would it be possible to disregard the rules in such situations and establish the SE without requiring the negotiation procedure to take place, if there is no one with whom to negotiate? Or must the six-month period first elapse so one can say: no agreement reached, standard rules apply? However, how can such period be calculated if no SNB has been established?

The SE-Directive contains no rules on the continuity of negotiations on employee involvement or even their results in case of a change of the Member State, in which the SE is proposed to be registered. Such a change in the terms of the merger will automatically result in the change of principal law applicable to the negotiation procedure, including the creation of the SNB. Suppose the parties to the merger decide to locate the seat of the SE in England, therefore the process of negotiations starts under English law and important steps are taken, perhaps including the decision on employee involvement. Then the general meetings of the participating companies alter the location and opt for Germany. According to the SE-Directive, the whole process must then be governed by German law. It remains to be seen, whether the German court of registration would be ready to recognise acts, legal or factual (creation of the SNB, voting within the SNB etc.) performed under English law, or whether it would insist upon their repetition under German law. There might be a chance for some continuity, if both laws contain rules so similar that no materially different result would be obtained by such a repetition. In any case, the greatest possible uniformity of the laws transposing the principal provisions of the SE-Directive into national legislations is very desirable here.

3. Restructuring after the formation of an SE

Another issue occupying expert minds throughout Europe is one on later restructurings of the SE and its possible impact on the employee involvement. Article 12 para. 4 of the SE-Regulation appears to give some instruments to combat any decrease in the quality and scope of the agreed quality and quantity of the involvement. It provides that the statues of the SE must not conflict at any time with the arrangements for employee involvement which have been so determined. The Czech draft bill makes use of the authorisation given by the following subparagraph. Section 7 of the draft bill not only empowers, but obliges the board of directors or the administrative board of the SE to amend the statutes of the SE without any further decision from the general shareholders meeting, if any of its provisions should conflict with the arrangements. The board must comply with the obligation without undue delay. In case of non-compliance or undue delay, the court may make an order winding-up the SE.

However, the rule applies only as long as the SE keeps the form of an SE. Once it abandons this legal form, the arrangements of employee involvement will be lost. Article 66 of the SE-Regulation expressly allowing the SE to be converted into a public limited-liability company governed by the law of the Member State in which its registered office is situated, should be read with special care. The article contains not one word on employee involvement. It is quite likely that the European public will get to hear of this provision in the future.

4. Standard rules for employee participation

A particular set of question arises in connection with the application of the standard rule for employee participation in an SE (Part 3 of the Annex), if no agreement is reached within the period specified in Art. 5 of the SE-Directive and the SE is established other than by transformation. The employees will then have the right to elect, appoint, recommend or oppose the appointment of a number of members of the administrative or supervisory body of the SE equal to the highest proportion in force in the participating companies concerned before the registration of the SE. The concept of the rule is clear: what applies is the best relevant *number*, not *the whole model of participation* which goes with the number. Yet the question is how to compare the various models established in participating companies from different company law jurisdictions in order to ascertain what is, in fact, this number, where each system guarantees a *different quality of participation*. One may e.g. land in real trouble deciding whether the highest proportion is three members of the supervisory board in one company, where the members are elected by the employees, or four members of the administrative board, if they represent the shareholders, the employees, though, have the right to veto their appointment, provided the future SE will be a two-tier one, the employee representatives will be sitting on the supervisory board and the employees will have the right to elect them. Not an easy task, indeed, if one bears in mind the main principle of the SE-Directive requiring that the application of the analysed standard rule should not result in a reduction in the standards of employee participation in any of the participating companies.

Waiting for the outcome of further Europe-wide discussions on such and similar issues, the expert group decided to propose wordings in the draft bill as close to the text of the provisions of the SE-Directive as possible. Only this attitude, it is believed, will leave the door open for a reasonable and uniform interpretation of the relevant norms, once the matters are clarified and resolved, ultimately by the European Court of Justice.

Denmark

Søren Friis Hansen

References: *Søren Friis Hansen* Ledelsesstrukturen i danske SE-selskaber, Juridiske emner ved Syddansk Universitet 2003 (Red. Bent Iversen), Djoef Publishing 2003, p. 73–95; *Jesper Lau Hansen* Nordic Company Law, Djoef Publishing, 2003; *Werlauff* SE – the Law of the European Company, Copenhagen 2002; *Werlauff*, The SE Company – A New Common European Company from 8 October 2004, European Business Law Review (EBLR), 14 (2003), p. 85–103.

I. Introduction

An SE with its registered office and head office located in Denmark, will, in accordance with the principles of Article 9 of the SE regulation, be governed by the rules that apply to "Aktieselskaber (A/S)" (= Public Limited Companies). Aktieselskaber are governed by the Act on Public Limited Companies of 1973. This act bears the Danish title "Aktieselskabsloven" (typically abbreviated "ASL"). While many amendments have been made to the Act since 1973, the fundamental system for public limited companies in Denmark remains unchanged from the original Act, which entered into force on January 1st 1974. The latest official version of the Act is "Lovbekendtgørelse nr. 9 of 9, February 2002".[1]

The Danish Act on Public Limited Companies was made in close co-operation with other Nordic countries; Norway, Sweden, and Finland.[2] Although the Nordic co-operation within the company law area was abandoned after Denmark's entry into the European Communities in 1973, the rules on public limited companies in the Nordic countries are still closely related, thirty years after the Danish Act was introduced.[3]

[1] The Act (as well as any Danish legislation in force) can be found at website of Retsinformation (www.retsinfo.dk). A version of the Act translated into English can be found at the website of the national Danish Authority which deals with company law matters; Erhvervs- og Selskabsstyrelsen (www.eogs.dk). Any information needed to contact this authority is also found at this site.

[2] See *Søren Friis Hansen*, in Ruth Nielsen & Boel Flodgren, Rätten (om)kring Øresund (DJOEF Publishing 2000), p. 67–85.

[3] See for a comparative study of the rules on public limited companies in the Nordic countries, *Jesper Lau Hansen*.

There is no doubt that the introduction of the SE into Danish law will require the Danish Parliament to adopt a special act, which will contain some provisions regarding the matters which can be decided by the Member States. On January 28th 2004 the Minister for Economy and Commerce presented an official draft for a Danish SE-Act to the Danish Parliament (Lovforslag L 142, available at: www.folketinget.de; in the following: "Draft").

II. Formation of an SE in Denmark

Under Article 2 Para. 5 of the SE-Regulation, Member States may provide that a company with its head office outside the Community, may participate in the formation of an SE, provided that the company is formed under the law of a Member State, and has a real and continuous link with a Member State. Since such a company may participate in the formation of a regular Danish PLC, that this provision will be adopted in Danish law (Draft, Art. 4).

Under Danish law, a Public Limited company must have its registered office and its head office in a Danish municipality. (ASL § 4, para 1, nb. 2). A Member State may, according to Article 7 of the SE-Regulation, impose on an SE the requirement that the head office and the registered office of an SE must be located at the same place within a Member State. Such a provision is introduced in the Draft (Art. 3).

Member States may adopt provisions concerning special protection of minority shareholders in connection with the transfer of the registered office of the SE (Art. 8 para. 5 SE-Reg.), the merger of an SE (Art. 24 para 2 SE-Reg.), and the formation of a holding SE (Art. 34 SE-Reg.). Such provisions will be applied to Danish SEs, so that minority shareholders may request the company to repurchase their shares (Draft, Art. 5 para. 1 and Art. 6 para. 1).

Danish authorities are not given the competence to oppose the merger of an SE (Art. 19 SE-Reg.) on grounds of public interest.

It is not expected that the possibility of providing for the relaxation of the requirements concerning a merger carried out by a company which holds 90% or more but not all the shares of another company conferring the right to vote at general meetings of another company, will be applied to a Danish SE (Art. 31 para 2 SE-Reg.).

The conversion of a Danish aktieselskab into an SE will not be made dependant on a favourable vote by a qualified majority in the organ in which the employees participate (i.e. the supervisory board or "bestyrelse", ASL § 49, stk. 2). This is due to the fact that the question of a conversion is considered to be a matter that shall be decided by the shareholders and that the protection of the employees under the Directive is sufficient.

Since 1998, Danish public and private limited companies have been able to express their share capital in either Danish kroner (DKK) or Euro. A similar provision applies to the publication of annual accounts of these companies (§ 16 in the Act on Annual Accounts (årsregnskabsloven, Lov nr. 448 af 7. june 2001).

III. Transfer of the registered office of an SE

Member States may lay down special requirements concerning the adequate protection of creditors and others before the issue of a certificate by the authorities in connection with the transfer of the registered office of an SE (Art. 8 para. 7 SE-Reg.). No such requirement will be imposed on a Danish SE before the certificate on the transfer of its seat out of Denmark can be issued.

Danish authorities will not be given the competence to oppose the transfer of the registered office of a Danish SE (Art. 8 para. 14 SE-Reg.) on grounds of public interest.

IV. Management system of a Danish SE

The managing director of a Danish PLC can be a member of the supervisory board (bestyrelsen), as long as the majority of the members of the supervisory board are not managing directors of that company (ASL § 51, stk. 2). Both the managing directors and the members of the supervisory board are responsible for managing the company (ASL § 54, para. 1, 1st sentence). The supervisory board can exercise power to manage the company (ASL § 54, stk. 1, and stk. 2). These two provisions alone make it clear that the management system of Danish PLCs must be labelled as **a one-tier system** under the provisions of the SE-Regulation (Art. 39 para. 3 and Art. 40 para. 1 SE-Reg.), even though there are actually two management organs in a Danish PLC[4].

The **two-tier system** (Art. 39–42 SE-Reg.) is therefore introduced as an alternative management system for Danish SE (Draft, Art. 8–10). Otherwise, companies that are planning to choose a two-tier system might be discouraged from choosing Denmark as the base for their SE.[5]

[4] See for a closer study of the management system of Danish SEs, *Søren Friis Hansen,* p. 73–95.

[5] *Werlauff* seems to assume that a Member State may deny a SE company the choice between the one-tier and the two-tier systems, cf. EBLR 14 (2003), p. 94. This view does not seem to be in accordance with the SE-Regulation, cf. *Søren Friis Hansen*, p. 77, *Lutter,* Betriebs Berater 2002, p. 4, and *Teichmann*, Zeitschrift für Gesellschafts- und Unter-

The management organ or the administrative organ of a Danish SE is not entitled to amend the statutes of the SE if these conflict with the arrangements for employee participation (SE-Regulation Art. 12 para. 4).

In a Danish PLC, there must be at least one managing director and three members of the supervisory board (ASL § 49, stk. 1 and § 51, stk. 1). Concerning the number of members in the organs of a Danish SE, the following fixed minimum numbers are suggested:

Management organ (two-tier, Art. 39 para. 4): One

Supervisory organ (two-tier, Art. 40 para. 3): Three

For a Danish SE the minimum number of members of the administrative organ will be fixed at three (Draft, Art. 12).

In a Danish SE, the right of the supervisory organ to require the management organ to provide the information necessary to exercise supervision, will be extended to the individual members of the supervisory organ (Art. 41 para. 3 2nd sentence).

In a Danish SE with a two-tier system, the supervisory organ will not be given the right for itself to make certain categories of transactions subject to authorisation (Art. 48, para. 1 SE-Reg.).

A Danish SE will be permitted to hold its first general meeting within 18 months of the incorporation of the SE (Art. 54 para. 1 SE-Reg., Draft, Art. 13).

The provision on Danish PLCs concerning the right of a shareholder to convene a general meeting (ASL § 70), is identical to that in SE-Regulation Art. 55 para 1. A lesser percentage than 10% will not be provided for a Danish SE.

Under Danish law, any shareholder of a company may request that an additional item is put on the agenda of the general meeting (ASL § 71). A similar provision will be provided for Danish SEs (Art. 56 SE-Reg., Draft, Art. 13).

Under Danish law, a majority of both 2/3rd of the votes at the general meeting and 2/3rd of the capital connected to shares giving a voting right and that are represented at the general meeting is required in order to amend the statutes of a PLC (ASL § 78). It will not be possible for a Danish SE to change the statute by simple majority (Art. 59 para. 2 SE-Reg.).

V. Involvement of employees in a Danish SE

Since 1973, employees of Danish public and private limited companies have had the right to elect two or more members of the supervisory organ of their company (ASL § 49, stk. 2). The rules on employee participation apply to com-

nehmensrecht (ZGR) 2002, p. 442. A Danish SE will under all circumstances be able to choose between a one-tier and a two-tier management system.

panies which have had 35 employees or more for a period of not less than three years. These rules apply to groups of companies, in which case the employees of the group can elect two or more members of the supervisory board of the parent company. The Danish rules on employee participation in groups apply, however, only to Danish parent companies and Danish subsidiaries.

It is likely that some minor adjustments will be necessary concerning the Danish rules on employee participation as a result of the introduction of the SE, but no details are as yet available on this point. However, no material changes to the Danish rules are expected.

France

Jacques-Louis Colombani

Literature on SE published in France: *Blanquet* Enfin la société européenne, Rev. du Droit de l'Union Européenne, 2001, p. 65 et seq.; *Blanquet* La Société Européenne n'est plus un Mythe, Rev. du droit int. comp. 2001, p. 139 et seq.; *Boucourechliev* Les voies de l'Europe des sociétés, J. C. P. (E), 30/05/96, 560, 18, p. 232; *Colombani* Le projet de société anonyme européenne: Dernier état des textes – Les Petites Affiches, 27 oct. 1993, n° 129; *Colombani* La Société Européenne: utilité d'un projet ancien pour le marché intérieur de demain, Thèse, Paris XI, Juillet 1998, Lille, ABES, 15 sept. 1998; *Colombani* La société par actions simplifiée (SAS) sera-t-elle un moteur pour la societas europaea (SE)?, Les Petites Affiches, 9 mars 1999; *Colombani* La SE est née à Nice – Les Petites Affiches, janv. 2001; *Colombani/Favero* Societas Europaea, Ed Joly, France 2002; *Favero* Plaidoyer pour une société Européenne, Petites Affiches 2 novembre 1998, p. 8; *Branger/Marini/ Colombani/Favero/Parleani* La Société Européenne, Gazette du Palais N° 92/93, mercredi 2 jeudi 3, avril 2003 (documentation of a conference held in the French Senat in june 2002); *Hopt/Menjucq/Wymeersch* La Société Européenne, 2003; *Menjucq* Droit International et Européen des sociétés, 2001; *Menjucq* La société européenne, Rev. des soc. 2002, p. 225 et seq.; *Menjucq* Société Européenne, juin 2002, Rép. sociétés Dalloz; La société européenne, numéro spéciale directive, Liaisons sociales, 2003.

I. Introduction

"Although I intend to leave the Description of this Empire to a particular Treatise, yet in the mean time I am content to gratify the curious Reader with some general Ideas."[1]

The current debates that are pending about the European Constitution reflect the incredible complexity of the definition of common standards and rules in order to live together. Some are afraid to be regarded as a micro nation and they suggest to "get back to the trees" in order to protect their countries from the effects of the globalisation. The European business community, more pragmatically, has been waiting for the European Company for more than forty years when negotiations suddenly succeeded "abracadabra-like"[2] at the summit

[1] Swift, Gulliver's travels, A voyage to Lilliput, Ch. VI: Of the Inhabitants of Lilliput; their learning, laws and customs, the manner of educating their children.

[2] *Baranger*, Gazette du Palais N° 92/93, Mercredi 2, Jeudi 3 avril 2003, p. 3.

of Nice. We will not go into the details of the history of negotiations that have been presented elsewhere by *Blanquet*.[3]

France is strongly determined to modernise its commercial law in order to welcome the changes and to keep an open approach of Europe.[4] Regarding the corporate organisation of the SE, the solutions which are consisting in a "rewriting" of the regulation that are proposed[5] are considered as "very strongly" expressed but the comments[6] are pleading for a discussion about the possible opportunity that could be offered by the regulation to the governments to introduce a national SA held by a single shareholder instead of a subsidiary SE.

From a national point of view, we will make a single reference to the different approaches that are proposed in France[7] in order to change the national

[3] *Blanquet*, in Societas Europaea, *Colombani/Favero*, Societas Europaea, p. 5 et seq. *Blanquet* summarises the different steps of the negotiations concerning the SE. She emphasizes the difficult challenge of our thesis which was to conciliate the different approaches to corporate governance within the European Common Market.

[4] A proposal for implementing the European Company has been presented by Senators *Branger* and *Hyest*, http://www.senat.fr/Leg/pp/03-152.html; http://www.lamylinereflex.fr/lamy/index.html, see also La Tribune, 22 jan. 2004. See also the press release of the French Prime Minister, dated 27th of june 2003, about the 1st conference on international investments, that took place in La Baule, http://www.france.diplomatie.fr/actu/article.asp?ART=35703.

[5] See the proposal presented both before the Senate and the National Assembly, by *MM. Marini*, Senator, and *De Roux*, Deputy, on October 9, 2003; see a question about the proposal that could introduce the opportunity to organise a "French SE" even a subsidiary one, on the scheme of the SAS, cahiers AGEFI 2003, *O. Dufour*; see also the complete proposal http://www.senat.fr/leg/ppl03-011.html; further to the recitals, the proposal does not deal with co-ordination measures or the implementation of the directive into French Law. "Beyond the coordination measures", it deals with a "kind of" implementation of the regulation and intends to create a "Société Anonyme Européenne Unipersonnelle" that could be introduced into French law under the light of the SE regulation. See F. Fages, M. Menjuc, JCP, Ed. Gen. 22 octobre 2003, aperçu rapide, act. 505; JCP, Ed. E. n° 42, 16 oct 2003. For a networking between French, Spanish and Portuguese companies, based on national/private agreements and "e-filing" of official documents and registration of the SE (without prejudice of the confidential information referred to in the directive, or questions about the possible and easy counterfeiting of national stamps) see the launching of the GEIE Euro-Aequitas, http//www.pointvirgule.com; http://www.euro-aequitas.net/; and the advertisement on the network: http://www.jurisclasseur.com/htm/top_index/top_index_actualites.htm?url=http://rb.juris-classeur.com/actualite/depeche/visu_news.html?date_new=2003-11-21&url_key=/data/13112003/13112003-102423.html&jour_jo=Mardi.

[6] http://www.editions-joly.com/services/jolynews/e-docs/00/00/01/E5/fiche_jolynews.md; see also *Olivia Dufour*, doubtful about the method, Petites Affiches, 23 oct. 2003, p. 4.

[7] AFEP, ANSA and MEDEF are pleading for another approach: the report "Pour un droit moderne des sociétés", is proposing a substantial transformation of French company law without assimilation between the SE and the national companies. The report

company law. A group of experts is currently working on the aspects of the SE that are not dealt with in the above exposed proposals. This group is working in France on behalf of Senator *Branger* and Senator *J. J. Hyest*. The spirit of the work is to enrich the current drafts and analysis with open, independent and plural approaches.[8] This group is focussed on the incorporation of the SE into French law, especially with regard to the implementation of the directive and the putting in place of the necessary machinery in order to allow a concomitant application of the texts. A report will be communicated shortly for the purpose of a public discussion.

Our three arguments in favour of the SE remain:

Firstly, the SE is essential for the realisation of the single European market, since it allows free movement of companies and capital and is flexible enough to be applicable directly in the countries which are applicant to join the EU.

Secondly, while at present companies wishing to set up business in another Member State have to undergo a costly and complex process in order to comply with the laws of that State; this could no longer be the case if a single body of rules was applicable throughout the EC. A fortiori, a global option for a single European accounting rule will help the system.

Thirdly, the installation of the SE will aid the transfer of technology in the internal European market. It could put in place a common system of financial information, and lead to a better protection of intellectual property rights.

Consequently, the SE will be an opportunity not only for France but also for all the players and the Member States that are interested in "win-win" strategies.

In our opinion, the SE allows some very specific operations that can not be set up without a real European legal structure. In their day to day management, the lawyers or legal counsels in the companies may experience the following:

Harmonisation of community law and the concentrations processes are creating juridical solutions different from those of yesterday.

There is a strong demand from top management to lower the costs of analyses, arbitration centres etc.

Specialisation of the business implies a new management of the teams.

pleads for a flexible subsidiary SE. WWW.ansa.fr; The Chambre Of Commerce of Paris, proposed a report "Pour une réforme du droit de la société anonyme non cotée" on october 23th 2003; see www.ccip.fr/etudes, p. 15. The report seems to be favourable to a closed European company that could be adopted in France on the grounds of the regulation, on the other hand, the report is realistic with regard to the provisions (directly applicable) of the regulation with regards to the corporate governance of a subsidiary. In the recitals of the last proposal of law by *Branger/Hyest* (see note 4) the idea of a link between the SAS and a new Société Anonyme Simplifiée has been exposed in order to satisfy the above claims.

[8] See, the complete list of the group of experts held by Senators Branger and Hyest on http://www.senat.fr/senateurs/branger_jean_guy/groupeSE.html.

Secrecy, independence, protection of the minorities, of the workers and creditors are in question into national laws.

Therefore, industry and especially the groups that are facing the practical lack of a common corporate structure were favourable to the SE.[9]

Prior to the Nice summit, however, the modern French doctrine in favour of the SE[10] faced severe scepticism.[11] The dominant authors in this time were strongly in favour of the classical operations and mergers.[12] Apart from the traditional debate about the legal definition of the "enterprise"[13], very few publications or books can be considered as 100% related to the precise topic of the

[9] *Favero*, Petites Affiches 2 novembre 1998, p. 8; *Favero*, les défenses anti OPA, Dictionnaire JOLY Bourse, 1999-2.

[10] *Colombani* La SE dernier état des textes, 27 oct. 1993, Petites Affiches n° 129 (explains the main contradictions in the current opinions about the SE; it tries to conciliate those points of view, explains the interest of the new drafts proposed by the Commission); *Colombani/Tétu/Tsoraklidis* Les arrêts Javico et Silhoutette, précisions ou contradiction de motifs dans la jurisprudence de la CJCE?, Petites Affiches 11 jan. 1999 (this study emphasizes the risks taken by industry in its blind approach to the exhaustion of rights; it proposes solutions and arguments in favour of the adoption of European legal instruments that could facilitate the management of the IP rights portfolios, furthermore this article pleads in favour of the adoption of a single commercial entity in order to rationalise the business made on the internal market); *Colombani* La Société Européenne: utilité d'un projet ancien pour le marché intérieur de demain, Thèse, Paris XI, Jul. 1998, Lille, ABES, 15 sept. 1998 (Jury, Pr May, Pr. Daigre, Pr Decoopman, Pr Sirinelli), Favero, Plaidoyer pour la société européenne, Les Petites Affiches, 2 nov. 1998 (Pleads for our thesis), *Colombani* Les Petites Affiches, 9 mars 99 (compares the new French Société par Actions simplifiée with the SE project and provides arguments for a flexible SE statute); *Colombani* Réflexion sur une politique de transfert des produits marqués – Les Petites Affiches, juil. 1999 (explaining strategies offered to the industry by the new exemption regulations about IP, this article emphasises the lack of the SE as a common corporate structure); *Colombani* La SE et Voilà Cadet Roussel! Les Petites Affiches, janv. 2001 (welcomes the adoption of the SE Statute).

[11] *Boucourechliev* Pour une SARL européenne, PUF 1973; then, making an express link with the works of *Hopt* in Germany and strongly against the project of SE as published and commented and in favour of the 5th directive and a "Close company": *Boucourechliev* Les voies de l'Europe des sociétés, J. C. P. (E), 30/05/96, 560, 18, p. 232. see also, Marini: "Réformer le droit des sociétés pour accroître notre compétitivité juridique", Droit et patrimoine, n° 54, nov. 1997.

[12] *Menjucq* Juris Classeur, Europe, 1998.

[13] *Luby* L'entreprise européenne, étude de droit des sociétés, thèse, Pau 1991, doubtful regarding the SE. For a statement on the deep differences between the national philosophies and definitions of the "enterprise" especially on the topic of the involvement of the employees, that where definitely regarded as obstacles on the road of the SE as a single corporate structure with national variations, *Luc et Pascal Julien Saint – Amand* Droit et Patrimoine, nov. 97, p. 47; for a new and challenging vision of the SE and the national laws of France, Italy, the Netherlands, Spain and Austria, see *Arlt/Bervoets/Grechenig/Kalss*, European Business Organization Law Review, 2002, p. 738.

last projects of regulation and directive that where achieving a single European legal entity (or European Company), where available in France.[14] At this time the idea to use the shadow "European Company" together with the SAS in a business context was, a fortiori supposed to be a very original solution and this theoretical hypothesis was supported by very few authors. Since the historic breakthrough, interest in the European Company has considerably increased[15] which can be proved by the activity of the French Senate who hosted two conferences in 2002/2003 on the topic of the European Company.[16]

Some are of the opinion that the SE may only be used in the strategies of the groups that only have a "European dimension, prima facie".[17]

This study will not cover the works that are also pending before the European Commission which could lead to national solutions in cross-border mergers which are different from the solution of the SE. The European Commission has presented a proposal for a Directive to make cross-border mergers easier, by overcoming obstacles caused by different national laws.[18] The proposal is presented as especially useful for small and medium-sized businesses who want to operate in more than one Member State, but not throughout Europe, and thus are not likely to seek incorporation under the European Company Statute. The proposed Directive would set up a cross-border merger procedure whereby mergers would be governed in each Member State by the principles and rules applicable to "domestic" mergers. The proposal, which covers all companies with share capital, both public and private limited-liability companies, aims to make cross-border mergers possible and easy all over the European Union by approximating the cross-border merger procedure to the procedures used for "domestic mergers" between companies governed by the laws of the same Member State.

[14] For instance, see *Vallée* La société anonyme européenne, Delmas, 1991, or Dictionnaire Permanent de Droit Européen des Affaires 1991, Société Européenne, under *M. Vaillant*'s supervision, *Marini*: pour un système optionnel, droit et patrimoine, n° 54, nov 1997, p. 57.

[15] *Hommelhoff* Einige Bemerkungen zur Organisationsverfassung der Europäischen Aktiengesellschaft, AG (2001) pp. 279 et sq.; *Parleani* Gazette du Palais N° 92/93, Mercredi 2, Jeudi 3 avril 2003, p. 9 et seq; *Colombani, Favero*, Societas Europaea, Ed Joly 2003, 167 pages about the SE.

[16] June 12, 2002 (see Senator *Branger*, Gazette du Palais N° 92/93, 2, 3 apr. 2003, p. 4); http://www.senat.fr/senateurs/branger_jean_guy/gazettedupalais.html#haut; october 3/4, 2002 (see *Hopt/Menjucq/Wymeersch*).

[17] *Davignon* Vers la société européenne, Le Monde 17 feb. 2001, p. 15; and, deeming to close the door to the SE as the daughter of an SAS, *Couret* la création de la SE, in: La société européenne, p. 27, n° 32; *Hopt* The European company (SE) Under the Nice Compromize: Major Breakthrough or Small Coin for Europe? Euriedia 2000, p. 465.

[18] http://europa.eu.int/comm/internal_market/en/company/company/news/index.htm.

This study will not cover the complementary proposal to update, clarify and broaden the scope of the European Community's Directive that provides for tax deferral in the case of cross-border mergers and divisions of companies, transfers of assets and exchanges of shares (90/434/EEC) that was presented by the Commission. This text opens the way to a new proposal on cross-border mergers, based on national agreements.[19]

The SE can be regarded as a lost cause;[20] anyway, we have to admit that both the Regulation and the Directive are applicable under article 70 of the Regulation and 16 of the Directive and, that October 8th 2004 can be taken as a checkpoint.[21] Senator *Branger* who is politically active in favour of the SE, takes the success of the European co-operation in company law, as a strong symbol. He is going ahead with the workers involvement and the free movement of the companies through the SE since the early 1991. He hosted the first international Moot Court about the SE which took place at the Palais du Luxembourg on May 20th 2003. This event was prepared under the high supervision of Rector *Hommelhoff* in Heidelberg of Dean *Faugere* and Pr. *Delcross* from the Faculté Jean Monnet, Sceaux (Paris XI) in France. The Moot Court conference has been a great success and received the support of the French Prime Minister *Jean-Pierre Raffarin*.[22] The scenario had been written, discussed and validated between a large number of European lawyers and, as described below, was dedicated to the creation of a closed holding company located in Germany. Senator *Hyest* presented the economic questions which were currently pending[23] before the French parliament.

[19] For a complete list of the current texts that are pending before the European Union, see http://europa.eu.int/eur-lex/fr/com/reg/fr_register_1710.html.

[20] *Bandrac*, Dom, introduction by Marini, Loi NRE et autres réformes, Joly 2002, p. 14.

[21] *Luby*, Enfin la société européenne! www.univ-tlse1.fr/liea/Chronique-sources/ Chron-2001.htm; *Colombani*, La société européenne pour l'exploitation de niches technologiques et pari pour la participation, colloque Sénat date butoir: 8 octobre 2004, colloque sénat, 12 juin 2002, Gazette du palais 3 avril 2003.

[22] May 20, 2003 (international moot court on the European Company, documentation published on the website of Senator Branger: http://www.senat.fr/senateurs/branger_jean_guy/colloque.html#haut).

[23] See, report on "initiative économique" Rap. 217 (2002–2003) – commission spéciale; http://www.senat.fr/rap/l02-217/l02-217.html; report on "modification du code de commerce relative aux mandats sociaux"; Rap. 13 (2002–2003) – commission des lois, http: //www.senat.fr/rap/l02-013/l02-013_mono.html.; see also, Loi n° 2003-721 1er août 2003, JO n° 179, 5 août 2003, Conseil constitutionnel, dec. N° 2003-477 DC, 31 juill. 2003. See about the security of the share holders and for substantial changes in the law on the financial security, http://www.senat.fr/senint/hyest_jean_jacques950391_2002_pjl02-166_2.html, and also the "avis" given on behalf of the "commission des lois": http://www.senat.fr/rap/a02-207/a02-207.html.

II. French company law and the SE

The on-going economic reforms reforms of the new economic regulations are the fruit of a technique called "codification à droit constant"[24] which has its virtues, but the method implies constant and global work for the legislator. The second is the obligation to deal with the issues presented by the European Company Statute, imposed on the governments in the context of three legislative areas:

A Regulation establishing the SE Statute that is directly applicable in every Member States.

A Directive on worker involvement, which will have to be implemented in national law in all Member States.

National bridges between the National Laws designated by the Regulation and Directive; and national co-ordination measures in order to let the regulation and the directive apply simultaneously.

Should we provide next some definitions that could be helpful for the reader?

1. The distinction between "Directors" and "Directeurs"

Particular attention should be given to terminology: In legal terms the French word "Directeur" is not a translation of "Director" in the sense of a member of the board of a company, but instead "Directeur" would usually be translated as "Manager". However, a "Director" being an individual appointed to the board of the company by the shareholders would normally be translated as an "Administrateur" or "Mandataire Social".

An "Administrateur" is solely an officer of the company (in French a "mandataire social"); he or she will not have a contract of employment with the company and thus does not benefit from the French employment law. The practical consequence is that an "Administrateur" can generally be dismissed from his or her position without notice or compensation, although the dismissal should not be vexatious. In many cases, an "Administrateur" or "Director" of a French company might also have a contract of employment, but this would be considered at French law to be totally separate from his position as an officer of the company. Such a contract of employment would relate to a specific function to be separated from his position of "Director" which might for example

[24] See for instance: *Terré/Outin-Adam* Codifier est un art difficile, D. 1994, Chron. P. 99; *Mathieu* La sécurité juridique: un produit d'exportation dorénavant made in France, D. 2000, n° 4, point de vue; – *Marini*, in Loi NRE et autres réformes, Joly 2002, p. 1.

be his capacity as financial manager, sales manager or H. R. Manager; this agreement would give the employee the full protection of French employment law provisions.

2. The legal regime of the SE and its national cousins SA, SAS, and SARL – in a nutshell

France has no legal definition of "company" ("enterprise") – this word can only be found in fiscal or economical provisions. From a legal perspective, a "company" is a form of organisation of a business. The legal regime of the SE will be the regime of the "sociétés anonymes" (*SA*).

Therefore we should briefly consider the three main French commercial entities: "sociétés à responsabilité limitée" (*SARL*), "sociétés anonymes" (*SA*), and "sociétés par actions simplifiées" (*SAS*).

The SARL must have a minimum of one shareholder, has no directors and is run by a gérant. This gérant can be a stockholder. If he owns a minority of the capital, he may have the benefit of an employment contract. If he has the majority, however, this is no longer possible.

An SA must have a minimum of seven shareholders. Two different types of management structure may be put in place: (i) the monistic type with a one-tier management structure, which consists of a board of directors ("conseil d'administration") comprising a minimum of three and a maximum of 18 directors ("administrateurs") appointed by and from the shareholders and (ii) the dualistic type with a two-tier management structure, which consists in a management board ("directoire") controlled by a supervisory board ("conseil de surveillance").The management board consists of one up to five members (seven members if the S.A. is a listed company). The supervisory board consists of a minimum of three and a maximum of 18 members appointed by the shareholders. The directors of an SA can be employed (and protected as far as pensions, social insurance, etc., is concerned) if they are assuming a management position on behalf of the company.

The S.A.S. can be governed by a sole shareholder, in this case, article L 432-6-1 of the "code du travail" does not apply.[25] Such an issue may be impossible a priori in an SE, even "French fashioned".

[25] Article L 227-9 of the commercial code provides: (In the SAS) "Les statuts déterminent les décisions qui doivent être prises collectivement par les associés et les formes et conditions qu'ils prévoient" – Article R 432-21, III, provides "Les statuts fixent les règles relatives aux modalités d'examen des demandes d'inscription des projets de résolution adressées par les comités d'entreprises". The representation of the workers through

The principal characteristic of the S.A.S. is the flexibility in organisation of the management of the company, the conditions in which shareholders' decisions can be adopted and the relationships between the shareholders, subject to the following minimum requirements set out by the Commercial Code: A chairman ("Président") must be appointed to represent the company vis-à-vis third parties. Some decisions, such as the approval of the accounts, the appointment of the statutory auditors, any amendment of the share capital or a merger, must be made by the shareholders in accordance with the provisions of the by-laws.

The by-laws may freely determine the organisation of the internal management of the company and provide, for example, for the setting up of committees, a supervisory board, etc. The new article L 227-6 of the French Commercial Code[26] introduces a new link between the corporate governance of the SA and the organisation of the SAS. The new law introduces a "Directeur Général" or "Directeur Général Délégué" in the SAS, these functions were traditionally assumed by the legal representatives of the SA. The shareholders and officers of an SAS can be either individuals or bodies corporate.

During the initial period of implementation of the SE in national law, the benefit of cross-border mergers that will give birth to a SE will be reserved to the SA. The SAS is finding favour though, with a number of foreign, particularly US, Japanese and Swiss corporations which are setting up subsidiaries in France. Using the SAS, foreign partners will be able to set up a daughter SE that could be a convenient way to organise a partnership between medium sized companies. This example was given during the above mentioned Moot Court which took place in the French Senate on 20th May 2003.

3. Is there a place for a closed and contractual SE located in France?

The SAS is a modern company form that serves as a flexible tool to those companies who regard the traditional stock corporation law as being too rigid.[27]

a "comité d'entreprise" is difficult: article L 432-6-1 of the code du travail provides "Le comité d'entreprise peut demander en justice la désignation d'un mandataire chargé de convoquer l'assemblée des actionnaires en cas d'urgence ...".

[26] LOI n° 2003-706 du 1er août 2003 de sécurité financière, Journal Officiel 177 du 2 août 2003, art. 118, http:www.adminet.com/jo/20030802/ECOX0200186L.html, the nes article provides: "Les statuts peuvent prévoir les conditions dans lesquelles une ou plusieurs personnes autres que le président, portant le titre de directeur général ou de directeur général délégué, peuvent exercer les pouvoirs confiés à ce dernier par le présent article."

[27] For an accurate overview, see, Lamy sociétés commerciales, 2003, 3968, and especially, *Bouere* Société Anonyme simplifiée et accords d'actionnaires, Petites affiches 13 mars 1991, p. 4, *Epstein/Barre* La société anonyme simplifiée ou la joint venture de droit français, Fusions et Acquisitions, apr. 1992, p. 44 ; *Field* Rapport du Groupe de travail sur la

The introduction of this new flexible form in the nineties of the last century is generally considered as a great success of the French legislator. However, its position in the context of the formation and running of an SE remains unclear. In France, the SAS is regarded as not being really a "société anonyme" but a separate legal form. The SE Regulation, however, in its appendices I and II only makes a reference to the "société anonyme", the "société à responsabilité limitée" and to article 48 EC.

The French government will determine whether the SAS will be considered as an SA (with exception of the provisions which are not compliant with the directives) or whether additional provisions are needed in order to comply with the directives on public companies whereby the SAS could have the benefit of mergers through the SE. A bridge could be adopted by the government in order to simplifying the transformation of the SAS into SA for the purpose of the creation of a European company. Anyway, a transformation of a national company into an SA is not very difficult.

Some are of the opinion that the SAS is not a company which complies with Art. 48 EC.[28] The question remains open. As it has been demonstrated during the "moot court" which took place at the French Senate on May 20 2003, the SAS gives to the players the opportunity to build some flexible links not only with the countries of common law.

A special regime has to be found for the corporate governance of a subsidiary SE held by a single share holder. In this case, under article 3 of the regulation, the company will be governed simultaneously by the law of the SA and the law of the SARL. A precision should be made on this point.

The demand is presently located in markets mainly in Europe or abroad and the SE can be helpful in simplifying the policies of a group wishing to play on the European market.

société anonyme simplifiée, CNPF, Commission économique, oct. 1990; *Germain* La société par actions simplifiée, JCP éd. E. 1994, I, n° 341; *Guyon* Présentation générale de la SAS, Rev. Sociétés 1994, p. 207; *Honorat* La SAS ou la résurgence de l'élément contractuel en droit français des sociétés, Petites Affiches 16 Août 1996, p. 4; *Le Cannu* Un nouveau lieu de savoir faire contractuel: la SAS, Defrénois 1994, p. 1345; les dirigeants de la SAS, Rev. Sociétés 1994, p. 239; la SAS pour tous, Bull. Joly 1999, p. 841, *Daigre* Faut-il banaliser la SAS ? JCP E 1999, n° 23, p. 977; *Paillusseau* La société anonyme, technique d'organisation de l'entreprise, Sirey, 1967, et la nouvelle société par actions simplifiées, le big bang du droit des sociétés, Dalloz 1999, p. 333; La SAS une nouvelle structure pour les PME et les personnes physiques, JCP E 2002, n° 11 p. 458, (*Paillusseau* could be regarded as the godfather of the SAS in France); *Stoufflet* Aménagements statutaires et actionariat de la SAS, Rev. Sociétés 2000, p. 239; *Guyon* L'élargissement du domaine des SAS, Rev. Sociétés 1999, p. 505, Les aspects communautaires et internationaux de la SAS, Rev. Sociétés 2000, p. 255.

[28] *Couret* Les techniques de constitution de la société européenne, in: *Hopt/Menjucq/Wymeersch.*, p. 27, n° 32.

A debate does exist in France about the possibilities of "corporate governance" which could be partly based on agreements;[29] the main advantage of the SAS lays in the fact that the principal source of obligations is the statue of the company itself.

The contractual sphere that exists in the SE has to be subject to analysis. Article 48 of the Regulation leads to thought concerning the contractual scope that already exists in the regulation. This article does not need to be redrafted and applies directly in each Member State.

1. An SE's statutes shall list the categories of transactions that require authorisation of the management organ by the supervisory organ in the two-tier system or an express decision by the administrative organ in the one-tier system. A Member State may, however, provide that in the two-tier system the supervisory organ may itself make certain categories of transactions that will be subject to authorisation.
2. Member State may determine the categories of transactions that must at least be indicated in the statutes of SEs registered within its territory.

The French government could read this Article in keeping with the provisions of Article 9 of the Regulation. This analysis should conduct to distinguish between the topics expressly or partly mentioned in the regulation (workers involvement, transfer of seat ...), and the domestic law on the "sociétés anonymes" which will be applicable to the other matters (pensions, intellectual property, fiscal issues, corporate governance...).

To the question "Why don't we create a closed and contractual European Company?"[30] the reply of the French Government could be: "Go ahead and create a European Company!"[31]

III. Formation of an SE

There are several ways to set up a European Company:

- The merger of two or more existing public limited companies from at least two different EU Member States;

[29] In particular: Favourable to the use of pacts in the SA: *Daigre/Sentilles-Dupont*, Pactes d'actionnaires, Joly editions 1995; for an overview about the complexe issues in France, see, Dialogues avec Michel Jeantin, Prospectives du droit économique, Dalloz 1999, http://www.glose.org/melan/m60.htm, see also *Marini* Le temps de la libre expression est passé, le temps de l'arbitrage est venu. L'Etat doit désormais donner le cap, Droit et Patrimoine, n° 54 nov. 1997, p. 6; *Bandrac* Dom, Loi NRE et autres réformes, Joly 2002, p. 129 et sq.

[30] *Huet* Et pourquoi pas une société européenne fermée?, D. Aff. 1998, n° 141.

[31] See Annex 1 to this book, about some questions that could be subject to discussion in France.

- The formation of a holding company promoted by public or private limited companies from at least two different Member States;
- The formation of a subsidiary of companies from at least two different Member States;
- The transformation of a public limited company which has, for at least two years, had a subsidiary in another Member State.

The present study will be focused only on the three first cases.

1. Participating companies the head offices of which are not located in the Community

The regulation[32] is expressly mentioning that "a Member State may provide" that a company, the head office of which is not in the Community, may participate in the formation of an SE, provided that company is formed under the law of a Member State, has its registered office in that Member State and has a real and continuous link with a Member State's economy. France may have no difficulties to apply this provision directly.[33]

A negotiation process could probably solve the questions that could be discussed in this case. E.g., French Company law authorises the SA (monistic or dualistic) to have or not to have a body representing the employees: In the case of the putting in place in France of a subsidiary SE, which is the subsidiary of a GmbH (with a system of *Mitbestimmung*) and of an SAS (without any employee's involvement), the only way to start with such a Joint Venture will be to find a win-win agreement between the players. France may probably adopt an open position regarding the social harmonisation and the mutual recognitions it implies.[34] Could this exercise be done more easily in a closed SE?

2. The SE: a convenient subsidiary that can move throughout Europe

The following scheme shows the different bodies playing in a group. The shareholders, the trade unions and the management can be spread into separate

[32] Art 2.5.

[33] See in France *Mayer* Droit International Privé, Domat, Montchrestien, 3e éd. P. 601, and about the French imperium in the social field, especially regarding the negotiations, Cass. soc., 14 may 1992, Vaulx distribution, D. 1993, p. 67, note *Decoopmann*.

[34] *Colombani/Favero*, p. 30, for the possibility of risk that some countries only recognize the organizations that are mirroring their national companies and the opportunity to create a number of new legal structures that will be adapted to the SE and sometimes disappear with it, see, *Parleani* Gazette du Palais N° 92/93, Mercredi 2, Jeudi 3 avril 2003, p. 13.

entities that are incorporated in different countries in Europe or abroad. The demand is presently located in markets mainly in Europe or abroad and the SE can be helpful in simplifying the policies of a group wishing to play on the European market. Each Member State should be able to decide which companies could be used for this purpose.[35]

a) The classical cross-boarder transaction

From a French point of view, and thanks to the discrete bridges[36] that are built for the SE between the European and local forums, let us describe below how the SE can be used as a subsidiary that could be set up between industrial partners in order to be present in a niche.[37]

(1) Map of the activities of a group

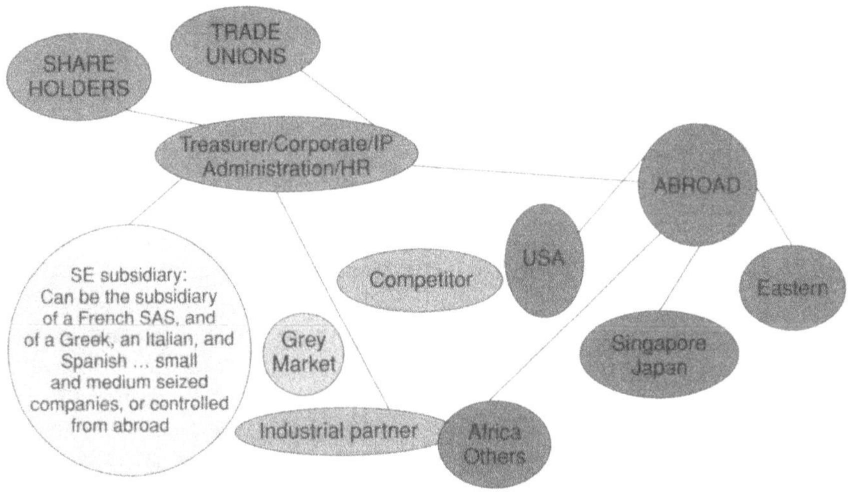

[35] *Davies* Employee Involvement, in *Hopt/Menjucq/Wymeersch,* pp. 79: a blocking attitude cannot be presumed on the part of the national representatives.

[36] *Béguin* Le rattachement de la société européenne, *Hopt/Menjucq/Wymeersch*, p. 33; *Colombani* La société européenne, utilité d'un projet ancien pour le marché intérieur de demain, p. 77; *Colombani/Favero*, pp. 166 et sq.; 218, 243, 248 et sq., 322.

[37] For a systematic work about the SE within the EC antitrust and concentration context, the IP policies, and for some specific strategies using the European "boat", see, *Colombani* La Société Européenne: utilité d'un projet ancien pour le marché intérieur de demain, Thèse, Paris XI, Jul. 1998, Lille, ABES, 15 sept. 1998, see also: *Favero* Plaidoyer pour la société européenne, Les Petites Affiches, 2 nov. 1998; *Colombani* Réflexion sur une politique de transfert des produits marqués – Les Petites Affiches, juil. 1999, *Colombani/Favero* Societas europaea, p. 31; La société européenne, Gazette du Palais, 3 apr. 2003.

(2) Classical transaction: Exchange of half the new shares of A and B between the holding companies

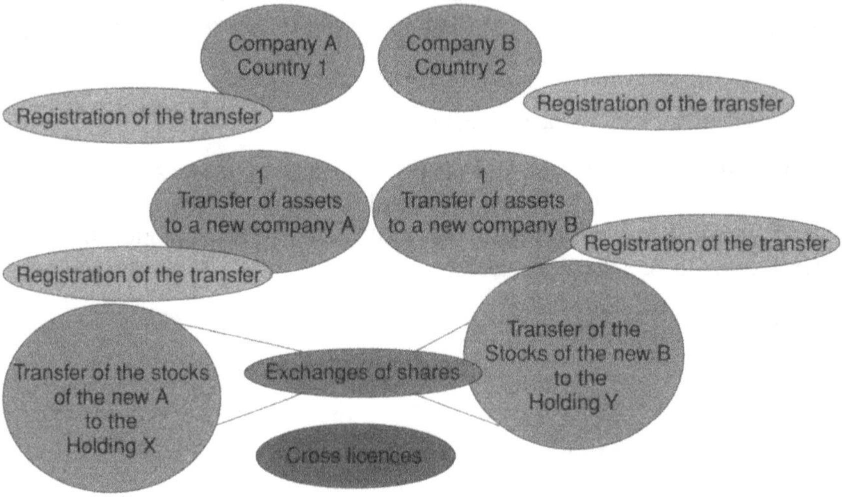

This scheme has the virtue to be quite usual. It has been used for example in the DEXIA Case.[38]

Most executives would prefer these schemes in order to set up cross-border business as long as they will not be fully comfortable with the rules of the SE. There is, however, a natural risk at the level of the transfer of IP rights. E.g., when the corporate department is separated from the IP one, or when the due diligences are managed too quickly, the process of registration of the transfers of portfolios before the national patent and trademark offices can be difficult. The practical risk for the purchaser is to face the impossibility of enforcement. Secondly, this scheme of co-operation is asking a few questions from the European Industrial Property side[39] e.g. in terms of exhaustion of rights and judicial and or administrative justification of a position.

Anyway, the SE will be an optional instrument for all the players and the above scheme of organisation will obviously remain and especially while the current work of the Commission on the relevant directives is not complete, especially if the SE is a closed company.[40]

[38] *Colombani/Favero,* p. 27.

[39] *Colombani* Réflexion sur une politique de transfert des produits marqués, Les Petites affiches, juillet 1999; *Colombani/Favero*, p. 31.

[40] Reg (CE) n° 1606/2002, JO L 243 11 sept. 2002, is bounding the public entities to follow the international IAS standards, as per Jan. 1rst 2005 and after this date in the field

In this case the parties can negotiate a common way of valuing their shares and stocks. A member of the holding can decide to leave the deal with cash compensation, if the possibility does exist (e.g.) in the State of incorporation.

b) Transaction using an SE: a simplification that implies negotiations on the transfers costs and a real co-operation between the member States and the European Entities which are in charge of the putting in place of the SE

We experienced such a negotiation in the moot court that took place at the French Senate on May 2003 supported by the French Prime Minister *J.-P. Raffarin*.

(1) The scenario

The scenario of the Moot Court was the following:

"A French SAS (200 employees) and an Austrian GmbH (150 employees) intend to found a common subsidiary in the form of a Societas Europaea (SE) ARCO SE – which will have its registered office in Paris (France) and will have 500 employees.

The SE's main object is the production of healthcare products; at the same time, the SE sets up a research and development centre for the development of new products. UNPOL SE, an SE formed in Poland by means of a merger of a Polish and a Hungarian company, decides to become a partner and to provide ARCOTEC with its support. Consequently, UNPOL has the benefit of one share from ARCO SE.

Meanwhile a Danish public limited liability company and a Swedish public limited liability company (50 employees each) are co-operating on a common R&D project on infusion technology.

of insurance, probably under the provisions of the proposal of directive, COM (2002) 259/2 final, jul. 9, 2002. The closed SE should make the choice of the IAS standard pursuant to article 5 of the regulation on the international accounting standards. If this choice is considered as locally impossible, the current methods of cross-border controls (e.g., global compliance with US GAP and national accounting systems) should continue to apply.
For an opinion about the lack of harmonisation in the accounting standards an the current work of the European Commission on this topic, see *Van Hulle* Les comptes annuels et les comptes consolidés de la SE, in *Hopt/Menjucq/Wymeersch*, p. 158: "Il s'ensuit que, pour les comptes annuels, le niveau d'harmonisation sera relativement réduit. Il pourra se trouver amélioré à la suite de la modernisation des directives comptables". France has transposed most of the options of the 4th directive n° 78/660 (J.O.C.E. n° L 222 dated 14 Aug. 1978) through a law which can be considered as quite modern: L. n° 83–353 dated 30 Apr. 1983 and D. n° 83–1020 dated 29 Nov. 1983, the obligations have been broadly extended.

The result produced by this research programme was so satisfactory that the two companies decided to file a jointly held European patent.

With a view to jointly exploiting the patent and expanding their production, the Nordic companies decide to merge and to form a European Company, HAMEK SE, with its registered office in Copenhagen (Denmark).

However, development and production of new medical instruments are expensive. HAMEK SE therefore approaches ARCO and offers to combine know-how and experience so that they can commercialise their products together.

The two SEs intend to place a new system for remote control of an infusion pump via a central display, on the market.

At the moment they do not plan the formation of a new company; on the contrary, both companies would remain free in their production and distribution decisions.

A German AG – TEC AG – (500 employees) learns about this co-operation.

TEC AG has a minority with 10%.

Like the other companies, it intends to enter the market for medical instruments. To achieve this aim, the German AG proposes to the other companies that they form a holding SE (ARCOTEC SE) with a share capital of 1,000,000.– Euro and its registered office in Heidelberg (Germany).

An expert evaluates the companies promoting the holding SE and ascertains the following values:

ARCO SE: 200,000 Euro
HAMEK SE: 800,000 Euro
TEC AG: 500,000 Euro.

Having established the holding SE, the management decides to introduce a common management structure in the group and to transform TEC AG into an SE.

Thereby the monistic management system can be applied in all of ARCOTEC's subsidiaries.

The Austrian shareholders of ARCOTEC propose the potential transfer of seat to Vienna (Austria), because of the excellence of the research of the Faculty of Medicine of the University of Vienna. The other shareholders consider the advantages of other Member States."

The aim was to discuss the best conditions for the company (law, economy, taxes, social system, infrastructure, and education …) in different Member States. We must state at first sight that some countries are already ready to practice the mergers between them (Denmark, Sweden), and that others are prepared as well to host a closed holding SE. Mr *Marc Favero* and Dr. *Silja Maul* launched the discussion about the best methods in order to open the holding or part of it.

(2) Procedure

Both the parties and the member States should designate independent bodies that will have the mission to verify the process utilised in the formation of the company. This could be done under the responsibility and control of the traditional chartered accountants and legal bodies that are currently working on the cross border operations.

Anyway, the players will have to distinguish between two periods: before and after the registration of the SE. The law of the parties should lead to determine the legal domicile that will govern the new SE.[41] In France, like in the other Member states, we will have to determine some guidelines for this independent evaluation, in order to recognise a priori the information given by the parties, under their responsibility.

We are, however, of the opinion that a European co-ordination office, or a body of national experts would be helpful in order to centralise the information about the SE. An independent body of experts, which could be chartered on a national or European level, could verify the compliance of the reports, social agreements, and financial information with the European requirements especially in tree fields:

Firstly in the case of mergers, the national laws might be written in keeping with the ratio legis of the SE, especially a consensus should be found about the transcription and the application of article 18 and 25 of the regulation.[42] *Secondly*, the same statement can be made about the "before and after principle". Prior to any movement or creation of an SE, the parties and third parties should be able to verify, if an agreement has been found about the workers involvement, under the provisions of Article 4 of the SE-Directive.[43] *Thirdly*, in order to prevent misuse of the cross border operation, a member State could decide under the provisions of Article 8 para. 14 of the SE-Regulation, that a competent authority can oppose the transfer on grounds of public interests.[44] France may pay special attention to these aspects.[45]

[41] See *Colombani/Favero*, p. 52, n° 174.

[42] For a precise example linked to the EADS case and the possibility of risk of non recognition of the national independent expertises that exists in the cases of mergers see *Colombani/Favero*, p. 75, n° 253.

[43] See *Colombani/Favero*, p. 61, n° 205.

[44] For the listed companies, which are supervised by a national supervisory authority (AMF in France or CNMV in Spain ...) this provision will create new responsibilities, see *Favero* in Colombani/Favero, p. 115, n° 417.

[45] *Hyest* rapport sur la loi en matière de sécurité financière, Sénat, 2003, http://www.senat.fr/rap/a02-207/a02-207_mono.html.

The process should facilitate for instance the putting in place of the SE in a few closed groups, and, by the way, France may especially decide to give an advantage to the companies which are playing the SE in order to cut the general and administration costs. This method could be shared by the other member States in a "win – win" approach.[46]

An SAS could be used for this purpose and have the gain, by the way of its social aspect but under the before and after principle and on a negotiated basis even if an SE may have at least three members seated at the board when the standard rules are applicable.[47]

Locally some place has to be made in company law to accommodate special cases, e.g., the French SAS, could be assimilated to a private "société anonyme", in order to gain the benefit of setting up an SE through mergers.[48] In the Member States the idea of a new national "european" company, which could be adopted only for the purpose of the SE could be discussed as an option.

(3) Minority Protection

Pursuant to Article 24 para. 2 of the Regulation, Member States may adopt provisions designed to ensure appropriate protection for minority shareholders who have opposed the merger. This provision would only make sense in the countries where this protection is not organised under domestic law; this is not the case in France.[49] A similar provision is contained in Article 34 of the Regulation with regard to the formation of a holding SE. The shareholders of the companies promoting the operation shall have a period of three month in

[46] *Teichmann* ECLR, Minderheitenschutz bei Gründung und Sitzverlegung der SE, Zeitschrift für Unternehmens- und Gesellschaftsrecht, De Gruyter Recht, 3/2003, p. 390.

[47] In favour of an "SAS de type européen", see for instance *Valuet* Droit et patrimoine, nov 1997, p. 57; in favour of the possibility of using the SAS as a national vehicle in order to set up an SE through the last project of the Commission see *Colombani*, Les Petites Affiches, 9 mars 1999, and in favour of a large contractual sphere of the future SE based in France see *Colombani/Favero*, p. 44, n° 142.

[48] For the basic schemes which can be played through the last regulation see *Colombani*, thèse , p. 236 et sq; *Colombani/Favero*, p. 72 et sq; *Colombani*, La société européenne pour l'exploitation de niches technologiques et pari pour la participation, Gazette du Palais, 3 avr. 2003, pp. 17 et sq; see also, *Wenz* Einsatzmöglichkeiten einer Europäischen Aktiengesellschaft in der Unternehmenspraxis aus betriebswirtschaflicher Sicht, Die Aktiengesellschaft, 1. Apr. 2003, pp. 185 et sq.

[49] Under Art. 18 of the Regulation, in the cases of mergers, the provisions of article L 236-5 should be applicable, as well as the current case law which is preventing the misuse of a majority, see *Lamy* Droit des sociétés, p. 1779, n° 1778, see also *Colombani/Favero*, p. 77, n° 262.

which to inform the promoting companies whether they intend to contribute their shares in the formation of the holding SE.[50]

In the cases of mergers, the SE-Regulation goes very far, when it provides under Article 25 para. 3, that the action of a minority could impeach the process.[51] From a practical aspect, this provision could be a major issue in the listed groups. In closed companies, held by a single body, the decision process might be easier.

(4) Opposition by public authority

Pursuant to Art. 19 of the SE-Regulation, a Member State may provide that any of the Member State's competent authorities opposes the merger. This provision can be understood especially bearing in mind recital n° 24 of the preamble that provides: "The SE should be enabled to transfer its registered office to another Member state. Adequate protection of the interests of minority shareholders who oppose the transfer, of creditors and of holders of other rights should be proportionate. Such transfer should not affect the rights originating before the transfer." As discussed above, we are of the opinion that the fair co-operation between the European authorities and the Member States, which are conducting the putting in place of the SE, will be a wager for the success of the SE.[52]

(5) Special Negotiating Body

In the case of a European Company created through a merger, the standard principles on participation of its workers would be applied when at least 25% of employees had the right to participate before the merger.[53]

[50] In France, when an SARL composed of multiple partners will be involved in the deal, the usual actions protecting the minority should be reinforced by a special expertise, under the provisions of article L 223-22 of the commercial code and D. n° 67–236, 23 mar. 1967, art. 45-1. See also *Colombani/Favero*, p. 85, n° 296.

[51] *Colombani/Favero*, p. 79, n° 270, 271.

[52] See *Colombani/Favero*, p. 118, n° 429, about the sleepless nights that are necessary in order to achieve the process, see *Davies* Employee Involvement in: *Hopt/Menjucq/Wymeersch*, pp. 79; about the impact in French Law of the new law n° 2003 706 du 1er Août 2003 that deals with financial security see *Pansier/Charbonneau* Présentation de la loi n° 2003-706 du 1er Août 2003 relative à la sécurité financière, Gazette du Palais, 27 et 28 août 2003.

[53] Directive, article 3, 7, see *Colombani/Favero*, p. 60; se also, about the role of the social partners *Davies*, Employee Involvement in: *Hopt/Menjucq/Wymeersch*, pp. 74 et seq.

Employment contracts and pensions are not covered by the Regulation. They would be subject to national law in the Member States where the headquarters and branches operated: This provision may be included in the auditing/evaluation process.

(6) Practical point of view

Let us propose the positive vision of a merger that can be planned in a closed group in which there are no special claims from the minorities or from the workers. The merger will take place between two countries highly compatible such as Denmark and Sweden or other partners.

In this case, the articles of the SE could be set up as follows:

- Title 1: form, name + "SE", object, registered office, duration, statutory provisions (in keeping with the law of the registered office);
- Title 2: contributions, corporate capital and shares;
- Title 3: board of directors, management and statutory auditor;
- Title 4: workers involvement, conditions of the participation;
- Title 5: general shareholders meetings;
- Title 6: corporate financial year, profits and reserves;
- Title 7: losses, dissolution and liquidation.

The exchange of the shares should be managed as follows:

Under French company law, an extraordinary general meeting has to resolve on the merger plan. The auditors may provide the general meeting with a clear statement about minority protection. In the meantime, the special negotiating body should be working on the following items that are subject to be included in the articles of association of the new SE (see Art. 4 of the SE-Directive):

- scope of the agreement;
- composition, number of members and allocation of seats on the representative body which will be the discussion partner of the competent organ of the SE in connection with arrangements for the information and consultation of the employees of the SE and its subsidiaries and establishments etc ...

If the standard rules are chosen, the following could appear in the agreement:

- composition of the body representative of the employees;
- standard rules for information and consultation;
- standard rules for participation.

c) Holding SE

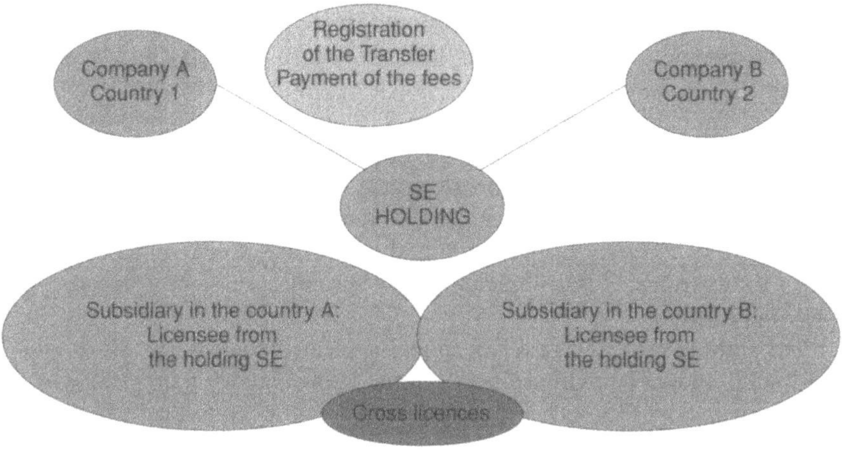

Such a corporate organisation seems realistic to us, especially from the fiscal point of view.[54]

We have listed the provisions that are mandatory in the regulation in order to set up a SE holding, if there is a difficulty the provisions concerning the mergers should be applicable.[55]

Co-ordination is necessary anyway, in order to enable the European travellers to cross the national rivers thanks to the bridge SE. For instance, no SE will be set up without an agreement or a provision in the bylaws about the involvement of the employees. This opportunity should be for them to make the choice of a demonstration of mutual understanding and respect by setting up social agreements that could appear different at first sight but that will nevertheless be more favourable than the previous existing system. Afterwards, the lawyers and the accountants will do what they are paid for.

From our point of view, it will be difficult to set up an effective and secure business through the SE as long as a European Register will not be in charge of the centralisation of the publications, and of the relevant questions linked to the SE. In France, the "Registre du Commerce et des Sociétés" which is cen-

[54] *Oplustil* Selected problems concerning the formation of a holding SE, German Law Journal, vol. 04, n° 02, 107, *Colombani/Favero*, pp. 86 et seq.

[55] Also *Largo Gil* Revista de derecho de sociedades 2002, 99, 103, *Teichmann* ECLR, Minderheitenschutz bei Gründung und Sitzverlegung der SE, Zeitschrift für Unternehmens- und Gesellschaftsrecht, De Gruyter Recht, 3/2003, p. 389 et seq, Colombani/ Favero, p. 83 et seq.

tralizing the information about the companies is closely linked and is working on a permanent basis with the national patent and trade mark office, which is gathering the relevant information about the "fonds de commerce". The national office provides interested parties with the information that is available in France.

This technique of twinning directives that have a certain direct effect through a regulation, has been used by the European Union in order to implement in the national legal systems the provisions of the new legal instruments of the European Commerce such as: Community Trade Marks or Designs.[56] The Industrial Property Lawyers are used in their day to day practice to deal with such instruments in co-operation with the European authorities, e.g. the OAMI in Alicante.

The authorities in charge of the global implementation of the SE throughout the EC should be well inspired from the French model in order to provide the Member states with such a co-ordination support or equivalent structure.

d) The SE as a subsidiary: a cross-boarder co-operation that opens a field of negotiations on the contractual sphere.

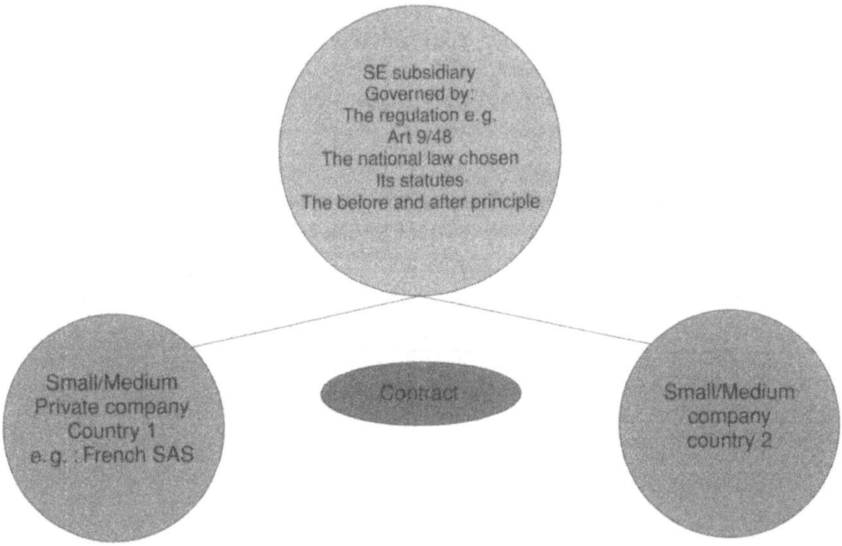

[56] For a French point of view see *Dreyfus* Marque dessins et modèles, strategies de défense et de valorisation, Delmas 2002, p. 176. Trade marks: For a complete study about the global business through the EC Trademark, see *Mostert* Famous and well-known marks, Butterworths, 1997, pp. 21 et sq; 294, 61 et sq.; 148. *Trade Marks*: First

120 000 Euros in minimum capital opens the SE to "small and medium" sized firms which are able to face international competition or to make joint ventures. The joint venture can be for instance found attractive for setting up Community programs in favour of innovation.

For example we can imagine that a Greek, an Italian, Spanish and a French Company located in France will use the SE to get together in order to comply with the European funds' requirements dedicated to help the projects in the Mediterranean Islands (e.g. Corsica, Sardinia, Sicily).

We can also imagine a case of a private holding created between medium sized companies in order to be present on a technological niche.

IV. Management system

1. General

The legal regime of the SE in France will consist of rules applicable to the SE that already includes the one-tier and the two-tier system of management. From this point of view the task of the legislator could be less difficult than in Austria[57] or Germany and other countries where the SE obliges the Member State to create a new management system.

Actually, it is possible in France to set up a SE even with a monistic structure or with the two-tier organisation. Furthermore, the involvement of the workers is not linked to the internal organisation but to the number of employees.

Directive 89/104/EEC of the Council, of 21 December 1988, to Approximate the Laws of the Member States Relating to Trade Marks (OJ EC No L 40 of 11.2.1989, p. 1); Council Regulation (EC) No 40/94 of 20 December 1993 on the Community trade mark; Commission Regulation (EC) No 2868/95 of 13 December 1995 implementing Council Regulation (EC) No 40/94 on the Community trade mark; Commission Regulation (EC) No 2869/95 of 13 December 1995 on the fees payable to the Office for Harmonization in the Internal Market (Trade Marks and Designs); Commission Regulation (EC) No 216/96 of 5 February 1996 laying down the rules of procedure of the Boards of Appeal of the Office for Harmonization in the Internal Market (Trade Marks and Designs). *Designs*: Council Regulation (EC) n° 6/2002 of 12 December 2001 on Community Designs – Commission Regulation (EC) n° 2245/2002 of 21 October 2002 implementing Council Regulation (EC) No 6/2002 on Community designs; Commission Regulation (EC) n° 2246/2002 of 16 December 2002 on the fees payable to the Office for Harmonization in the Internal Market (Trade Marks and Designs) in respect of the registration of Community designs; Directive 98/71/EC of the European Parliament and of the Council of 13 October 1998 on the legal protection of designs. *Patents*: Proposal for a Council Regulation on the Community patent – Text revised by the Presidency – Document 10404/03 (PI 53).

[57] *Arlt/Bervoest/Grechenig/Kalss*, European Business Organization Law Review, 2002 p. 738.

The statements that are made about the new economic regulation and the power of the board of the employees should not be changed by the adoption of the SE.[58] In accordance with the principle "before and after", the companies may draft an agreement fully compliant with the provisions of the directive especially with Art. 4 para. 2, and then decide to make an express reference to this agreement in the bylaws. This method has been used by the students in the above mentioned moot court in order to find a win – win agreement during the moot court.

Therefore pursuant to the provisions of Article 3 para. 2 lit. a) i) of the Directive, the Special Negotiating Body should be composed by one representative for ten percent of the employees. These representatives will be elected to the board of employees of the SE.

However this negotiation, even compliant with the directive, should not lead to a reduction of the involvement in the management of the new company of the workers who are coming from Member States in which the "co-management" is mandatory.[59]

Such an agreement should be easier to find in the closed companies or in countries that are flexible or admit the workers at the board on a voluntary basis.[60] Anyway, we shall plead for a negotiated and flexible approach.[61]

2. Two-tier system:

The option which is contained in Article 39 para. 2 of the Regulation and that offers to the Member States require or permit the statutes to provide that the member or members of the management organ shall be appointed and removed by the general meeting. The current law should not be amended on this point,[62] but could be adapted in order to welcome the SE in France.

The same remark can be made about the option offered by Article 39 para. 3, 39 para. 5 and 40 para. 3. The option actually makes sense in the Member Sta-

[58] When a "comité d'entreprise" is mandatory, *Bandrac* Dom, Loi NRE et autres réformes, Joly 2002, pp. 235 et seq.

[59] *Le Cannu* La direction de la société européenne, in: *Hopt/Menjucq/Wymeersch*, and, especially with regards to the social aspect of the SE, combined with its classical contractual sphere, see p. 103.

[60] For an example in Italy: *Arlt/Bervoest/Grechenig/Kalss*, European Business Organization Law Review, 2002 p. 749.

[61] *Teichmann*, German Law Journal april 1st 2003 (see: www.germanlawjournal.com).

[62] *Colombani/Favero*, pp. 105 et seq; for a comparison between five Member States see *Arlt/Bervoets/Grechenig/Kalss*, European Business Organization Law Review, 2002, p. 738.

tes that have not chosen this type of organisation.[63] Italy can be taken as an extraordinary example of adaptation; the new law is providing a large scope of corporate governance as well as codes of conducts and corporate governance codes.[64] In France the law is currently changing and article L 225-94-1 of the commercial code shall be redrafted.[65] The French two-tier SE might nevertheless stay "French fashioned".[66]

3. One-tier system

Regarding the "classical" mode of corporate governance, the regulation is very precise, but will neither operate a great change in French law.[67] For instance, Article 43 para. 2 "The number of members of the administrative organ or the rules for determining it shall be laid down in the SE's statutes". This provision is especially interesting when considering that the SAS is linked to the SA.

A provision, which have probably been adopted under German influence, is the one according to which the administrative organ shall consist of at least tree members where employee's participation is regulated in accordance with the directive.[68] This could be considered as a potential issue in the companies that are currently managed by less than tree directors.

4. Rules common to both systems

Article 47 para. 1 of the Regulation provides that a Member State may permit a company "or other legal entity" to be a member of an organ of the SE. This provision could be another chance for the SAS or for a new SA which may be less flexible than the SAS.[69]

[63] *Colombani/Favero*, p. 104: Belgium, Denmark, Spain, the UK, Greece, Luxembourg and Sweden are concerned.

[64] *Padovini*, Gesellschafter, 2/2002, pp. 86 et sq; and for a bet on the possible competition between Italy, the Netherland and France: *Arlt/Bervoets/Grechenig/Kalss*, European Business Organization Law Review, 2002, p. 748.

[65] See *Hyest*, Rapport, prec., Modification de dispositions du code de commerce relatives aux mandats sociaux http://www.senat.fr/rap/l02-013/l02-013.pdf.

[66] For an opinion about the opportunity to introduce a Katalog in French Law, see, *Le Cannu* Le fonctionnement de la SE, in: *Hopt/Menjucq/Wymeersch*, p. 110.

[67] See *Colombani/Favero*, pp. 108 et seq.

[68] *Colombani, Favero*, Societas Europaea, n° 386, p. 109; See also, the point made by Le Cannu, October 3/4, 2002 (*Hopt/Menjucq/Wymeersch.*), p. 112.

[69] *Colombani/Favero*, n° 394, p. 110.

France is currently evaluating the opportunity to change the current dualistic system pursuant to article 48 para. 1 and 2 of the Regulation. Also the second point providing that, "A Member State may determine the categories of transactions which must at least be indicated in the Statutes of SEs" is subject to analysis. France may have the choice to provide the SE with a strong contractual sphere and this could be a safer option especially for the creditors.

V. General meeting

Pursuant to Art. 54 para. 1 of the Regulation, the first general meeting has to be held at any time in the 18 months following a SE's incorporation, in France this option should be managed under the provisions of article L 225-7 of the commercial code.[70]

We are thoughtful about the opportunity that is given to the Member States in the Regulation under Articles 55 and 56. Less than 10% of the stockholders should be able to convene a general meeting (Art. 55) and to put additional items on the agendas (Art. 56). Article 55, seems[71] to allow this right only to the holders of stocks that are linked to subscribed capital.[72] Anyway a minority should respond in court of any misuse.[73] The courts thereby could have a key position in the management of the conflicts.

Pursuant to Article 55 para. 3 of the Regulation, if no meeting is held on the request within two months, the competent judicial or administrative authority may order that a general meeting be convened. In France with regard to the urgent aspect of such an issue, the relevant procedure should be the "Référé".[74] A practical point could rise about the calculation of the delay of two month if the national law is not more precise than the regulation. The same question remains with regard to Art. 56.

With regard to the amendment of the statutes (Art. 59 para. 1 of the Regulation), we are of the opinion that in France a majority under the provisions of article L 225-96 will be sufficient for any amendment of the statutes.

70 *Colombani/Favero*, n° 1.1, p. 101.

71 *Rojo* Les investisseurs, in: *Hopt/Menjucq/Wymeersch*, p. 123.

72 *Colombani/Favero*, p. 101.

73 *Rojo* Les investisseurs, in: *Hopt/Menjucq/Wymeersch*, p. 122.

74 *Colombani/Favero*, p. 101, n° 1.2.

VI. Transfer of seat

We experienced in the above mentioned Moot Court, that the SE has a direct effect on the "sex appeal" of the national legislations. Each country is showing a nice and good face in order to attract new companies! We would say that this new wave in company law is refreshing our old continent in a pleasant way. From a practical side, however, our opinion remains that the management nerve of a group should be difficult to locate.[75]

A balance must be found on a few points:

Firstly, regarding the option that is included in Article 7 providing that a Member State may in addition impose on SE's registered in its territory the obligation of locating their head office and their registered office at the same place. In France, the "siège réel" theory would be sufficient. Anyway, after a period of probation and of definition of the procedures linked to the travelling SE, and pursuant to Article 69, the Regulation could generally allow this option.

Secondly, the possible opposition by public authorities provided by Article 8 para. 14 will have to be debated in the light of the current European case law.[76] Pursuant to Articles 43 EC and 48 EC, a company formed in accordance with the law of a Member State and having its registered office is exercising its freedom of establishment in another Member State may be recognised by the host Member State in its legal capacity and its capacity to be a party to legal proceedings. This rule may a fortiori be applicable to the SE.[77]

The issues of the protection of minority shareholders under Article 8 para. 5 and the protection of creditors under Article 8 para. 7 should be regarded by the legislator with the same eyes as those that are used in order to translate the process of international merger or of setting up a holding SE into local laws.[78]

[75] *Colombani*, Sénat 12 juin 2002, Gazette du Palais, 2, 3 apr. 2003, p. 24.

[76] See *Colombani*, thèse, pp. 81 et sq., pp 281 et sq.; *Favero* Plaidoyer pour une société européenne, op. cit; *Menjucq* La circulation internationale des sociétés, Les Petites Affiches, 4 mai 2001, n° 89, CJCE, 27 sept. 1988, case. 81/47 Daily Mail; CJCE, 26 june 2001, case C-212/99, Commission/Italy, about the non discrimination in the free movements of workers; CJCE, 5 nov. 2002, case Überseering BV.

[77] *Menjucq* Droit international et Européen des sociétés, Montchrestien, Domat, 2001, n° 226 et sq; *Colombani/Favero*, pp. 117 et seq.

[78] See *Colombani/Favero*, pp. 113 et seq: "Un formalisme adapté à une structure mobile".

VII. Involvement of employees

It is the first time in France that a preliminary condition about the involvement of the workers shall be mandatory prior to the first registering of a company.[79] In the case of a merger, for example, the parties shall try to reach an agreement on employee involvement prior to the incorporation of the SE in order to secure the business. It was difficult to find a medium position between no participation at all and the various national models. The principles that are of direct effect have been introduced in the regulation that offers a few simple options to the governments, and the standard principles coming from the directive have been discussed above.

We may add that out of the Moot Court experience we feel that not only in France each organ of the SE must be negotiated and shaped through a common guideline which can make the things easier.

The directive will conduct the managers who want to try the SE to provide regular reports on the basis of which there must be regular consultation of and information to a body representing the companies' employees. These reports must detail the companies' current and future business plans, production and sales levels, implications of these for the workforce, management changes, mergers, divestments, potential closures and layoffs. Anyway the directive will not significantly change the French labour law. In the classical cases of mergers or scission (which is impossible through the SE), when a "comité d'entreprise" is concerned the negotiation process is mandatory in France.[80] France will neither have to redraft its company law nor its social law in order to host the SE. The coherence of the involvement of employees can be achieved by the election or designation of the representatives.

Contrary to previously, when the parties are unable to negotiate a mutually satisfactory agreement, and the companies involved in the creation of an SE were previously covered by participation rules, a European Company would apply standard principles on the participation of its workers. This would be the case of a European Company created as a holding company or joint-venture.

In a group with several subsidiaries a co-ordination board could exist to manage the workers involvement issues. Such issues remain the same throughout the various European subsidiaries or establishments. In some European

[79] *Parleani*, Gazette du Palais N° 92/93, Mercredi 2, Jeudi 3 avril 2003, p. 13.

[80] Cass. Soc., 9 oct. 1990, RJS, 1991/1.3, obs. *Pélissier*; JCP, éd. E., 1991 II 196, note Deprez; *Catala/Bonnet*, Droit social européen, Litec 1991, p. 205, *Colombani*, thèse, supra, pp. 307 et sq.; *Colombani/Favero*, supra, pp. 49 et sq. See also, *Moreau* A propos de "l'affaire Renault", Dr. Soc., n° 5, 1997, p. 493; TGI Nanterre, référés, 4 avril 1997 et CA Versailles, 7 mai 1997, obs. *A. Lyon Caen*.

countries the idea of worker involvement is relatively new and not so extensive as in other countries. In others it is fully based on negotiation between the social partners. The court who will be competent to solve potential conflicts may be the general jurisdiction: Tribunal de Grande Instance.

VIII. Fiscal issues

Last but not least, we should mention the main fiscal issues. Presently we can hear two current visions of the mutual recognition of the companies:

1. Free movement for all the companies and a single tax policy throughout Europe, that sounds nowadays like a former option.
2. Transfer and mergers through the SE, this option considers the SE like a national company and is careful of the sovereign power of the Member States on their international tax policy.

The European Company must be registered in the Member State where it has its administrative head office. This is according to the Commission, the only system that allows effective supervision of the whole SE, so as to avoid the SE being used for doubtful practices such as tax fraud or money laundering. In the meantime, the governments are working on a tax code that would be subject to a European tax policy.

There would be a fiscal advantage in creating a European Company by merger registered in the most favourable Member State for tax purposes but operating through subsidiaries located in the Member States. As proposed by Senator *Branger* (see note 4), the existing bilateral conventions could be amended in order to cover the SE.

IX. Conclusion: Will the SE significantly change the national philosophies of the company law?

We are of the opinion that the answer to this question will be quite the same in each country, and we can bet that it will be certainly a more or less a soft no![81]

But, and there is a "but", the SE will probably allow new strategies and we have the chance to have the support of our countries to think about it. The SE will be an optional tool that will be broadly opened to all national entities. This instrument can lead to a common practice of business and social law. Beyond

[81] *Luby* La societas europaea beaucoup de bruit pour rien, ou si peu! Dr. Sociétés, fib. 2002, Chr. 2 p. 4.

the current practices, the SE is a challenging topic for the European businessmen lawyers and Member States no only from a technical point of view. First contacts with countries from Central Europe, such as Romania and Kosovo, prove that such instruments could be of some help for countries accessing the EU in the future.

From the human side, the SE can be a bridge over trouble water: this options of simplicity and efficiency; the possibility given to the managers to cut the general and administration cots prior to social costs will only come true if all the parties in charge of the SE on a political level are active to help the managers who decided to go ahead on this bridge.

While it is difficult to imagine a SE only dedicated to national business, the way of playing the SE, with a common regulation, is a way of mutual recognition. This way implies generosity, tolerance, and probably sometimes the players will have to compromise before finding the appropriate solutions. We wish the SE and its players will live under the Government of Reason,[82] so that the Societas Europaea and its crews, could have pleasant travels.

[82] *Swift* Gulliver's travels, A voyage to the country of the Houyhnms,, Ch.XII: the author's veracity.

Germany

Christoph Teichmann

The German Federal Ministry of Justice has published a **discussion draft** on the SE Implemention Act (Diskussionsentwurf für das Gesetz zur Ausführung der Verordnung (EG) Nr. 2157/2001 des Rates vom 8. Oktober 2001 über das Statut der Europäischen Gesellschaft (SE) – SE-Ausführungsgesetz –) which is available online at www.bmj.bund.de/gesetzgebungsvorhaben; printed in Die Aktiengesellschaft, Heft 4, April 2003, p. 204 et seq.

Literature on the SE published in Germany since 2001 (for earlier literature see the references in: *Schwarz* Europäisches Gesellschaftsrecht, 2000, p. 640, and *Habersack* Europäisches Gesellschaftsrecht, 2nd edition, 2003, S. 396):* *Blanquet* Das Statut der Europäischen Aktiengesellschaft (Societas Europaea „SE") – Ein Gemeinschaftsinstrument für die grenzübergreifende Zusammenarbeit im Dienste der Unternehmen, ZGR 2002, 20; *Brandi* Die Europäische Aktiengesellschaft im deutschen und internationalen Konzernrecht, NZG 2003, 889; *Brandt* Überlegungen zu einem SE-Ausführungsgesetz, NZG 2002, 991; *Brandt* Der Diskussionsentwurf zu einem SE-Ausführungsgesetz, DStR 2003, 1208; *Brandt/Scheifele* Die Europäische Aktiengesellschaft und das anwendbare Recht, DStR 2002, 547; *Bungert/Beier* Die Europäische Aktiengesellschaft, EWS 2002, 1; *Buchheim*, Europäische Aktiengesellschaft und grenzüberschreitende Konzernverflechtung, 2001; *Casper* Der Lückenschluß im Statut der Europäischen Aktiengesellschaft, FS Ulmer, 2003, S. 51; *Ebert* Das anwendbare Konzernrecht der Europäischen Aktiengesellschaft, BB 2003, 1854; *Ebke* Die Europäische Aktiengesellschaft ist da – und jetzt?, EWS 2002, 1; *Förster/Lange* Steuerliche Aspekte der Gründung einer Europäischen Aktiengesellschaft, DB 2002, 288; *Forstmoser* Monistische oder dualistische Unternehmensverfassung? Das Schweizer Konzept, ZGR 2003, 688; *Götz* Ist die Europäische Aktiengesellschaft eine überzeugende Option für die Praxis? ZIP 2003, 1067; *Gruber/Weller* Societas Europaea: Mitbestimmung ohne Aufsichtsrat?, NZG 2002, 297; *Habersack* Das Konzernrecht der „deutschen" SE, ZGR 2003, 724; *Heinze* Die Europäische Aktiengesellschaft, ZGR 2002, 66; *Henssler* Unternehmerische Mitbestimmung in der Societas Europaea, FS Ulmer, 2003, p. 193; *Herfs-Röttgen* Arbeitnehmerbeteiligung in der Europäischen Aktiengesell-

* List of abbreviations: AG = Die Aktiengesellschaft; AuR = Arbeit und Recht; BB = Betriebs-Berater; DB = Der Betrieb; DStR = Deutsches Steuerrecht; EuZW = Europäische Zeitschrift für Wirtschaftsrecht; EWS = Europäisches Wirtschafts- & Steuerrecht; FS = Festschrift; NZA = Neue Zeitschrift für Arbeitsrecht; NZG = Neue Zeitschrift für Gesellschaftsrecht; RdA = Recht der Arbeit; RIW = Recht der Internationalen Wirtschaft; SZWR/RSDA = Schweizerische Zeitschrift für Wirtschaftsrecht/Revue suisse de droit des affaires; WM = Wertpapier-Mitteilungen; ZGR = Zeitschrift für Unternehmens- und Gesellschaftsrecht; ZHR = Zeitschrift für das gesamte Handelsrecht und Wirtschaftsrecht; ZIP = Zeitschrift für Wirtschaftsrecht.

schaft, NZA 2001, 424; *Hirte* Die Europäische Aktiengesellschaft, NZG 2002, 1; *Hopt* Europäische Aktiengesellschaft – per aspera ad astra?, EuZW 2002, 1; *Hopt* The European Company (SE) under the Nice compromise: Major breakthrough or small coin for Europe?, Euredia, European Banking and Financial Law Journal, 2000/4, p. 465; *Hommelhoff* Einige Bemerkungen zur Organisationsverfassung der Europäischen Aktiengesellschaft, AG 2001, 279; *Hommelhoff* Satzungsstrenge und Gestaltungsfreiheit in der Europäischen Aktiengesellschaft, FS Ulmer, 2003, p. 267; *Hommelhoff* Zum Konzernrecht in der Europäischen Aktiengesellschaft, AG 2003, 179; *Hommelhoff/Teichmann* Die Europäische Aktiengesellschaft – das Flaggschiff läuft vom Stapel, SZWR/RSDA 2002, 1; *Ihrig/Wagner* Diskussionsentwurf für ein SE-Ausführungsgesetz, BB 2003, 969; *Jaecks/Schönborn* Die Europäische Aktiengesellschaft, das Internationale und das deutsche Konzernrecht, RIW 2003, 254; *Jahn/Herfs-Röttgen* Die Europäische Aktiengesellschaft – Societas Europaea, DB 2001, 631; *Kallmeyer* Europa AG: Strategische Optionen für deutsche Unternehmen, AG 2003, 197; *Kallmeyer* Das monistische System der SE mit Sitz in Deutschland, ZIP 2003, 1531; *Kersting* Societas Europaea: Gründung und Vorgesellschaft, DB 2001, 2079; *Klapdor* Überlegungen zur Besteuerung der Europäischen Aktiengesellschaft, EuZW 2001, 677; *Kleinsorge* Europäische Gesellschaft und Beteiligungsrechte der Arbeitnehmer, RdA 2002, 343; *Kloster* Societas Europaea und europäische Unternehmenszusammenschlüsse, EuZW 2003, 293; *Köstler* Die Mitbestimmung in der SE, ZGR 2003, 800; *Kraushaar* Europäische Aktiengesellschaft (SE) und Unternehmensmitbestimmung, BB 2003, 1614; *Kübler* Leitungsstrukturen der Aktiengesellschaft und die Umsetzung des SE-Statuts, ZHR 167 (2003), 222; *Kübler* Barabfindung bei Gründung einer Europa-AG?, ZHR 167 (2003), 627; *Lange* Überlegungen zur Umwandlung einer deutschen in eine Europäische Aktiengesellschaft, EuZW 2003, 301; *Lutter* Europäische Aktiengesellschaft – Rechtsfigur mit Zukunft?, BB 2002, 1; *Maul* Konzernrecht der „deutschen" SE – Ausgewählte Fragen zum Vertragskonzern und den faktischen Unternehmensverbindungen, ZGR 2003, 743; *Menjucq* Das „monistische" System der Unternehmensleitung in der SE, ZGR 2003, 679; *Merkt* Die monistische Unternehmensverfassung für die Europäische Aktiengesellschaft aus deutscher Sicht, ZGR 2003, 650; *Nagel* Verschlechternde Regelungen und Vereinbarungen zur Mitbestimmung in der Europäischen Aktiengesellschaft, AuR 2001, 406; *Neye* Kein neuer Stolperstein für die Europäische Aktiengesellschaft, ZGR 2002, 377; *Neye/C. Teichmann* Der Entwurf des Ausführungsgesetzes zur Europäischen Aktiengesellschaft, AG 2003, 169; *Oplustil/Schneider* Zur Stellung der Europäischen Aktiengesellschaft im Umwandlungsrecht, NZG 2003, 13; *Pluskat* Die neuen Vorschläge für die Europäische Aktiengesellschaft, EuZW 2001, 524; *Pluskat* Die Arbeitnehmerbeteiligung in der geplanten Europäischen AG, DStR 2001, 1483; *Reichert/Brandes* Mitbestimmung der Arbeitnehmer in der SE: Gestaltungsfreiheit und Bestandsschutz, ZGR 2003, 767; *Schulz/Geismar* Die Europäische Aktiengesellschaft – Eine kritische Bestandsaufnahme, DStR 2001, 1078; *Schulz/Petersen* Die Europa-AG: Steuerlicher Handlungsbedarf bei Gründung und Sitzverlegung, DStR 2002, 1508; *Schwarz* Zum Statut der Europäischen Aktiengesellschaft, ZIP 2001, 1847; *C. Teichmann* Die Einführung der Europäischen Aktiengesellschaft – Grundlagen der Ergänzung des europäischen Statuts durch den deutschen Gesetzgeber, ZGR 2002, 383; *C. Teichmann* Vorschläge für das deutsche Ausführungsgesetz zur Europäischen Aktiengesellschaft, ZIP 2002, 1109; *C. Teichmann* Minderheitenschutz bei Gründung und Sitzverlegung der SE, ZGR 2003, 367; *C. Teichmann* The European Company – A Challenge to Academics, Legislatures and Practitioners, www.germanlawjournal.com, Vol. 4 No. 4; *C. Teichmann* Gestaltungsfreiheit im monistischen Leitungssystem der Europäischen Aktiengesellschaft, BB 2004, 53; *C. Teichmann* Austrittsrecht und Pflichtangebot bei Gründung einer Europäischen Aktiengesellschaft, AG 2004, 67; *Theisen/Wenz* (ed.) Die Europäische Aktiengesellschaft, 2002; *Veil* Das Konzernrecht der Europäischen Aktiengesellschaft, WM 2003, 2169; *Wagner* Die Bestimmung des auf die SE anwendbaren Rechts, NZG 2002, 985; *Wenz* Einsatzmöglichkeiten einer Europäischen Aktiengesellschaft in der Unternehmenspraxis aus betriebswirtschaftlicher Sicht, AG 2003, 185; *Wiesner* Der Nizza-Kompromiss zur Europa-AG – Triumph oder Fehlschlag?, ZIP 2001, 397.

I. Introduction

The European Company is nearing legal realisation in stages. After many decades of long drawn out negotiations in Council and Parliament, the necessary statutory measures were passed on 8 October 2001 – the Council Regulation (EC) No. 2157/2001 on the statute for a European company (SE),[1] and the Council Directive 2001/86/EC supplementing the Statute for a European company with regard to the involvement of employees.[2] For the arrival of the first real SE – the abbreviation is for Societas Europaea – 8 October 2004 must be awaited, as the texts provide for a transition period of three years, by the expiry of which the member states must have adjusted their legislation to the new legal form.

The primary legal basis of the SE consists of the SE-Regulation and the SE-Directive. A regulation applies automatically in the member states (Art. 249 para. 2 EC Treaty), and requires, by its nature, no implementing legislation in the member states. However, the SE-Regulation does not contain complete provisions on the substantive issues. It deals with formation, the structure of the SE and the transfer of registered office, but otherwise refers mostly to national law.[3] In most cases, reference is made direct to the national law on public limited companies, although in some case the national legislature is authorised to make specific provisions for the SE. Some of these discretionary areas or legislative requirements, such as minority protection on setting up an SE, the one-tier structure, and the provisions on the transfer of registered office, have considerable significance from a German point of view. These issues are dealt with in Parts A to C of this contribution, and are considered in the light of the discussion draft ***(DiscD)*** of the SE Implementation Act, issued by the Federal Ministry of Justice in March 2003.[4] The SE-Directive by its nature requires

[1] OJ EC of 10.11.2001, L 294/1; referred to throughout as "the SE-Regulation" or "the Regulation".

[2] OJ EC of 10.11.2001, L 294/22; referred to throughout as "the SE-Directive" or "the Directive".

[3] On the law applicable to the SE cf. especially *Brandt/Scheifele*, DStR 2002, 547ff.; *Wagner*, NZG 2002, 985ff.

[4] Accessible in Internet under www.bmj.bund.de/gesetzgebungsvorhaben. Cf. *Neye/C. Teichmann*, AG 2003, 169, on the draft.

implementation in national law (Art. 249 para. 3 EC Treaty). The associated questions are dealt with in Part D.

II. Formation of an SE

Four primary ways are provided for the formation of an SE (Art. 2 SE-Regulation) – formation by merger, the formation of a holding SE, the formation of a subsidiary SE and the transformation into an SE.[5] Once formed, the SE can form a subsidiary SE (secondary formation), or with other companies form a new SE by merger, a holding SE or subsidiary SE (Art. 3 SE-Regulation).

1. Participation of companies having head offices outside the EU

In principle, only a company which is formed under the law of a member state of the Community and having its registered office and its head office in the Community, can form an SE.[6] However, the member states may provide that a company, the head office of which is not in the Community, may participate in the formation of an SE provided that company is formed under the laws of a member state, has its registered office in that member state and has a real and continuous link with a member state's economy (Art. 2 para. 5 SE-Regulation).[7]

According to the *real seat theory* (Sitztheorie), hitherto followed in Germany, the law applicable to a company corresponds to the place of its main administration.[8] However, the *real seat theory* does not refer directly to the substantive law of the state where the main administration is situated, but to the entire legal system including its private international law. If this state follows the incorporation theory, a further reference to the law of the state of incorpo-

[5] For detailed conditions and the formation procedure in each case, cf. Art. 2 and Art. 15ff. of the Regulation and, in the literature, *Neun*, in: Theisen/Wenz (ed.), Die Europäische Aktiengesellschaft, 2002, p. 51ff.

[6] This arises in detail out of the various paragraphs of Art. 2 of the Regulation.

[7] By "registered office", the SE-Regulation always means only that according to the statutes (*Schwarz*, ZIP 2001, 1847, 1849).

[8] *Großfeld* in: Staudinger – Internationales Gesellschaftsrecht, Neubearbeitung 1998, marginal note 108f.; *Kindler* in: Münchener Kommentar-Internationales Handels- and Gesellschaftsrecht, 3. ed., 1999, marginal note 378ff. In how far the real seat theory still applies after the "Überseering" and the "Inspire Art" judgement of the ECJ (Case C-208/00, 5 November 2002, and Case C-167/01, 30 September 2002, http://curia.eu.int/en/content/juris/index.htm) is not a subject for discussion here.

ration comes into question. If the state of incorporation also follows the incorporation theory and if the company was properly formed there, its existence would not be put into question from a German point of view.[9]

In some cases, the real seat theory would permit a company having its main administration outside the Community to participate in the formation of an SE in Germany. The German legislature is faced with the question whether it should permit the companies mentioned in Art. 2 para. 5 SE-Regulation to form an SE with registered office in Germany – the German legislature has, of course, no jurisdiction on the formation of an SE outside Germany. There appears to be no urgent practical need for this. In any event, such a provision could be seen by German companies as prejudicial, because thus far location of registered office and main administration in different states is not permitted to them. The new German discussion draft does not, therefore, avail of the authority granted by Art. 2 para. 5 SE-Regulation.

2. Minority protection on formation

The SE-Regulation deals quite extensively with the procedure for formation by merger or formation of a holding SE, without attention to the interests of possible minorities in the national companies concerned. Instead, the national legislatures are authorised to make provisions for the protection of minorities in companies subject to their laws.

a) Merger

The procedure of merger of two public companies to become an SE is, on the one hand, sketched in the SE-Regulation and, on the other hand, is supplemented by the reference in Art. 18 to the national law on mergers, implementing the third directive. In addition, provisions can be made for the protection of minorities which oppose the merger (Art. 24 para. 2 SE-Regulation). German law has some provisions for minority protection in the case of mergers which, according to the present DiscD, should be applicable to the formation of an SE.

[9] The "Überseering" judgement of the ECJ (cf. footnote 8) is not relevant here, because in that case a company had transferred its registered office *to Germany.* Art. 2 para. 5 of the Regulation addresses only companies having their registered offices outside the Community. As stated already, in that case, even on application of the real seat theory, one reaches an assessment of the existence of the company according to the law of its incorporation.

(1) Review of the exchange ratio

§ 15 Transformation Act (*Umwandlungsgesetz*) grants shareholders in the case of national mergers, the possibility of having the exchange ratio reviewed by a court. If the exchange ratio is found to be unfair, the shareholders receive compensation in cash. § 6 DiscD makes the same provision for the case of merger to an SE. This applies whether the company which is subject to German law, is the transferring or acquiring company, because the shareholders in an acquiring company suffer a loss by an excessively high exchange ratio, just as those of the transferring company do by an excessively low exchange ratio.[10]

One may doubt whether the provision of Art. 24 para. 2 SE-Regulation permitting to protect shareholders "opposing" the merger does also cover the review of the exchange ratio, since this obviously is to benefit also shareholders who are in favour of the merger.[11] On the other hand, it should not make any difference whether a shareholder is opposing the merger as a whole or only some of the conditions linked to the merger – such as the exchange ratio. Usually a shareholder opposing the exchange ratio would have to oppose the merger which means he would have to challenge the merger resolution of the general meeting. Under German law, however, this very issue is solved by putting away the procedure for challenging the resolution – which would block the whole merger – and introducing a particular judicial review of the exchange ratio (*Spruchverfahren*) allowing to carry on with the merger and to litigate on the exchange ratio at the same time. This particular procedure of German (and Austrian) law has been acknowledged in Art. 25 para. 3 SE-Regulation for the very reason to render it applicable on the formation process of a European Company.

Interest on the cash compensation applies from the expiry of the day on which the merger is registered and announced in the state in which the SE has its registered office, according to the law applicable there (§ 6 para. 3 DiscD). The registration is, according to Art. 15, para. 2 together with Art. 13 SE-Regulation, to be published in the future state of the registered office of the SE according to the provisions made under the first directive. Furthermore, the registration is, according to Art. 14 para. 1 SE-Regulation, to be published in

[10] Such a provisions should be incorporated into the Transformation Act for national mergers, at the next opportunity. So far the German Transformation Act protects only shareholders in the transferring company, as has been criticised in the literature. For example, *Baums*, Gutachten F zum 63. Deutschen Juristentag, 2000, p. 120ff., and *Martens*, AG 2000, 301, 303ff.

[11] For this discussion see *Deutscher Anwaltverein*, NZG 2004, 76; *Ihrig/Wagner*, BB 2003, 969, 972; *Schindler*, ecolex 2003, issue 6, Script 26, 1, 5/6; *C. Teichmann*, ZGR 2003, 367, 384/385.

the Official Journal (OJ) of the EC. The DiscD does not attach legal consequences to this publication, as it is purely of declaratory character.[12]

An obligation of the commercial registers to mutually inform each other may possibly be derived from Art. 8 para. 11 SE-Regulation, because the interests are the same in cases of cross-border merger and transfer of registered office. For the protection of third parties, an analogy to Art. 8 para. 13 SE-Regulation could be considered. Because of doubt as to the competence of the national legislatures, the DiscD does not take a position on this issue. Further consideration at the European level will have to be given to the question of co-operation between the commercial registers.

(2) Offer of cash compensation (appraisal right)

Minority shareholders who wish to leave the company because of the merger, are protected by § 7 para. 1 DiscD. This provides that every merging company must make a reasonable cash offer to its shareholders for the purchase of their shares. This basic rule and details are derived from §§ 29ff. Transformation Act. As in the case of the review of the exchange ratio, the protection applies equally to the shareholders of a transferring as well as to those of an acquiring company.

The shareholders have two months within which to accept the cash offer. This period begins with the registration of the merger (§ 7 para. 4 sentence 1 DiscD). The SE is therefore ultimately liable for payment of the purchase price, because the merging company is extinguished by the registration. Payment in return for the shares constitutes a purchase of its own shares by the SE. The DiscD here, in § 7 para. 1 sentence 2, adopts German law provisions which permit a German company to acquire its own shares for this purpose.[13] The shareholders can have the amount of the cash payment reviewed by a court. The result is binding on the receiving company and its shareholders (Art. 25 para. 3 sentence 4 SE-Regulation).

The proposal to offer dissenting shareholders a right to withdraw from the company has given rise to criticism in the discussion following the publication of the DiscD. It has been pointed out that the comparable rule in German law

[12] Art. 14 para. 1 of the Regulation expressly states: "shall be published for information purposes". In addition, the SE-Regulation connects legal consequences always to the entry in the register of the state where the registered office of the SE is situated, and not on the notice in the OJ (cf. Art. 16 para. 1, Art. 27 para. 1, Art. 37 para. 9 of the Regulation).

[13] This comes from an option in Art. 20 para. 1 lit. d) of the second directive (77/91/EEC).

(§ 29 Transformation Act) only provides for a withdrawal of minority shareholders if the merger results in a change of legal form. However, the European Company – at least one having its seat in Germany – will not be much different from a German *Aktiengesellschaft* since the Regulation to a great extent refers to the national law of public limited-liability companies (see Art. 9 of the Regulation). A proposal more consistent with existing rules of German law may be to restrict withdrawal rights of the minority to such cases in which the future SE has its seat outside Germany.[14]

(3) Exclusion of the right to challenge the merger resolution

The special feature of §§ 6 and 7 DiscD is that shareholders, even in the case of an unreasonable exchange ratio or inadequate cash compensation, cannot challenge the merger resolution.[15] If there is a dispute on these issues, it will be dealt with in a separate court proceeding which will not prevent the registration of the merger and cannot have the result of reversing the merger. This allows for the legal certainty which is all the more necessary in the case of cross-border formations for the companies participating in the merger. The provisions in German law on this court proceeding were in the course of amendment at the time of drafting the DiscD.[16] The DiscD was awaiting the outcome of the amendment and therefore does not yet refer to the court proceedings.

(4) The Position of shareholders of a foreign company

The minority protection provided in the DiscD applies only to shareholders of companies which are subject to German law. The authority granted under Art. 24 para. 2 SE-Regulation applies only to such companies. However, in a merger by which an SE is formed, a public company from another member state (cf. Art. 2 para. 1 SE-Regulation) must be involved, and possibly that state may not have the same protective mechanism as that in German law. In that case, the procedure for reviewing the exchange ratio and the cash compensation applies only if the shareholders of merging companies situated in other Member States which do not provide for such procedure, explicitly accept the procedure (Art. 25 para. 3 sentence 1 SE-Regulation). The German legislature will

[14] See for this proposal *Kalss*, ZGR 2003, 593, 624 et seq., and *C. Teichmann*, AG 2004, 67 et seq. Also *DAV* (above note 11), NZG 2004, 75, 77, and *Kübler*, ZHR 167 (2003), 627 et seq.

[15] § 6 para. 1 and § 7 para. 5 DiscD.

[16] The law has been passed in the meantime: *Spruchverfahrensneuordnungsgesetz*, BGBl. I, 838; cf. the introduction by *Neye*, NZG 2002, 23, DStR 2002, 178, ZIP 2002, 2097 and FS Wiedemann, 2002, 1127ff.

provide that the shareholders of companies situated in other Member States are enabled to participate in the German proceedings through a special representative, and thereby have the opportunity of articulating their interests.[17]

b) *Holding SE*

The SE-Regulation also provides special minority protection in the case of the formation of a holding SE (Art. 34 SE-Regulation). German law in this case also proposes a review of the exchange ratio and the cash compensation offered, which corresponds largely to that provided for the merger (§§ 9 and 10 DiscD).

In the case of the formation of a holding, the protection mechanism of the merger may seem out of place at first sight. The special characteristic of a merger is that a minority shareholder is at the risk of losing his shares against his will, by having to exchange his shares for shares in the receiving company, while in the case of the formation of a holding, every shareholder is free to exchange his shares or not. Contrary to the case of a merger, the formation of a holding does not lead to the extinction of the original companies.[18]

Nevertheless, there are strong arguments in favour of providing a similar protection of minority shareholders in the case of the formation of a holding, as that provided in the case of a merger. The SE-Regulation prescribes a special procedure for the formation of a holding, which strongly resembles that for a merger. The Regulation does not stop at the mere exchange of shares, but requires also a preparatory resolution of the general meetings of all participating companies (Art. 32 para. 6 SE-Regulation). This resolution is to be preceded by preparation of draft terms and a formation report (Art. 32 para. 2–5 SE-Regulation). This constitutes, in many respects, a broad front for court challenges from minorities – especially in the central area of the determination

[17] Cf. *C. Teichmann*, ZGR 2002, 383, 429 and in Theisen/Wenz (ed.), Die Europäische Aktiengesellschaft, 2002, p. 573, 586f. It was also proposed that shareholders in the companies situtated in other Member States be granted the right to their own review of the exchange ratio and cash compensation (*C. Teichmann*, ZGR 2002, 383, 429; also *Neun*, in: Theisen/Wenz (ed.), Die Europäische Aktiengesellschaft, 2002, p. 51, 126f.). However, the authorisation in Art. 24 para. 2 of the Regulation does not extend that far, it authorises only provision for companies governed by German law.

[18] A similarity between Merger-SE and holding SE is therefore questioned in various ways precisely on this issue of the minority protection: *Casper*, FS Ulmer, 2003, 51, 61; *Neun* in: Theisen/Wenz (ed.), Die Europäische Aktiengesellschaft, 2002, 51, 141f. Leaving the question unresolved: *Oplustil*, German Law Journal, Volume 4 No. 2 (February 2003), http://www.germanlawjournal.com, in No. 16ff.; stressing the similarity of the procedures: *C. Teichmann*, ZGR 2003, 367, 389.

of the exchange ratio. Unlike in the case of a merger (Art. 25 para. 2 SE-Regulation), the Regulation does not provide for the issuance of a certificate conclusively attesting to the completion of the pre-formation acts and formalities. The holding SE may not, however, be registered until it is shown that the formalities referred to in Art. 32 have been completed (Art. 33 para. 5 of the Regulation). The authority registering the SE will therefore be attentive to possible claims by shareholders that the resolution of the general meeting suffers any legal defect.

Consequently, a challenge to the resolution of the general meeting could block the formation of the holding. For that reason, the DiscD excludes the challenge suit and provides, in compensation, a review of the exchange ratio and the cash compensation offer (§§ 9, 10 DiscD). The scope of this provision may, as already pointed out for the merger, be restricted to such holding SEs as have their seat outside Germany.[19]

3. Particulars of the formation procedure and court jurisdiction

In the case of the formation of an SE by merger, under Art. 21 SE-Regulation certain information on the participating companies, the future SE and the protection of creditors and minority shareholders has to be published. The Regulation does not specify the time and manner of this publication. § 5 DiscD is intended to provide clarification as to the procedure to be followed. The data under Art. 21 SE-Regulation are to be disclosed when the merger plan is filed to the register which is to publish same together with the publication of the merger required by § 61 para. 2 Transformation Act.[20]

According to Art. 7 sentence 1 SE-Regulation, the SE must have its registered office and its head office in the same member state. § 2 DiscD provides, in addition, that the registered office according to the statutes should normally be at the same location as a plant of the company, its management centre, or administration centre. This is based on Art. 7 sentence 2 SE-Regulation and conforms to the national law on public companies, which has a corresponding provision at § 5 para. 2 Stock Corporation Act (*Aktiengesetz*).[21]

[19] For further discussion of the appraisal right in case of the formation of a holding SE (and, in particular, the possible conflict with capital market rules on a public offer) see *C. Teichmann*, AG 2004, 67, 73.

[20] § 61 para. 2 Transformation Act applies by the reference in Art. 18 of the Regulation.

[21] Art. 7 s. 2 of the Regulation authorises explicitly only to impose on SEs the obligation of locating their registered office and their head office in the same place. This should also permit national legislatures to introduce a less onerous provision. (cf. *Brandt*, NZG 2002, 991, 994).

Art. 12 para. 1 SE-Regulation deals with the registration of the SE in the state in which it has its registered office, in a register "designated by the law of that member state". One may question whether such an express provision is at all necessary. For clarity, § 3 DiscD provides that the SE is to be entered in the commercial register in accordance with the relevant provisions on public companies.

The commercial register also has jurisdiction, according to § 4 DiscD, for other procedures provided for in the Regulation.[22] It is to issue the certificate attesting the completion of the acts and formalities to be accomplished before the transfer of registered office (Art. 8 para. 8 SE-Regulation), as well as the pre-merger acts in case of a merger (Art. 25 para. 2 SE-Regulation). The legality of a merger shall be scrutinised by the commercial register as regards the part of the procedure concerning the completion of the merger and the formation of the SE (Art. 26 para. 1 SE-Regulation).

The SE-Regulation is incomplete in this respect concerning the formation of a holding SE. No certificate attesting to the proper completion of the procedure in the companies which intend to form a holding SE is required, although the procedure required is similar to that for a merger. In particular, a resolution of these companies is required (Art. 32 para. 6 sentence 1 SE-Regulation). The danger of this resolution being challenged has been referred to above. A German commercial register may therefore be faced with the question as to how it should proceed if it ascertains that a shareholder has challenged the resolution on the formation of the holding SE. As the SE-Regulation does not require that provision be made for this situation, the DiscD, at this stage, makes no such provision. A provision could be considered requiring the filing of a certificate, with the application for registration, that no challenges are pending.[23] Such a provision could be supported on the basis of Art. 68 para. 1 SE-Regulation, as this clarification seems to be necessary, at least in the case of the formation of a holding SE under German procedural law.

According to Art. 15 SE-Regulation, German law is applicable to the further procedure in the formation of a holding SE. The question has been raised in the literature on this issue as to who is actually the "founder" in the meaning of this provision.[24] The parallel to the merger procedure suggests a clarifying provision based on § 36 para. 2 sentence 2 Transformation Act. The "founders"

[22] This follows the legislative requirements of Art. 68 para. 2 sentence 1 SE-Regulation.

[23] A comparable provision is contained in § 16 para. 2 Transformation Act for national mergers.

[24] *Neun* in: Theisen/Wenz (ed.), Die Aktiengesellschaft, 2002, p. 51, 148f.; *Oplustil*, German Law Journal, Volume 4 No. 2 (February 2003), www.germanlawjournal.com, in No. 24.

would then be the companies which intend to form a holding SE.[25] Any other solution would be very impractical, as possibly all the many shareholders of the participating companies would have to be seen as "founders". The Regulation does not provide an explicit authority for such a view, with the result that only recourse to Art. 68 para. 1 SE-Regulation remains. So far, the DiscD contains no provision on this issue.

The SE-Regulation requires that the national legislatures make suitable provisions for the case that an SE breaches Art. 7 SE-Regulation, according to which the registered office and head office of the company must be in the same member state.[26] As the location of the registered office must be stated in the statutes, German law provides the fall back on the procedure of "liquidation through official act", according to § 262 para. 1 No. 5 Stock Corporation Act (§ 49 DiscD). The winding-up procedure, as provided for in § 144a Act on Matters of Free Court Jurisdiction (*Gesetz über die Angelegenheiten der freiwilligen Gerichtsbarkeit*), fulfils the statutory requirements of Art. 64 SE-Regulation.[27] The company is required to remedy the defect in the statutes within a reasonable period. If the defect is not remedied, the court shall expressly declare the breach. This judgement is subject to appeal. When the judgement comes into legal effect, the company is deemed to be wound-up.

The DiscD does not take up the proposal made in the literature[28] that a special court be created for SE proceedings.[29] Certainly, legal questions which have not so far arisen in national corporate law, could arise in connection with SEs. But these SE specific questions will always concern the interpretation of European law, which can only be finally decided by the ECJ. The preliminary proceeding under Art. 234 EC Treaty should be adequate for this purpose.

III. Structure of the SE

The greatest degree of freedom is allowed by the Regulation in the area of the structure of the company. Firstly, the freedom of the SE itself to choose between the one-tier or two-tier system of administration. Secondly, the freedom of the national legislatures, which can, for the system its laws do not so far provide for, pass legislation specifically applicable to the SE.

[25] See on this issue also *C. Teichmann*, ZGR 2003, 367, 392.

[26] Cf. Art. 64 and Art. 68 para. 2 the Regulation.

[27] Cf. *Ch. Teichmann*, ZGR 2002, 383, 457 ff.

[28] *Brandt*, NZG 2002, 991, 995.

[29] Cf. *Neye/Ch. Teichmann*, AG 2003, 169, 174.

1. Two-tier system (management organ/supervisory organ)

An SE with a two-tier system has a management organ and a supervisory organ [Art. 38 b) SE-Regulation]. This corresponds to the German model of management board and supervisory board.[30] The authorisation in Art. 39 para. 5 SE-Regulation to create a two-tier system for the SE, applies only to those member states, whose corporate law does not so far know this system. Where the two-tier system already exists national law applies, in addition to the rudimentary provisions of Art. 39 ff. SE-Regulation. The SE with the two-tier system will, if it has its registered office in Germany, function in principle as a German public company with management board and supervisory board.[31]

The Regulation does, however, provide for a small number of possibilities of regulation for those states the law of which already knows the two-tier system. The DiscD avails of this opportunity by calling on provisions parallel to national corporate law on public companies. For example, § 13 DiscD adopts the provisions of § 105 para. 2 sentences 1 and 2, Stock Corporation Act on members of the supervisory board taking over management functions.[32] §§ 14, 15 DiscD follow §§ 76 para. 2 and 95 para. 1 Stock Corporation Act, in relation to the number of members of the management and supervisory organs.[33] The number of members of the management and supervisory organs depends, however, on the rules which are applicable to the employees' co-determination rights. Part D of this contribution is referred to in this respect. The provisions on information which may be demanded (§ 16 DiscD) and the specification of matters requiring approval of the supervisory organ (§ 17 DiscD), are based on § 90 para. 3 sentence 2 or § 111 para. 4 Stock Corporation Act.[34]

[30] Cf. the methodology of the German two-tier system, especially in: Hopt/Kanda/Roe/Wymeersch/Prigge (ed.), Comparative Corporate Governance – The State of the Art and Emerging Research, 1998, contributions of *Hopt* (p. 227), *Theisen* (p. 259) and *Semler* (p. 267).

[31] For theory and practice of the German two-tier system see in: Hopt/Kanda/Roe/Wymeersch/Prigge (editors), Comporative Corporate Governance – The State of the Art and Emerging Research –, 1998, the contributions by *Hopt* (p. 227), *Theisen* (p. 259) and *Semler* (p. 267).

[32] Basis: Art. 39 para. 3 sentence 4 the Regulation.

[33] Basis: Art. 39 para. 4 sentence 2 and Art. 40 para. 3 sentence 2 of the Regulation.

[34] Basis: Art. 41 para. 3 sentence 2 or. Art. 48 para. 1 sentence 2 of the Regulation.

2. One-tier system (administrative organ)

The German legislature can introduce the one-tier system with only one administrative organ, on the basis of Art. 43 para. 4 SE-Regulation.[35] The intention of the European legislature is that the SE is an option not only for major companies but also for small and medium sized companies. In addition, it is an option for groups operating throughout Europe to organise their subsidiaries throughout Europe in the legal form of an SE.[36] The German DiscD is intended to open these opportunities to SEs by flexibly structuring the one-tier system on the basis of the law on private limited liability companies. Smaller and medium sized companies are often neither subject to co-determination nor quoted on a stock exchange, likewise often the case with subsidiaries. The DiscD, therefore, provides a basic model which ignores the influence of co-determination and stock exchange quotation. On co-determination, provisions will be made when the Directive is being implemented, and for companies quoted on a stock exchange, the question of how far an amendment of the German Corporate Governance Code[37] can render statutory provisions superfluous needs to be discussed.

a) Management of the company by the administrative organ

"The administrative organ shall manage the company, specify the guidelines for its activity, and supervise their implementation". This formula in § 21 para. 1 sentence 1 DiscD, is based on French law and illustrates the characteristic of the one-tier system, namely, that the highest management of the company resides in one organ.[38] This applies notwithstanding delegation of management

[35] Alone by means of the statutes of the SE would probably not be possible [cf. Art. 9 para. 1b) of the Regulation]: The SE is subject to the provisions of its statutes "where expressly authorised by this Regulation". According to Art. 38 b) of the Regulation, the statutes decide only the form of the management system (one-tier or two-tier), not, however, its broader organisation. This is deducible as the corollary out of the strict limits authorised for the statutes in the following Article.

[36] The considerations as to the uses of the SE which were taken into account in the drafting of the Regulation is clear from *Blanquet*, ZGR 2002, 20, 34ff. As to the application of the SE-Regulation to small and medium sized companies, op. cit., p. 52.

[37] Details thereof under www.corporate-governance-code.de.

[38] Cf. Art. L. 225-35 Code de commerce: "Le conseil d'administration détermine les orientations de l'activité de la société et veille à leur mise en œuvre." Likewise Art. 716a Swiss Law of Obligations: "The administrative council has the following non-transferable and indispensable tasks: (1) the highest management of the company and the issuing of the necessary instructions ...".

functions to third persons or within the organ. The final responsibility for the management of the company rests with the administrative organ. This is a significant difference to the two-tier system in which the management responsibilities are spread over two organs.

The highest management by the administrative organ permits concentration of strategic decisions and the delegation only of the task of implementing such decisions. This is particularly appropriate for the management structure of small and medium sized companies and subsidiaries in a group. This principle also affects the legal position of the managing directors, which will be discussed below. The DiscD deliberately avoids granting the managing director a status comparable to that of the German management board (*Vorstand*). Only by making this clear distinction between the two management systems, can the one-tier model become an alternative. The structure of the Regulation prohibits too close a similarity between the two systems, which expresses clearly in Art. 38b, that the SE should be able to choose between the two systems.

§§ 18ff. DiscD provides fairly comprehensive provisions on the administrative organ. This is because the provisions applicable to the supervisory board of a German public company have been largely adopted – with changes where necessary. For example, the appointment, removal and composition of the administrative organ, the personal qualifications of its members and contracts with members of the administrative organ (§§ 20, 22, 23 and 30ff. DiscD). Likewise, the provisions on the internal procedures, the calling of meetings and the passing of resolutions by the administrative board, are based on the corresponding provisions of the Stock Corporation Act (*Aktiengesetz*), relating to the supervisory board (§§ 38ff. DiscD). One can regard this as over-regulation in comparison to other jurisdictions where significantly less legal text is required.[39] However, in view of the thorough regulation of the management in the two-tier system, it seems appropriate to add regulation of the issues which are provided for in the Stock Corporation Act also to the one-tier model. Otherwise, in order to close gaps in the DiscD, the question would always arise whether the provisions of the Stock Corporation Act apply by analogy. This would cause unnecessary legal uncertainty, and raise unwanted questions of principle, as to whether and to what extent provisions of the two-tier model can be employed to close gaps in the one-tier model.

[39] For example, the Swiss Law of Obligations, Art. 707ff.; The French Code de commerce, on the other hand, in Art. L. 225-17ff. also regulates extensively similar to the German law. See the criticism of *Merkt*, ZGR 2003, 650, 654.

b) *Adjustment of the one-tier system to German public company law*

Because of the many references in the SE-Regulation to German public company law, the one-tier system must also be compatible with the general law on public companies, which is characterised by the principle that in every public company there are two separate organs. In many cases, the law assumes that the management board and supervisory board work together, in certain respects. General German law on public companies is applicable to an SE with its registered office in Germany; this follows directly from the application of the SE-Regulation and is not subject to any revision by the national legislature. Therefore, the act implementing the European Company in Germany cannot remain silent on the question of who takes over these competences and obligations in the one-tier system.[40]

(1) *Imposition of the tasks of the management board and supervisory board on the administrative board*

In so far as the tasks of the supervisory board are concerned, it is natural that they be assigned to the administrative organ in the one-tier model. This is expressly provided for in § 21 para. 5 sentence 1 DiscD. The management board presents greater difficulty. It not only directs the day-to-day business, but is also, in a public company, the organ which in many respects, is responsible for the strategic direction of the company.[41] This is clear from its many obligations to report to the general meeting, for example, on capital increases and inter-company agreements[42] or – very generally – the obligation to provide information in accordance with § 131 Stock Corporation Act. Such basic management functions must, in the one-tier system, be assigned to the administrative organ, as the organ primarily responsible for the highest management of the company. § 21 para. 5 sentence 1 DiscD therefore assigns to the administrative organ, not only the legal responsibilities of the supervisory board, but also, in principle, those of the management board. Furthermore, the DiscD explicitly mentions some other tasks which the management board performs in the two-tier system. These include the preparation and implementation of resolutions of the general meeting, at the request of the general meeting (§ 21 para. 1 sentence 2 DiscD), and the calling of the general meeting in the event of the loss of half of the

[40] This is discussed in more detail by *C. Teichmann*, BB 2004, 53 et seq.

[41] The management tasks of the management board have recently been extracted by *Fleischer*, ZIP 2003, 1 ff.

[42] Report on the exclusion of the right to preferential shares (§ 186 para. 4 sentence 2 Stock Corporation Act), Report on inter-company agreements (§ 293 a Stock Corporation Act). On other statutory management tasks, *Fleischer*, ZIP 2003, 1, 6.

nominal capital (§ 21 para. 4 DiscD).[43] This represents the obligation of the administrative organ, as the highest management organ, to the shareholders of the company.[44]

(2) Separation of functions by the introduction of a managing director

In addition, there are tasks of the management board, which are assigned to the on-going management and in a one-tier system need not be carried out by the administrative organ itself. For example, commercial register applications, or the sending of information to shareholders in preparation for the general meeting. If the act implementing the SE does not provide for these matters, the administrative organ will be responsible for all such tasks, meaning that, for example, for every commercial register application, the notarised signatures of members of the administrative organ in the number required to validly represent the company, required by § 12 para. 1 Commercial Code, would have to be obtained. In a company subject to co-determination or quoted on a stock exchange, this would hardly be desirable. The appointment of a managing director to whom such management tasks can be delegated, is indicated.

The provisions of the general law on public companies which require that the management board and supervisory board work together, and thereby provide a certain "looking over the shoulder", are even stronger arguments for the appointment of a managing director. The most important examples are the preparation of the annual accounts by the management board and their approval by the supervisory board (§§ 170ff. Stock Corporation Act), and the distribution of tasks between both organs in Corporate Group law (in particular §§ 311ff. Stock Corporation Act, preparation of the dependency report by the management board and review of the report by the supervisory board). Many of these provisions are elements of internal corporate governance, another example being § 111 para. 2, third sentence whereby the supervisory board is mandating the auditor and not the possibly biassed management organ. If these tasks were assigned, as a whole, in the one-tier system to the administrative organ, the graduation intended in the law on public companies, and which is the expression of quite a useful control mechanism, would be defeated.[45] The examples of the annual accounts and the dependency report are good illustrations of that. These are documents of the highest importance, for which the organ competent for the highest management should be responsible. Their pre-

[43] Stock Corporation Act § 83 or § 92.

[44] The managing director (shortly in the text) must inform the administrative organ if he becomes aware of the loss of half of the nominal capital (§ 24 para. 3 DiscD).

[45] *C. Teichmann*, BB 2004, 53, 57 et seq.

paration, on the other hand, requires proximity to day-to-day business, which, in the two-tier system, only the management board has, and which cannot automatically be attributed to the administrative organ in the one-tier system. Ultimately, the separation of the preparation of the document and its final review, provide an element of self-control, which should not be surrendered unnecessarily. The legislative basic model for the one-tier system, therefore, provides for this separation of functions.

§ 24 para. 1 DiscD for these reasons mandatorily prescribes the appointment of at least one managing director. According to § 44 DiscD, he is to be responsible for the preparation of the annual accounts, and, according to § 46 DiscD, he is the party addressed by those regulations, which in the two-tier system are addressed to the management board.[46] He also undertakes notifications to the Commercial Register, in so far as such tasks are, in the Stock Corporation Act, assigned to the management board (§ 24 para. 1 sentence 7 DiscD, and § 42 DiscD). In the discussion on the implementing legislation, it will have to be clarified, whether the managing director will be assigned other competences of the management board, for example, the notification in preparation for the general meeting.[47]

Authority for this provision seems, on first sight to be dubious. While, under the SE-Regulation, the national legislature can assign the on-going business matters to the managing director (Art. 39 para. 1 sentence 2 or Art. 43 para. 1 sentence 2 SE-Regulation), this applies only "under the same conditions as for public limited-liability companies that have registered offices within that Member State's territory". As the German law on public companies does not provide for a managing director, these authorising provisions are not intended for it.[48] The corollary that this structure is intended only for those states which already have it, cannot, however, be drawn from this.[49] A member state such as Ger-

[46] *Maul* in: Theisen/Wenz (ed.), Die Europäische Aktiengesellschaft, 2002, p. 399, 427ff. has recently convincingly shown that the distribution of functions within a group should be catered for already in the statutory basic model and not only when a company becomes part of a group.

[47] According to § 125 Stock Corporation Act. On the contrary, the calling of the general meeting should, because of the importance of this event for the relationship between the management and the shareholders, be assigned to the administrative organ (the basic provision of § 21 para. 5 sentence 1 DiscD suffices for this).

[48] Cf. *Ch. Teichmann*, ZIP 2002, 1109, 1113f., whereas *Henssler*, FS Ulmer, p. 193, 208, apparantly pleads for applying these provisions (also *Kallmeyer*, ZIP 2003, 1531). Background to these provisions is the speciality of the Scandinavian law which is close to the one-tier system but employs one single organ for day-to-day business.

[49] *Hirte*, NZG 2002, 1, 8 tends in this direction; see also recently *DAV* (above note 11), NZG 2004, 75, 81 et seq. with fundamental criticism against the one-tier model of the DiscD.

many, the laws of which do not provide for the one-tier system, can rely in general on the authorisation in § 43 para. 4 SE-Regulation. The additional authorisation in Art. 43 para. 1 sentence 2 SE-Regulation is intended only to provide those states, the laws of which already regulate the one-tier system, and which therefore are not provided with SE specific provisions according to § 43 para. 4 SE-Regulation, with authorisation to regulate this one concrete point, as an exception.[50]

c) Position of the managing director

The introduction of the managing director is not a return to the two-tier system, as he has a clearly different position to that of a management board in a two-tier system. The management board directs the business "in its own responsibility",[51] and is not subject to any instructions, and can be removed prior to the end of its period of office, only for good cause.[52] The management board enjoys, therefore, considerable legal independence. On the contrary, the managing directors are subject, personally and materially, to the administrative organ. They will be appointed by it and can by removed by it at any time (§ 24 para. 1 and para. 5 DiscD). Externally, they have unrestricted representative authority for the company (§ 28 para. 1 DiscD). Internally, they are, however, obliged to comply with instructions and restrictions decided by the administrative organ (Art. 24 para. 2 DiscD). Their position is, therefore, comparable to that of a managing director of a GmbH (private limited liability company).[53] This corresponds to the above mentioned purpose, of providing the SE with possible uses for which the GmbH is typically applicable in national law. Reliance on the GmbH law is also intended to facilitate application of practice and court judgements to the initially novel management system.

[50] One may argue that such an authority was not necessary, in view of the reference of Art. 9 para. 1c) ii) of the Regulation to national law. It was, however, a wish of the Swedish negotiating delegation that this be clarified, because it seemed to be unclear what system the Scandinavian law should be attributed to, and what consequences this could have for the law applicable subsidiarily. This is also the reason why the same authorising provisions are found in the section on the two-tier model (Art. 39 para. 1 p. 2 of the Regulation) as well as in the section on the one-tier model (Art. 43 para. 1 p. 2 of the Regulation).

[51] § 76 para. 1 Stock Corporation Act, similarly formulated in Art. 39 para. 1 sentence 1of the Regulation.

[52] § 84 para. 3 Stock Corporation Act.

[53] § 28 para. 2 DiscD is derived from § 37 para. 1 Act on Limited Liability Companies (GmbHG).

The one-tier model of the DiscD also offers an SE significantly more freedom of choice than the two-tier model of the Stock Corporation Act.[54] The number of managing directors is left open, managing directors can also be members of the administrative organ. The only restriction is that the number of **non-executive** directors on the administrative organ must be greater than that of **executive** directors (§ 24 para. 1 sentence 2 DiscD).[55] Each company is therefore free to decide whether and to what extent it finds personnel overlap beneficial, for example, because of improved flow of information, which is, in any event, ascribed to the one-tier model. A tighter management structure, which is of special interest to smaller companies and groups with subsidiaries, is therefore possible. As the administrative organ may, at least in companies with a capital of not more than three million Euro, consist of less than three persons, the one-tier system provides a very slim management structure for smaller companies, ultimately reducible to an administrative organ of one, and one managing director.[56]

With the introduction of the managing director, the basis is laid for separation of function in companies with co-determination and listed companies. For listed companies, the freedom granted by the DiscD will have to be restricted.[57] The DiscD leaves open the question of whether this will be effected in the German Corporate Governance Code, or by special legislation for listed companies. In companies subject to co-determination, the composition of the administrative organ depends on whether an agreement is made or the default provision applies.[58]

[54] For a detailed analysis of the flexibility of the one-tier system *C. Teichmann*, BB 2004, 53 et seq. with further references to the ongoing debate on the appropriate structure of the one-tier system in Germany.

[55] For the determination that certain members of the organ should exclusively have supervisory functions, cf. also *Theisen/Hölzl* in: Theisen/Wenz (ed.), Die Europäische Aktiengesellschaft, 2002, 247, 279. A mandatory right of approval, as in § 111 para. 4 sentence 2 Stock Corporation Act, as proposed by *Theisen/Hölzl*, seems unnecessary, as the administrative organ as the highest management organ, by virtue or its authority to instruct, can reserve to itself any decision which it considers important. In addition, Art. 48 para. 1 sentence 1 of the Regulation must be so understood that the statutes must provide some regulation of this question.

[56] If the administrative organ consists of only one person, this person cannot at the same time be the managing director, as otherwise a breach of § 24 para. 2 sentence 1 DiscD would occur, according to which the majority of the members of the administrative organ cannot be managing directors.

[57] Concrete proposals in: *Theisen/Hölzl*, in: Theisen/Wenz (ed.), Die Europäische Aktiengesellschaft, 2002, p. 247, 277ff.

[58] On co-determination cf. D.

3. General meeting

The SE-Regulation provides the national legislatures with only limited freedom in regard to the procedure and organisation of general meetings. In addition, according to § 53 SE-Regulation, the general corporate law of the state in which the SE has its registered office, applies. The Regulation provides for the right of minorities holding at least 10% of the shares, to demand the calling of a general meeting and the making of additions to its agenda (Art. 55 para. 1 and Art. 56 SE-Regulation). The national legislatures are authorised to fix a lesser quota. § 47 DiscD reduces the quota to 5%. This corresponds to the provision of § 122 of the German Stock Corporation Act.

IV. Transfer of registered office

1. Protection of minority shareholders

Protection of minorities is especially necessary when a company transfers its registered office, because, in doing so, it becomes subject to another legal jurisdiction. The referral provisions of the SE-Regulation mean that, on many issues, the law of the state where the registered office is situated applies to the SE. § 11 DiscD therefore provides minority shareholders who do not want to participate in the transfer of registered office, with a right of withdrawal in return for reasonable cash compensation.[59] This provision is based on the same principle and actual implementation procedure as that relating to a merger.[60] A challenge based on the inadequacy of the cash compensation is also excluded in this case (§ 11 para. 2 together with § 7 para. 2 DiscD).

2. Protection of creditors

The creditors, like the minority shareholders, also require protection when a transfer of registered office of a SE takes place.[61] § 12 DiscD provides for the right to demand security, restricted, however, to creditors which can credibly establish that the satisfaction of their claims is endangered by the transfer.[62]

[59] This is based on Art. 8 para. 5 of the Regulation.

[60] Cf. above

[61] Art. 8 para. 7 of the Regulation therefore provides that the certificate on the proper conduct of the transfer of registered office is issued only after the company has provided evidence that the interests of the creditors are adequately protected in accordance with the requirements of the state in which the registered office has hitherto been situated.

[62] Cf. the preliminary considerations on this provision; *Ch. Teichmann* in: Theisen/Wenz

This is an attempt to strike a balance between the interest of the company in a rapid completion of the transfer of its registered office and those of the creditors in the security of their claims. The requirement that satisfaction of the claims should be endangered is intended to illustrate that a transfer of registered office as such, does not represent a sufficient risk in itself. It would be a contradiction of the basic principle of a European-wide legal form if the transfer of registered office within the internal market were to be seen as endangering the rights of contractual partners. In addition, Art. 8 para. 16 SE-Regulation maintains the former jurisdiction for "old creditors". Certainly, the transfer of registered office may, in some cases, be intended to render it more difficult for creditors to recover their debts. The affected creditors must, however, according to § 12 para. 2 DiscD, be in a position to establish that their fears are well founded. This could be, for example, in a case where the transfer of registered office is connected with the transfer abroad of significant assets.[63]

Art. 8 para. 7 sentence 2 SE-Regulation permits member states to extend minority protection provisions to such debts as have arisen prior to the transfer of registered office. § 12 para. 2 DiscD avails of this in modified form. Debts which have arisen prior to or by fifteen days after the publication of the planned transfer, are included. The period of 15 days is derived from § 15 para. 2 Commercial Code, in accordance with the fundamental principle that a fact, which has been duly published, is deemed to be known after the expiry of fifteen days, even if not actually known.[64] Extension of the period until the actual transfer itself, seems less sensible as this would put the company at the risk that new creditors would constantly emerge, demanding security and thereby delaying further the transfer of registered office.

3. Merger combined with transfer of registered office

The interest of the creditors in protection in the case of transfer of registered office also applies to the formation, by merger, of an SE which will have its registered office abroad. The German company would thereby be extinguished, and liability for the debts pass to the SE (Art. 29 SE-Regulation). The Regulation refers in Art. 24 to creditor protection in rather a guarded form. The law of the member state applies to protection of the interests of creditors "taking into

(ed.), Die Europäische Aktiengesellschaft, 2002, p. 573, 595ff. and., ZGR 2002, 383, 460ff.

[63] On the risks to creditors, also *Wenz* in: Theisen/Wenz (ed.), Die Europäische Aktiengesellschaft, 2002, p. 171, 213f.

[64] § 15 Commercial Code in turn based on Art. 3 para. 5 sentence 2 of the first directive (68/151/EWG).

account the cross-border nature of the merger". The protection of creditors contained in the German Transformation Act should therefore be adjusted to the cross-border character of the merger. However, German law applies only deferred creditor protection to mergers. Under § 22 Transformation Act, creditors can, within six months after the registration of the merger, notify their claims in writing and possibly demand security. This would not be adequate in the case of a cross-border merger, if, precisely because of the cross-border character, satisfaction of the debts was endangered. The distribution of interests is then similar to that in the case of the transfer of registered office. Whether a court can cater for this by extension of § 22 Transformation Act alone, seems questionable. Even though the SE-Regulation does not explicitly require that legislation be introduced on this point, the member states will ultimately have the decision, because of the reference to national law, as to how it will deal with the cross-border element. § 8 DiscD therefore refers to the provisions on transfer of registered office.

V. Involvement of employees

1. Legislative requirements

On the formation of an SE, the management organs of the participating companies must negotiate on the involvement of the employees in the future SE (Art. 4 SE-Regulation). A special body is to be formed by the employees for this purpose, composed proportionately by employees from the participating companies. The management organs of the companies and the employees' negotiating body can then make an agreement on the involvement of the employees in the SE. If they do not succeed in doing so, a default provision applies (Art. 7 SE-Regulation). This prescribes that a body representative of the employees be established, which is entitled to information and hearing rights. If co-determination already applies in one of the participating companies, it continues to apply to the SE.

Provision on this issue by the national legislatures will range from the procedure for the installation of the special body to the concrete implementation of the default provision. No proposal has so far been made by the Federal Economic and Labour Ministry. It is to be assumed, however, that the default solution applicable if negotiations fail, will correspond to the existing German provisions on co-determination, i.e. in public companies with 500 or more employees, one third of the supervisory board members are employee representatives.[65]

[65] Provided in § 76 Shop Constitution Act 1952 (BetrVG 1952).

In companies with over 2000 employees, one half of the members of the supervisory board are employee representatives.[66] However, the chairman of the supervisory board then has a casting vote in the event of a tie (§ 29 para. 2 sentence 1 Co-Determination Act). As the chairman is usually a representative of the shareholders,[67] there is a slight imbalance in favour of the shareholders, even in supervisory boards which are equally constituted.

It will be the task of the legislatures to integrate co-determination into the one-tier model. So far, co-determination has been tailored to the two-tier system, as employee representatives sit on the supervisory board, not on the management board. In order to adequately transfer this to the one-tier system, presumably a distinction will have to be made between executive and non-executive members of the administrative organ.[68] Employee representatives will then presumably occupy the positions of non-executive members, which would correspond to their supervisory capacity in their position as members of the supervisory boards in the two-tier system. The number of seats in the one-tier system should be derived from the one employees usually occupy in the two-tier system. An adaption to the one-tier system would mean that employees will be granted the same number of the non-executive members of the administrative board as they would be granted within a supervisory board under the two-tier system. One can imagine that this very issue is highly sensitive in the political debate and will be difficult to solve within the legislation impelenting the directive.[69]

2. Risks and opportunities provided by the negotiations

Although German business sees co-determination as a hindrance in European competition, the SE-Directive also provides opportunities. If a negotiated solution is arrived at, the statutory provisions will not apply. This can be used by

66 Provided in the Act on Employees' Co-determination (MitbG). For further analysis of German co-determination see in Hopt/Kanda/Roe/Wymeersch/Prigge (editors), Comparative Corporate Governance – The State of the Art and Emerging Research, 1998, the contributions of *Geruml Wagner* (p. 341) and *Roe* (p. 361).

67 This is in the discretionary procedure of § 27 MitbG: The chairman must be elected with a majority of 2/3rds; if this does not happen, only the shareholders' representatives vote in the second round, and the employees' representatives elect the deputy chairman.

68 Cf. for example, *Henssler*, FS Ulmer, p. 193ff.; *Ch. Teichmann*, ZGR 2002, 383, 444ff.

69 The standard rules of the SE-Directive may be interpreted either way (see *C. Teichmann*, BB 2004, 53, 56): The more formal interpretation would lead to the conclusion that employees will be granted the same proportion of seats in the one-tier organ than they would have in a supervisory board; a more systematic interpretation would lead to compare the number of non-executives in both systems.

the negotiating partners to develop a co-determination model tailored to the needs of the company, taking the interests of both sides more fairly into account than is possible under the straightjacket of the statutory provisions. For example, the expensive procedure for the election of employee representatives is an unwelcome cost factor, from the point of view of the companies. A more flexible approach could result in cost savings.[70] Also in regard to the size of German supervisory boards, often the source of complaint, the negotiated solution could offer improvement. The employees will also appreciate that some basic decisions will be listed which will require the consent of the administrative organ. In this way, employees would be more closely involved in decision making.

From the point of view of the employees, the possibility of negotiation also contains the risk that co-determination may be circumvented. Reduction of co-determination rights may also be a goal of the negotiations. If German employees are in a minority in the special negotiation body, they could be outvoted by employees from other states. However, a resolution to reduce co-determination rights requires a specially qualified majority.[71]

The concern of German employees is also directed to the cases in which an SE with a lesser number of employees is formed. In that case, co-determination at a lower level could be negotiated, and the number of employees later increased, without co-determination having to be adjusted in accordance with the new numbers – e.g. exceeding 500 or 2000 employees. It is to be expected, however, that the German legislature will provide for such eventualities. According to recital 18 to the SE-Directive, the principle that the rights of employees should be protected applies, not only to the formation of an SE, but also to all structural amendments of an already formed SE. Together with Art. 11 SE-Directive, the legislature may well be authorised to make provision for such situations,[72] for example, a duty to renegotiate in such a case, could be considered.[73]

[70] Cf. also *Köstler* in: Theisen/Wenz (ed.), Die Europäische Aktiengesellschaft, p. 323f.

[71] Art. 3 para. 4 SE-Directive.

[72] Art. 11 SE-Directive states: "Member States shall take appropriate measures in conformity with Community law with a view to preventing the misuse of an SE for the purpose of depriving employees of rights to employee involvement or withholding such rights".

[73] This is demanded by *Köstler* in: Theisen/Wenz (ed.), Die Europäische Aktiengesellschaft, p. 327.

Greece

Evanghelos Perakis

Literature on SE published in Greece: *Anastassopoulou* Proposal of an EC Regulation on the Statute of the European Société Anonyme, Deltio Syndesmou AE & EPE, 1989, issue 1642, 360; *Arachovitis* On the Right of Establishment of Companies inside the EEC and the Creation of a European Commercial Company, Nomikon Deltion Trapezis tis Ellados 1965–66, 63; *Douvlis* in Commentary of the Law of the SA (Perakis, ed.), vol. 1, 2002, p. 149, Iordanidis The indirect introduction of new forms of governance through the recent Regulation on the Statute of the SE: The two-tier system, Episkopisi Emporikou Dikaiou, 2002, 972; *Kravaritou-Manitaki* The Representation of Employees in the Undertakings according to Community Law, Armenopoulos 1982, 611; *Konstas* The Participation of Employees in the Management of the Company according to Community Law, 1980, 95; *Leontakianakos* The Corporate Law of the European Community, Nomiko Vima 1985, 1349, 1365; *Mouzoulas* European Company and the Adjustment of the Law of Corporations in the European Community, Archio Nomologias, 417; *eiusdem* The Directive Proposal of the EC Council for the Status of Employees in the European Company, Deltion Ergatikis Nomothessias 1991, 65; *eiusdem* The Control of the Management of the Société Anonyme. The Paradigm of the European Company and the Perspectives of Evolution of the Greek Legislation, Acts of the 3rd Hellenic Congress of Commercial Law, 119, 165; *Païda* The Law of Sociétés Anonymes Ia, 103; *Panagopoulos* The European Company Limited by Shares and the European Public Company, Efimeris Ellinon Nomikon 1967, 722; *Papadimopoulos* Approximation and Integration of Corporate Law in the European Community, Elliniki Epitheorissi Europaïkou Dikaiou 1995, 865, 885; *Perakis* The Regulation 2157/2001 on the SE: A dubious solution to an old problem, Dikaio Epihiriseon & Etairion, May 2003; *Samara-Douvlis* The Harmonization of Greek Corporate Law with Community Law, 1983, 21; *Sarikas* The Integrated Type of the European Société Anonyme – Societas Europaea, Dioikitiki Dikaiosyni 1971, 41; *Stoïkos* The Control of the Management of the Société Anonyme. The Paradigm of the European Company and the Perspectives of Evolution of the Greek Legislation, Acts of the 3rd Hellenic Congress of Commercial Law, 159; *Tritaris* The Elaboration of the European Société Anonyme in the framework of the EEC, Archio Nomologias 1972, 346; *Varvitsiotis* The European Economic Community and the Corporate Law, Nomiko Vima 1968, 932; *Vassileiou* A Regulatory Attempt of Groups of Companies in the framework of EEC, Nomikon Deltion Trapezis tis Ellados 1972–74, 45, 46.

I. Introduction

The Greek company form, which is the equivalent of the SE, is the "anonymi etaireia" (ανώνυμη εταιρία = société anonyme) (hereinafter "SA"). A Greek SA is mainly governed by Law 2190/1920, as amended and as now in force. However, some legislative material on SAs can be found outside of Law 2190/1920: in the Commercial Code (of French origin) there are still some provisions on the SAs, and there are quite a few other laws (such as the recent law 3016/2002 on corporate governance) containing company law rules. Capital market legislation also contains company law relating to the functioning of the SA or the transfer of its shares.

Greece follows the continental tradition of company law (SAs are commercial companies), uses the "classic" methods of protecting and preserving capital, as laid down by the EC directives, follows the one-tier system and has fully complied – save for possible interpretative details – with the EC Company Law Directives.

Greece is expected to amend its legislation in the near future in order to render the formation and the functioning of the SE fully possible. However, since there has not been any work or draft of a work presented so far regarding this matter, the purpose of the present note is to point out some elements of Greek law to the extent that it is pertinent to the SE, without, however, making too many guesses as to the choices that Greece will eventually make within the options provided by Regulation 2157/2001 (the "Regulation") and Directive 2001/86/EC. At the moment, it is also unknown if the legislator will proceed to a special regulation concerning the SE alone or if this will be an opportunity for making a more general amendment of the general law of the SAs. The author considers the latter to be highly unlikely.

A delicate matter will also be the extent to which the statutes of a future "Greek" SE will be allowed to complement the Regulation. Although in matters regulated by the Regulation itself this will be only possible to the extent it is expressly authorized by the latter (cf. article 9 para. 1b[1]), some more flexibility may be allowed to the extent that national (Greek) law is applied (cf. article 9 para. 1c, iii).

II. Formation of a European Company

According to article 15, the formation of an SE is to be governed by the law applicable to public limited liability companies of the member state in which the SE establishes its registered office. The Greek legislation on SAs provides for the drawing up of a notarial deed containing the instrument of incorporation and the statutes (or "articles of association") of the company, an examination by an administrative authority of the legality of the formation require-

[1] In the following reference to articles is made to the articles of the Regulation.

ments, the registration of the new company in the registry of SAs (which is the determining moment for the acquisition of its legal personality), and the publication of an announcement about such registration in the Government Gazette. Some delays are usually caused during the phase of the administrative examination, although companies with an initial capital not exceeding 300,000 euros (therefore all SEs starting with the minimum capital under article 4 of the Regulation) have to be registered on the same day. This formation procedure will have to be followed also by "Greek" SEs. In the absence of a "universal" commercial register in Greece, the Greek legislator will have to decide whether the registry of the SEs will be the same as that of the SAs (this should be expected), or a separate register will be instituted (cf. article 12 para. 1).

An SE will be formed as provided in article 2, by companies qualifying under that article. Para. 5 of this article 2 will not be applicable in Greece, where the system of the "real seat" ("siège reel") is followed.

1. Formation by merger

In most of the matters concerning the formation by merger, the law of the member state governing each merging company shall apply "taking into account the cross-border nature of the merger", with regard to the protection of creditors, bondholders and holders of securities other than shares (article 24 para. 1). Greece has complied with the 3rd EC directive on mergers. However, there is some special legislation concerning mergers (mainly law 2166/1993), which provides for fiscal incentives and exemptions. This legislation has been criticized for deviating to some extent from the above directive, but, in principle, it should be also applicable to SEs (article 10).

The Greek legislator will have to decide if the publication provided for in article 21 will contain particulars additional to those listed in that article (rather unlikely). Regarding the protection of minorities opposing the merger (article 24 para. 2), a right of exit is likely to be granted, or a right to review the share-exchange ratio. In general Greece follows the system of nullity of the merger in the event of an unfair ratio rather than that of a separate compensation procedure (cf. also article 25 para. 3).

It is not known whether Greece will opt for the possibility of a public authority blocking the participation of the national company upon grounds of public interest (as per article 19).

2. Formation of a holding SE

This is a formation procedure unknown to (although not impossible under) Greek law. For the protection of minority shareholders opposing the operation, and for the protection of creditors and employees (article 34), rights of exit, review of the exchange ratio, compensation or granting of securities (depending on the persons to be protected) will be possible measures.

3. Formation of a Subsidiary SE

There are no special legislative measures for this operation, which is the simplest of all.

4. Conversion of an existing SA into an SE

The only legislative measure to be taken here concerns the possible need of a qualified majority or unanimity in the organ of the company within which employee participation is organized. But this is not applicable in Greece where co-determination models for SAs are not provided.

III. Management system of the European Company – the organs of the SE

1. The organ managing the company

Greek law adopts the board system. An SA is managed by a board of directors consisting of at least three members, who may or may not be shareholders or shareholders' representatiaves. It is appointed and removed *ad nutum* by the general meeting. If so empowered by the statutes, the board can entrust certain of its functions to a managing director or to other managers of the company.

Following the Regulation, Greek law will need to be amended, in order to make the two-tier system available for SEs also. True, article 39 refers to a *possibility* of member states introducing this system, if not provided in their laws ("... a member state *may* adopt ..."), but the preamble to the Regulation (no. 14) is very clear in this respect ("... an SE *should* be allowed to choose between the two systems ..."). It is not expected, however, that the legislature will also provide Greek SAs with the option of using the two-tier model, an option that already exists in France. Article 43 para. 4 is not applicable to Greece.

Regarding the two-tier system it has to be noted that the options of article 39 paras. 1 and 2 are not applicable in Greece, since this system is unknown there.

On the other hand, one cannot be sure what attitude the Greek legislature will eventually adopt in regard to the options of articles 39 paras. 3 and 4, 40 para. 3 and 41 para. 3.

Regarding the one-tier system, it is expected that Greek law will provide for the possibility of the appointment of one or more managing directors for the current management of the company's affairs, as is the case with Greek SAs (see article 43 para. 1). It is also expected that the minimum number of members of the board of directors will be fixed at three, as in Greek SAs (article 43 para. 2).

On the references to national law by articles 47–51, the following should be noted: Greek law does not prohibit legal entities being members of the administrative organ of a Greek SA (although in practice this is not frequent), and therefore the same will apply to SEs (article 47 para. 1). Similarly, it does not provide for disqualification of certain persons from being appointed members of the management organ (cf. article 47 para. 2). However, it is generally admitted that the statutes of a Greek SA may provide for certain eligibility conditions for members of the management organ (cf. article 47 para. 3). It should also be noted that one or more shareholders may be allowed by the statutes of an SA (which may also determine the modalities of the exercise of such a right and the minimum shares required) to directly appoint up to 1/3rd of the total number of directors. (cf. article 47 para. 4). Regarding the civil liability of the members of the management, supervisory and administrative organ of an SE, these will be governed by the rules applicable to the Greek SAs (article 51) – therefore these members will be obliged to exercise the same care as they would in their own interests and consequently liable for the corresponding degree of negligence ("diligentia quam in suis"), with the exception of the managing director who is liable for any negligence. Finally, the attitude of the Greek legislator on the matters mentioned in article 48 paras 1 and 2 is for the present unknown.

2. The general meeting

The general meeting of an SE is generally conceived and regulated by the Regulation in the general lines as the corresponding Greek rules. Therefore the Greek rules regarding the "organisation and conduct of the general meeting together with voting procedures" (see article 53) will be smoothly applied to the SEs registered in Greece. Greek law provides only for an "ordinary" meeting held once a year and not for more frequent meetings (cf. article 54 para. 1 first sentence). It also provides that the first fiscal period may be longer than one year, if so provided by the statues. The first annual meeting may be held in the 24 months following incorporation. For SEs, however, a maximum period of

18 months will have to be respected (see article 54 para. 1, second sentence). The general meeting of a Greek SA may not be convened by persons other than the board of directors (cf. article 54 para. 2). It has also to be noted that under Greek law, the general meeting has to be convened following a request made by a 1/20th minority; the same percentage will be needed for SEs (article 55 para. 1). The same applies to the right of the minority to request that additional items be put on the agenda of a forthcoming general meeting (article 56).

The general meeting decides with the majority of the votes cast. However, Greek law provides for higher majorities (2/3rd) in certain cases, such as the increase or the reduction of capital, the issuance of a debenture loan, the conversion or dissolution of the company and some other important matters. But under certain conditions the statutes may allow for a simple majority in the case of an increase of capital or the issue of a debenture loan. Despite article 59 para. 1, this simple majority could also be provided for SEs, because of article 5 of the Regulation. The option provided by article 59 para. 2 is not expected to be used.

3. Auditors

The Regulation does not contain provisions for auditors. Therefore the corresponding provisions of Greek law, to which reference is made in article 61, will be applied. Greek company law reflects the second and the eighth directives in this respect.

IV. Transfer of seat/registered office

As already noted, Greece follows the system of the "real seat" ("siège reel"). It does not accept a genuine transfer of the seat and therefore a change of a company's nationality (with maintenance of the legal personality) is not considered possible, although some authors suggest that this is possible if the other state, either as "sending" or "receiving" state, has legislation which would be compatible with Greek law (for example, if the foreign state would recognize the transfer of a Greek company to such a state).

In any event, article 8 will be a novelty in regard to the transfer.

Future legislation on the SE will have to fix the requirements for securing the interests of creditors before the "competent authority" delivers the certificate provided for in para. 8 of article 8, and therefore before the transfer takes place (see para. 7). Such requirements may be the provision of security or guarantees, to be ordered by the court.

Protection of minority shareholders who oppose the transfer (for example, through exit rights) will also be an issue to be considered in such legislation (as per para. 5 of article 8). It is not known whether Greece will opt for the possibility of a public authority to block the transfer upon grounds of public interest (as per para. 14).

It should be mentioned, finally, that Greece will have to provide for the "appropriate" measures in the cases provided in article 64 para. 1 (i.e. when the "head office" of a "Greek" SE is no longer in Greece). Such a measure is likely to be the revocation of the administrative act establishing the SE. In such a case, the SE will be liquidated, as envisaged by article 64 para. 2.

V. Involvement of employees

Involvement of employees is perhaps the most difficult topic, since Greek law does not provide for any mandatory scheme of employee participation in the organs of an SA, and there has been no discussion until now on the measures to be taken by the legislator in respect of the involvement in the SE. Therefore, it does not seem possible to make any prediction for the time being as to the manner in which Directive 2001/86/EC will be implemented.

VI. Other issues

Under article 5 of the Regulation, Greek law shall be applicable to all "Greek" SEs in respect of the capital and changes thereto, as well as regarding the shares, the bonds and similar securities. Greece has complied with the relevant EC Directives and therefore there will be no problems in that respect. It should be noted that Greek SAs can issue only shares and bonds. There are no other securities issued by them (the "founder's certificates" are not real "securities"). Greek law shall be also applicable to the publication of documents and particulars (article 13), as well as the annual and consolidated accounts, their auditing and their publication (article 61).

Greek law on SAs will be also applicable to SEs regarding liquidation, insolvency, cessation of payments and similar procedures (article 63).

Finally, the implementing Greek legislation will have to designate the competent authorities "within the meaning of articles 8, 25, 26, 54, 55 and 64" (article 68).

Hungary

Gabor Kozma

I. Introduction

Law No CXLIV of 1997 on Commercial Companies (Gt.), which provides, inter alia, for the transformation and organisation of commercial companies,[1] or the acquisition of influence in such companies, is the basis of Hungarian company law. The first part of the Gt. contains general provisions, applicable to all company forms, while in the second part special regulation of the various company forms is provided. In addition, Law No. CXLV of 1997 on Commercial Registers, access to the registers and the register court procedure, Law No. XLIX of 1991 on Bankruptcy and Liquidation or winding-up and Law No. CXX of 2001 on the Capital Markets, are relevant.

Although Hungarian company law is, to a great extent, harmonised with Community Law,[2] the Hungarian legislature had not responded so far to the authority provided in the SE-Regulation[3] to issue special regulations and by implementing the co-determination Directive,[4] which has relevance to the formation of an SE. Nevertheless, we will here make some suggestions for special regulations which may be deduced from the existing company law principles.

[1] The most important company forms are the general partnership (VIII. Chapter), the limited partnership (IX. Chapter), the limited liability company (XI. Chapter) and the public limited company (XII. Chapter).

[2] The implementation of the first, (68/151/EEC), the second (77/91/EEC), the third (78/855/EEC), the sixth (82/891/EEC), the twelfth (89/667/EEC) and the eleventh (89/666/EEC) Directives is already complete (cf. § 321 Gt.).

[3] Council Regulation (EC) No. 2157/2001 of 8 October 2001 on the Statute for a European company (SE).

[4] Council Directive 2001/86/EC of 8 October 2001 supplementing the Statute for a European company with regard to the involvement of employees.

II. Formation of an SE

1. General

In Hungarian law, a (public) company is formed either by a closed group or in a public procedure. In the first case, the founders undertake to take-up all the shares in a closed company (§ 206 Gt.). A closed company is one whose shares are not publicly traded (§ 177 para. 2 Gt.). In contrast, a public company can, under § 212 para. 1 Gt., be formed in a public procedure by subscription of its shares. A public company is characterised by the fact that all or some of its shares are traded in public (§ 177 para. 3 Gt.). By transformation,[5] only a closed Hungarian company can be formed.[6] This does not, however, apply to a company formed by merger, if the receiving company or all participants in the merger are public companies.[7]

According to Hungarian law, the cash contributions on the formation of a company may not be less than 30% of the founding capital, and not less than 10 million Forint, § 203 para. 2 Gt. If the company comes about by transformation, this provision does not apply to the relationship of contributions-in-kind and cash contributions. This will change in the future, as § 203 para. 2 Gt. will be repealed in the present draft law amending the Gt., on 01.01.2005.[8]

2. Merger

Under current law, the existing provisions of harmonised Hungarian law are applicable to the procedure for establishing an SE with its registered office in Hungary, unless the Regulation contains a specific provision (Art. 18 SE-Regulation). The second stage in the establishment refers to the newly formed SE, although the law of the state in which the future registered office will be situated is applicable to the entire founding procedure,[9] subject to the provisions in the Articles of Association (Art. 15 para. 1 SE-Regulation). We will, therefore, outline the merger procedure under Hungarian law.

[5] In Hungarian law, transformation includes merger and division, § 59 para. 2 Gt.

[6] § 60 para. 3 Gt.

[7] § 76 para. 1 Gt.

[8] § 34 para. 5 of Law No XLIX of 2003 amending the Gt. and the Ct.

[9] It is, however, disputed whether Art. 15 para. 1 SE-Regulation applies even before entry, as the SE at this point has no registered office (cf. *Teichmann*, ZGR [Zeitschrift für Unternehmens- und Gesellschaftsrecht] 2002, 383, 414).

a) First resolution of the general meeting

The SE-Regulation does not regulate the procedure prior to the arrangement of the merger, and therefore, national law applies, in accordance with Art. 18 SE-Regulation. Hungarian transformation law lays down the following procedure for the merger of two companies: firstly, under § 62 para. 2 Gt., a General Meeting is called at which it is ascertained whether the shareholders are agreeable to the merger, and a resolution on the intended legal form is taken. This resolution does not, however, give effect to the merger, but rather gives the management the authority to take the measures necessary to implement the merger. The need for this provision is created by § 233c) Gt. which states that the General Meeting has sole competence to decide on a merger, and the board is not therefore entitled to decide the matter. In addition, the considerable costs in advance of the merger would be useless expenditure if the General Meeting later rejected the merger.[10] A 3/4^{ths} majority of the votes present is required for the passing of the resolution at the first General Meeting, according to § 237 para. 1 Gt.

Finally, the shareholders must declare whether they intend to become shareholders in the successor company, i.e. the SE. This is not a legally binding declaration, firstly, because the statute expressly refers to "an intention", and secondly, according to § 62 para. 3 Gt., drafts of the documents necessary for implementation of the merger must be presented (cf. under b) only if the shareholders have voted for the merger at the first General Meeting.

b) Duties of the management board after the first general meeting

(1) Merger plan

The management or administrative organs of the merging companies prepare a merger plan, in accordance with Art. 20 para. 1 SE-Regulation. This brings up the question of whether this provision is definitive, or whether reference is made to the national laws of the merging companies, in the meaning of Art. 18 SE-Regulation. As under Hungarian transformation law, (§ 64 para. 1 together with § 75 para. 1 Gt.), a merger agreement has to be concluded, this would be an additional condition for the implementation of the merger. The question of whether a merger agreement in its legal effect acquires a greater importance than the merger plan. It is disputed that both the merger agreement and the merger plan can be classified as organisational acts in the corporate law sense. It is, however, doubtful whether the merger plan has contractual characteristics like the merger agreement. The fact that the parties can add further points to

[10] Cf. on founding §§ 62, 63 Gt.

the merger plan indicates that it has (Art. 20 para. 2 SE-Regulation).[11] In spite of some contrary opinions in the literature,[12] it can be said that Art. 20 para. 1 SE-Regulation contains a definitive provision. The founding companies from various Member States must act in compliance with the same rules, at least where the merger requires a common approach.[13] A merger agreement between the merging companies is not, therefore, necessary on the founding of an SE.

(2) Balance sheet and inventory

If the General Meeting has approved the merger, the management board is then obliged and entitled, in accordance with § 62 para. 3 Gt., to prepare draft closing accounts[14] and inventories of the founding companies as of a date specified by the General Meeting, and a draft opening account and inventory for the new successor company. The purpose of this provision is to assist the shareholders in assessing the financial position of the companies, and the financial effects of the merger, and so to enable them to make a well based decision on the merger.[15]

This provision can apply to the founding of an SE. only to a limited extent. Firstly, because of Art. 18 SE-Regulation, the obligation to prepare the above mentioned drafts only applies if the founding companies have their registered offices in Hungary, and, secondly, the drafts as far as the new company is concerned must be presented only if it will have its registered office in Hungary, so that it will be subject to Hungarian law by the reference in Art. 15 SE-Regulation. In the latter case, as the opening accounts must also contain the assets of the founding companies,[16] companies registered abroad will be compelled in practice to prepare draft accounts, even if the law of their home states does not so provide. This raises the question of whether the interim accounts, for the information of the shareholders, provided for in Art. 11 para. 1c) of the Merger Directive,[17] can take the place of the drafts mentioned. The fact that both the interim accounts and the above mentioned draft final accounts are to be prepar-

[11] *Neun*, in: *Theisen/Wenz* (ed.), Die Europäische Aktiengesellschaft, 2002, 79f.

[12] *Hirte*, NZG (Neue Zeitschrift für Gesellschaftsrecht) 2002, 1, 3.

[13] *Teichmann*, ZGR 2002, 383, 419f.

[14] Under § 63 para. 1 S. 2 in place of a closing account, the last annual accounts can be used, if the date of account is not longer than 6 months before the second General Meeting.

[15] *T. Nagy Erzsébet*, in: *Sárközy Tamás* (ed.), Társasági törvény, cégtörvény, 1997, 136.

[16] § 136 para. 2 Sztv. (Act No. C of 2000 on Accountancy).

[17] Third Council Directive 78/855/EEC of 9 October 1978.

ed by the same method and with the same headings, is an argument in favour of this view.[18] It should be noted that the Hungarian provision is more onerous in regard to deadlines, and presents greater demands with regard to the up-to-date nature of the financial information on the company.[19] According to § 63 para. 1 Gt., the accounts and inventory must be checked by the supervisory board and an independent expert.

(3) Draft method of calculation of settlement with the withdrawing shareholders

Because of the reference by Art. 18 SE-Regulation, the management board of an Hungarian founding company is also obliged, according to § 62 para. 3 Gt., to prepare a Draft Method of Calculation of Settlement with the Withdrawing Shareholders. This serves the purpose firstly, of enabling the shareholders to assess the financial and economic effects of the merger, and secondly, it is very closely related to the above mentioned draft accounts, because it represents the difference between the final accounts of the founding companies and the opening accounts of the SE.[20] The amount of the cash settlement depends, according to § 64 para. 3 Gt., on the relation of the capital disclosed in the draft accounts and the subscribed capital of the founding companies.

(4) Merger report

The SE-Regulation does not prescribe a merger report. According, by Art. 18 SE-Regulation, national law applies. In a merger company, which is subject to Hungarian law, the management board must provide a merger report, as required by § 76 para. 3 Gt., at the same time as the merger plan, in which the merger

[18] Cf. Art. 11 para. 2 Merger Directive together with § 136 para. 3 Sztv.

[19] According to Art. 11 para. 1 lit. c) Merger Directive, the interim account must be prepared as of a date which is not prior to the first day of the third month before the preparation of the merger plan. The merger plan must, according to Art. 6 Merger Directive, be published at least one month prior to the day of the General Meeting at which the resolution on the merger will be taken. According to § 64 para. 1 Gt., there cannot be more than three months between the date of the drafts and the time of the (second) General Meeting resolution on the merger, unless the date of the last annual accounts is not more than six months prior to the second General Meeting; in this case also, the last annual accounts can be taken.

[20] According to § 62 para. 4 Gt. the difference between the final accounts of the founding company and the opening accounts of the successor company consists of the following: (a) the contributions of new shareholders in the successor company, (b) the additional contributions of the existing shareholders to which the merger is subject, (c) the settlement payments to the withdrawing shareholders.

and, in particular, the share exchange ratio, must be legally and financially explained and justified. In this report, any special difficulties in arriving at a valuation must be mentioned.[21]

The merger report can be dispensed with only if one of the merging companies is the sole shareholder of the other.[22]

c) *Merger account*

Under European merger law, one or more independent experts[23] audit the merger plan and provide a written report for the shareholders.[24] In a separate audit, the auditor will be appointed by the management board of the Hungarian company.[25] Although Hungarian law also recognises a joint audit,[26] joint appointment of the auditor in the sense of Art. 22 para. 1 SE-Regulation, cannot take place, precisely because he is not appointed by a court or official authority. An amendment of the Gt. would, therefore, be desirable in this regard, so that the founding companies could avail of the time and expense saving involved. Unlike the SE-Regulation 1991 draft at Art. 21, the present SE-Regulation does not itself provide any regulation of the content of the audit report, with the result that this gap must also be filled by national law, in accordance with the reference of Art. 18 SE-Regulation.[27] The practical implications of this issue is that Hungarian transformation law, which is already harmonised, prescribes elements to be contained in the expert report over and above the standard content prescribed in the Merger Directive. The experts must explain, for example, whether the merger report of the management board is justified and whether the intended merger, in their opinion, prejudices the existing creditors.[28]

[21] Cf. Art. 9 Merger Directive.

[22] § 77 para. 5 Gt. together with § 76 para. 3 Gt.

[23] According to some opinions in the literature, non-independent experts can be appointed (cf. *Schwarz*, ZIP [Zeitschrift für Wirtschaftsrecht] 2001, 1851), as this can be deduced from the wording of Art. 22 para. 1 SE-Regulation. According to *Teichmann*, on the contrary, Art. 22 para. 1 SE-Regulation means "special audit in each company/common audit of both companies" (*Teichmann*, loc.cit. [Fn. 13], 423f.).

[24] Art. 10 Merger Directive.

[25] This is not specifically dealt with in the Gt., but follows from the general authority of the management board to manage, § 21 para. 1 together with § 240 para. 1 Gt. In addition, the auditor can be appointed by the register court only in the context of the protection of minority shareholders, if the General Meeting has failed to take a resolution on the application for a special audit of the last annual accounts or of a business transaction which took place within the past two years, § 51 para. 3, 4 Gt.

[26] § 72 para. 3 Gt.

[27] *Neun*, loc.cit. (Fn. 11), 103.

[28] § 76 para. 5 Gt.

In the case of a merger by takeover, an audit in accordance with Art. 31 para. 1 SE-Regulation is not required if a solely owned subsidiary is merged with the parent company. This is fully consistent with Hungarian merger law, so that the merging companies need not provide an audit. Neither is an audit required in the case of a merger by a new formation, under § 77 para. 5 Gt. This is not, however, the result of the reference under Art. 31 para. 1 sentence 2 SE-Regulation, which refers only to possible additional conditions of national law in relation to merger by takeover,[29] but rather to that under Art. 18 SE-Regulation. For the merger of two companies, one of which is owner of at least 90% of the shares of the other, the same rules apply as in the case of the preparation of a merger report,[30] although not only the merger variations provided for in Art. 31 para. 2 SE-Regulation, but also, for the above reasons, to a merger by a new formation.

d) *Disclosure under § 77 para. 1 Gt. and notification under Art. 21 SE-Regulation*

The merging companies are obliged, under § 77 para. 1 Gt., to file the merger plan, the merger report and the expert report with the competent Commercial Register, 30 days prior to the day of the General Meeting at which the resolution approving the merger plan will be taken.

Notice of the intended merger must, according to § 21 SE-Regulation, be published in the official bulletin of the Member States to the law of which the founding companies are subject. Unlike the draft regulation of 1991, the present Regulation does not state when this publication must take place. Following the logic of the Regulation, publication can be required only when the merger plan has been prepared.[31] On the other hand, the interests of the shareholders, and the formulation "intended name and registered office",[32] would indicate that the publication take place prior to the General Meeting at which the merger plan must be approved.[33] It is therefore suggested that the publication of the data required by Art. 21 SE-Regulation should be linked to the disclosure under § 77 para. 1 Gt. It remains doubtful, however, who is obliged to perform the duty of making the publication of the data required under Art. 21 SE-

[29] The wording of Art. 31 para. 1 sentence. 2 SE-Regulation: "National law governing each merging company shall nevertheless apply" is in favour.

[30] Cf. under B.II.2.d).

[31] *Teichmann*, loc.cit. (Fn. 13), 422.

[32] After the approving resolution, name and registered office are determined.

[33] *Neun*, loc.cit. (Fn. 11), 114f.

Regulation. While § 7 Ct. contains the list of resolutions to be published by the register court itself, according to § 65 para. 1 Gt. the companies themselves are obliged to announce the merger in two successive issues of the official bulletin, within 8 days after the passing of the resolution. On the one hand, § 65 para. 1 Gt. would be analogously applicable with regard to the persons who are obliged to make the publication, on the other hand, it is also possible that the implementation law would place the obligation of notifying the matters specified in Art. 21 SE-Regulation to the register court when filing the documents required § 77 para. 1 Gt., on the merging companies, and the court would publish these by adding to the list under § 7 Ct.

e) Second resolution of the general meeting

The second General Meeting decides on the drafts specified in § 62 para. 1 Gt.,[34] in particular, the merger plan, also by a 3/4^{ths} majority,[35] within three months after the ***effective date of the merger***[36] (§ 64 para. 1 Gt. together with Art. 23 para. 1 SE-Regulation). Under § 64 para. 1 Gt., the amount of the settlement with the withdrawing shareholders and the manner of payment, as well as the specification of the shareholders' participation in the intended subscribed capital of the successor company, must be decided at this General Meeting.[37] After the passing of the resolution approving the merger by the two General Meetings, the companies are obliged under § 65 para. 1 Gt., to announce the merger within 8 days after the resolution, in two successive issues of the official bulletin.[38]

The merger is also to be notified to the employees' representative organ.

f) Application and registration of the merger

Application to register the merger must be made to the competent Commercial Register within 60 days after the acceptance of the articles of association of the SE, according to § 36 para. 1 Ct. The register court reviews, according to Art. 25 para. 1 SE-Regulation, the correctness of the procedure in the founding companies and issues a certificate to the effect that the procedure has been correctly

34 Cf. under B.II.2.a)–c).

35 § 237 para. 1 Gt.

36 Unless the date of the last annual accounts is not more than six months prior to the second General Meeting, in which case the last annual accounts can be taken.

37 *T. Nagy Erzsébet*, loc.cit. (Fn. 15), 142f.

38 As to the items to be published cf. § 65 para. 2 Gt.

followed (Art. 25 para. 2 SE-Regulation). The register court is obliged, under § 44 para. 3 together with § 42 para. 1–3 Ct., to decide on the application within 60 days of the making of the application. If this time limit is not complied with, the chairman of the register court, according to § 42 para. 3 Ct., shall, within 8 days after the expiry of the period, take the necessary measures to process the application for the registration of the merger. If the decision of the court is not made within these 8 days, the merger will, on the 9th day after the expiry of the 60 day period, be entered with the content in the application, § 42 para. 3 Ct. The period of 60 days also applies to the issue of the certificate, and if the court fails to issue the certificate, the application of § 42 para. 3 Ct. remains per definition excluded. If the SE has its registered office in Hungary, Art. 26 SE-Regulation and § 42,44 para. 3 apply accordingly.

3. Holding SE

a) *Expert report*

As in the case of merger, a joint auditor may be appointed to prepare a written report for the shareholders of all companies, Art. 32 para. 4 SE-Regulation. Although in the case of a merger, a joint appointment of an auditor in the sense of Art. 22 para. 1 SE-Regulation is not possible in Hungary precisely because a joint auditor will not be appointed by a court or official authority, this is possible in the case of a formation of a holding SE. The only condition is the consent of all companies involved.

b) *Majority*

As the formation of a holding company is not specifically regulated in Hungarian law, difficult questions as to the majority required for the passing of the resolutions at the General Meetings of the various companies, arise. Art. 32 para. 6 SE-Regulation provides only that the General Meetings must agree, from which it can be inferred that a simple majority would suffice. It has been suggested that this gap be closed by passing special regulations at national level.[39] Against this view, it can be argued that an express authority is not provided in the SE-Regulation.[40] The gap could be closed by analogous application of Art. 18 SE-Regulation which deals with the majority requirements in the

[39] *Brandt*, NZG 2002, 991, 995.

[40] *Teichmann*, Ausführungsgesetz in Deutschland, in: Theisen/Wenz: Die Europäische Aktiengesellschaft, 2002 S. 587f.

case of a merger.[41] This, however, is controversial,[42] because the conditions for analogous application are not fulfilled. Firstly, the gap is not an unplanned one,[43] and secondly, the necessary similarity of the material is missing.[44] If one also takes into account that, according to Art. 32 para. 2, 4th sentence together with Art. 33 para. 2 SE-Regulation, the contribution of shares carrying more than 50% of the voting rights is required for the effective formation of a holding SE, it can be concluded that a simple majority is adequate for the formation of a holding SE.

c) Basic capital of the holding SE

On the formation of a holding SE, the shareholders in the founding companies exchange their shares for shares in the new holding SE,[45] and this constitutes a pure contribution-in-kind. However, under Hungarian law, 30% and not less than 10 million Forint of the basic capital must be contributed in cash (§ 203 para. 2 Gt.). Following the reference in Art. 15 SE-Regulation, this means that the founders of a holding SE are obliged to contribute cash up to a total of 30% of the basic capital in addition to their shares.[46] § 203 para. 2 Gt. on the proportion of cash contributions to contributions-in-kind will, however, be repealed with effect from 01.01.2005[47] so that this problem will not arise in the future on the formation of a holding SE.

4. Subsidiary-SE

The SE-Regulation does not provide detailed regulation of the formation of a Subsidiary-SE, but instead, refers, in Art. 36 SE-Regulation, to the national laws of the founding companies. Under current Hungarian law, the managing organ is entitled to form a subsidiary.[48] The procedure follows that for the for-

[41] *Teichmann*, loc.cit. (Fn. 13), 435.

[42] Cf. *Casper*, Der Lückenschluss im Statut der Europäischen Aktiengesellschaft, in: Festschrift für Peter Ulmer zum 70. Geburtstag, 2003, 60ff.

[43] This can be deduced by a historical interpretation, as the 1991 draft had an explicit provision on the majority required in the formation of the holding (Casper, loc.cit. [Fn. 45] S. 60).

[44] The difference is that the minority shareholders – unlike as in the case of a merger – are not obliged to contribute their shares to the holding (*Neun*, loc.cit. [Fn. 11], 142).

[45] *Berke*, in: Miskolczi Bodnár (ed.), Európai társasági jog, 2000, 126.

[46] This is a case of a formation by a closed group.

[47] § 34 para. 5 of Law No XLIX of 2003 amending the Gt. and the Ct.

[48] This can be deduced from the list of cases reserved to the exclusive decision of the

mation of a national company, and is not further dealt with here. It appears, however, to be problematic that the SE-Regulation specifies no means of protection for minority shareholders,[49] which may have the result that this formation option could be used to circumvent the merger provisions. It is thinkable that a subsidiary could first be formed, and subsequently all necessary assets of the founding companies transferred to it, as a single successor.[50] It is therefore proposed that the procedural rules for the other forms be applied analogously, if the formation of a Subsidiary-SE is intended to achieve the same financial effects as those of a merger or a holding.[51] However, it should be pointed out that there is already a Hungarian draft law according to which the conclusion of an agreement between a company and one of its affiliated companies for the transfer of assets requires the prior consent of the General Meeting, if the consideration provided by the company exceeds 10% of the basic capital.[52]

5. Conversion

An SE can also come about by the conversion of an existing company into an SE. In that event, the question of whether the procedure outlined in Art. 37 SE-Regulation is definitive, arises. If the gap in the Regulation is planned, national law is invoked. Although Art. 37 para. 7 refers explicitly to Art. 7 of the merger directive, Art. 37 SE-Regulation is devoid of any reference to the preparation and implementation of a general meeting, so that it can be concluded that the Hungarian provisions on the conversion procedure (§ 59ff. Gt.) apply. As the change of legal form and the merger constitute a conversion within the meaning of the Gt., the rules on mergers (§ 59ff. Gt.) with the exception of the special rules applicable to mergers (§ 72ff. Gt.) apply mutatis mutandis.

III. Protection of minority shareholders and creditors

On the formation of an SE by merger or of a holding SE, the issues of the protection of minorities and of creditors are closely linked, and are catered for in the Regulation by the authorisation to the Member States to provide this pro-

General Meeting (cf. e.g. § 233 Gt. for a plc AG, or § 150 para. 2 Gt. for a limited liability company).

49 E.g. Preparation and audit of a merger plan or approval of the General Meeting.

50 *Casper*, loc.cit. (Fn. 45) S. 63.

51 *Teichmann*, loc.cit. (Fn. 13), 438.

52 § 8 para. 1 and 3 of Law No XLIX of 2003 amending the Gt. and the Ct.

tection to creditors (Art. 34 SE-Regulation) and shareholders (Art. 24 para. 2, Art. 34 SE-Regulation), who do not agree to the formation of the SE. In addition, the issue is also very important in the case of the transfer of registered office of the SE, and in respect of which the Member States are also authorised to pass appropriate measures in the interests of the minority shareholders and the creditors. (Art. 8 para. 5 and 7 sentence 2 SE-Regulation).

1. Protection of minority shareholders

a) *General*

The Gt. provides many regulations for the protection of the minority shareholders in an Hungarian company. The following are the most important of the measures provided, but the list is not exhaustive: application for the appointment of an auditor by the register court,[53] and an action in the name of the company against the shareholders, the members of the management and supervisory boards or the auditor, if the General Meeting rejects the application, or if a resolution is not tabled.[54] Usually, shareholders who represent at least 10% of the voting rights granted by the basic capital are entitled to these rights. The right to call a General Meeting,[55] and application to add to the agenda of the General Meeting,[56] which are provided for in the Gt., are also dealt with in Art. 55 para. 1 and Art. 56 sentence 1 SE-Regulation, although the Member States may provide for a lesser percentage.[57] If it is determined in the articles of association of an Hungarian plc. that a shareholder may hold at most 10% of the voting rights, or if no shareholder holds more than 10% of the voting rights, directly or indirectly, the above rights can be exercised by shareholders representing 5% of the voting rights granted by the basic capital.[58]

In addition, each individual shareholder or member of the management and supervisory boards can apply for a court review of resolutions of the company organs on the basis of breach of the law or of the articles of association.[59]

[53] The auditor is appointed by the register court, if the General Meeting has failed to take a resolution on the application for a special audit of the last annual accounts or of a business transaction which took place within the past two years. § 51 para. 3–4 Gt.

[54] § 51 para. 5 Gt.

[55] A lesser percentage can be specified in the statutes, § 51 para. 1–2 Gt.

[56] § 230 Gt.

[57] Art. 55 para. 1 and Art. 56 S. 2 SE-Regulation.

[58] § 51 para. 6 Gt.

[59] The challenge does not delay the implementation of the resolution, although the court has discretion to defer the implementation, § 47 para. 5 Gt.

b) Protection of minority shareholders on formation and transfer of registered office

Hungarian transformation law provides for the protection of shareholders withdrawing because of a merger, as follows: the management organ is obliged, inter alia, to produce a draft of the modalities for compensating the shareholders withdrawing due to the merger (§ 62 para. 3 Gt.). The second General Meeting resolves on the acceptance of the draft required by § 62 para. 3 Gt.[60] (§ 64 para. 1 Gt.), i.e. practically, therefore on the merger itself. The withdrawing shareholders are determined in accordance with § 62 para. 3 last sentence Gt., according to which only the shareholders in the successor company are entitled to accept the articles of association of the successor company. Those who do not wish to be shareholders in the future SE must refuse to accept the articles of association. Thereafter, the amount of the compensation for the withdrawing shareholders must be fixed at this General Meeting, as well and the manner of payment. According to § 64 para. 3 Gt., the amount of compensation depends on the relationship of the capital shown on the accounts and the subscribed capital of the founding company. The register court reviews, according to § 44 para. 1 Ct., whether the entry of the matters applied for is in accordance with the law. With regard to the minority protection, this means that the certificate under Art. 25 para. 2 SE-Regulation will not be issued if the amount of the compensation for the withdrawing shareholders is not in accordance with the legally prescribed relationship of capital to subscribed capital.

In the case of the formation of a holding SE, the Hungarian legislator should provide special regulations for the protection of minority shareholders, and for this purpose it would seem advisable to declare the provisions of the Gt. relating to the protection of minority shareholders of a merging company to be applicable to the founding of a holding.

Likewise, the Hungarian legislator should avail of the authorisation in Art. 8 para. 5 SE-Regulation, by issuing specifically SE provisions on the reasonable protection of shareholders who oppose a transfer of registered office. Again, the protection measures relating to mergers, could be adapted.

2. Protection of creditors

Effective protection of creditors in the event of a transfer of registered office or merger with an SE, the registered office of which is in another Member State, is of the greatest significance. According to Art. 24 para. 1 a) SE-Regulation, the

[60] Cf. under B.II.2.a)–c).

rules to which the merging companies are subject, taking account of the cross-border nature of the merger, are applicable to the protection of the creditors. The interests to be protected are the same in the case of a transfer of registered office.

The creditors of an Hungarian company can demand security if they can credibly establish that their debts which have not become payable, but have come into existence prior to the publication of the merger resolution, are endangered. This can and must take place prior to the second publication, i.e. prior to the implementation of the merger (§ 66 para. 2 together with § 77 para. 4 Gt.). The Hungarian legislator need not take any action in this regard, although application of this provision to the transfer of registered office would be advisable in the implementing statute.

IV. Management and supervision

Art. 38b) SE-Regulation provides the SE with the choice between the monistic and dualistic systems of management. The latter is already known to Hungarian law, while the monistic system is an innovation. Following a short analysis of the provisions of the SE-Regulation on the separation of management and supervisory boards, we will deal here with issues relevant to the Hungarian legislature for the introduction of a monistic model.

1. The dualistic management system

a) Management organ

According to Art. 39 para. 4 sentence 1 SE-Regulation, the number of members of the management organ is determined by the articles of association, although the Member States can set a minimum or maximum number, Art. 39 para. 4 sentence 2 SE-Regulation. Under current Hungarian corporate law, the management board consists of at least three, at most, eleven *natural* persons.[61] § 244 provides an exception, according to which it can be determined in the founding document of a company, that, instead of the management board, a general director, who exercises the rights of the management board, can be appointed. It would be advisable, in the implementing act, to declare this provision to be applicable to the management organ of the SE also. A legal person cannot be a member of a board of management, so that Art. 47 SE-Regulation

[61] § 240 para. 2 sentence 1 Gt.

does not apply to an SE with its registered office in Hungary. According to § 240 para. 2 sentence 2 Gt., the chairman is elected by the management board from among its members.

A management board member may, at any one time, be on the management board of, at most, three companies. He is obliged to inform the company of which he is managing director, of his appointment to the management boards of other companies, § 22 para. 1 Gt. In addition, a person who has been convicted of a crime cannot be appointed as a member of a management board,[62] if prohibited by a court order from exercising an occupation,[63] and if he has been managing director of a liquidated company for at least a year, in the two years prior to the court decision on the liquidation, unless his appointment was made precisely to avoid the liquidation.[64]

As the members of the management board are appointed[65] and removed[66] by the General Meeting, the Hungarian legislator should leave this possibility open, and ***avail of the authorisation*** in Art. 39 para. 2 sentence 2 SE-Regulation.

The management board members are subject to instructions from the General Meeting,[67] which can, according to § 22 para. 4 Gt., withdraw their management authority to the extent foreseen in the articles of association. This does not apply to a one-person company, in which case the shareholder can issue written instructions to the management board members, or withdraw an area of competence. In such a case, the management board or member will be relieved of liability under § 29 Gt.[68] Likewise, § 22 para. 4 Gt. is not applicable if a shareholder holds more than 3/4[ths] of all voting rights, § 22 para. 6 Gt.

While the management board exercises its rights and performs its duties collectively, distribution of tasks or competences between the members can be provided for in the rules of procedure of the management board, § 241 para. 1 Gt.

The members of the management board must, in their management of the company, exercise the care of a prudent businessman taking the interests of the company into account, § 29 para. 1 sentence 1 Gt. In the case of culpable breach of duty, they are liable jointly and severally to the company for damages.[69] If the damage is caused by a resolution of the management board, those

[62] For the duration of the legal effect of the judgement, § 23 para. 1 Gt.

[63] Only in the case of a company the business objects of which are identical, for the duration of the legal effect of the judgement, § 23 para. 2 Gt.

[64] For three years after the liquidation order comes into legal effect, § 23 para. 3 Gt.

[65] § 19 para. 3 Gt.

[66] § 30 para. 1 lit. b) Gt.

[67] § 22 para. 2 Gt.

[68] § 22 para. 5 Gt.

[69] § 29 para. 1. 2 Gt. together with § 29 para. 2 S. 1 Gt.

members who were absent when the vote was taken, or who voted against the resolution, and who notified the supervisory board in writing of this within 15 days after the vote, are relieved of liability. If third parties are damaged due to acts of a member of the management board in the course of the management of the company, the company is liable in accordance with § 29 para. 3 Gt.

b) Supervisory organ

The number of members of the supervisory organ is determined by the articles of association (the statutes), according to Art. 40 para. 3 sentence 1 SE-Regulation. Here also, the Hungarian legislator should avail of the authorisation provided by Art. 40 para. 3 sentence 2 SE-Regulation, by declaring the Hungarian provisions, according to which the supervisory board shall have a minimum of three and a maximum of five natural[70] persons as members,[71] to be applicable to the SE. No limit is set to the number of supervisory organ appointments one person may have, unlike the position of management board members, although a supervisory organ member is obliged to inform the other companies in which he is a member of the supervisory board, in writing within 15 days of accepting his appointment.[72]

The members of the supervisory organ are, under § 38 para. 4 Gt., liable without limitation and collectively, for damage suffered by the company due to breach of their supervisory duties.

2. The monistic system of management

By the monistic system, the Regulation introduces an important element of freedom of organisation. Although the Member States the legal systems of which do not know this system, are not obliged, according to Art. 43 para. 4 SE-Regulation, to introduce it, they will be compelled in practice to do so, as the provisions of the SE-Regulation apply even in the absence of special provisions, if the SE decides for the monistic model.[73] In particular with regard to employee co-determination,[74] difficulties could be encountered in the absence of such

[70] This is not explicitly stated in the Gt., but follows from § 34 para. 2 Gt., according to which members of the supervisory board must act personally.

[71] § 31 para. 1 Gt.

[72] § 32 ss, 1 Gt.

[73] *Bungert/Beier*, EWS 2002, 1, 3.

[74] In the dualistic model, the employees participate in the supervision of the management, in the monistic system, they have, in contrast, the possibility of participating in the management.

provisions. The Hungarian legislator is therefore provided with the opportunity of freely structuring the monistic model, although, of course it is advisable to look at other legal systems.

The separation of management and supervisory functions could be the solution for the integration of co-determination in the monistic model. Convergence of the dual and monistic systems is spoken of in this regard.[75] The French and English systems could serve as examples.

While some opinions in the literature express doubts about the possibility of introducing separation of functions between inside and outside directors,[76] special provisions similar to the French law could be introduced. In this context also, the flexible nature of English law, which does not mandatorily impose a management system and leaves the design of the optimal management system to the company itself, should be noted. For Hungary, a form of SE specific regulation could be presented, if the separation of functions was achieved by the attribution of tasks to the administration board and the managing directors, or by precise demarcation of liability of managing directors from that of members of the administration board.[77] In addition, it should be left to the articles of association (statutes) to provide, as in English law, whether one or more managing directors are responsible for the day-to-day business or not.[78]

V. Employees' co-determination

There are many connections between the Regulation and the Directive on Employees' Co-determination. "*The rules on the involvement of employees in the European Company are laid down in Directive 2001/86/EC and those provisions thus form an indissociable complement to this Regulation and must be applied concomitantly*". It remains to be seen how the Hungarian legislator implements the SE Directive. For this reason, we will here deal only with the default provisions for co-determination in Appendix Part 3 SE Directive.

According to the default provisions, the SE is not obliged to introduce an agreement on employees' co-determination, if none of the participating companies had such provision prior to the entry of the SE in the Commercial Register. The same applies in the case of the formation of an SE by conversion/

[75] *Teichmann*, loc.cit. (Fn. 13), 447.

[76] *Hirte*, loc.cit. (Fn. 12), 8.

[77] Recital 14 SE-Regulation (extract) "the respective responsibilities of those responsible for management and those responsible for supervision should be clearly defined."

[78] *Teichmann*, loc.cit. (Fn. 43), S 606.

transformation. On the other hand, if the employees were entitled to co-determination rights prior to the entry of the SE, future co-determination shall be in accordance with the prior highest degree of co-determination. Hungarian co-determination provisions prescribes that employees in companies with more than 200 employees are entitled to one third of the seats on the supervisory board.[79] This does not create a major obstacle to the attractiveness of an SE with registered office in Hungary, because the relatively low threshold of the number of employees is no disadvantage. It can be anticipated that any SE will have a considerably greater number of employees, in any event.

VI. Conclusion

The Regulation represents an advance in so far as the legal pre-requisites for a corporate legal form for companies active on a cross-border basis are provided. Although practical questions such as tax issues and corporate group law questions are not dealt with, it can be assumed that the SE will have a future in competition between companies and legal forms. The advantages include cost savings in subsidiaries or plants in other Member States due to a unitary organisation structure, simplified and therefore more effective management, (one General Meeting, one management and administration organ), and even the European "logo".[80]

The processing and harmonisation of the monistic model to existing management systems seems, however, to be problematical, at least in Hungary. The international experience shows, however, that appropriate, even creative, solutions for flexible corporate structuring can be developed in practice.

[79] § 36 para. 1 together with § 31 para. 2 lit. c) Gt.

[80] *Blanquet*, ZGR 2002, 20, 36.

Ireland

Rossa Fanning

References: *Courtney, Thomas B.* The Law of Private Companies, 2nd Edition, Butterworths Ireland Ltd (2002); *Keane, Ronan* Company Law 3rd Edition, Butterworths Ireland Ltd (2000).

I. Introduction

The passing of the EU Council Regulation on the Statute for a European public limited liability company or Societas Europaea ('SE') was finally accomplished on 8 October 2001. The SE was over 30 years of deliberation in the making,[1] an extraordinarily protracted gestation period by any yardstick.

Yet, the reaction in Ireland is notable only in the sense that Sherlock Holmes considered the dog that did not bark to be noteworthy. There has been virtually no public or academic interest in the topic and there is, as of October 2003, no formal indication from either the Office of the Attorney General (the Office responsible for the drafting of Irish domestic legislation) or the relevant Government Department (Enterprise, Trade and Employment) as to progress as of yet made in the preparation of implementing legislation in advance of the coming into effect of the SE on 8 October 2004.[2]

[1] Council Regulation (EC) No 2157/2001 refers in its own preamble at Paragraphs (8) and (9) to some of the relevant history: "*(8) The Statute for a European public limited-liability company (hereafter referred to as 'SE') is among the measures to be adopted by the Council before 1992 listed in the Commission's White Paper on completing the internal market, approved by the European Council that met in Milan in June 1985. The European Council that met in Brussels in 1987 expressed the wish to see such a Statute created swiftly. (9) Since the Commission's submission in 1970 of a proposal for a Regulation on the Statute for a European public limited-liability company, amended in 1975, work on the approximation of national company law has made substantial progress.*"

[2] As provided for by Council Directive 2001/86/EC, Article 79. Interestingly, it would appear that responsibility for implementing the Regulation falls upon the Company Law (EU) section of that Department whilst responsibility in respect of the Directive falls upon the Industrial Relations section of the same Department, perhaps increasing the likelihood of discrete domestic legislation at the implementation stage.

Even the Company Law Review Group, a body charged under Irish domestic law with the specific function of advising the relevant Minister in this area,[3] make, in their First Report of 31 December 2001 only a passing reference to the SE.[4]

The leading Irish textbook on Company Law[5] makes the obvious observation as to why the imminent introduction of the SE has had little impact in this jurisdiction thus far: "*In relative terms, the SE is likely to be of very limited interest to the vast majority of Irish corporators.*"[6]

There are a plurality of reasons as to why this is self-evidently so. The SE is a variant of the Public Limited Company (PLC)[7] – a type of company that is numerically scarce to vanishing point amongst Irish registered companies. There were 914 PLCs registered in Ireland on 31 December 2001 out of a total of 130,516, just 0.6% of the total, expressed as a percentage.

Moreover, the SE-Regulation purports – for the moment anyway[8] – to regulate only a very specific breed of PLC, setting out its limited objective in paragraph 10 of the Preamble as follows, "*... it must be possible at least to create such a company as a means both of enabling companies from different Member States to merge or to create a holding company and of enabling companies and other legal persons carrying on economic activities and governed by the laws of different Member States to form joint subsidiaries.*"

[3] Section 68(1) of the Company Law Enforcement Act, 2001 provides "*The Review Group shall monitor, review and advise the Minister on matters concerning- ... (f) the approach to issues arising from the State's membership of the European Union, insofar as they affect the operation of the Companies Acts.*"

[4] Paragraph 1.9.1 (at p.11) simply states "*... It is also noted that the Council has approved the statute for the European Company, which must become operable no later than 2004.*"

[5] *Courtney, Thomas B.* The Law of Private Companies 2nd Edition, Butterworths Ireland Ltd (2002).

[6] *Ibid.* at p. 42. Perhaps intentionally, the author emphasises his own point by allocating just three-quarters of one page to the topic in an extremely comprehensive text book (albeit primarily concerned with Private Companies) of 1,628 pages of text excluding appendices, contents pages and the index.

[7] Article 10 of the Regulation renders this expressly the case: "*... an SE shall be treated in every Member State as if it were a public limited liability company formed in accordance with the law of the Member State in which it has its registered office.*"

[8] The greater significance may lie in the potential future expansion of the SE. Paragraph 10 of the Preamble of the Regulation, dealing with ambit, is expressly qualified by its commencing clause: "*Without prejudice to any economic needs that may arise in the future ...*" In light of the difficulties experienced in reaching agreement on the present Regulation, any future expansion of the ambit of the SE must be very speculative at this stage.

It follows from all of this that any discussion of the likely shape of the implementation rules that will bind the Societas Europaea to Irish company law is both tentative and speculative at this time, and is accordingly brief.

It might be considered, however, that certain general considerations will inform the Irish approach. First, in light of the apparent unlikelihood of significant usage of the SE in this jurisdiction, there will be little appetite to choose options that involve any significant discordance with existing domestic law, or that would likely provoke any significant reshaping of domestic law.

As against that, it is worth noting that Ireland has experienced a marked upsurge in enthusiasm for revision and amendment of domestic company law in recent years. In March 1999, the Government approved the implementation of the recommendations in the report of the Working Group on Company Law Compliance and Enforcement (the McDowell Report) which included as one of its primary recommendations that "*[t]here is a vital urgency in ensuring that Ireland, as a potential place in which to do business and from which to do business, has a first class system of company law which places Ireland in the forefront as a contender for the location of international commerce.*"[9] The consequential establishment of a statutorily-based Company Law Review Group, in addition to the enactment of amending legislation in 1999 and 2001 is indicative of the appetite for reform and change in this area.[10]

It seems reasonable to suggest therefore, that Ireland will be anxious, in the method of its implementation of the SE, to reconcile the competing desires to retain stability and continuity in its existing domestic law on the one hand, and on the other hand, to ensure that the SE is seen as having been properly and adequately implemented in this jurisdiction in a manner that does not diminish the generally perceived attractiveness of Ireland as a location for international business over the past decade or so.

Although the Regulation will be of direct effect in Ireland from 8 October 2004, the accompanying Directive will not.[11] This does create an interesting backdrop to the decision as to *which level* of Irish law the two pieces of European legislation will be implemented at. European legislation is introduced either by means of primary legislation, i.e. by an Act of the Oireachtas (Parliament) or by means of secondary legislation, (a so-called Ministerial Order or

[9] Government Publications (Pn. 6697), 30 November 1998, p. ix, paragraph 63.

[10] Two Acts of the Oireachtas (the Irish Parliament) were passed in 1999: the Companies Amendment Act, 1999 and the Companies (Amendment) (No 2) Act, 1999. The Company Law Enforcement Act, 2001 has created a new executive agency with new responsibilities; the Office of the Director of Corporate Enforcement.

[11] Although it is of course the case that the implementation deadline for the Directive of 8 October 2004 is provided by Article 14 thereof to be the same date of 8 October 2004.

Regulation, which is simply promulgated by the relevant Government Minister without the approval of Parliament).

There is a strict constitutional rule that legislation which contains "*principles and policies*" must be introduced by way of primary legislation, as the Constitution reserves, under Article 15.2.1°, the exclusive power of lawmaking to the Oireachtas.[12] Legislation necessitated by Ireland's membership of the European Union is immune from constitutional challenge under Article 29.4.7°. However, if the discretion left to Ireland in the manner of the implementation of the SE in fact abdicates the determination of at least some "*principles and policies*" to Ireland, then it would be constitutionally illegitimate to implement the Regulation by way of secondary legislation. This argument has not found sympathy with the Irish Supreme Court when it has been raised in other factual contexts[13] but would arguably be once again stateable here were secondary legislation the chosen method. The question of whether the original European legislation is in the form of a Regulation or a Directive is not decisive; an analysis of the amount of discretion left to the Member State is required in each case.

II. Formation of a European Company

Article 2 of the Regulation provides that a European Company can be created:

- through a merger between companies or the creation of a holding company;
- by the creation of a joint subsidiary;
- through the conversion of an existing public limited-liability company into an SE, provided it for at least two years has had a subsidiary company governed by the law of another Member State.

The option of creating an SE is available to a company the head office of which is not within the Community, provided the company is formed under the law of a Member State, has its registered office in that Member State and has a real and continuous link with a Member State's economy. Article 3 specifies that an SE will be regarded as a public limited-liability company governed by the law of the Member State in which it has its registered office.

It is not entirely apparent what additional provision Ireland will be required to make over and above the existing rules for the formation and registration of PLCs, which apply by virtue of Article 15 of the Regulation.

[12] See, *inter alia*, *Cityview Press Ltd. v. An Chomhairle Oiliúna (AnCO) [1980] IR 381* and *Laurentiu v. Minister for Justice [1999] 4 IR 26*.

[13] *Meagher v. Minister for Agriculture [1994] 1 IR 329* and *Maher v. Minister for Agriculture [2001] 2 IR 139*.

Under Irish company law, these can either be formed *ab initio* or by the conversion of a private company. There are basic requirements for the filing in the Companies Registration Office of a memorandum and articles of association, in addition to a special form known as Form No A1.[14]

There is also a requirement that such companies offer their shares to the general public, the process being initiated by way of a *prospectus*. The sale is normally conducted *via* the Stock Exchange by way of a *flotation* of the company. Irish law in this area need not be considered here in any detail,[15] but it is of course, heavily influenced by European Community law already.[16]

The procedure whereby an Irish company metamorphoses from private to public is now governed by section 9 of the Companies (Amendment) Act, 1983 which stipulates that the Company must pass a special resolution to that effect and must comply with various other statutory formalities.

Some additional provisions to Ireland's existing provisions on company registration will be required. In particular, the Article 3 provision stipulating that "*An SE may itself set up one or more subsidiaries in the form of SEs*" will require some changes to be made to the current registration system.[17] It is not thought, however, that this will be particularly problematic.

[14] This form requires that various details be inserted including:
- the name of the company
- the company's registered address
- the name, address and signature of the secretary
- particulars of the directors, including their signatures (section 43 of the Companies (Amendment) (No 2) Act, 1999 requires the entering into of a bond in the amount of € 25,394.76 in the event that no director is resident in the State. There is an exemption from the requirement where the Registrar of Companies certifies that "*the company has a real and continuous link with one or more economic activities that are being carried out in the State.*")
- the signatures of two subscribers / solicitor acting
- a Declaration of Compliance that all the requirements of the Companies Acts have been complied with
- a declaration that the company is being formed for the purpose of carrying on an activity in the State
- the completion of a "*Capital Duty*" Statement.

[15] For a more detailed account of the Irish law in this area see *Courtney*, Chapter 28 and *Keane*, pp 85–94.

[16] For instance, the requirements governing the content of a prospectus in Section 44 of the Companies Act, 1963 are amended by the European Communities (Transferable Securities and Stock Exchange) Regulations, 1992. Similarly, the information that must be provided on an application for a listing on the Irish Stock Exchange is set out in the Schedules to the European Communities (Stock Exchange) Regulations, 1984 which domestic legislation in turn implemented the Listing Particulars Directive (80/390/EEC of 17 March 1980).

[17] Article 3 will also quite clearly fashion a substantive change to Irish law insofar as it

The Article 19 provision envisaging an optional "public interest" challenge by "competent authorities" of a relevant Member State to the formation of an SE by merger is entirely novel and it is not known at this stage whether it would appeal to Ireland.

III. Management system of the European Company

Article 38 of the Regulation offers a polarised choice for European Companies as between "*either a supervisory organ and a management organ (two-tier) system or an administrative organ (one-tier system) depending on the form adopted in the statutes.*"

Irish companies are almost certain to opt for the one-tier option, the administrative organ corresponding to the board of directors under Irish company law. There is no equivalent to the "*supervisory organ*" under Irish company law and it would seem highly unlikely, given a much more familiar alternative, that it would be opted for here.

The rules in relation to the management of a one-tier system are set out in Articles 43–51 of the Regulation.

Article 43 paragraph 1 states that "*[t]he administrative organ shall manage the SE. A Member State may provide that a managing director or managing directors shall be responsible for the day-to-day management under the same conditions as for public limited-liability companies that have registered offices within that Member State's territory.*" Ireland might be considered unlikely to make any specific provision in this regard given that the default articles of association that would apply[18] confer a discretion upon the board of directors in the delegation of their powers to the Managing Director. Model Article 112 of Table A states "*The directors may entrust to and confer upon a managing director any of the powers exercisable by them upon such terms and conditions and with such restrictions as they may think fit and either collaterally with or to the exclusion of their own powers, and may from time to time revoke, withdraw, alter or vary all or any of such powers.*" In any event, the delegation of authority by the board of directors will in turn depend on the management powers that the board them-

will render the provision implementing the Twelfth Directive on single-member private limited liability companies – implemented in Ireland by the European Communities (Single-Member Private Limited Companies) Regulations, 1994 – applicable to SEs.

[18] 'TABLE A' is a set of 'model' Articles of Association contained in the First Schedule to the Companies Act, 1963. These Articles are by no means binding, but are applicable unless excluded or varied.

selves are granted; their own powers may or may not be as extensive as those contained in Model Article 80 of Table A.

Paragraph 2 of Article 43 provides that in the first instance, the number of members of the administrative organ shall be laid down in the SE's statute, subject to the stipulation of a Member State. Ireland might be thought unlikely to go beyond its current provisions. These require a minimum of two directors, even for single-member companies and impose no upper limit.[19] There is, however, a requirement that one of the directors be resident in the State[20] and there is a statutory maximum of 25 on the number of directorships that an individual may hold, though this will be of little consequence as PLCs are exempted from this restriction.[21] The stipulation that the administrative organ shall consist of at least three members where employee participation is regulated in accordance with the Directive is most unlikely to have application.

Article 47, Paragraph 1 provides that an SE's statutes may permit a company to be a member of one of its organs, *provided that the law applicable to public limited-liability companies in the Member State in which the SE's registered office is situated does not provide otherwise*. Ireland is a jurisdiction where the law does provide otherwise as only natural persons can become directors of companies; there is an express prohibition in section 176(1) of the Companies Act, 1963 on companies having a body corporate as a director. Thus, a company will not be permitted to be a member of an "*administrative organ*." Conversely, a company can lawfully become a member of another company, subject to any constraints provided this is *intra vires* its objects clause.[22]

IV. Transfer of seat / registered office

Article 7 of the Regulation provides that "*[t]he registered office of an SE shall be located within the Community, in the same Member State as its head office. A Member State may in addition impose on SEs registered in its territory the obligation of locating their head office and their registered office in the same place.*" The latter optional additional requirement is thought unlikely to be imposed on

19 Section 174 of the Companies Act 1963 stipulates the requirement of two directors. Model Article 97 in Table A allows a company to vary the number of its directors by ordinary resolution.

20 Section 43 of the Companies (Amendment) (No 2) Act, 1999 imposes such a restriction, although permitting a bond to be entered into in the amount of € 25,394.76 in the event that no director is resident in the State.

21 Section 45 (3) (a) (i) of the Companies (Amendment) (No 2) Act, 1999.

22 *Re Barned's Banking Co. (1867) LR 3 Ch 105.*

Ireland as there is currently no obligation on companies to have their head office and their registered office located in the same place.[23]

Detailed rules outlining a system providing for the transfer of an SE's registered office are contained in Article 8.

Paragraph 2 of Article 8 permits the management or administrative organ of an SE to draw up a transfer proposal and publicise it in accordance with Article 13, *without prejudice to any additional forms of publication provided for by the Member State of the registered office.* At present, Ireland simply requires under section 113 (3) of the Companies Act, 1963 that "*[n]otice of any change in the situation of the registered office of a company shall be given within fourteen days after the date of the change to the registrar who shall record same.*"[24]

Paragraph 5 of Article 8 provides that "*[a] Member State may, in the case of SEs registered within its territory, adopt provisions designed to ensure appropriate protection for minority shareholders who oppose a transfer.*" Ireland has a general minority petition procedure which may be invoked in circumstances where a petitioner claims that the affairs of the company or the powers of the directors are "*being exercised in a manner oppressive to him or any of the members*" or "*in disregard of his or their interests as members*". It would seemingly be open to a minority shareholder to proceed under this existing provision. However, there are more narrowly tailored remedies for minority shareholders to challenge specific decisions; for instance an alteration of the rights of a class of shareholders by special resolution amending the articles of association may be the subject of a court application by the holders of at least 10% of the shares affected.[25] It is simply impossible at this stage to predict whether such a specific remedy will commend itself in this jurisdiction, although apparently envisaged by the statement in paragraph 14 that "*[r]eview by a judicial authority shall be possible.*" The prescription of a two-month moratorium in paragraph 6 seems designed to facilitate such a challenge and paragraph 14 expressly extends to Member States the option of permitting the competent authorities (including a supervisory financial authority where appropriate) of a Member State the entitlement to challenge any proposed transfer, though solely on grounds of "*public interest.*"

[23] See section 113 of the Companies Act, 1963, as amended by section 4 (1) of the Companies (Amendment) Act, 1982.

[24] There are special registration requirements provided for companies formed or registered abroad by Part XI of the Companies Act, 1963 but these rules now have no application to limited companies incorporated outside the State which establish a *branch* within the State, pursuant to the European Communities (Branch Disclosures) Regulations, 1993 (which would certainly be the case with any SE).

[25] See section 78 of the Companies Act, 1963.

Paragraph 7 of Article 8 includes a provision requiring the SE to satisfy the competent authority[26] that issues the required certificate that, in respect of any liabilities arising prior to the publication of the transfer proposal, the interests of creditors and others *have been adequately protected in accordance with requirements laid down by the Member State where the SE has its registered office prior to the transfer.*

At present, creditors have no particular safeguards afforded to them under Irish law in respect of any changes to the location of a company's registered office. What seems contemplated here is the introduction of some special provision to prevent creditors of a company in one jurisdiction being disadvantaged or prejudiced in some way by a transfer of a registered office. One answer to any such problem is the Brussels Convention, 1968 on the service of legal proceedings and documents outside a jurisdiction.[27] However, it would seem competent for Ireland to introduce a measure analogous to the validation procedure applicable where a company seeks to enter into guarantees or provide security in connection with loans, quasi-loans and credit transactions in favour of directors and similar persons,[28] and indeed, the '*whitewash*' procedure whereby companies can provide financial assistance in connection with the purchase of their own shares.[29]

V. Involvement of employees

As is well known, the issue of the involvement of workers was a major stumbling block in the prolonged lead-up to the SE. There is and was a very great disparity between the laws of the various Member States regarding the degree of worker involvement in company decision-making organs. Whilst certain Member States such as Germany have long had institutionalised systems of worker co-determination "*Mitbestimmung*" and others favour company works councils, Ireland remains, with the United Kingdom, on something of a limb in providing in its domestic law no institutionalised system of employee representation, other than, in Ireland's case at least, for state enterprises.

26 Perhaps the Registrar of Companies in Ireland.

27 The Convention was incorporated into Irish law by the Jurisdiction of Courts and Enforcement of Judgments Act, 1988. See also Order 11A of the Rules of the Superior Courts, 1986 (as amended).

28 See section 34 of the Companies Act, 1990.

29 See section 60 (2)–(11) of the Companies Act, 1963.

In the case of state enterprises, the Worker Participation (State Enterprise) Acts of 1977[30] and 1988 represent an important exception to the otherwise voluntarist system of Irish industrial relations. Worker directors are statutorily entrenched in state-owned, commercial companies. Private sector employers have always preferred a voluntarist approach and there is no statutory provision made for board-level employee participation in the private sector.

The original 1977 legislation established the following principles of participation:

The direct election of full-time employees to one-third of the seats on the board of directors in applicable state-controlled trading companies;

The franchise extended to all full-time employees;

Candidates for election could be nominated only by a trade union or other organisation (such as a staff association), which is recognised for collective bargaining purposes by the company concerned;

The term of office of the elected worker directors was to be three years;

The worker directors held the same status as any other directors and were therefore entitled to the same rights and to assume similar responsibilities;

Elections were to be conducted under the proportional representation system.

The Act did not make any attempt to influence structural arrangements below board level, such as relationships among worker directors, trade unions, and employees.

The 1988 Act provides for the introduction of arrangements for sub-board structures in the state sector. In recognition of the fact that different circumstances apply to individual companies, that Act allows management and worker representatives to choose from a wide range of sub-board participatory institutions.

As a proportion of the total Irish workforce, the Acts cover well under 10 per cent of employees, and its scope has been diminishing with continued privatisation of this sector. Employee representatives have seats on single-tier/unitary boards of directors. However, they are in the minority on these boards as they only account for one-third of board membership, rendering their role more of

[30] The 1977 Act granted the right of employee representation on the boards of such state companies as the national airline (*Aer Lingus*), the national transport company (*CIÉ*), the national electricity generator and producer (ESB), the national sugar beet producer (Irish Sugar), the national fertiliser manufacturer (*Nitrigin Éireann*) and the national peat producer and processor, (*Bord na Móna*). Subsequently, the application of the right was extended to the postal service (*An Post*), the then national telecommunications company (*Bord Telecom*), the national steel producer, (*Irish Steel*), gas producer and distributor, (*Bord Gáis*) and health insurer (*VHI*).

advocate and watchdog on behalf of employees rather than ultimate decision-maker.

Private sector employers have traditionally opposed the introduction of legislation enforcing the introduction of employee participation structures, favouring a voluntarist approach, arguing that statutory provisions would have a negative impact on foreign direct inward investment, especially with regard to investment from US multinationals. This fear is also one shared by the Industrial Development Agency (IDA) and successive governments.

All of this is by way of background to the likely Irish attitude to the Directive providing for worker participation. That Directive in its original draft[31] set out mandatory participation options on worker participation that proved unacceptable to all Member States. The solution arrived at by the Davignon group of experts took, as its starting point, the *realpolitik* that complete harmonisation on this issue would not be possible and accepted the corollary approach of an absence of minimum requirements.

The final Directive establishes a machinery for the negotiation of worker participation in an SE with the primary purpose of avoiding the dilution of rights already enjoyed by employees in countries that make existing provision for such rights. The Directive does impose an obligation on Ireland however to establish rules of participation and specifies some mandatory content for those rules.

There is a requirement contained in Article 3 for the establishment of a 'special negotiating body' to be charged with "*the task of determining by written agreement, arrangements for the involvement of employees within the SE.*" The SNB is composed of elected or appointed members, with seats allocated in proportion to the number of employees employed in each Member State by the participating companies. The basic rule is that Member States have one seat for every 10%, or fraction thereof, of the total EU workforce of the participating companies employed there. These SNB negotiations must be completed within six months, which period may be extended to a total of one year by agreement. In many ways the most important feature of the Directive is its provision of a set of default rules where no agreement is reached. Involvement is a broad concept, including the provision of information to and consultation of employees and, in certain circumstances where this previously existed in the participating companies, board-level participation. The Directive also lays down rules on issues such as confidentiality, protection of employee representatives, its relationship with other provisions and compliance.

Accordingly, although not particularly intrusive, the compromise reached on the employee participation measures is likely to be of some concern in this

[31] Document 5269/93, Brussels, 10 March 1993.

jurisdiction to large private sector companies, although it would clearly be applicable only to very few of them. But what decisions must Ireland take surrounding implementation?

Paragraph 2(b) of Article 3 provides that "*Member States shall determine the method to be used for the election or appointment of the special negotiating body who are to be elected or appointed in their territories.*" Given the precedent referred to above of the 1977 and 1988 Acts, which have operated without great difficulty, it might be thought that Ireland would seek to borrow some of the features contained there in respect of the method of election of the members to the special negotiating body, such as, for instance, the three year term of office and the method of election by proportional representation. Other features, however, such as the sole power of nomination being reserved to trade unions or similar organisations would certainly be inappropriate here in all cases given that the same paragraph goes on to state that "*Member States shall provide that employees in undertakings or establishments in which there are no employees' representatives through no fault of their own have the right to elect or appoint members of the special negotiating body.*" Obviously, further modification, perhaps by the introduction of a type of constituency system, will be required in order to ensure representation by one member representing each participating company with employees in Ireland.

Paragraph 6 of Article 3 – the option not to open or to terminate negotiations and instead rely on the rules of information and consultation of employees already in force – clearly will not apply in Ireland.

The option to lay down budgetary rules in paragraph 7 of Article 3 might commend itself to Ireland in order to ensure that the SNB is not seen as being relatively more expensive or inconvenient in this jurisdiction.

The provision in Article 6 that the legislation applicable to the negotiation procedure shall be that of Ireland in cases where the registered office of the SE is within Ireland is somewhat unhelpful given that there is no legislation presently applicable to this type of process. There is, of course, a battery of employment and industrial relations legislation but nothing specifically in this area.

It is impossible to speculate upon the precise content of Ireland's "*standard rules*" required by Article 7, beyond what is prescribed in the Annex. Similarly, it is not possible at this stage to indicate what precise shape the reservation and confidentiality provisions contained in Article 8 will ultimately take. Article 11 is clearly unlikely to apply to Ireland at all, whilst Article 12 might possibly see the statutory allocation of an oversight/disciplinary function to an officer created under 2001 legislation, the Director of Corporate Enforcement.

Italy

Federico Pernazza/Valentina Allotti

Literature on the SE published in Italy: *Ambrosiani* Società europea e fusione internazionale, Le società, 2002, first part, 1351 and second part, 1499; *Ballarino* Sulla mobilità delle società nella Comunità europea. Da Daily Mail a Überseering: norme imperative, norme di conflitto e libertà comunitarie, Rivista delle società, 2003, 669; *Bianca* La società europea: considerazioni introduttive, Contratto e impresa – Europa, 2002, I, 479; *Carbone* La corporate governance della società europea nel reg. n. 2157/2001: tra norme materiali uniformi e tecniche di diritto internazionale privato, Diritto del commercio internazionale, 2002, 133; *Caterino* Il regolamento della società europea e la connessa direttiva sul coinvolgimento dei lavoratori, Giurisprudenza commerciale, 2002, I, 479; *Draetta-Pocar* (editors) La Società europea. Problemi di diritto societario comunitario, Giuffrè, Milano, 2002; *Enriques* Capitale, azioni e finanziamento della Società europea: quando meno è meglio, Rivista delle società, 2003, 375; *Fimmanò* Società europea: ultimo atto, Rivista delle società, 1994, 994; *Guaccero* La società europea a confronto con la società per azioni italiana a seguito dell'attuazione delle direttive CEE, Giustizia Civile, 1993, II, 237; *Malatesta* Prime osservazioni sul regolamento CE n. 2157/2001 sulla società europea, Rivista del diritto internazionale privato e processuale, 2002, 613; *Paciello* La società europea, Rivista di diritto dell'impresa, 2001, 317; *Pocar* Le statut de la société européenne: une étape importante dans l'évolution du droit communautaire, Rivista del diritto internazionale privato e processuale, 2002, 585; *Principe* (editor) Lo statuto legale di società europea, ESI, Napoli, 2002.

I. Introduction: Applicable law

The SE-Regulation regulates the European company (hereunder "SE") both directly by providing for substantive rules and indirectly by making reference to national laws on public limited-liability companies (Art. 9). However, the Regulation just provides for the general framework and refers to Member States' company law for several and fundamental aspects of the "Statute" for an SE. Thus, substantive rules on SEs derive from the co-ordination between European rules and national laws, as far as they are referred to by the Regulation.

In addition, the application of several provisions of the Regulation requires the previous implementation of the Directive on workers' involvement: e.g. the entry into force of the Regulation must be deferred so that each Member State may incorporate into its national law the provisions of the Directive, to ensure the concomitantly application of the two texts; an SE may not be registered unless an agreement for employees involvement has been concluded (Art. 12, para. 2).

It is therefore necessary to ascertain how the relevant national law completes the Regulation in order to determine the "Statute" of an SE. Three classes of national provisions of law are to be considered: (i) the provisions of law adopted by Member States relating specifically to an SE; (ii) the provisions of Member States' law which would apply to a public-limited liability company formed in accordance with that Member State's law; (iii) the provisions of Member States' law adopted in implementation of the Directive on workers' involvement.

1. The provisions of law adopted by Member States relating specifically to an SE

As to the first class of provisions, the Regulation provides that Member States shall make such provision as is appropriate to ensure the effective application of the Regulation (Art.s 9 and 68). Sometimes, the adoption of specific provisions is necessary for the applicability of the Regulation: e.g. Art. 12 para. 1 requires each Member State to designate by law a register where an SE shall be registered; Art. 64 para. 2 requires the adoption of the measures necessary to ensure that an SE which fails to regularise its position in case of infringement of the "real seat arrangement" is liquidated; Art. 68 para. 2 provides that each Member State shall designate the competent authority to issue a certificate attesting the completion of the acts and formalities required for the transfer of the registered office and the formation by merger.

Sometimes, the adoption of specific provisions on an SE is merely optional: that is the case when the Regulation allows Member States to choose different solutions from those provided for by its own rules, especially as far as the governance structure is concerned.

At present, Italy has not adopted any specific provision on an SE, nor have the issues raised by the Regulation been directly confronted under the new company law (legislative decree 17 January 2003, n. 6).[1] However, it is evident that the Regulation on the "Statute" for an SE has been taken into consideration while drawing the main lines of the new company law; this is especially evident with reference to the new rules on corporate governance. The new company law has introduced two new systems of governance for public limited-liability companies, the one-tier and the two-tier system, besides the traditional one, consisting of three organs: the general meeting of shareholders, the administrative

[1] The implementation of the directive on workers' involvement is provided for in the draft bill concerning implementation of European legislation in Italy, currently under discussion in the Parliament (www.parlamento.it, S2254).

organ and the body of auditors (collegio sindacale). Both the two new systems are largely inspired by the Regulation on the "Statute" of an SE, as explicitly affirmed in the Report to the draft law. Equally inspired by the Regulation on the SE is the new provision on the minimum legal capital required for a public limited-liability company; the new Art. 2327 c.c. requires that the subscribed capital shall not be less than EUR 120.000 as well as provided for in Art. 4 para. 2 of the Regulation.

2. The provisions of Member States' law which would apply to a public-limited liability company formed in accordance with that Member State's law

As to the second class of provisions, the Regulation refers to the provisions of Member States' laws which would apply to a public limited-liability company formed in accordance with the law of the Member State in which the SE has its registered office (Art. 9). Reference to national law aims at integrating the "Statute" of the SE on the basis of its being treated as if it were a public limited-liability company (Art. 10). Since national law concurs in determining the "Statute" of an SE, the uniformity of rules pursued by the European legislator is affected (recital 4 and 6). From this standpoint, differences in national laws can turn out into competition between legal systems.[2]

3. Provisions of law applicable for the companies involved in the formation of an SE

Reference to national law is often made to regulate acts realised by companies involved in the formation of an SE, i.e. the general rule set forth in Art. 18 for the formation of an SE by merger.

In this case, the Regulation determines conditions and ways of formation of an SE, including the criteria to determine the law applicable to different parts of the procedure for such a formation. The application of national law is therefore justified in that it concerns acts and operations realised by "national" com-

[2] On the issue of competition between legal systems and the company law reform in Italian literature see *Ballarino* Sulla mobilità delle società nella Comunità europea. Da Daily Mail a Überseering: norme imperative, norme di conflitto e libertà comunitarie, Rivista delle società 2003, 669; *Benedettelli* Mercato comunitario delle regole e riforma del diritto societario italiano, Rivista delle società 2003, 699; *Portale* Riforma delle società di capitali e limiti di effettività del diritto nazionale, Le società 2003, vol. 2 bis 261.

panies, formed in accordance with the law of the Member State referred to by the Regulation.

Problems of construction may arise where the Regulation neither deals with a specific issue nor it makes a general reference to national law, as it is the case with Art. 32 para. 6 on the needed majority required for the decisions of the general meeting of promoting companies to approve the formation of an SE holding. Provisions on the formation of an SE – mandatory for national companies willing to form an SE – pertain to the SE regulation as well as provisions on the governance structure to be applied by the SE itself. Based on this assumption, any gap in the Regulation should be filled, mutatis mutandis, accordingly to the general rule set forth in Art. 9.[3]

A different but strictly related question is to ascertain whether or not a specific issue is regulated by the Regulation.

4. Relevant Italian laws

With reference to Italian law, this refers to the new company law provided by legislative decree 17January 2003 n. 6 (referred to as d. lgs. 6/2003), which amended the civil code (codice civile, referred to as c.c.) and the special procedure law provided for disputes in the companies area by legislative decree 17 January 2003, n. 5 (referred to as d. lgs. 5/2003). Where an SE registered in Italy has securities traded in regulated markets reference should be made also to the provisions in the Consolidated Law on Financial Intermediation (legislative decree 24 February 1998, n. 58, referred to ad d. lgs. 58/1998). Legislative decree 6/2003 has been recently amended also in order to ensure a better coordination with the law applicable to listed companies. Finally, the Italian private international law on companies is equally applicable to an SE by means of the general cross-reference to national law (article 25 of the law 31 May 1995, n. 218, referred to as L. 218/1995).

Wide reference to national law is justified by the progress in the approximation of national company law, so that "on those points where the functioning of an SE does not need uniform Community rules reference may be made to the law governing public limited-liability companies in the Member State where it has its registered office" (recital 9). However, since the Regulation refers to national law also for aspects not covered by the Regulation itself, the scope of

[3] For a different opinion see *Teichmann* The European Company – A Challenge to Academics, Legislatures and Practitioners, 2003 German Law Journal, Vol. 4, No. 4 (available under www.germanlawjournal.com); *Oplustil* Selected problems concerning the formation of a holding SE, German Law Journal, 2003 Vol. 4, No. 2, 107 (www.germanlawjournal.com).

competition between legal systems increases. Reference to national law for aspects not covered by the Regulation engenders the recognition of the "equivalence" between national provisions even in the absence of any approximation of national laws.

II. The formation of an SE

1. General

An SE may be formed by means of a merger, by formation of a holding SE, by formation of a subsidiary SE or by conversion of an existing public limited-liability company into an SE.

The Regulation provides for general provisions to determine who is entitled to participate in the formation of an SE, to set forth the conditions for the registration and its effects and the publication of documents and particulars concerning an SE. It then provides for a general clause according to which "the formation of an SE shall be governed by the law applicable to public limited-liability companies in the Member State in which the SE establishes its registered offices" (Art. 15 of the Regulation).

The Regulation then provides for specific provisions on the different means for the formation of an SE; among these conditions, the formation by merger is the more complex since it turns out in a cross-border merger, governed for the first time in the Regulation.

a) Legal entities entitled to form an SE (Art. 2)

An SE may only be formed by public limited-liability companies, private limited-liability companies, companies and firms within the meaning of Art. 48 of the Treaty and other legal bodies governed by public or private law (Art. 2). An SE may thus be considered as a "second degree company", in the sense that it may be formed only by legal entities. The Regulation further distinguishes entities entitled according to the different means of formation: formation by merger and by conversion of an existing company is reserved to public limited-liability companies; formation of an SE holding is allowed to both public and private limited-liability companies; formation of an SE subsidiary is allowed to any legal entity considered in Art. 2.

In order to be able to form an SE the participating companies need to be subject to the law of different Member States. This "international" requirement, however, is to be ascertained according to the provisions of each Member State private international law; therefore, the risk of different evaluation according to the different legal system occurs: it may engender uncertainties as to the scope of application of the Regulation itself.

Art. 25 of Italian private international law (L. 218/1995) provides that the law of the country according to the law of which they have been formed governs companies. However, Italian law is to be applied also when the head office or the main activities of the company are located in Italy. Therefore, companies formed according to Italian law – whether they operate in Italy or not – and companies formed according to a foreign law that are "connected" to Italy pursuant to Art. 25 are subject to Italian law in the meaning of Art. 2 of the Regulation. Consequently, when two companies, both having their head office in Italy, even if one has been formed in a different country, form an SE the "international" requirement may lack.[4]

A similar problem arises in determining the scope of application of Italian law in the formation of an SE. In fact, when reference is made to national law to be applied to "national" companies participating in the formation of an SE, the national conflict of laws system is to be used to ascertain whether a company is subject to that law. In fact, Art. 18 provides that for matters not covered by the Regulation, "each company involved in the formation of an SE by merger shall be governed by the provisions of law of the Member States to which it is subject that apply to mergers of public limited-liability companies".

On the contrary, when reference to national law is made to determine the law applicable to an SE, the Regulation provides for a uniform element to ascertain the relevant national law, that is the place of the registered office (Art. 9 and 7).

b) Instrument of incorporation and statute

General provisions on the formation of an SE are scanty and leave wide room for national laws to fill the gaps. National laws play an important role especially with reference to the instrument of incorporation and its contents (art. 2328 c.c.) and the scrutiny over the legality of the formation for the registration.

According to Italian law, the statutes of an SE shall be an official document (notarial deed); it shall include, inter alia,[5] the following particulars: the mana-

[4] For a comment on Überseering decision and its effects on Italian private international law see *Carbone* La riforma societaria tra conflitto di leggi e principi di diritto comunitario, Diritto commercio internazionale, 2003, 89. See also case C-167/01, judgment of 30 September 2003, Kamer van Koophandel en Fabrieken voor Amsterdam and Inspire Art Ltd., and its possible effects on national private international law.

[5] Article 2328 c.c. implemented articles 2 and 3 of the Second Council Directive 77/91/ EEC of 13 December 1976 on coordination of safeguards for the protection of the interests of members and others.

gement system of the company,[6] the duration of the company; when the duration is unlimited, the exit right[7] for shareholders must be provided. According to art. 2328 c.c., para. 2, the statute providing for the internal arrangements and the management of the company is deemed to be part of the instrument of incorporation. It further specifies that in case of conflicts between provisions of the instrument of incorporation and those of the statute the latter are to prevail.

The new company law expressly provides for the possibility to include arbitration and mediation clauses in the statute. In particular, according to article 34 of legislative decree 5/2003, arbitrators may finally settle all disputes arising out or in connection with the company statute among shareholders or between the company and shareholders; however, the arbitration clause cannot be included in the statute of companies whose securities are widely distributed among the public.

The arbitration clause is binding on the company and the shareholders; the instrument of incorporation may provide that the arbitration clause is binding also on directors and members of the body of auditors: in this case, the clause shall be effective from the date of the acceptance of their mandate.

The general meeting shall approve any amendment to the instrument of incorporation in order to introduce, modify or delete an arbitration clause with a special qualified majority (2/3 of the equity capital). Dissenting or absent shareholders may withdraw within the following 90 days.

The legislative decree 5/2003 has also introduced mandatory provisions on arbitral proceedings, which differs partially from the general one set forth in the arbitration law 25/1994.

When the instrument of incorporation contains a mediation clause, the dispute cannot be litigated in court unless the mediation procedure has been previously engaged. The court, on request of one of the parties, may suspend the trial and fix a term (from 30 to 60 days) within which the mediation procedure must be engaged. The cause of suspension elapses after 6 months from the suspension decree.

[6] The company law reform provides for three different management systems: the one-tier, the two-tier and the so called "traditional" one. The management system chosen shall be included in the articles of associations; the default model is the traditional one (art. 2380 bis c.c.).

[7] New provisions on exit rights have been introduced by d. lgs. 6/2003 (articles 2437–2437 quinquies). According to those provisions, the shares are first offered to other shareholders, and only if not sold, to third parties; as a last resort, the company itself buys out those shares (artiche 2437 quater). For a first comment see *Sandulli – Santoro* (editors) La riforma delle società, Giappichelli, Torino 2003, 877–901).

c) Scrutiny on legality of the formation

Reference to national law is especially relevant as far as scrutiny on the legality of the formation of an SE is concerned. This aspect is not directly governed by the Regulation; it just provides for specific provisions on the formation by merger (Art.s 25 and 26).

An SE cannot be registered in Italy – and then shall not acquire legal personality – absent a scrutiny of the legality of the instrument of incorporation, carried out by a notary according to article 2330 c.c. Possible conflicts between the statute and the arrangements for employees involvement (Art. 12 para. 4) are to be object of such scrutiny, which should not be limited to the adoption of those arrangements, but also on their compatibility with the statute.

d) The SE as a different legal form

Is the SE a different legal form from public limited-liability companies formed in accordance with the laws of Member States? The question is relevant for the applicability of national measures for minority protection when the formation of an SE implies a conversion of the legal form of the promoting company and no special safeguards are provided for in the Regulation. As a general principle, it seems appropriate to grant a comparable protection to minority shareholders when dealing with the formation of a "national" company as well as with the formation of a European company.

Various provisions of the Regulation support this idea. First of all, Art. 2 para. 4 and 37, according to which an SE may be formed by conversion of an existing public limited-liability company.[8]

Moreover, Art. 3 provides that for the purpose of the formation of another SE, "an SE shall be regarded as a public limited-liability company governed by the law of the Member State in which it has its registered office" and Art. 10 provides that "subject to this Regulation, an SE shall be treated in every Member State as if it were a public limited-liability company formed in accordance with the law of the Member State in which it has its registered office". The idea underlying both provisions seems to be that an SE can be compared to a national public limited-liability company but is basically different in kind; that is the reason why a specific and express equivalence is to be provided.

[8] In Italy, articles 2498–2500 novies c.c. provide for the conversion of companies without winding up and creation of a new legal person.

2. Formation by merger (Art. 17 to 31)

The formation of an SE by merger is a cross-border merger. The Regulation introduces a common regulation for such merger and determines the law applicable to the participating companies and to the SE. By doing so, major problems arising in the context of a cross-border merger are superseded, although the proposed tenth directive on cross-border mergers has never been adopted (a new proposal was published on November 18, 2003, COM(2003) 703 final).

a) Procedure and minority protection

The rules on the formation by merger are largely inspired by the provisions set forth in the directive on domestic mergers (78/855/CEE of 9 October 1978). The formation of an SE by merger may be carried out by the procedure for merger by acquisition or the procedure for merger by formation of a new company. In the first case, the acquiring company shall take the form of an SE when the merger takes place. Although, according to Art. 10, an SE shall be treated in every Member State as if it were a public limited liability company, an SE may be considered a legal form different from a public limited-liability company subject to Italian law. In this case, taking the form of an SE implies a conversion of the Italian acquiring company. Italian law on conversion of companies is therefore applicable; in particular, article 2437 c.c. entitles an exit right to shareholders if they dissented or were absent in the general meeting deciding on the conversion.

The Regulation provides for only one procedure for merger irrespective of the kind of the merger. In the procedure two ideal phases can be distinguished. The first one concerns the acts and operation carried out by each participating company. Relevant national law, for those aspects not covered directly by the Regulation, governs this part (Art. 18). The provisions of law of the Member State where the SE locates its registered office govern the second phase, concerning the merger and the formation of an SE (Art. 15). Consistently, the scrutiny on the legality of merger is divided in to two part: as regards the part of the procedure concerning each merging company, the legality shall be scrutinised in accordance with the law on mergers of public limited-liability companies of the Member States to which the merging company is subject; as regards the part of the procedure concerning the completion of the merger and the formation of an SE, the legality of merger shall be scrutinised by the authority competent to scrutinise that aspect of the legality of mergers of public limited liability companies in the Member State of the proposed registered office of the SE.[9]

[9] New provisions on merger have been introduced by d.lgs. 6/2003 (articles 2501–2505

b) Documents annexed to the draft terms of merger

Apparently, the Regulation does not require the report by the management or administrative body on the draft term of mergers; however, the need of such report can be deemed by the provision of Art. 31, para. 2; in any case, the report is required by the directive on domestic mergers, which is made applicable by Art. 18.

Similarly, the Regulation does not explicitly provide for the publication of an accounting statement and other documents that shareholders are entitled to inspect before the general meeting; again, it is to be assumed the applicability of provisions on the publication of the aforesaid documents by virtue of the reference to the merger directive and, in case of an Italian merger company, of article 2501 quater c.c.

c) Decision on merger (Art. 23)

The general meeting of each of the merging companies shall approve the draft terms of mergers (Art. 25). Lacking any provision in the Regulation, the decision shall require the same majority required by the law of the Member State to which the merging company is subject. In case of an Italian merging company, the decision shall require the same majority provided for the amendment of articles of association (articles 2502 and 2365 c.c.). Where there is more than one class of shares, the decision concerning a merger shall be subject to a separate vote by at least each class of shareholders whose rights are affected by the transaction according to article 2376 c.c.

Article 2502 para. 2 c.c. enables the general meeting to modify the draft terms of merger provided that amendments do not affect the rights of shareholders or others. It is not clear whether such provision is compatible with the provisions of the Regulation requiring the merging companies to approve draft terms of merger in the same terms (Art. 26, para. 3).

d) Scrutiny on the legality of merger (Art. 25 to 26)

Art. 25 states that as regards the part of the procedure concerning each merging company the legality of merger is scrutinised by the competent authority of the Member State to which the merging company is subject, in accordance to the law on mergers of public limited liability companies. The competent authority shall issue a certificate conclusively attesting to the completion of the pre-merger acts and formalities.

quater); *Perrino* La riforma della disciplina delle fusioni di società, Rivista delle società 2003, 507.

Art. 26 provides that a court, notary or other authority competent in the Member State of the proposed registered office of the SE shall scrutinise the legality of the procedure concerning the completion of the merger and the formation of the SE; to that end, each merging company shall submit to the competent authority the certificate referred to in Art. 25 within six months of its issue together with a copy of the draft terms of merger approved by that company. The scrutiny should ensure that the merging companies have approved draft terms of merger in the same terms and that arrangements for employee involvement have been determined pursuant to directive 2001/86/EC. The competent authority shall also satisfy that the SE has been formed in accordance with the requirements of the law of the Member State in which it has its registered office in accordance with Art. 15.

For an SE with its registered office in Italy, therefore, the scrutiny should ensure that requirements for the formation of a public limited liability company, as set forth in the civil code, have been complied with.

Each Member State shall designate the competent authority within the meaning of Art.s 25 and 26. The Italian law on mergers provide that the legality of decisions on mergers shall be scrutinised by a notary and then registered in the Register of undertakings (artt. 2502 bis e 2436 c.c.). The terms of merger – which ends up in the instrument of incorporation in case of the procedure of merger by the formation of a new company – shall be published and registered in the Register of undertakings (art. 2504 c.c.).

e) Formation of an SE by merger with a subsidiary company (Art. 31)

Art. 31 provides for a simplified procedure for the formation of an SE in case of merger with a subsidiary company. Notwithstanding the special provision, the general meeting of each merging companies is to approve the draft terms of mergers.

Articles 2505 and 2505 bis c.c. provide for the procedure of merger by acquisition of a subsidiary company. According to these special provisions, the management or the administrative body can take the decision on merger, if it is provided by the statutes. The directive on domestic mergers expressly allows this possibility. It is not quite clear whether those provisions are applicable to an SE with its registered office in Italy or Art. 31 is to be considered mandatory; but, if we assume that the acquiring company is to be converted in an SE, a resolution by the general meeting with a qualified majority shall be requested (article 2500 sexies).

3. The formation of an SE holding (Art. 32 to 34)

The formation of an SE holding engenders the formation of a controlling company or parent company in the form of an SE, in which more than 50% of shares conferring permanent voting rights of the companies promoting the operation shall be conferred. Shareholders of the participating companies shall receive shares in the SE, as well as it happens in the formation of an SE by mergers.

Art. 32 provides that the management or administrative organs of the companies promoting the operation shall draw up, in the same terms, draft terms for the formation of the holding SE; the minimum content of the draft terms is set forth in the Regulation. The draft terms shall fix the minimum proportion of the shares in each of the companies promoting the operation, which the shareholders must contribute to the formation of the holding SE. In any case, that proportion shall be shares conferring more than 50% of the permanent voting rights, since only under this condition the SE shall control the promoting companies.

The general meeting of each company promoting the operation shall approve the draft terms of the formation of the holding SE. Art. 32 para. 6 does not provide for any majority requirements.[10] If this is a gap in the Regulation, it should be filled by national law.

Italian company law does not provide for a comparable procedure for the formation of a holding company; therefore, the question would be to determine whether the "ordinary" shareholder meeting[11] or the extraordinary shareholder meeting,[12] deciding with the qualified majority requested for the amendment of the articles of association[13] should be competent in this case. According to the general principle of Italian company law, the ordinary meeting is competent unless it is provided in a different way by the law. However, the formation of an SE holding by an Italian company renders the latter a "controlled company" in the meaning of articles 2497 quater c.c. on exit rights within group of companies. According to this article, when a company becomes part of a group (or is no longer part of a group) and it engenders an alteration of the conditions of the business carried out, shareholders are granted an exit right.

Moreover, Art. 34 of the Regulation provides that a Member State may adopt provisions designed to ensure protection for minority shareholders who

[10] For a discussion on the gap and how it could be filled, see *Teichmann* and *Oplustil* (see above note 3).

[11] Articles 2364 and 2364 bis c.c.

[12] Article 2365 c.c.

[13] Article 2365 c.c.

oppose the operation, creditors and employees: Italian legislator could therefore require a qualified majority when adopting measures to ensure the effective application of the Regulation.[14]

4. Formation of an SE subsidiary (Art. 35 to 36)

The formation of an SE subsidiary requires the subscription of its shares by the participating companies. The procedure is the same as the one provided for the formation of a company being subject only to the national law. Companies, firms and other legal entities participating in such an operation shall be subject to the provisions governing their participation in the formation of a subsidiary in the form of a public limited liability company under national law (Art. 36).

As to the Italian law, the provision on considerations in kind shall be applicable (artt. 2342–2345 c.c.).

5. Conversion of an existing public limited-liability company into an SE (Art. 37)

The Regulation allows domestic public limited-liability company to reorganise their business on a Community scale. According to Art. 37, para. 4, the management or administrative organ of the company in question shall draw up draft terms of conversion and a report explaining and justifying the legal and economic aspects of the conversion. The general meeting of the company in question shall approve the draft terms of conversion together with the statute of the SE.

In case of conversion of an Italian public limited-liability company majority required are those required for the amendment of the statute (artt. 2365, 2368 and 2369 c.c.).

Assuming that the conversion into an SE determines a change in the legal form of the company, provisions on the exit right should be applicable (art. 2437 c.c.). The applicability of rules provided for the conversion of an Italian company into another Italian company to the formation of an SE aims at granting an equal protection to minority shareholders in the two situations.

[14] Moreover, according to article 33 para. 2 the holding SE shall be formed only if the shareholders of the companies promoting the operation have assigned the minimum proportion of shares in each company in accordance with the draft terms of formation.

6. Formation of an SE and group of companies

The formation of an SE may end up in the formation or re-organization of group of companies. The Regulation, however, does not introduce any rules dealing with parent-subsidiary relationship, in that no specific Regulation was deemed necessary for an SE. The Regulation simply refers to the rules and general principles of private international law where an SE exercises control and where it is a controlled company (recital 17 of the Regulation).

The rules and Regulations of an SE therefore seem analogous under this profile to those that in reality are applicable to other companies of national law. In particular, "where one undertaking controls another governed by a different legal system, its ensuing rights and obligations as regards the protection of minority shareholders and third parties are governed by the law governing the controlled undertaking, without prejudice to the obligations imposed on the controlling undertaking by its own law, for example the requirement to prepare consolidated accounts" (recital n. 16 of the Regulation).

The Italian new company law provides for specific rules on group of companies. In particular, it regulates the liability of parent companies, introduces new transparency obligations and provides for special right of exit for subsidiary company's shareholders.[15]

III. Management systems of the European Company

1. Introduction

The Discussion of management systems for SE with their seat in Italy must recognise the fact that national legislation to implement the Community Regulation is still lacking, so that all the comments that follow are based on a mere comparison of the Community provisions with the rules for Italian public limited-liability companies (Società per Azioni – S.p.A.) in their new formulation following the reform of which in legislative decree 17 January 2003 n. 6 independently of any measures that may be introduced specifically for SE.[16]

The task is certainly facilitated by the recent reform, in which the system of organisation of the S.p.A. is one of the most topical and innovative aspects; the

[15] Articles 2497–2497 sexies c.c. For a first comment see Sandulli – Santoro (editors) La riforma delle società (see above note 7).

[16] Due to the uncertainty caused by the reform the Italian literature concerning the coordination of the SE-Regulation and the Italian company law is still limited. For the most recent contributions see references above.

monolithic structure of the S.p.A. as regulated in the code of 1942 has been abandoned and a notable degree of flexibility has been introduced[17].

From 2004, in fact, Italian S.p.A. will be able to choose between three organisational models: the traditional model, the two-tier model and the one-tier model. It is significant that the government report presenting the reform indicated the SE as one of the models taken as a reference by the legislator for both the national two-tier and the one-tier organisational systems[18]. It is therefore logical that, since two organisational systems of the national S.p.A. are modelled on the SE, coordination with national legislation should not be excessively difficult for SE with their seat in Italy.

However the question must be asked whether SE with their seat in Italy can also adopt the traditional management system, following its bringing approximately into line with one of the models provided for an SE.

In examining the coordination profiles of the two sources, the order followed will be that of the Regulation, starting from the rules common to the various

[17] The literature about the reform of the Italian company law is very wide; for a general perspective see *ex multis*: *Abbadessa* Il nuovo ruolo dell'assemblea nella società per azioni, in Associazione Disiano Preite (editor), Verso un nuovo diritto societario, Il Mulino, Bologna, 2002; *Ambrosini* (editor) La riforma delle società. Profili della nuova disciplina, Giappichelli, Torino, 2003; *Associazione Preite* Il nuovo diritto delle società, edited by Olivieri – Presti – Vella, Il Mulino, Bologna, 2003; *Assonime* Guida alla riforma delle società di capitali. Principali novità e regole di transizione, Roma, 2003 and http: //www1.assonime.it/assonime/pubblicazione/pub notestudi A.nsf/; *Benazzo – Patriarca – Presti* (editors) Il nuovo diritto societario fra società aperte e società private, Milano 2003; *Benedettelli* Mercato comunitario delle regole e riforma del diritto societario italiano, Rivista delle società, 2003, 699; *Buonocore* (editor) La riforma del diritto societario. Commento al d. lgs. nn. 5–6 del 17 gennaio 2003, Giappichelli, Torino, 2003; *Carbone* La riforma societaria tra conflitto di leggi e principi del diritto comunitario, Diritto del commercio internazionale 2003, 89; *D'Alessandro* Un nuovo ruolo per l'assemblea nella società per azioni, in Associazione Disiano Preite (editor), Verso un nuovo diritto societario, Il Mulino, Bologna, 2002; *Galgano* Il nuovo diritto societario, in Trattato di diritto commerciale e di diritto pubblico dell'economia, edited by Galgano, XXIX, Cedam, Padova, 2003; *Mosco* Dove si forma la volontà sociale? Il ruolo dell'assemblea nella s.p.a.: considerazioni generali, in Associazione Disiano Preite (editor), Verso un nuovo diritto societario, Bologna, 2002; *Perrino* La riforma della disciplina delle fusioni di società, Rivista delle società 2003, 507; *Portale* La riforma delle società di capitali e limiti di effettività del diritto nazionale, Le società 2003, 261; *Ragusa Maggiore* Trattato delle società. II. Le società di capitali. La società per azioni. Formazione della società per azioni, Cedam, Padova, 2003; *Sandulli – Santoro* (editors) La riforma delle società (see above note 7); *Santosuosso* La riforma del diritto societario – autonomia privata e norme imperative nei DD. Lgs. 17 gennaio 2003, nn. 5 e 6, Giuffrè, Milano, 2003.

[18] Relazione al decreto legislativo recante riforma organica della disciplina delle società di capitali e società cooperative, in attuazione della legge 3 ottobre 2001, n. 366, Rivista delle società, 2003, p. 112ff., § 6.

systems of administration and then examining the rules for the individual models separately.

2. The general meeting

a) Competence (Art. 52)

The general meeting of shareholders decides on the matters indicated in the Regulation, in the national law for application of Directive 2001/86/EC, and also on matters for which responsibility is given to the general meeting by law or by the statute under the national law of the Member State in which the SE has its seat.

For an SE with its seat in Italy, the competencies of the general meeting will presumably differ according to whether or not there is a supervisory organ. In addition to the competencies provided for in the Regulation (changes to the statute, election and recall of members of the administrative organ and of the supervisory organ[19]), Italian law on S.p.A. assigns the general meeting the competence to decide on company actions against members of the administrative organ or the supervisory organ for liability, and to approve the annual accounts, or, in the case of the two-tier system, only on distribution of the profits,[20] to appoint the members of the *collegio sindacale,*[21] auditors and liquidators and, in the case of companies with no supervisory board, to authorise decisions of the management board for which the statute so requires.[22]

b) Frequency, call and agenda (Art. 54, 55 and 56)

The minimum annual frequency (within six months of the end of the financial year[23]) is common to the Regulation and to Italian law.

[19] Art. 39, para. 2, allows the national law to either require or leave to the company statute any requirement for the election and recall of members of the management board to be decided by the general meeting. This faculty has not been provided for in Italy for the national S.p.A.

[20] In S.p.A., the statute may require that, in the event of failure to approve the annual accounts or on request by at least one third of the members of the management board or supervisory board, competence for approval of the annual accounts may be assigned to the general meeting (2409 terdecies c.c.).

[21] The *collegio sindacale* is the special supervisory board provided for in the traditional system: see *infra* paragraph. 3.d).

[22] On the general meeting in the reformed Italian S.p.A. *see* the articles mentioned in note 17 from *Abbadessa, D'Alessandro*, *Mosco* as well as *Lener* L'assemblea nella riforma del diritto societario, Rivista di diritto commerciale, 2002, 463.

[23] If reasons are given, the statute may require that the call can be within 180 days of the end of the financial year.

The Regulation assigns competence for calling the general meeting to all the company organs. In the case of S.p.A., however, the competence is restricted to the administrative board or management board, and only in case of default to the *collegio sindacale* (article 2406 c.c.) and the supervisory board (article 2409-quaterdecies c.c.) respectively. In view of the reference in Art. 54, para. 2, to national legislation, the latter will apply in full to SE with their seat in Italy.

On the right of shareholders to call a general meeting, the provisions of the Regulation and of Italian law are identical, whereas in the case of S.p.A. they do not have a right to add to the agenda of the general meeting; a special provision in either national law or statutes will therefore be required for SE concerning the procedures and the time limits applicable to such requests.

c) Quorum and majority (Art. 57 to 59)

The Regulation states that the decisions of a general meeting shall be taken by a majority of the votes validly cast, excluding votes attaching to shares in respect of which the shareholder has not taken part in the vote or has abstained or has returned a blank or spoilt ballot paper. The required majority can only be raised by national legislation and this seems to be the approach in the Italian law, which requires a quorum of 50% and an absolute majority, or higher if provided for in the statute, on first convocation. On second convocation a majority of the votes present is sufficient unless the statute requires a greater majority.

For changes to the statute, the Regulation requires a majority of two thirds of the votes cast or any higher percentage imposed by national legislation, but also allows national legislation to reduce the requisite majority to a simple majority, if at least half of the capital subscribed is represented in the general meeting.

The Italian law for the S.p.A is much more restrictive. The votes of at least half the share capital are required on first convocation, whereas on second convocation at least one third of the capital must be represented, with a vote in favour by two thirds of those present. The statutes may, however, require larger majorities.[24]

On that basis, it is reasonable to suppose that the more rigorous rules imposed on S.p.A. will apply to SE with their seat in Italy. Otherwise, the SE could be an attractive option for Italian companies that wanted to reduce required majorities.

[24] Lower majorities are envisaged for companies that make recourse to the capital market (that is, whose securities are widely held by the public or are quoted).

3. Administrative and supervisory organs

a) Rules common to the one-tier and two-tier systems

(1) Duration in office of administrative organs (Art. 46)

The Regulation leaves the duration in office of the organs to the statute, though imposing a maximum of six years. In S.p.A. the maximum duration in office for directors is three years in both the one-tier and traditional systems (articles 2383, para. 2, c.c. and 2409-noviesdecies, para. 1, c.c.) and also for members of the management board (article 2409-novies c.c.)[25] and is fixed at three years for the members of the *collegio sindacale* (article 2400, para. 1, c.c.),[26] for auditors (article 2409-quater, para. 2, c.c.), and for members of the supervisory board (article 2409 duodecies, para. 2, c.c.).[27] It is therefore to be hoped that in adoption of the SE, there will be a specific provision allowing the statute to permit a longer duration, as otherwise a conflict would arise between the Community rule, which seems to indicate that the statute should determine duration in office, and the more restrictive national legislation.

(2) Legal entity as director (Art. 47)

The possibility that a company or other legal entity may be a member of an organ is not envisaged for S.p.A. and, following the prevailing opinion concerning the law in force before the recent reform,[28] it was contrary to some provisions. Lacking specific contrary provisions in the new general company act, it is theorically possibile, althought not probable, that the law implementing the regulation include a specific provision allowing legal entities to be designated as directors

In Italy, legal entities can be members of organs in an European Economic Interest Grouping (EEIG).

[25] The appointment of members of the management board expires on the day of the meeting of the supervisory board called to approve the annual accounts for the last year of their term of office.

[26] More specifically, the *collegio sindacale* remains in office until the general meeting that approves the annual accounts for the third year of its term of office, but ceases from office only when the new *collegio sidacale* has been formed.

[27] Or until the first general meeting after the end of the three year term.

[28] See *ex multis Minervini* Gli amministratori di società per azioni, Milano, 1956, 90; *Fré* Società per azioni, in Commentario del codice civile a cura di Scialoja – Branca, Bologna 1982, 444; *Ferri* Le società, in Trattato di diritto civile fondato da Vassalli, Torino, 1989, 640; *contra Guerra* Può la carica di amministratore di società essere ricoperta da un'altra società?, Rivista delle società, 1956, 697.

(3) Right of appointment of a shareholders minority (Art. 47)

Following Art. 47, the Regulation shall not affect national law permitting a minority of shareholders or other persons or authorities to appoint some of the members of a company organ. The provision is relevant in Italy in two main cases: in relation to the right of a minority of shareholders to appoint at least a member of the *collegio sindacale* of the supervisory organ and of the *comitato per il controllo sulla gestione* in the listed companies[29] and with reference to the right of appointment of the State and of public entities.[30]

(4) Transactions authorised by the supervisory board or remitted to an express decision of the administrative organ (Art. 48)

The Regulation leaves it to the statutes to specify the transactions that must be authorised by the supervisory board, allowing Member States to provide that, under the two-tier system, the supervisory board may itself make certain categories of transactions subject to authorisation. Member States may also indicate the categories of operations that must appear in the statutes of SE registered within their territory.

There is no binding provision in the two-tier system of management for Italian S.p.A. for an authorisation role of the supervisory organ; the statutes may provide that the supervisory organ votes on strategic, industrial and financial plans set by the management organ but this approval does not affect the responsibility of the managers. Therefore it seems likely that a provision of such content will be introduced for SE registered in Italy, since a different measure would be discriminatory.[31]

On the contrary, the national law provides for limits in the delegation applicable to the management organ in the two-tier system and to the administrative organ in the monistic and traditional systems.[32] The provision should be applied to the SE adopting the monistic system, following Art. 48, para. 2.

[29] See article 148 of the legislative decree 24 february 1998, n. 58. Generally, the right of appointment of the minority of shareholders may be provided for by statute.

[30] See articles 2449 and 2450 c.c. as reformed by legislative decree 17 february 2003, n. 6.

[31] In Italian literature it is discussed whether such an authorisation role could be assigned to the general meeting of shareholders, as it is expressely provided for the one-tier system: see *Rectio* L'assemblea nel progetto di riforma delle società di capitali, Consiglio Notarile Milano (November 2002–March 2003), Riunioni di studio sulla riforma delle società, www.notarlex.it.

[32] In relation to the traditional system see article 2381, para. 4, c.c., to which articles 2409-novies c.c. (two-tier system) and 2409-noviedecies c.c. (monistic system) make reference: delegation is excluded for the competences concerning annual accounts, modifications of the capital, mergers and divisions: see *Cagnasso* Brevi note in tema di delega di potere gestorio nelle società di capitali, Le società, 2003, 801 ff.

(5) Obligation to confidentiality (Art. 49)

The obligation of members of the company's organs to confidentiality is not explicitly spelled out for S.p.A. but is assumed to be one of the rules of conduct they are obliged to comply with, violation of which would involve liability for any damage to the company.

(6) Quorums (Art. 50)

The Regulation provides that, in general, a quorum shall be at least half of the members, while decisions can be taken by a majority of the members present. However, the Regulation itself provides for specific derogations and also allows others to be introduced in the statute.

The rules correspond to those in Italy for both the administrative board (article 2388) and the *collegio sindacale* (article 2404 c.c.) in the traditional model and for the administrative board in the one-tier model (article 2409-noviesdecies c.c.), as well as for the management board (article 2409-undecies c.c.) and the supervisory board (article 2409-quaterdecies c.c.) in the two-tier-system.

Derogations to the quorum regulations may increase, but not lower it. Derogations to a decision-taking majority regulations may raise or lower it.

(7) Liability (Art. 51)

The rule regarding the liability of members of management, supervisory and administrative organs does not pose any problems of implementation with the national regulations on S.p.A. since it refers totally to the latter.

b) Two-tier system

(1) The management organ (Art. 39)

The Regulation assigns responsibility for management of the SE to the management organ. The competence of the management board of Italian S.p.A. is apparently limited to "management of the enterprise" (article 2409-novies c.c.), i.e. to the activities included in the object of the company, but they have to carry out all the activities concerning the functioning of the company (i.e. call the general meeting; etc.) thus in reality attaining identity with the SE model.

The Regulation allows national legislation to assign responsibility for current management to one or more managing directors, as in national regulations. Italian law allows the board to delegate functions other than operations on the company's capital, issue of bonds, preparation of the annual accounts and preparation of merger and division projects. The board has in any case power to arrogate every decision to itself, and to impart directives; it evaluates organisation of the administration and the company's accounting, its strategic planning and the general course of operations.

Members of the management organ of an SE are appointed by the supervisory board, unless national legislation requires or allows them to be appointed by the general meeting under the same conditions as for public limited-liability companies that have registered offices within its territory (Art. 39 para. 2). Italian law on S.p.A. adopting the two-tier system does not allow members of the management board to be appointed by the general meeting. However, it may be questioned if the option could be provided specifically for SE, considering the similarity between the system that would thus be created for SE and the traditional system for administration of S.p.A., where both the management organ and controlling organ are designated by the general meeting (see below para. II.4).

The prohibition on membership of both management organ and supervisory organ is exactly the same as for S.p.A. (Art. 39 para. 3). However, in S.p.A. it is not possible for a member of the supervisory board to temporarily replace a member of the management board; and a specific provision for SE will therefore be introduced in order to specify a restrictive time limit.

The number of members of the SE's management board is left to the statute, unless there is a different provision in national law. In Italy it can be presumed that the minimum number of two for directors of an S.p.A. (article 2409-novies c.c.) will also be applied to SE.

(2) The supervisory organ (Art. 40)

The Regulation restricts itself to assigning the supervisory organ a supervisory role, though it allows the statute to specify categories of actions that require prior authorisation from it. In S.p.A., on the other hand, the functions of the supervisory board are predetermined,[33] and there is no possibility for the stat-

[33] In particular, in S.p.A. the supervisory board appoints and recalls the members of the management board, approves the annual accounts, monitors compliance with the law, the statute and principles of good administration. It also monitors the adequacy of the organisational, administrative and accounting structure and its functioning, and company actions for liability against management board members; it reports to the general meeting on the monitoring activities performed.

ute to subject management operations to prior authorisation by the supervisory organ; the statute may, however, provide that the supervisory organ votes on strategic, industrial and financial plans set by the management organ but this approval does not affect the responsibility of the managers (art. 2409-terdecies, para. 1, f-bis).

Coordinating the two approaches, the statute of an SE with its seat in Italy could indicate operations subject to prior authorisation by the supervisory board in addition to the functions proper to that board. However, it seems improbable that Italy will exercise the options of Art. 48, para. 1 and para. 2 of the Regulation, beyond the limits provided for by art. 2409-terdecies, par. 1, f-bis, since a management function for the supervisory board, even in the form of prior authorisation, is ruled out for S.p.A.

Members of the supervisory board are appointed by the general meeting, in S.p.A., as in SE, but clauses of the statute recognising to the minority shareholders a right of appointment are not forbidden; following Art. 47, para. 4, the same principle may be applied to the SE having seat in Italy. In S.p.A. there is no provision for employees having a right to appoint one or more members of the board and it must be presumed that Italy in implementing Directive 2001/86/EC will not adopt that form of employee involvement.[34]

The regulation leaves the number of members of the supervisory organ to the statute or national law. Italian law provides for a minimum of three members for the supervisory board (article 2409-duodecies c.c.), as, in general, for all the organs having relevant role of control.[35]

(3) Information and verification (Art. 41)

The obligation of the management board to supply information and the supervisory powers of the supervisory board of which in Art. 41 SE-Regulation are directly applicable to SE. It should be noted that in S.p.A. the members of the supervisory board may attend meetings of the management board and in that way obtain direct knowledge of the activities of the management organ (article 2409-terdecies, para. 4, c.c.).

With regard to the option for the national legislator to enable each member of the supervisory board to require individually the management board to pro-

[34] As an exception, the minority shareholders in the listed companies have the right to appoint at least one member of the *collegio sindacale*; admitting the SEs with seat in Italy to choose the traditional system, the provisions applies.

[35] The *collegio sindacale* in the monistic system is composed by three or five members (article 2397 c.c.); the control committee (*comitato per il controllo sulla gestione*) internal to the administrative organ in the national monistic system is composed by at least three members in the companies that have recourse to the capital market.

vide information (Art. 41 para. 3), it should be mentioned that Italian law allows each member of the board of an S.p.A. to make individual inspections. Therefore, it is highly probable that the above-said authorisation will be exercised for the SE with seat in Italy.

c) *The one-tier system*

The one-tier system delineated in Art. 43 to 45 of the Regulation provides for a minimum organisational structure comprising general meeting and administrative organ. There is no provision for any control instrument within the company, apart from the accounting controls which must in any case be organised to comply with the eighth Directive.

The Italian law on S.p.A. does not go so far, providing for some form of internal control in every organisational model: the *collegio sindacale* in the traditional model, the supervisory board in the two-tier model, the internal controls committee *(comitato per il controllo sulla gestione)* in the administrative board of the one-tier model.

Following article 2380 c.c., if the statute of the S.p.A. does not provide otherwise, the traditional system is applicable. Therefore, when the statute provides for a single administrative organ without making reference to the so-called monistic system, *ex lege* a *collegio sindacale* must be appointed and its role is that one regulated by the code. Nevertheless, the statute may adopt the monistic system that implies some provisions concerning a controlling committee internal to the administrative organ called "*comitato per il controllo sulla gestione*". It may be questioned if this forced option is coherent with the SE-Regulation, where the monistic system does not provide specifically for any control entity, and if the SE located in Italy may adopt the "pure" European one-tier model. In the light of Art. 9, para. 1, c) ii, both the solutions are possible, because the Regulation does not provide for organs charged of mere legality control as the *collegio sindacale* nor regulates the internal committees of the administrative organ. Therefore, the Italian provisions for S.p.A. are applicable and it is up to the statute to adopt the traditional or the monistic model.[36] In the one-tier system for S.p.A., management is entrusted to the administrative board which, if the statute or general meeting so permits, may delegate part of its competencies to an executive committee or to one or more of its own members. In such a case, the other members of the administrative board are not liable for the actions of their delegates unless they are aware of the facts that have given rise to the liability and have not done all in their power to prevent the occurrence of

[37] Following art. 2381 the administrators have to ask complete information to the delegates before assuming any relevant decision but they have not power of inspection.

damage to the company.[37] Art. 43 para. 1 of the Regulation can be implemented in these terms.

The minimum number of directors in the one-tier S.p.A. is not stated explicitly, but is conditioned by the need for a management control committee within the board. Since there is no provision for this committee in SE, in the absence of specific indications in national legislation, the SE could even have a sole director, as is indeed permitted by the Regulation other than in the hypotheses of which in Art. 43 para. 2. There is no maximum number of directors for an S.p.A. and it is unlikely that such a provision would be introduced specifically for SE.

The few other rules in the Regulation relating to the administrative organ do not require national measures for their implementation. It need only be said that it is foreign to the Italian legal tradition for employee representatives to take part directly in a company's management organs and it is therefore improbable that such a form of involvement will be introduced for SE.

d) The traditional system

Until the reform in 2003, S.p.A. were organised on a model in which a single administrative organ was flanked by a *collegio sindacale*, a body entrusted with checking compliance with the law and statute and, in the case of unlisted companies, auditing the accounting system and the annual accounts.

Following the reform, S.p.A. can choose between the traditional organisational model, the two-tier model and the single-tier model. Does the same option exist for SE having their seat in Italy?

The question relates to the flexibility of the organisational structure of the SE in the light of Art. 9 and 39 of the Regulation. In Art. 9, the statutes as a source of regulation of the SE are pertinent for matters to which there is an explicit reference in the Regulation (letter b) and, together with the national provisions, for matters not regulated by the Regulation or only partly regulated by it.

As regards organisational structure, and in particular for the one-tier system, the Regulation does not leave it to the statute to create further organs. Their introduction can therefore be hypothesised only if one takes the view that organisational structure is among the matters only partly regulated by the Regulation. This interpretation can be accepted with reference to the competences, powers and responsibilities of organs, but not to their specification, if the introduction of additional organs would result in an unacceptable compression of the role of those delineated in the Regulation.

[37] Following art. 2381 the administrators have to ask complete information to the delegates before assuming any relevant decision but they have not power of inspection.

Neverthless, the addition of a *collegio sindacale* to the organisational structure of an SE that adopts the one-tier system would not affect the role of the administrative organ: the *collegio sindacale* is charged of the control of mere legality and has powers of inspection and information to the shareholders.

For an SE that adopts the two-tier system, on the other hand, the question arises whether the supervisory organ can in practice be regulated in the same way as a *collegio sindacale.*

Certainly, the supervisory board can be elected directly by the general meeting (Art. 39 para. 2) like the *collegio sindacale* in the S.p.A. (article 2400 c.c.). There is also consistency in the rules on incompatibility, on the number of members, and on powers of information and vigilance. However, there is a conflict in terms of functions. The supervisory board of an SE authorises the operations specified in the statute under Art. 48, whereas an action of such importance in the company's management is not permitted to the *collegio sindacale* of an S.p.A. Since Art. 48 of the Regulation assigns listing of the operations that require prior authorisation from the supervisory organ to the statute, national law cannot prevent such a function being assigned to it, but only lay down its minimum contents (Art. 48 para. 2). However, since this competence is not envisaged in a compulsory manner for the supervisory organs of S.p.A, it is reasonable to suppose that the Italian law implementing the Regulation will make no binding provision for it. In that case, the statutes might even list no requirement for prior authorisation[38] thus bringing the role of the supervisory board of an SE substantially into line with that of the *collegio sindacale* in a S.p.A.

IV. Transfer of the registered office

The registered office of an SE shall be located within the Community in the same Member State as its head office (Art. 7). Thus, the Regulation adopts the so called "real seat" arrangement.

1. The "real seat" arrangement and its effects (Art. 7)

Choosing the real seat arrangement as the relevant element to determine the law applicable to an SE in the case of matters not regulated by the Regulation should ensure the application of the law of the Member States more strictly

[38] The obligation to list the categories of transactions requiring authorisation by the supervisory organ is formulated in a way to seem substantially be remitted to the shareholders, within the limits allowed by the national law.

connected with the SE from an economic viewpoint. The Regulation, however, does not provide for any definition of "head office" and seems to ignore that tasks usually pertinent to the head office of a company may likely be carried out in different Member States, as it can happen within multinational groups of companies.

According to Italian law, the place where the main administrative activities are carried out should be considered as the head office of a company. At this end, relevance should be given not only to the place where the general meeting and administrative bodies meet, but also to the place where the organisational and management structure of the company are located, provided that different company establishments and third parties refer to it as the head office. In any case, a co-ordination between the notion of head office and fiscal residence of a company seems appropriate especially in case of transfer of the seat.

2. Secondary establishment of an SE

The Regulation does not determine the law applicable to the secondary establishment of an SE located in a Member State different from the head office. According to Art. 10, the SE shall be treated by the Member State in which its branch is located as if it were a public limited-liability company formed in accordance with the law of the Member State in which it has its registered office. With reference to Italian law, provisions on the branch of "foreign" company are to be applied.[39]

An SE formed according to the law of another Member State which has a secondary establishment in Italy shall be subject, for each branch, to Italian law on the publication of the documents and particulars concerning the company pursuant to article 2506 c.c.

3. Infringement of the "real seat" arrangement (Art. 64)

The registered office of an SE must be located in the same Member State as its head office from its formation and for the life of the company. When an SE no longer complies with the requirement laid down in Art. 7, the Member State in which the SE's registered office is situated shall take appropriate measures to oblige the SE to regularise its position within a specified period (Art. 64).

[39] Articles 2507–2510 c.c. For a first comment, *A. Berlinguer* Commento agli artt. 2507–2510 in Sandulli – Santoro (editors) La riforma delle società (see above note 7).

Breach of the real seat arrangements turns out to be a cause for the winding up of the company in addition to those provided by the italian law on public limited-liability companies (see article 2448 c.c)

The Regulation does not determine the authority competent to ascertain the said infringement and to adopt the appropriate measures to oblige the SE to regularise its position; each Member State shall thus designate the competent authority. In any case, the Regulation requires from the Member State in which the SE's registered office is situated to provide for a judicial remedy with regard to any established infringement. That remedy shall have a suspensory effect on the procedures laid down to regularise its position.

In case of breach of Art. 7 and pending the procedure to regularise the infringement pursuant to Art. 64, it is not clear which "office" may be relied on against thirds parties: whether the registered office or the head office. The Regulation only deals with the issue of reliance of thirds parties while ruling on the transfer of the seat, providing that "on publication of an SE's new registration, the new registered office may be relied on against third parties" (Art. 8, para. 13).

At this regard, the relevant Italian law provides that when registered office and head office of a company are located in different places, third partied may rely also on the latter (art. 46 cc.).

The registered office of an SE may be transferred to another Member State; such transfer shall not result in the winding up of the SE or in the creation of a new legal person (Art. 8, para. 1). Art. 25, para. 3 of the Italian private international law allows the transfer abroad of the registered office, provided that the operation is carried out pursuant to the requirements provided for by the law of the countries concerned. The transfer of the registered office of an SE does not create any problem since the legal personality is acquired directly by virtue of the Regulation and it is recognised and enforceable in any Member State (Art. 1, para. 3 and Art. 16).

4. Procedure for the transfer of the registered office (Art. 8)

The procedure for the transfer of the registered office is articulated into four parts: (i) the drawing up of the transfer proposal; (ii) the publication of the transfer proposal; (iii) the decision on the transfer of the registered office by the general meeting; (iv) the certification attesting the completion of the acts and formalities of the procedure.

The management or administrative organ shall draw up a transfer proposal; its minimum content is defined by the Regulation itself. The management or administrative organ shall also draw up a report explaining and justifying the legal and economic aspects of the transfer and explaining the implications of the transfer for shareholders, creditors and employees (Art. 8, para. 3). The transfer proposal shall be published according to the law of the Member State where the SE registered office is located (Art. 13). Anyway, an SE shareholders and creditors are entitled to examine at the SE's registered office the transfer proposal.

The transfer of the registered office shall require a decision by the general meeting taken by a majority which may not be less than two thirds of the votes cast, unless the law applicable to public limited-liability companies in the Member State in which an SE's registered office is situated requires or permits a larger majority (Art. 59).

5. Scrutiny on the procedure for the transfer of the registered office (Art. 8 para. 8)

A court, a notary or other competent authority in the Member State in which the SE has its registered office shall carry out the scrutiny on the procedure for the transfer of the registered office. The competent authority shall issue a certificate attesting to the completion of the acts and formalities to be accomplished before the transfer (Art. 8, para. 8). The new registration may not be effected until the certificate issued by the competent authority has been submitted. The registration is subject to the formalities required for registration in the country of the new registered office.

Thus, two different kind of scrutiny can be distinguished: the scrutiny on the procedure for the transfer, carried out by the competent authority of the members state where the SE is registered (by the notary, if the SE transfers the registered office from Italy) and the scrutiny on the completion of the formalities required for registration in the country of the new registered office carried out by the competent organ (by the Register of undertakings, if the SE transfers the registered office to Italy).

6. Transfer of the registered office and law applicable to an SE

Since the registered office is the relevant element to determine the law applicable to the SE for all those aspects not governed by the Regulation, the transfer of the registered office from a Member State to another should entail the change of the law applicable to an SE. As a consequence, only the organisational aspects directly ruled by the Regulation itself or by the statute will not be affected by the said change; however, since the European legislator mainly referred to national laws to govern these aspects, the impact of the transfer of the registered office on the structure of the SE will ultimately be determined according to the legislation of the Member State of destination.

V. Involvement of employees in the SE

The considerations obtained from the numerous references to the Directive, set forth in the Regulation, are that: (i) the regulation of the SE must be completed by the Directive as far as the involvement of the employees is concerned, otherwise the SE could not be registered (Art. 12 para. 2 of the Regulation); (ii) would not acquire legal personality (Art. 16 para. 1 of the Regulation), its registered office could not be transferred under the provisions of the Regulation (Art. 8 para. 2, lit. c; (iii) the statutes of the SE must not conflict with the arrangements for employees involvement; should such a conflict arise, the statute is to be amended (Art. 12 para. 4 of the Regulation); (iv) the Authority competent to scrutinise the legality of the merger shall ensure that arrangements for employee involvement have been determined pursuant to the Directive (Art. 26 para. 3 of the Regulation): at this regard, it is doubtful whether the authority simply has to ensure the provisions of rules on the issue or the conformity of such rules to the standards provided for in the Directive (pursuant to Art. 7 and Annex to the Directive).

According to the Directive, the employee involvement may be fulfilled either actively, through their participation in the decision-making process, or passively, through information and consultation mechanisms (Art. 2 para. 1 lit. h of the Directive).

As for the passive involvement, information and consultation may be achieved by the establishment of a representative body or alternatively by defining information and consultation procedures, according to an agreement reached by the parties – that is the undertaking and its employees (Art. 4, para. 2, lit. f of the Directive); in any case, information and consultation mechanisms should allow the representative body (or the employees) to acknowledge and evaluate all the issues concerning the SE and to express opinions which may be taken into account in the decision-making process within the SE.

As for the active involvement, participation means the influence of the body representative of the employees and/or the employees' representatives in the affairs of the company by way of, i) the right to elect or appoint some of the members of the company's supervisory or administrative organ; or ii) the right to recommend and/or oppose the appointment of some or all of the members of the company's supervisory or administrative organ (Art. 2 para. 1 lit. k of the Directive).

The goal reached by the Directive is that: (i) information and consultation procedures should be ensured in all cases of creation of an SE, by means of an agreement entered into by the parties, according to Art. 4, or of the implementation by the Member States of the Standard Rules, pursuant to Art. 7 and the Annex; (ii) participation rights should be ensured – by means of an agreement or by applying the Standard Rules – if and when such participation existed within the participating companies before the formation of an SE (recital no. 11).

The concrete procedures of employee information and consultation as well as participation should be defined primarily by means of an agreement between the parties concerned or, in the absence thereof, through the application of Standard Rules (recital no. 8).

It is worth stressing that in any case Member States shall provide rules (the Standard Rules) for the information and consultation procedures as well as for the participation according to the standards set forth in the Directive. However, the application of the rules on participation is mandatory only when and if participation procedures existed within the participating companies before the registration of an SE (see para. 3, part III, of the Annex stating that "if none of the participating companies was governed by participation rules before registration of the SE, the latter shall not be required to establish provisions for employee participation").

Moreover, Member States have the option of not applying rules relating to participation in the case of formation of an SE through a merger (Art. 7 para. 3 of the Directive).

Standard Rules must satisfy the provisions set out in the Annex, and thus: (i) the representative body shall have the right to be informed and consulted at least once a year on the progress of the business of the SE and its prospects (that is, on structure, economic and financial situations, the probable development of the business and of production and sales, the situation and likely trend of employment, investments, and substantial changes concerning organisation, introduction of new working methods or production processes, transfers of production, mergers, cut-backs or closures of undertakings, establishments or important parts thereof, and collective redundancies); (ii) where there are exceptional circumstances affecting the employee's interests to a considerable extent (relocation, transfers, the closure of establishments or undertakings or collective redundancies), the representative body shall have the right to be informed and to meet at its request the competent organ of the SE to be informed and consulted; (iii) where the competent organ decides not to act in accordance with the opinion expressed by the representative body, this body shall have the right to a further meeting with the competent organ of the SE.

Although the meetings referred to above shall not affect the prerogatives of the competent organ (lit. c, part II, Annex of the Directive), the impact of information and consultation procedures on the decisional process of an SE is significant in terms of time and when relating to the mediation of conflicting interests.

The Directive proposes a model for employee involvement, specific for an SE, taking into consideration its international nature. Therefore, the risk that such a model becomes the pattern to which other draft Directives will refer must be avoided (such as the V, on the limited-liability company, the X, on cross-borders mergers, and the XIV, on the cross-border transfer of the registered office). The employee involvement suggested for an SE, even if burdensome, is optional (in that it is applicable only if and when an SE is formed). It is therefore advisable not to adopt such a model for the general company law applicable to Member States' companies, without further exams and discussions about its suitability.

Italian law already provides for information and consultation procedures, deriving from European laws (Cfr. Directive n. 94/45/CE on the establishment of a European Works Council or a procedure in Community-scale undertakings and Community-scale groups of undertakings for the purposes of informing and consulting employees), from national laws (L. 29 December 1990, n. 428, art. 47 on the transfer of undertakings and L. 23 July 1991, n. 223 on collective redundancies) and from collective agreement practices.

Art. 13 para. 1 of the Directive deals with the issue of the links between the Directive and other provisions providing that: where an SE is a Community-scale undertaking, the provisions of the Directive 94/45/EC shall not apply; where the special negotiating body decides in accordance with Art. 3 para. 6 not to open negotiations or to terminate negotiations already opened, Directive 94/45/EC shall apply.

Moreover, the Directive provides that provisions on the participation of employees in companies' bodies provided for by national legislation and/or practices other than those implementing this Directive shall not apply to an SE (Art. 13 para. 2 of the Directive).

Finally, Art. 13 para. 3 of the Directive states that the Directive shall not prejudice the existing rights to involvement of employees provided for by national legislation and/or practice in the Member States other than participation in the bodies of an SE (i.e. the rules on the transfer of undertakings and on collective redundancies, as well as the collective bargaining practices). With reference to this regulation it seems that the standard rules adopted pursuant to the Directive shall not provide for a level of employee involvement less than the one already existing.

The Netherlands

Michiel Huizinga/Martha Meinema

Literature on the SE published in the Netherlands since 1 January 2001: *Bellingwout* Verplaatsing van een Europese vennootschap (SE), Ondernemingsrecht 2001, p. 356–361; *Buijs* De Europese vennootschap, een Brussels virus voor het nationale medezeggenschapsrecht, Ondernemingsrecht 2001, 181–182; *De Kluiver* De Verordening op de Europese Vennootschap (SE): haarlemmer olie of levertraan?, WPNR 2002, 245–246; *Dortmond* De Europese vennootschap en juridische fusie, Ondernemingsrecht 2001, p. 190–193; *Gepken-Jager* „The New European Company: opportunity in diversity", Ondernemingsrecht 2003, 336–341; *Huiskes* De Europese NV deel 2: Grensoverschrijdend ondernemen als Europese Vennootschap, Juridisch up to date 2002, 14–19; *Kiersch/Ter Huurne* Het Statuut van de Europese vennootschap, Ondernemingsrecht 2001, 183–190; *Klomp/De Jong* De Societas Europea, een gerealiseerde droom of een onwerkbaar compromis?, Ondernemingsrecht 2002, 106–107; *Ministerie van Justitie* Ambtelijk Voorontwerp Uitvoeringswet Verordening Europese vennootschap met Memorie van Toelichting, April 2003; *Sociaal-Economische Raad* Advies Nr. 03/08: De rol van de werknemers in de Europese Vennootschap, 20 juni 2003; *Ter Huurne* Voorontwerp Uitvoeringswet Verordening Europese Vennootschap, Ondernemingsrecht 2003, 222–223; *Timmerman* De medezeggenschap van de Europese vennootschap; een eerste verkenning vanuit Nederlands gezichtspunt, Ondernemingsrecht 2001, p. 199–201; *Timmerman* Schijnmedezeggenschap, Ondernemingsrecht 2003, 243; *Van Olffen* De Europese NV; kapitaal- en aandelenstructuur, Ondernemingsrecht 2001, p. 194–195; *Wiggers* Hij is er (bijna): de Europese Vennootschap!, V&O 2001, 194–197; *Winter* De Europese Vennootschap als sluis voor in- en uitvoer van vennootschapsrecht, Nederlands Juristenblad 2002, p. 2034–2040; *Winter* De Europese Vennootschap: besturen in rangen en standen, Ondernemingsrecht 2001, p. 195–199.

I. General

On 21 November 2003, the Dutch Government introduced a legislative proposal into Parliament for the implementation of the SE-Regulation (the Implementation Act concerning the SE-Regulation, referred to as "IAR").[1] The provisions of the IAR are largely identical to draft implementation clauses pre-

[1] Voorstel van wet tot uitvoering van verordening (EG) Nr. 2157/2001 van de Raad van de Europese Unie van 8 oktober 2001 betreffende het statuut van de Europese vennootschap (SE) (Uitvoeringswet verordening Europese vennootschap), Tweede Kamer, vergaderjaar 2003–2004, 29 309, nrs. 1–2, 3, 4.

pared by the Ministry of Justice, which were published in April 2003,[2] accompanied by explanatory notes concerning the implementation of the SE-Regulation in general and the Ministry's draft clauses in particular (the "Notes").[3] Below, we discuss the implementation of the SE-Regulation in the Netherlands in accordance with the IAR in the light of the Ministry of Justice's Notes. The final Act may, however, differ from the IAR, since amendments may be made during the legislative procedure.

The general Dutch company law rules concerning public limited-liability companies ("NVs") have a gap-filling function on the basis of Art. 9 (1) lit. c (ii) SE-Regulation. These rules are laid down in Book 2 of the Dutch Civil Code (*BW*). References to these provisions are cited as "Art. 2: 12 BW", meaning Article 12 of Book 2 Dutch Civil Code.

II. Formation

1. General

Title II of the SE-Regulation, entitled "Formation", contains provisions on the formation of an SE by way of merger, creation of a holding, transformation and formation of a subsidiary. In view of Art. 15 (1) SE-Regulation, the law applicable to public limited-liability companies in the Member State in which the SE establishes its registered office has a gap-filling function in respect of formation matters not (fully) covered in the Regulation. First, we will discuss some issues which are relevant for all manners of formation. After that, the various forms of formation will be examined in more detail.

a) Statement of no objection

According to Article 2: 64 (2) BW, the formation of an NV requires a statement of no objection from the Minister of Justice. The statement may only be refused if, in view of the aims or references of the person(s) who will solely or jointly

[2] Ambtelijk Voorontwerp van een Wet houdende uitvoering van verordening (EG) Nr. 2157/2001 van de Raad van de Europese Unie van 8 oktober 2001 betreffende het statuut van de Europese vennootschap (SE) (Uitvoeringswet verordening Europese vennootschap), downloadable at http://www.justitie.nl/themas/wetgeving/wetgeving_in_voorbereiding/privaatrecht/index.asp.

[3] Memorie van Toelichting bij het Ambtelijk Voorontwerp Uitvoeringswet verordening Europese vennootschap, downloadable at http://www.justitie.nl/themas/wetgeving/wetgeving_in_voorbereiding/privaatrecht/index.asp.

determine the company's policy, there is a risk that the company shall be used for illegal purposes or that its activities will prejudice creditors (Art. 2: 68 (2) BW). A statement of no objection is also required in connection with a merger (Art. 2: 332 BW) and the transformation of an NV into a private limited liability company (Art. 2: 183 (1) in connection with 2: 125 (1) BW). We assume that, in view of Article 15 (1) Regulation, this requirement will be applicable to all forms of formation of an SE.[4]

b) *Registration and publication*

The registration of SEs in the Netherlands takes place at the commercial register (*handelsregister*) as referred to in Art. 2 Commercial Register Act 1996 (*Hregw*) (Art. 6 IAR in connection with Art. 12 SE-Regulation) and must be announced in the State Gazette (*staatscourant*) (Article 17 Hregw in connection with Art. 15 (2) and 13 SE-Regulation).[5]

c) *Minimum capital*

The SE's issued capital must at least amount to 120,000 Euro (Art. 4 (2) SE-Regulation). In accordance with Art. 2: 80 (1) BW, it may be arranged that only part of the issued capital, with a minimum of 25%, is paid up at formation; the remaining part has to be paid up as soon as the company requests. However, the paid-up part of the issued capital at the formation of an SE may not be less than 45,000 Euro, since this is the minimum paid-up capital requirement for an NV (Art. 2: 67 BW).[6]

d) *Independent experts*

Auditors (*registeraccountants* and *accountants-administratieconsulenten*) qualify as independent experts as referred to in the SE-Regulation (e.g. Art. 22, 32 (4) and 37 (6)), see Art. 2: 393 (1) and 2: 94 a (1) BW.

e) *Companies with head office outside the Community*

In the IAR, it is proposed to exercise the option laid down in Art. 2 (5) SE-Regulation. Consequently, a company would also be able to participate in the

[4] See also the Notes p. 12. Differing *Winter* Ondernemingsrecht 2001, p. 198.

[5] Art. 17 Hregw was implemented in accordance with Directive 68/151/EEC, see *Schutte-Veenstra* Tekst & Commentaar Ondernemingsrecht, 2002, Hregw Art. 17 aant. 2.

[6] Notes p. 6. See also *Van Olffen* Ondernemingsrecht 2001, p. 194.

formation of an SE in the Netherlands if its head office is not in the Community, provided that it is formed under the law of a Member State, has its registered office in that Member State and has a real and continuous link with a Member State's economy (Art. 2 IAR).[7]

2. Merger

a) *General*

SEs may be formed through a merger of public limited-liability companies in accordance with Art. 2 (1) and 15 to 31 SE-Regulation. With respect to issues not or only partly regulated by the SE-Regulation, each company involved is governed by Member State law that applies to mergers of public limited-liability companies in accordance with the Merger Directive (Art. 18 SE-Regulation).[8] In the Netherlands, these provisions have been laid down in Articles 2: 309 to 334 BW.[9]

b) *Terms of merger and publication*

The management or administrative organs of each of the merging companies shall draw up draft terms of merger, containing the items mentioned in Article 20 SE-Regulation. These draft terms of merger must be identical (Art. 26 (3) SE-Regulation). It is debatable whether Art. 20 Regulation is exhaustive or merely constitutes a minimum of what has to be contained in the terms of merger.[10] If Art. 20 is exhaustive, a number of items which are required for the terms of merger concerning a "domestic" merger would not have to be included in the terms of an SE merger (cf. Art. 18 SE-Regulation).[11]

[7] The reason is that the Netherlands follows the "incorporation theory", i.e. a company having its registered office in the Netherlands may have its head office and/or main activities abroad, see Notes p. 3–5 and 41. See also MvT bij Uitvoeringswet verordening Europese vennootschap (explanatory memorandum to IAR), Tweede Kamer, vergaderjaar 2003–2004, 29 309, nr. 3, p. 7.

[8] Directive 78/855/EEC.

[9] *Van Schilfgaarde* Van de BV en de NV, 2001, p. 336.

[10] *Teichmann* Die Einführung der Europäischen Aktiengesellschaft, ZGR 2002, 383–464, p. 418/419 takes the view that Art. 20 is exhaustive. The Notes p. 14, seem to take the same position.

[11] See Articles 2: 312 (2) and 2: 326 BW, which contain the following items in addition to the matters referred to in Art. 20 SE-Regulation: (i) the compensatory rights conferred on persons who, other than as shareholders, have special rights against the merging com-

With respect to the publication of the merger, the Government proposes not to impose additional requirements as mentioned in Article 21 SE-Regulation, since national requirements applicable to "domestic" mergers shall apply on the basis of Art. 18 in connection with Art. 9 (2) lit. c (ii) SE-Regulation.[12] Shareholders and persons with a special right against the merging NV (such as a profit-sharing right or the right to subscribe for shares) must have access to the terms of merger and the other relevant documents at such company's head office and – during 6 months following the completion of the merger – at the head office of the SE.[13] In view of Article 21 SE-Regulation, the proposed merger and the filing of the terms of merger have to be announced in the State Gazette. The companies promoting a merger must also make an announcement in a Dutch national newspaper, referring to the merger and stating the commercial register and the entry number under which the terms of merger and the ancillary documents have been filed, as well as the address at which these can be obtained (Art. 2: 314 (3) BW).

c) *Explanatory memorandum and auditors' report*

The management board of the NV has to draw up an explanatory memorandum, setting out the reasons for the merger, the expected consequences for the companies' activities and an explanation from a legal, social and economic point of view (Art. 2: 313 (1) BW in connection with Art. 18 SE-Regulation).

pany, such as profit distribution or share subscription rights, and their effective date, (ii) the proposed members of the management board and supervisory board of the acquiring company, (iii) the intentions concerning the termination and/or continuation of activities, (iv) the persons who have to approve the merger resolution, (v) the number of shares in the acquiring company held by any party to the merger that will be cancelled.

[12] See Notes p. 14 and MvT bij Uitvoeringswet verordening Europese vennootschap (explanatory memorandum to IAR), Tweede Kamer, vergaderjaar 2003–2004, 29 309, nr. 3, p. 13. The terms of merger must be filed with the commercial register (Art. 2: 314 (1) BW), as well as the following documents (if and to the extent that the companies involved in the merger are under a statutory duty to make their annual accounts and reports public): (i) the three most recent annual accounts of all companies involved in the merger, including an auditor's opinion, (ii) the three most recent annual reports of all companies involved, (iii) if the filing date lies six months after the end of the fiscal year of the companies involved, interim accounts or draft annual accounts of such companies (see Art. 2: 314 (2) BW).

[13] Furthermore, if a Dutch company promoting a merger has established a works council, such company must enable the works council to render its advice with respect to the proposed merger (Art. 25 Works Council Act). This would also apply to a "Dutch" SE (see below).

The memorandum further has to contain information[14] on the valuation methods that were used to calculate the share-exchange ratio and the amounts of compensation (if any), as well as the valuations to which these methods lead (Art. 2: 327 BW). The terms of merger, and, in particular, the explanatory memorandum, must be scrutinised by an auditor (Article 2: 328 BW in connection with Art. 18 and 22 SE-Regulation).[15] In principle, each company involved will have to appoint its own expert, but the President of the Enterprise Chamber of the Amsterdam Court of Appeal may allow the merging companies to appoint only one auditor, if they file a joint request (Art. 2: 328 BW in connection with Art. 22 SE-Regulation).[16]

d) *General Meeting*

The NV's general meeting of shareholders has to approve the SE merger (Art. 23 SE-Regulation),[17] which is in line with Dutch company law (Art. 2: 317 BW).[18] In view of Art. 18 SE-Regulation, the merger resolution is subject to the same requirements as an amendment of the statutes, unless the statutes provide differently (Art. 2: 317 (3) and (4) BW).[19] However, the resolution must, in any event, be taken with a two-thirds majority of the votes if less than 50% of the

[14] Such as particular difficulties of valuation and determining the exchange ratio, the methods used to arrive at the proposed exchange ratio and whether such methods are adequate in the case at hand.

[15] The auditor has to give a fairness opinion with respect to the proposed exchange-ratio. Furthermore, he must confirm that, in view of Dutch generally accepted accounting principles, the sum of the amounts of net asset value of each of the disappearing limited companies at least equals the aggregate of the par value of the shares issued by the SE plus the aggregate amounts of further compensation to be paid by the SE (Art. 2: 328 (1) BW). Finally, he must draw up a report in which the contents of the explanatory memorandum are discussed.

[16] However, such a request will not be granted easily if there are minority shareholders involved. See the recent decisions of the Enterprise Chamber: JOR 2001, 112 and JOR 2002, 25.

[17] Such resolution can only be taken after at least one month has passed from the date on which each of the companies promoting the merger announced that the terms of merger have been filed, Article 2: 317 (2) BW.

[18] However, it must be assumed that the exception to this rule, according to which the management board of an acquiring NV is authorised to resolve on the merger (Art. 2: 331 BW), is not applicable to the formation of an SE by way of merger. See *Dortmond* Ondernemingsrecht 2001, p. 191.

[19] The statutes of the NV may, for example, contain provisions on the majority requirement and on approval rights that certain company organs (such as the supervisory board) or certain shareholders may have in connection with the decision to merge.

NV's issued capital is present or represented (Art. 2: 330 (1) BW). If there are separate classes of shares, the approval of each meeting of holders of a specific class of shares whose rights are affected is also necessary. Finally, in NVs to which the "large company regime" applies (see below), the supervisory board must approve the proposal to merge.

e) Intra-group mergers

In respect of mergers between a subsidiary and a parent company holding 100% of its shares, certain statutory merger formalities do not apply (Art. 2: 333 BW in connection with Art. 31 (1) SE-Regulation)[20]. Dutch law does not contain any special provisions with respect to mergers between a company holding 90% or more (but not all) of the shares or voting rights in its subsidiary. There is no intention to introduce such special provisions in respect of SEs on the basis of Article 31 (2) SE-Regulation.[21]

f) Scrutiny of legality

The Dutch legislative proposal suggests the appointment of the Dutch civil-law notary as the authority that scrutinises the legality of the creation of an SE by way of merger as referred to in Art. 25 and 26 SE-Regulation (Art. 20 IAR). Under the general Dutch merger provisions, the civil law notary must scrutinise whether all formalities have been fulfilled and all (required) resolutions have been formally taken.[22] It seems, however, that in respect of an SE merger, the civil law notary must also scrutinise and conclusively attest[23] that the resolution

[20] Cf. MvT bij Uitvoeringswet verordening Europese vennootschap (explanatory memorandum to IAR), Tweede Kamer, vergaderjaar 2003–2004, 29 309, nr. 3, p. 13.

[21] See Notes p. 18. See also MvT bij Uitvoeringswet verordening Europese vennootschap (explanatory memorandum to IAR), Tweede Kamer, vergaderjaar 2003–2004, 29 309, nr. 3, p. 14

[22] He does not, however, have to scrutinise the material validity/unavoidability of the legal acts concerning the merger (Art. 2: 318 (2) BW). Moreover, mergers may be nullified afterwards if a reason to nullify a merger resolution existed (Art. 2: 323 (1) lit. c BW). See, for a recent example of a shareholder challenging a merger, the decision of the Amsterdam district court of 6 January 2002, JOR 2002, 61 (Leyinvest/Vendex KBB).

[23] Notably, in the Dutch version of the SE-Regulation, in Art. 25 (2) the words "waaruit afdoende blijkt dat" are used. Thus, the Dutch version seems to require a lower level of certainty with respect to the completion of the pre-merger acts and formalities when issuing the certificate than the German and English versions. The German version reads here: "aus der zweifelsfrei hervorgeht", whereas the English version speaks of "conclusively attesting to".

taken by the general meeting of the NV is valid and not liable to be set aside, as such a merger (as opposed to "domestic" mergers) cannot be nullified once registration has taken place (Art. 30 SE-Regulation).[24] This requirement could lead to a material delay of SE mergers involving NVs, because shareholders' resolutions of an NV can be challenged during a period of one year after they have been made public (Art. 2: 15 BW). Only when this one year period has passed, and no shareholder has opposed the merger resolution, would the civil law notary be able to *conclusively* confirm that all pre-merger acts and formalities have been completed. The Dutch legislative proposal does not contain specific provisions concerning this issue. In our view, a solution would be to explicitly deviate from Art. 2: 15 BW by restricting the period of time during which shareholders are able to oppose merger resolutions in respect of SEs, to one or two months.

g) Protection of creditors

Creditors of a company proposing to merge can oppose the merger within one month after the date on which all companies have announced the filing of the terms of merger (Art. 2: 316 (2) BW in connection with Art. 24 (1) lit. a SE-Regulation).[25] The civil law notary may not execute the merger deed as long as the court has not decided on the opposition and the opposition has not been withdrawn (Art. 2: 316 (4) BW). There are no special protection mechanisms for bondholders deviating from these creditor protection rules (Art. 24 (1) lit. b SE-Regulation). Holders of securities other than shares carrying special rights against a company which will cease to exist in the course of a merger, are entitled to compensation if they are not granted an equal right against the acquiring company (Art. 2: 320 BW and Art. 24 (1) lit. c SE-Regulation).

h) Protection of minority shareholders

The Dutch legislative proposal does not contain any specific measures to protect minority shareholders with regard to the creation of an SE by way of merger (cf. Art. 24 (2) SE-Regulation).[26] This is in line with general Dutch company

[24] Article 2: 323 (1) BW is therefore not applicable to SE mergers, see also *Dortmond* Ondernemingsrecht 2001, p. 193.

[25] The court may rule that the opposing creditor must be provided with security or some other kind of guarantee with respect to his claims. If the court finds, however, that an opposing creditor has already enough security for his claim(s), or if the financial position of the acquiring company (i.e. the SE) does not render less comfort than the financial position of the original debtor, it will refuse the creditor's opposition.

[26] See Notes p. 13 and 15, basically stating that shareholders should consider the possi-

law, which has no statutory minority protection regime in the sense of the German *Konzernrecht*: unfair treatment of minority shareholders by the majority is judged on the basis of general legal concepts. However, there are arguments in favour of introducing special protection for minority shareholders who oppose the formation of an SE by way of a merger. Firstly, the rights accruing to (minority) shareholders in an SE that is registered in another Member State may differ markedly from the rights they have under Dutch law.[27] Secondly, once an SE has been registered, the merger can no longer be annulled (Art. 30 SE-Regulation, see above). Thus, if a shareholder challenges the merger decision (e.g. on grounds of reasonableness and fairness), the attesting certificate could only be issued after the judgment dismissing such shareholder's claim can no longer be appealed. Until that moment, the civil-law notary will not be able to attest conclusively to the completion of the pre-merger acts and formalities (Art. 25 (2) SE-Regulation), since the merger decision may finally be annulled. This would give shareholders the opportunity to materially delay SE mergers. By providing for special protective measures, minority shareholders might have less ground to challenge SE merger decisions. Such protection could *inter alia* be achieved by introducing special majority requirements for the merger resolution.[28] Alternatively, reasonable compensation could be granted to shareholders who oppose the merger. We are of the view that, if minority shareholders would be offered special compensation rights, the opposition against an SE merger (decision) should not prevent the registration of the SE, in order to enhance the efficiency of the merger procedure (cf. Art. 25 (3) SE-Regulation).

i) Opposition by the State

The Netherlands intends to exercise the option provided for in Art. 19 SE-Regulation, stipulating that the Minister of Justice may oppose the involvement of an NV in the creation of an SE by way of merger, on grounds of public interest (Art. 7 IAR). The opposition can be challenged by the NV before the

ble implications of the SE merger prior to resolving on it. This point of view does not, however, seem to fully appreciate the specific position of minority shareholders, who (although they may understand the implications of a merger) are not able to influence the outcome of the merger resolution.

[27] E.g. voting rights, prior approval rights, the right to contest shareholders' resolutions and the right to request an investigation into the company's business.

[28] As was suggested by *Dortmond* Ondernemingsrecht 2001, p. 192. However, such a requirement might hinder the formation of SEs by way of merger and thus discriminate against SEs in favour of "regular" NVs. This seems to violate the SE-Regulation, see Art. 10 SE-Regulation.

Enterprise Chamber of the Amsterdam Court of Appeals. Reference is made to our remarks with respect to the State opposition against a transfer of seat (below).

j) *Completion*

The civil law notary will execute a notarial deed confirming the merger only after receiving the certificates referred to in Art. 25 (2) SE-Regulation in respect of each non-Dutch merging company and successfully completing scrutiny of the merger requirements with respect to the NV (Art. 25 (1) SE-Regulation) and the merger as a whole (Art. 26 (1) SE-Regulation).[29] The SE may then be registered (Art. 27 (1) SE-Regulation). Registration shall be published in the State Gazette (Art. 28 SE-Regulation). Within one month after registration, the SE must notify all relevant public registers of the merger (Art. 2: 318 (4) BW in connection with Art. 29 (3) SE-Regulation). With respect to registered property (such as real estate), the keeper of the land registry has to be provided with all relevant documents in order to record the merger.[30]

3. Holding

a) *Draft terms and publication*

The draft terms for the formation of a holding SE, including an explanatory memorandum, shall be drawn up by the management board (*bestuur*) of the NV and by the management or administrative organs of each of the other companies which promote the transaction (Art. 32 (2) SE-Regulation). Furthermore, an auditor's report shall be drawn up (Article 32 (4) and (5) SE-Regulation).[31] The draft terms and the auditor's report are to be filed at the commercial register at least one month prior to the general meeting deciding on the formation of a holding SE (Art. 8 (1) IAR). These documents must also be available for the shareholders at the office of each Dutch company involved in

[29] Art. 2: 318 BW, requiring that a notarial deed is passed in connection with the completion of a merger, applies to the creation of an SE through a merger in view of Art. 18 Regulation; see Notes p. 16.

[30] *Dortmond* Ondernemingsrecht 2001, 192.

[31] According to the Notes p. 18–19, the provisions concerning auditor's review in the event of a merger (Art. 2: 328 BW) apply mutatis mutandis to the review in connection with the formation of a holding SE. This includes the appointment procedure if only one auditor is preparing the report for all companies involved (cf. Art. 32 (4) second sentence SE-Regulation).

the formation of the holding SE.[32] The filing must be announced in a national newspaper, mentioning the commercial register number and the address at which these documents are available (Art. 8 (3) IAR).

b) *General meeting*

The general meeting of each company involved must approve the creation of the holding SE (Art. 32 (3) SE-Regulation).[33] The Regulation does not contain any provisions with respect to the majority requirements of such a resolution, nor does the Government express its intention to provide for regulation in respect of this matter. Therefore, it must be assumed that a simple majority will suffice if the statutes of the NV do not provide otherwise. After all, the formation of a holding SE does not lead to the dissolution of the companies promoting the same, and the position of the other shareholders does not, in principle, change.

c) *Prospectus and offering memorandum*

Under Dutch securities law, it is forbidden to offer securities at issuance outside a restricted circle or to make announcements with respect to such an offer, unless a prospectus is published or an exception applies (Art. 3 WTE 1995). The fact that the holding SE will issue shares to the shareholders willing to exchange their shares, is announced through the publication of the terms for formation and the general meeting's calling notice. It may be argued that this qualifies as (an announcement of) a securities offer requiring a prospectus. Furthermore, a public bid may not be made for securities that are listed on a Dutch stock exchange or that are regularly traded in the Netherlands, unless an offering memorandum has been published and a number of procedural rules have been followed (Art. 6a WTE 1995). The offer made to the shareholders of the companies promoting the holding SE might qualify as a public bid for shares, if such shares are listed or traded regularly in the Netherlands. Consequently, an

[32] It is not clear why these documents are not to be held at the disposal of holders with a special right against the Dutch company, such as a profit-sharing right or the right to subscribe for shares, as it is the case in connection with a merger (Art. 2: 314 (2) BW, to which the Notes, p. 44 explicitly refer). See also MvT bij Uitvoeringswet verordening Europese vennootschap (explanatory memorandum to IAR), Tweede Kamer, vergaderjaar 2003–2004, 29 309, nr. 3, p. 14.

[33] With respect to NVs, general meetings have to be called at least 15 days in advance (Art. 2: 115 BW). The calling notice must indicate which matters are to be resolved (Art. 2: 114 BW).

offering memorandum would also have to be published. The Netherlands does not seem to intend to regulate this matter. A solution could be to provide that the formation of a holding SE is exempt from these securities regulations.[34]

d) Formation formalities

The Regulation does not regulate the formation of a holding SE in full detail. According to Art. 15 SE-Regulation, non-regulated questions in connection with the formation of a holding SE having its registered seat in the Netherlands are governed by the Dutch rules applicable to the formation of NVs. Thus, a declaration of no objection must be granted by the Ministry of Justice and a deed of formation, including the company's statutes, is to be passed before a Dutch civil law notary (Art. 2: 64 (2) BW). The exchange of shares in the companies promoting the formation of the holding SE qualifies as a contribution in kind (Art. 2: 80b BW). Accordingly, the incorporators have to draw up a description of the contributions in kind, together with a valuation of the same and the valuation methods that have been used (Art. 2: 94a (1) BW).[35] An auditor must render an opinion with respect to this description, in which he declares that the value of the contribution according to Dutch GAAP is at least equal to the amounts that must be paid up on the shares issued by the company (Art. 2: 94a (2) BW).

e) Protection of minority shareholders, creditors and employees

It is not proposed to introduce any protection for minority shareholders, creditors and employees in connection with the formation of a holding SE, because, unlike in the merger scenario, the companies promoting the formation of a holding SE continue to exist (Art. 32 (1) SE-Regulation).[36] In the absence of specific minority protection in general Dutch company law (see above), there is no reason to introduce specific minority protection in connection with the creation of a holding SE. The same goes for creditors and employees of the Dutch companies involved: their contractual counterparts continue to exist, and they will have the same position as before the formation of the holding SE.

[34] This would, however, only be a feasible option if it is deemed that the SE-Regulation offers the same level of protection to shareholders as the relevant securities regulations.

[35] However, persons receiving shares at issuance must not necessarily participate in the formation and persons participating in the formation must not necessarily subscribe for shares in the company they form (Article 2: 64 (2) BW).

[36] See Notes p. 20 and MvT bij Uitvoeringswet verordening Europese vennootschap (explanatory memorandum to IAR), Tweede Kamer, vergaderjaar 2003–2004, 29 309, nr. 3, p. 15.

f) Scrutiny of formalities and publication

As soon as the conditions for formation of a holding SE have been fulfilled, this shall be made public through the filing of a declaration at the commercial register and by inserting an announcement in a national newspaper (Art. 9 IAR). The SE-Regulation stipulates that a holding SE cannot be registered until it is shown that the formalities and conditions set out in Articles 32 and 33 (2) SE-Regulation have been fulfilled (Art. 33 (5) SE-Regulation). The Government suggests that the commercial register will perform this review.[37] It is, however, not clear whether the commercial register is equipped to this end. An alternative would be to determine that the civil law notary who is involved in the formation of the holding SE scrutinises the formation formalities and conditions. This may prove more efficient and would be in line with the rules governing the formation of an SE by way of merger.

4. Subsidiary

a) Formation by companies, firms and other entities governed by national law

"*Companies and firms within the meaning of the second paragraph of Art. 48 of the EC Treaty*" are entitled to form a subsidiary SE (Art. 2 (3) SE-Regulation). Consequently, all firms, entities and co-operatives with a profit-making purpose, i.e. NVs (public companies) and BVs (private companies),[38] general partnerships (*maatschap* or *v.o.f.*) as well as limited partnerships (*c.v.*), mutual companies (*onderlinge waarborgmaatschappijen*) and cooperative associations (*coöperaties*), but not proprietorships (*eenmanszaken*), may do so.[39] Furthermore, Art. 2 (3) SE-Regulation refers to "*other legal bodies governed by public or private law*", which includes the state (*Staat der Nederlanden*) and (regional and other) entities of public law, e.g. provinces (*provincies*) and cities (*gemeenten*), but also entities without a profit-making purpose, such as associations (*verenigingen*) and foundations (*stichtingen*).[40]

[37] Notes p. 19–20.

[38] As Art. 2 (3) SE-Regulation does not make a difference between public and private limited-liability companies.

[39] Notes p. 4.

[40] By explicitly referring both to "companies and firms within the meaning of the second paragraph of Article 48 of the EC Treaty" (which does not include entities without a profit-making purpose) and to "other legal bodies governed by public and private law" (which includes entities without a profit-making purpose), Art. 3 section 2 of the Regulation must be deemed to have a broader spectrum than Art. 48 of the EC Treaty, thereby including entities without a profit-making purpose. Cf. the Notes p. 4–5.

The persons setting up a subsidiary SE are subject to the national provisions governing their participation in the formation of a public limited-liability company (Article 36 SE-Regulation). Under Dutch law, the management board of an NV is authorised to resolve on the formation of a subsidiary in the form of an NV, under certain circumstances subject to the approval of the supervisory board, if the company is subject to the "large company regime" (see below). In future, the management board may have to obtain the approval of the general meeting of shareholders as well, if the formation of a major subsidiary would bring about the transfer of all or materially all of the company's business to a third party (see the newly proposed Art. 2: 217a BW).[41] With respect to the formation formalities, the same rules apply as in the event of formation of an NV (see Art. 15 SE-Regulation). A statement of no objection must be granted by the Minister of Justice and a deed of formation, including the company's statutes, is to be passed before a Dutch civil-law notary (Art. 2: 64 (2) BW).

b) Formation by an SE

An SE can itself form a subsidiary in the form of an SE (Art. 3 (2) SE-Regulation). Generally, the same rules apply as with respect to the formation of a subsidiary SE by entities formed under national law. The decision-making process within the SE is governed by Articles 38 to 60 SE-Regulation and the national provisions applicable to the SE on the basis of Article 9 (1) (c) SE-Regulation. If the SE setting up the subsidiary has its registered office in the Netherlands (which need not necessarily be the case), it may be assumed that the same rules apply as with respect to NVs.

5. Transformation

An NV may be transformed into an SE in accordance with Articles 2 (4) and 37 SE-Regulation. The management board (*bestuur*) of the NV has to draw up the terms of transformation and the report concerning the transformation (Article 37 (4) SE-Regulation). The draft terms, including the report, shall be filed at the commercial register, whereupon the filing shall be announced in a national newspaper (Art. 10 IAR). An auditor has to certify that the company's net assets are at least equal to the paid-up and requested part of its issued capital (*gestort en opgevraagd deel van het kapitaal*) plus non-distributable reserves

[41] Wijziging van boek 2 van het Burgerlijk Wetboek in verband met aanpassing van de structuurregeling, Tweede Kamer, vergaderjaar 2001–2002, 28 179 (see below).

(Art. 2: 98 (2) BW in connection with Art. 37 (6) SE-Regulation). Transformation may force many NVs to increase their issued capital, as NVs must have an issued capital of at least 45,000 Euro (Art. 2: 67 BW), whereas the minimum for SEs amounts to 120,000 Euro (see above).

The NV's general meeting has to approve the transformation and the SE's statutes (Art. 37 (7) SE-Regulation). The resolution requires the same majority as a resolution to merge, being a two-thirds majority of the votes, unless at least 50% of the issued capital is present or represented at such meeting, in which case a simple majority is sufficient.[42] The transformation into an SE requires a notarial deed containing the SE's statutes (Art. 2: 18 (2) BW in connection with Art. 15 (1) SE-Regulation). If the relevant NV is subject to the "large company regime" (see below), the proposal to transform into an SE is subject to the approval of the NV's supervisory board (*raad van commissarissen*) (Art. 2: 164 (1) lit. g BW). The Netherlands does not intend to provide that, in this case, the supervisory board's approval requires a qualified majority (cf. Art. 37 (8) SE-Regulation).[43]

III. Board Structure

1. General

SEs may either have a one-tier or a two-tier board system (Article 38 SE-Regulation). The rules governing the SE's board structure are only partly embodied in the SE-Regulation, and issues not covered by the SE-Regulation are to be dealt with in the national implementation rules and the provisions applicable to public limited liability companies in the Member State where the SE has its registered office (Art. 9 (1) lit. c under (ii)). Accordingly, we will first discuss the corporate governance of Dutch public companies (NVs).

[42] Furthermore, if the transformation is detrimental to the rights of holders of a certain class of shares, the meetings of holders of such shares have an approval right with respect to the transformation (Art. 2: 330 BW in connection with Art. 37 (7) Regulation and Art. 7 of Directive 78/855/EEC). It must be assumed that the resolution to transform into an SE may (also) be made subject to the approval of other shareholders, such as priority shareholders (Article 15 (1) Regulation).

[43] See Notes p. 21–22.

a) NV board structure

NVs may choose either a two-tier system with a management board (*bestuur*) and a supervisory board (*raad van commissarissen*), or a one-tier system with only a management board. The rules governing the management board of one-tier NVs do not deviate significantly from the two-tier regime: in essence, the existing Dutch one-tier system is nothing more than a two-tier system without a supervisory board. A number of provisions concerning the governance of companies are of an enabling nature and may be modified by the company's statutes. However, to NVs that fit the description of a "large company" (Art. 2: 153 (2) BW),[44] a strict mandatory regime which is set out in Articles 2: 152 to 164 BW applies (the "large company regime"). Under the large company regime, companies must adopt a two-tier structure in which the employees have certain participation rights as to the appointment of supervisory directors. The supervisory board has the power to appoint and remove the members of the management board, to adopt the annual accounts and to approve important (business) transactions. Furthermore, supervisory board members are appointed in accordance with the system of "controlled co-optation", which includes a certain form of employee participation; this system is set out in more detail below. International holdings or subsidiaries of international corporations are subject to a more lenient regime (the so-called "mitigated regime"). In that case, the general meeting of the shareholders has the power to appoint and remove executive directors and to adopt the annual accounts. Consequently, the governance structure of NVs depends, to a large extent, on the distinction between companies that do and do not qualify as "large".

b) Applicability of the large company regime to an SE

The Dutch Government takes the view that the "large company regime" is not directly applicable to the SE.[45] It argues that the rules concerning the appointment of members of the supervisory board (the system of "controlled co-opta-

[44] "Large companies" are companies that fulfil the following criteria during at least three consecutive years: a) an issued and paid-up capital, including reserves, exceeding 13 million Euro; b) a works council having been installed; c) directly or indirectly (e.g. through subsidiaries) employing at least 100 employees in the Netherlands on a regular basis. However, subsidiaries of "large companies", group finance companies and international holding companies are exempt from the regime. Currently, an amendment of the "large company regime" is being proposed (see below).

[45] Notes p. 24–25. See also MvT bij Uitvoeringswet verordening Europese vennootschap (explanatory memorandum to IAR), Tweede Kamer, vergaderjaar 2003–2004, 29 309, nr. 3, p. 4. *Timmerman* Ondernemingsrecht 2003, 243 takes the same view.

tion") are set aside by the SE-Regulation (Art. 40 (2)), and that the Dutch employee participation rules which are contained in the large company regime are "overruled" by the SE Directive (Art. 13 (2), see below). With respect to the other provisions of the large company regime – i.e. the rules concerning the appointment and removal of members of the management board, the adoption of the annual accounts and the approval of certain important transactions – it maintains that these neither apply, nor should be declared applicable to SEs, as the large company regime as a whole constitutes a balanced governance system of which the Dutch employee participation provisions form the centrepiece.[46] The employee participation of the SE depends on arrangements made between the company and a special group of employee representatives (or, as the case may be, the applicable standard rules), and therefore may well deviate from the mandatory Dutch participation rules. Applying some provisions of the large company regime to SEs without applying the mandatory participation provisions would (in the view of the Ministry) disturb this carefully balanced system.

The Regulation seems indeed to leave little or no room for directly applying some (and not all of the) provisions of the large company regime to SEs, since many of the issues covered in these provisions are already addressed in the Regulation in a way that does not allow an automatic "gap-filling" function under Art. 9 (1) lit. c (ii) SE-Regulation. Nevertheless, not striving for alignment of the law applicable to the SE and to the "large" NV could have negative implications. First, the large company regime does not only have the aim of granting participation rights to employees, but also of providing for the effective control and supervision of management by a separate corporate organ with a strong and independent position:[47] the supervisory board may appoint and remove members of the management board and has the power to approve important transactions. This system of corporate governance may be weakened in SEs with a two-tier structure as compared to NVs subject to the large company regime. Secondly, if the position of the supervisory organ in two-tier SEs would be far weaker than the position of the supervisory board in "large" NVs, the level of employee participation in SEs would "indirectly" decrease.[48] It is

[46] Notes p. 25–26. See also MvT bij Uitvoeringswet verordening Europese vennootschap (explanatory memorandum to IAR), Tweede Kamer, vergaderjaar 2003–2004, 29 309, nr. 3, p. 5–6.

[47] This is especially important in large companies, where an effective control of management by the shareholders does not necessarily exist. See *Asser/Maeijer* 2-III, 2000, No. 16, 364–365, 379 and 381, and *Van Schilfgaarde* Van de BV en de NV, 2001, no. 137. The importance of the independent position of the supervisory board in the corporate governance structure of Dutch companies was also stressed in the Report of the Dutch Commission on Corporate Governance of 25 June 1997 (the "Peters Report").

[48] Cf. *Timmerman* Ondernemingsrecht 2003, 243.

unclear whether this would be in line with the "before-and-after" principle laid down in the SE Directive and the provision that all aspects of employee participation shall continue to apply to SEs formed by way of transformation (Articles 3 (6), 4 (4) SE Directive and part 3 (a) Annex to the SE Directive).[49] Thirdly, the mandatory nature of the employee participation regime in the NV could thus be undermined, as NVs subject to the "large company regime" would have an incentive to transform into SEs in order to decrease the influence of employees on the management.

On the other hand, not applying the mandatory provisions of the large company regime to SEs could also have advantages. The regime applicable to SEs would be more flexible than the rules applicable to large NVs., as the (general meeting of) shareholders could decide which checks and balances are needed. It would thus be possible to design a "tailor-made" system of corporate governance for each company, instead of having to rely on inflexible mandatory rules as are contained in the large company regime. These advantages would presumably exist to a lesser extent in companies with a wide range of shareholders where it seems difficult for the general meeting to effectively control the management.[50]

One way of dealing with this issue could be to exercise some of the options the SE-Regulation offers, thereby making a distinction in the implementation act between SEs that qualify as "large" and SEs that do not.[51] This way, the "large" SE regime could, to a great extent, be aligned to the governance structure of "large" NVs, whereas SEs that do not qualify as "large" would have all the advantages of a flexible structure. On the other hand, the introduction of an extra distinction might be deemed to complicate the SE system even further and make the governance structure of "large" SEs less flexible. The relevant Member State option rights are discussed in more detail below.

[49] However, according to the Dutch Government the powers and rights of the organ with respect to which the employees can exercise participation rights are not relevant for the "before-and-after" test laid down in Part 3 (a) of the Annex to the SE Directive. On the contrary, the Government argues that "participation rights" in the meaning of the SE Directive only concern the employees' rights in respect of the composition of the relevant company organ, see MvT bij Voorstel van Wet rol werknemers bij de Europese vennootschap (explanatory memorandum to IAD), Tweede Kamer, vergaderjaar 2003–2004, 29 298, nr. 3, p. 59.

[50] The Sociaal-Economische Raad, an advisory organ, consisting of employers' and employees' representatives and independent members, is divided with regard to this issue. See p. 24–26 of its draft advice with respect to the implementation of the SE Directive (hereafter the "Draft Advice"), which has been published on the internet (www.ser.nl).

[51] Applying a strictly mandatory regime to all SEs (even to those that do not qualify as "large companies") could be held to be discriminatory in the sense of Art. 10 Regulation, as it would be prejudicial to "small" SEs compared to "small" NVs.

2. Two-tier system

a) Management organ

(1) Duties and approval rights

The management organ is entrusted with the management of the SE (Art. 39 Regulation). As the SE-Regulation does not contain any provisions as to *how* the management organ has to fulfil its duties, Dutch law will in this respect apply to the SE (cf. Art. 9 (1) lit. c under (ii) Regulation). Accordingly, the members of the management organ have collective powers and responsibilities in respect of the management of the company (cf. Art. 2: 9 BW).[52] They may, for internal purposes, arrange a distribution of tasks in board regulations. Such a distribution does not, however, restrict the management's collective responsibility. The Government does not intend to deviate from these principles by making use of the Member State option right in Art. 39 (1) 2nd sentence SE-Regulation.[53] Accordingly, a "Dutch" two-tier SE will not be able to appoint managing directors who are responsible for the current management in addition to the management organ.

The management organ is, in principle, independent in the exercise of its duties (Art. 39 (1) SE-Regulation). In accordance with Dutch law, the management organ of a company must observe the interests of the company as a whole, including its businesses and subsidiaries, and take all relevant interests of the company's stakeholders (including the company's employees) into account.[54]

(2) Appointment, suspension and removal

Members of the SE's management organ are generally appointed and removed by the supervisory organ (Art. 39 (2) SE-Regulation). The Government proposes that the general meeting be enabled to exercise these powers (if the statutes so determine), irrespective of the size of the SE (Article 11 (1) IAR in connection with Art. 39 (2) 2nd sentence SE-Regulation)[55]. As was discussed above, this

[52] Notes p. 26.

[53] Notes p. 26.

[54] With respect to the duties of the management board under Dutch law see *Asser/Maeijer* 2-III, 2000, No. 291–293; *Van Schilfgaarde* Van de BV en de NV, 2001, No. 42.

[55] According to MvT bij Uitvoeringswet verordening Europese vennootschap (explanatory memorandum to IAR), Tweede Kamer, vergaderjaar 2003–2004, 29 309, nr. 3, p. 16, exercising this option would align the legal regime applicable to SEs to the provisions concerning NVs that are not subject to the large company regime. Furthermore, it is

would be in line with the rules applicable to regular NVs and to NVs subject to the "mitigated regime", but not with the "large company regime".[56] As an alternative, it may be stipulated that the general meeting only has this right in SEs which do not qualify as "large". As a consequence, the general rule of Art. 39 (2) SE-Regulation would only be applicable to SEs qualifying as "large".[57] This would bring the SE's regime more in line with Dutch company law. Moreover, it is not clear whether the Dutch proposal not to distinguish between companies that qualify as "large" and those that do not, is in conformity with Art. 39 (2) 2nd sentence Regulation, as the option is only allowed *under the same conditions as for public limited-liability companies.*

If an SE arranges for the appointment of the members of the management board by the general meeting, Art. 11 (2) IAR explicitly declares Art. 2: 133 and 134 BW directly applicable. Accordingly, the SE's statutes may stipulate that appointments by the general meeting be made on the basis of a binding proposal, containing at least two names (Art. 2: 133 (1) BW in connection with Art. 47 (4) SE-Regulation). Binding proposals may be drawn up by another company organ (such as the supervisory organ), by certain shareholders (such as priority shareholders) or by a third party (such as the state).[58] The general meeting may, however, deviate from such binding proposals with a two-third majority representing more than 50% of the issued share capital (Art. 2: 133 (2) BW). Furthermore, if the statutes stipulate that the general meeting's decision to remove members of the management organ requires a special majority, such majority may not exceed two-thirds of the votes representing more than 50% of the issued share capital (Art. 2: 134 (2) BW).

The SE-Regulation does not contain any provisions as to when and under which conditions members of the management organ may be suspended or removed. Therefore, we assume that Dutch company law applies to this matter (Article 9 (1) lit. c under (ii) SE-Regulation), according to which the organ authorised to appoint management organ members may suspend or remove them

argued that the proposed Art. 11 (1) IAR will enhance the functionality of the SE as a subsidiary in a group of companies.

[56] Reference is made to Art. 2: 132 and 2: 134 BW, according to which the general meeting has the power to appoint and remove supervisory board members. If, however, an NV qualifies as a "large company", these powers are mandatorily entrusted to the supervisory board (Art. 2: 162 BW).

[57] Similar *Hommelhoff* Zur Organisationsverfassung der Europäischen AG, AG 2001, p. 283, who suggests that the German legislator (only) make use of the option right in Art. 39 (2) 2nd sentence SE-Regulation in respect of companies not subject to (mandatory) employee co-determination.

[58] *Van Schilfgaarde* Van de BV en de NV, 2001, No. 44.

at all times (Art. 2: 134 (1) BW).[59] Furthermore, the supervisory organ is authorised to suspend each member of the management organ, unless the statutes provide otherwise (Art. 2: 147 (1) BW).

(3) Members

There are no statutory provisions in Dutch law disqualifying natural persons from serving as members of the managing board of an NV (cf. Art. 47 (2) SE-Regulation). Nevertheless, before a company can be incorporated, anybody who will (co-)determine the company's management (such as members of the management organ) is subject to a previous "screening" by the authorities for the purpose of obtaining a statement of no objection (see above). Proposed members of the management organ of SEs to be incorporated shall equally be subject to such screening.[60] Furthermore, the statutes may contain special conditions of eligibility for members of the management board if these are to be appointed by the general meeting (cf. Art. 47 (3) SE-Regulation and Art. 2: 132 (2) BW).[61] According to Dutch law, companies or other legal entities can act as member(s) of the management body of an NV, in which case the person(s) managing such "managing company" carries the responsibilities of the management board (Art. 2: 11 BW). The same applies to the SE (Art. 47 (1) 1st sentence SE-Regulation). There is no intention to set a minimum or a maximum number of members for the management organ, as Dutch company law does not provide for such a rule (Articles 39 (4) 2nd sentence SE-Regulation).[62]

b) Supervisory organ

(1) Duties

The supervisory organ must supervise the management organ (Art. 40 SE-Regulation). In accordance with Dutch company law, it must also supervise the

[59] On the other hand, Article 46 (1) SE-Regulation provides that members of company organs shall be appointed for a period determined in the statutes, which may not exceed six years. It could be argued that this period of time must be regarded as a fixed period and that members of company organs cannot be dismissed in between, unless for urgent cause, which would preclude Art. 2: 134 (1) BW. We tend to believe that Article 46 (1) does not constitute such a fixed appointment period, but that it merely confirms that members of the managing organ must step down after a certain period of time.

[60] See Notes p. 12.

[61] The general meeting may, however, disregard such conditions with a two-thirds majority representing more than 50% of the issued capital (Art. 2: 132 (2) 2nd sentence BW).

[62] See Notes p. 27.

general course of affairs of the company (Art. 2: 140 (2) BW) and advise the management organ, if and when required. Like the management organ, the supervisory organ must act in the interests of the company as a whole, including its businesses and subsidiaries, and take all (relevant) interests of the company's stakeholders (including the company's employees) into account.[63] The members of the supervisory organ have collective powers and are therefore collectively responsible for their supervision of the company's management. The Dutch Government does not intend to determine that individual members of the supervisory organ may require the information they need to exercise their supervisory duties (Art. 41 (3) 2nd sentence), as this would conflict with the principle of collective responsibility.[64]

According to the SE-Regulation, the supervisory organ may not interfere with the management of the SE (Art. 40). Art. 2: 146 BW, which provides that the supervisory organ may (only) represent the company when a conflict of interest arises between the company and one or more members of the management organ, will most likely also apply to the SE (Art. 9 (1) lit. c (ii) SE-Regulation). A supervisory organ member may be "delegated" to the management organ for a certain period of time. The Member States can regulate how long such delegation may last (Art. 39 (3) SE-Regulation), but the IAR does not impose a time limit. Instead, Art. 12 IAR declares Art. 2: 134 (4) BW applicable to the SE, which provides that the company's statutes have to contain provisions concerning the interim-management of the company in the event of a vacancy on the management board or absence of any management board members. It is, however, questionable whether the Netherlands may declare this provision applicable to SEs, as the SE-Regulation already seems to cover this matter in full. In any event, provisions in the SE's statutes that will be based upon Art. 12 IAR will have to be in line with Art. 39 (3) SE-Regulation.

(2) Approval rights

The SE-Regulation provides that the supervisory organ is to supervise the management organ, and that the statutes must list the categories of transactions that require the supervisory organ's approval (Art. 48 (1)). Unlike the "large company regime" for NVs (cf. Art. 2: 164 BW), the Dutch implementation proposal does not lay down a list of categories of transactions which

[63] With respect to the duties of the supervisory board see *Asser/Maeijer* 2-III, 2000, No. 341; *Van Schilfgaarde* Van de BV en de NV, 2001, No. 68.

[64] However, *Winter* Ondernemingsrecht 2001, p. 197, suggests that the statutes may provide that members of the supervisory organ have such individual information rights.

require the approval of the supervisory organ (Art. 48 (2) SE-Regulation).[65] In our view, an option would be to determine that the statutes of "large" SEs must at least make the categories of transactions mentioned in Art. 2: 164 BW subject to the supervisory organ's prior approval. This would bring the SE regime more in line with Dutch company law (including the large company regime) and might also enhance the two-tier SE's system of corporate governance.[66]

Apart from the approval rights of the supervisory board in the large company regime, Dutch company law contains additional (or alternative) control mechanisms: the statutes may stipulate that certain categories of transactions be subject to the prior approval of another organ of the company (Art. 2: 129 (3) BW), or require management to observe directives of the general meeting (or another organ) concerning the general course of the company's business (cf. Art. 2: 129 (4) BW).[67] It is not yet clear whether these control mechanisms will also apply or be available, respectively, to SEs in the Netherlands; this ultimately depends on the interpretation of Art. 9 (1) lit. c Regulation.[68]

(3) Appointment and removal

The general meeting has the power to appoint members of the supervisory organ (Art. 40 (2) SE-Regulation). The statutes may determine that up to one third of the members of the supervisory organ may be appointed by others (Art. 2: 143 BW in connection with Art. 47 (4) SE-Regulation). This provision can be used to give certain shareholders or even outsiders (for example, a bank or the state) influence over the company.[69] The Regulation does not clearly state

[65] Neither does it propose to provide that the SE's supervisory organ can supplement the approval list in the statutes, see the Notes p. 32–33. See also *Winter* Ondernemingsrecht 2001, p. 198.

[66] Leaving the supervision of management completely to the SE's statutes could be particularly problematic in "large" SEs, which often have a strongly dispersed shareholder structure. This was one of the reasons why the Netherlands introduced the large company regime for NVs in the year 1971; see *Asser/Maeijer* 2-III, 2000, No. 16, 364–365; *Van Schilfgaarde* Van de BV en de NV, 2001, No. 137.

[67] Furthermore, a legislative proposal will give the general meeting of shareholders a prior approval right with respect to transactions that significantly change the identity of the company (e.g. a transfer of all or materially all of the company's business).

[68] If Art. 48 SE-Regulation is to be deemed to cover the issue of management control only partly (see Art. 9 (1) under c), such additional or alternative control mechanisms would be allowed. If it must be deemed to fully and exhaustively cover this matter, such additional mechanisms would not be allowed. Since this question concerns the interpretation of European law, it can only be finally decided by the European Court of Justice.

[69] *Van Schilfgaarde* Van de BV en de NV, 2001, No. 71.

who has the right to suspend and remove members of the supervisory organ. We assume that this matter is governed by national law in view of Art. 9 (1) lit. c SE-Regulation. This would mean that the organ or person authorised to appoint members of the supervisory organ also has the right to suspend or remove them (Art. 2: 144 (1) BW). If employee participation arrangements apply to the SE, a different appointment and removal regime may be applicable.

(4) Members

The Dutch proposal does not stipulate that the SE's supervisory organ must have a certain minimum or maximum number of members (cf. Article 40 (3) SE-Regulation).[70] The statutes may contain special requirements of eligibility for members of the supervisory organ representing the shareholders (Art. 47 (3) SE-Regulation in connection with Art. 2: 142 (1) BW).[71] In conformity with Dutch law, legal entities cannot be members of the supervisory organ (cf. Art. 47 (1) 1st sentence SE-Regulation).[72]

3. One-tier system

a) General

Member States may adopt the appropriate measures in relation to SEs where no provision is made for a one-tier system in relation to public limited liability companies with registered offices within its territory (Art. 43 (4) SE-Regulation). Although Dutch law is familiar with the concept of a one-tier system, the rules applicable to one-tier companies do not contain detailed provisions with respect to the supervision and control of the company's management (as in the large company regime). Furthermore, the one-tier system is generally only available for small NVs, as "large" NVs are subject to the large company rules and must install a supervisory board, unless an exemption applies. It must therefore be assumed that the Netherlands is authorised to regulate the one-tier system for "Dutch" SEs in full detail on the basis of Art. 43 (4) SE-Regulation. How-

[70] See Notes p. 28. Art. 2: 158 (3) BW, which requires a minimum of 3 members for "large" companies, is therefore not applicable on SEs.

[71] Such requirements do not apply to members who are appointed on the basis of an employee co-determination scheme.

[72] Art. 2: 140 (1) BW does not enable legal entities to act as supervisory directors of other legal entities.

ever, the Government proposes to make use of this regulatory option in a rather restricted manner (Articles 13 and 14 IAR).[73]

Although Article 14 IAR explicitly refers to members of the administrative organ who do not have an executive role, and thus a distinction is made between "executive" and "non-executive" members of the administrative organ, executives and non-executives are still held to be collectively responsible for both day-to-day management and strategy.[74] It is yet not quite clear how a distinction between executives and non-executives may be made[75] and which consequences such a distinction will have regarding their respective powers and responsibilities. It is, for example, unclear which powers non-executive members have to supervise executive members.[76] More importantly, it is unclear whether they are merely responsible and liable for their supervision of the executive members, or whether they are also liable for the company's management just as the executive members. The latter would, for instance, imply joint and several liability in case of bankruptcy for not filing the annual account at the commercial register (Art. 2: 138 BW). Also, it is questionable whether all members of the administrative organ, including the non-executive members, have an equal right to represent the company and to be actively involved in the (day-to-day) management of the SE. Finally, it needs to be clarified how conflicts of interest between the company and (executive) members are to be dealt with.

The lack of clarity in the distinction between "executive" and "non-executive" members also influences the gap-filling function of Dutch law in view of Art. 9 (1) lit. c under (ii) SE-Regulation, more specifically whether certain provisions concerning the supervisory board should be analogously applied to non-executive members. Will, for example, Art. 2: 146 BW, which determines that supervisory board members represent the NV if a conflict of interest arises with a management board member, be (analogously) applicable to non-execu-

[73] See Notes p. 30–31 and MvT bij Uitvoeringswet verordening Europese vennootschap (explanatory memorandum to IAR), Tweede Kamer, vergaderjaar 2003–2004, 29 309, nr. 3, p. 18–19.

[74] See Notes p. 30.

[75] The Notes p. 22, suggest this is achieved by way of an internal arrangement between the members of the management organ themselves. In view thereof, the Dutch proposal determines that the administrative organ must have at least three members, because an effective supervision would not be possible if the administrative organ would only have one or two members (see Notes, p. 46 and MvT bij Uitvoeringswet verordening Europese vennootschap (explanatory memorandum to IAR), Tweede Kamer, vergaderjaar 2003–2004, 29 309, nr. 3, p. 19).

[76] The Notes p. 46 and MvT bij Uitvoeringswet verordening Europese vennootschap (explanatory memorandum to IAR), Tweede Kamer, vergaderjaar 2003–2004, 29 309, nr. 3, p. 19, refer to non-executive members as "supervising members".

tive members? Also, should non-executive members as a group have the right to suspend executive members, analogously applying Art. 2: 147 BW which concerns the supervisory board?

Indeed there seems to be a strong case for introducing a functional distinction between the roles of "executive" and "non-executive" members of the administrative organ in the SE[77] as this corresponds with the international efforts to strengthen corporate governance.[78] Moreover, the SE-Regulation seems to start from the principle that a clear distinction is made between management and supervision.[79] In this light, it seems advisable that the Netherlands introduces more detailed rules covering the functioning of the administrative organ and the legal rights and duties of executive and non-executive members,[80] especially in respect of "large" SEs.[81] Should the Netherlands not provide for detailed regulation, there will be many gaps to be filled with respect to the one-tier system. Such gap-filling could, for example, be accomplished by inserting detailed rules for the functioning of the administrative organ in the SE's statutes. It is, however, not clear to what extent the Regulation would allow such a practice.[82] Furthermore, even if such regulation in the statutes were permitted, the question remains which general company law rules are applicable to one-tier SEs in view of Art. 9 (1) lit. c SE-Regulation, and whether or not an SE may deviate from those rules in its statutes.

[77] Meaning a functional division of management and control; see in respect of German company law *Teichmann* ZGR 2002, 383–464, p. 447–455.

[78] *Theisen/Hölzl* Die Spitzenverfassung der SE, in: *Theisen/Wenz* (Eds.) Die Europäische Aktiengesellschaft, Stuttgart 2002, p. 279.

[79] Recital 14 points out that a clear division of tasks and responsibilities inside the administrative organ should be made, and Articles 43 (1) 2nd sentence and 48 (1) SE-Regulation suggest that supervision of the SE's management is taken care of within the administrative board. See *Hommelhoff* Zur Organisationsverfassung der Europäischen AG, AG 2001, p. 284; *Winter* Ondernemingsrecht 2001, p. 197; *Teichmann* ZGR 2002, 383–464, p. 447–455.

[80] See also *Winter* Ondernemingsrecht 2001, p. 197–198. The *Sociaal-Economische Raad*, an advisory organ, consisting of employers' and employees' representatives and independent members, is divided with regard to this issue. See p. 33–36 of its Draft Advice as referred to in fn. 50.

[81] Similar in respect of the implementation act in Germany: *Teichmann* ZGR 2002, 383–464, p. 451.

[82] See *Neye/Teichmann* Der Entwurf für das Ausführungsgesetz zur Europäischen AG, AG 2003, p. 175, who argue that the implementation of the one-tier structure (solely) in statutes would violate the (system of) the Regulation.

b) Administrative organ

We assume that the general rules governing the management board of an NV will be applicable to the administrative organ of a one-tier SE (insofar as these do not deviate from the SE-Regulation). Consequently, the rules applicable to the administrative organ will be basically the same as those relevant to the management organ in the two-tier system. Reference is made to our remarks above concerning the two-tier system. Only a small number of distinctions would exist. Firstly, the minimum number of members of the administrative organ is three (Art. 13 IAR in connection with Art. 43 (2) SE-Regulation). Secondly, not all of the members of the administrative organ may be legal entities, as "non-executives" must all be natural persons (see Art. 14 IAR). The general meeting has the right, in principle, to appoint members of the administrative organ, but employee participation arrangements could result in other applicable rules (Art. 43 (3) SE-Regulation). Whether any provisions concerning the supervisory board of an NV are analogously applicable to (non-executive) members of a one-tier SE, as touched upon above, remains to be discussed.

The Netherlands does not intend to make use of the Member State's option right established by the second sentence in Art. 43 (1) SE-Regulation to introduce managing directors who are responsible for the SE's day-to-day management, since national law does not provide for such a distinction.[83] As with the two-tier board structure, no list of categories of transactions that require an express decision by the administrative organ is deemed appropriate (see Art. 48 (2) SE-Regulation). The same remarks as set out above apply.

4. Liability

Under Art. 51 SE-Regulation, the (internal) liability of members of company organs is determined by national law. Since members of the management board have collective powers and responsibilities, each of them is in principle jointly and severally liable for damage sustained by the company as a result of mismanagement (cf. Art. 2: 9 BW). That member must then have *seriously* neglected his duties.[84] Furthermore, in determining whether an individual member is

[83] The Notes p. 30 suggest that the leading principle in the administrative organ should be collective responsibility of non-executive and executive members for both the day-to-day management and the strategy, and that the introduction of managing directors would mean a deviation from this principle.

[84] HR 10 January 1997, NJ 1997, 360; HR 4 April 2003, JOL 2003, 204.

liable, an internal distribution of tasks may play a role.[85] If a company or other legal entity acting as a member of the management organ or (in the one-tier system) of the administrative organ, is liable to the SE, each natural person acting as management board member (*bestuurder*) of such company or entity is jointly and severally liable to the SE (Art. 2:11 BW).[86] Members of the supervisory board are, in principle, also jointly and severally liable for damage sustained by the company as a result of failure to perform their duties (Art. 2: 149 in connection with Art. 2: 9 BW). In the light of the remarks above, it will have to be clarified how a division between executive and non-executive members will play a role in determining the liability of individual board members in the one-tier system.

Dutch law does not, in principle, provide for direct shareholder litigation against members of company organs. Through the piercing the veil doctrine, members of the management board may be held liable to creditors of the company. It must be assumed that this applies to the SE as well. Members of an SE's administrative or management organ, as well as of the supervisory organ, can also be held liable in bankruptcy (by the trustee) or to third parties.[87]

IV. Transfer of seat

1. Transfer proposal

The SE-Regulation enables an SE to transfer its registered office to another Member State. The management organ or administrative organ is required to draw up a transfer proposal, containing the items listed in Art. 8 (2) SE-Regulation. As Art. 7 SE-Regulation states that the registered office of an SE shall be located in the same Member State as its head office, the transfer of the registered office will at the same time include the transfer of the head office. The loca-

[85] HR 10 January 1997, NJ 1997, 360.

[86] See Notes p. 31–32.

[87] See Notes p. 34: it must be assumed that the rules governing external liability are applicable on the basis of Art. 9 (1) lit. c SE-Regulation. Consequently, in the case of bankruptcy, the trustee may initiate litigation against members of company organs on the basis that they have apparently neglected their duties (cf. Articles 2: 138, 149 BW). Furthermore, a member of the management organ or the administrative organ may be held liable to third parties for publishing misleading accounts (Art. 2: 139, 150 BW) in connection with a prospectus which is deemed misleading or on the basis of the general rules of tort. Liability based upon tort may arise if a manager has contracted with third parties on behalf of the company, although he knew that the company would not be able to fulfil its obligations under the contract.

tion of the registered office may, however, differ from the location of the head office (e.g. registered office in Eindhoven, head office in Amsterdam). It then seems appropriate to include a reference to the transfer of the head office in the transfer proposal (cf. Art. 7, 2nd sentence SE-Regulation).[88]

2. Publication

Art. 8 (2) SE-Regulation requires that the transfer of seat is published in accordance with Art. 13 SE-Regulation, which provision (in turn) refers to the Member State's implementation laws based upon Directive 68/151/EEC. The Dutch legislative proposal sums these requirements up in Art. 3 IAR, stipulating that the transfer proposal be entered into the commercial register and be announced in a national newspaper. No extra publication requirements (which the Member States may introduce on the basis of Art. 8 (2) SE-Regulation) are deemed necessary.[89]

3. Attesting certificate

The Dutch Government proposes to appoint the civil law notary as the competent authority to issue a certificate attesting to the completion of the acts and formalities in connection with the transfer (Art. 20 IAR in connection with Art. 8 (8) SE-Regulation). A number of acts and formalities may be distinguished. Firstly, the civil-law notary has to ensure that a decision to transfer the seat is taken in accordance with Art. 8 (6) SE-Regulation. Secondly, the SE must satisfy the civil-law notary that the interests of creditors and holders of other rights have been adequately protected (Art. 8 (7) SE-Regulation). Thirdly, the notary may not issue a certificate as long as a Member State opposes the transfer (Art. 5 IAR).[90]

In respect of the first matter, it is questionable whether the civil-law notary's duty is limited to checking whether such resolution has been formally taken, or whether he must scrutinise the material validity and the security of the resolution against challenge.[91] In the first case, an SE could transfer its seat on the

[88] *Bellingwout* Ondernemingsrecht 2001, p. 359.

[89] Notes p. 7.

[90] According to Art. 8 (14) SE-Regulation, the transfer shall not take effect if the competent authority opposes it.

[91] Cf. *Wenz* Grenzüberschreitende Sitzverlegung, in: *Theissen/Wenz* (Eds.) Die Europä-

basis of a shareholders' resolution that is annulled afterwards. This might give rise to far-reaching legal uncertainty. In the latter case, the civil-law notary would not be able to render the certificate until the period in which the shareholders' decision may be challenged has ended, i.e. one year (Art. 2: 15 BW). To diminish legal uncertainty, restricting the period of time within which the shareholders' resolution to transfer the seat may be challenged to two months, might be considered.

4. Protection of creditors

According to Art. 4 (2) IAR, a creditor of the SE may oppose the transfer proposal within a period of two months after its publication. The SE has to give any opposing creditor security or other guarantees to meet its liabilities, on penalty of validating the opposition, unless the creditor already has received sufficient guarantees or the financial position of the SE offers sufficient security that the SE will be able to meet its liabilities (Art. 4 (1) IAR). It is unclear whether the reference in the proposed Art. 4 (1) IAR to the financial position of the SE constitutes an effective protection of the SE's creditors, as the SE's financial position is not affected by the transfer of seat alone. Even if an SE were to transfer all its assets abroad, the company's financial position would not change. Thus, the main risks for creditors in connection with a transfer of seat of their debtor, being transactions negatively affecting their possibility of taking recourse,[92] would not be covered.

If a creditor opposes the proposal in good time, the civil-law notary may not issue the attesting certificate (Art. 8 (8) SE-Regulation). Art. 4 (4) IAR provides that the certificate may only be issued after the opposition is withdrawn or the court's decision to dismiss it is enforceable. However, according to Dutch law, the court may declare its decision enforceable with anticipation.[93] Thus, an SE may have received the attesting certificate and consequently transferred its registered office, while the judgment is reversed in appeal. Therefore, Art. 4 (5) IAR determines that the court of appeal may order that a guarantee be provid-

ische Aktiengesellschaft, 182–244, p. 228 and 230. This question can ultimately only be answered by the ECJ, as it concerns the interpretation of Art. 8 (8) of the SE-Regulation.

92 *Wenz* Grenzüberschreitende Sitzverlegung, in: *Theissen/Wenz* (Eds.) Die Europäische Aktiengesellschaft, 182–244, p. 214.

93 Notes p. 42; see also MvT bij Uitvoeringswet verordening Europese vennootschap (explanatory memorandum to IAR), Tweede Kamer, vergaderjaar 2003–2004, 29 309, nr. 3, p. 9.

ed, connected with a penalty for not doing so. The Dutch Government proposes to extend creditor protection to liabilities that arise prior to the seat transfer (cf. Art. 8 (7) 2nd sentence SE-Regulation).[94]

5. Opposition by the State

Art. 8 (14) SE-Regulation opens the possibility for Member States to oppose a transfer on grounds of public interest. The Government proposes to exercise this option by giving the Minister of Justice the right to oppose the transfer on grounds of public interest within two months after publication of the transfer proposal (Art. 5 IAR). It is suggested that a public interest may be at stake if a privatised company with a public task proposes to transfer its seat.[95] In defining "public interest", the case-law of the European Court of Justice must be taken into account,[96] a factor which will probably leave little room for opposing the transfer.

The state's opposition is disclosed by filing at the commercial register. The SE may appeal against the opposition at the Enterprise Chamber of the Court of Amsterdam. Only when the opposition is withdrawn, or its dismissal is irrevocable, may the notary issue the attesting certificate. Thus, the opposition of the state against a transfer of seat effectively blocks a seat transfer, until it is finally decided upon, whereas the opposition of a creditor may be set aside in advance by the court. Moreover, it is the SE that has to commence proceedings when the Minister of Justice opposes (instead of the other way around). The opposition procedure, though a civil law remedy, thus resembles in fact a public law remedy. From a systematic point of view, it might be preferable to provide for a public law remedy, i.e. an administrative decision, open to judicial review. It is, however, not quite clear whether the Regulation would permit this. Furthermore, it is debatable whether the Enterprise Chamber would actually be the appropriate court to judge whether the state may block a seat transfer on grounds of public interest, since that is not a matter of company law.

[94] Notes p. 42; see also MvT bij Uitvoeringswet verordening Europese vennootschap (explanatory memorandum to IAR), Tweede Kamer, vergaderjaar 2003–2004, 29 309, nr. 3, p. 9.

[95] Notes p. 43; see also MvT bij Uitvoeringswet verordening Europese vennootschap (explanatory memorandum to IAR), Tweede Kamer, vergaderjaar 2003–2004, 29 309, nr. 3, p. 11.

[96] See the recent judgement on "golden shares" of 4 June 2002, C-483/99 (Commission v. French Republic), where the ECJ adopts a restrictive approach. In its judgement of 5 November 2002, C-208/00 (Überseering), the ECJ mentions, among other things, the protection of the interests of the fiscal authorities as a possible ground of public interest.

6. Protection of minority shareholders

In principle, the decision to transfer the SE's seat is taken by the general meeting with a majority of at least two thirds of the votes cast (Art. 8 (6) in connection with Art. 59 SE-Regulation). However, since the Netherlands intends to make use of the option in Article 59 (2) SE-Regulation, a simple majority of the votes cast may suffice where at least half of an SE's issued capital is present or represented (Art. 17 IAR). A certain level of minority shareholder protection may be achieved through Art. 60 SE-Regulation, providing that, where an SE has two or more classes of shares, the decision will be subject to a separate vote by each class of shareholders whose class rights are affected. It will be interesting to see what the European Court of Justice will define as a "class of shares", since Member States' national law may differ on this subject.

There is no intention of adopting supplementary provisions for the protection of minority shareholders, as the seat transfer does not involve any change in the company's net equity, thus the explanatory memorandum to the Dutch legislative proposal.[97] Nevertheless, the rights of shareholders may be affected by the transfer, since they may differ from one Member State to another in view of Art. 9 (1) lit. c, 52 and 53 SE-Regulation.[98] In our view, not only the fact that the rights of minority shareholders may diminish, but also the practical implications of a seat transfer (attending a general meeting in another Member State, receiving information in a different language) may justify a higher level of minority protection. Moreover, in the absence of minority shareholder protection, shareholders will have an incentive to challenge the shareholders' decision concerning the transfer of seat. It is unclear which consequences such litigation may have for the seat transfer, as it is questionable whether the notary must wait until the court's judgement on such a shareholder's claim is irrevocable, or whether he may issue the attesting certificate as soon as the judgment is enforceable.[99]

[97] Notes p. 7.

[98] For example, shareholders of an NV representing at least 10 percent of the issued share capital or a nominal value of 225.000 Euro may request the Enterprise Chamber of the Amsterdam court of appeals for an investigation of the company. Such investigation may result in the court taking rather far-reaching measures, such as the annulment of resolutions, the suspension or removal of directors, the appointment of interim directors, temporary transfers of shares, temporary deviation from the company's articles of association and even the winding-up of the company. These and other measures may also be sought in preliminary relief. It must be assumed that the right to request an investigation is also applicable to shareholders of a "Dutch" SE, in accordance with Art. 9 (1) lit. c under (ii) SE-Regulation. If a "Dutch" SE would transfer its seat to another Member State, this kind of minority shareholder protection would disappear.

[99] In the latter case, the SE would be able to transfer its seat although the annulment has

A higher level of minority shareholder protection may be achieved by stipulating that the transfer decision is to be taken by qualified majority. Such a requirement, which would be in line with the rules governing the transformation of an NV into an SE (Art. 37 (7) SE-Regulation), could be introduced by not exercising the option in Article 59 (2) SE-Regulation. The qualified majority requirement would then be applicable to all (other) resolutions concerning the amendment of the SE's statutes as well. Another, more preferable way of achieving minority protection would be to implement a provision stating the conditions under which a transfer may take place, e.g. to offer reasonable compensation to the minority shareholder(s) opposing the seat transfer. In order to enhance the efficiency of the seat transfer procedure, it should then be stipulated that the fact that minority shareholders claim compensation from the SE does not prevent registration in another Member State.

7. Holders of depositary receipts (*certificaten*)

Under Dutch law, a special category of holders of depositary receipts (*certificaten*) exists. A company that wants to limit its shareholders' influence may decide to implement a structure in which shares in its capital are being held by a trustee-like institution, the administration office (*administratiekantoor*), which issues depositary receipts giving the holder(s) a right to the economic benefit of the shares. The administration office, in its formal capacity as shareholder, exercises the voting rights, having regard to the interests of both the company and the holders of the depositary receipts. Nevertheless, Dutch law grants certain shareholder rights to holders of depositary receipts as well (e.g. the right to request an investigation, the right to seek annulment of a decision). Since the SE-Regulation does not contain provisions with respect to depositary receipts, it must be assumed that an SE may have holders of depositary receipts, just as an NV (cf. Art. 9 (1) c ii SE-Regulation).[100]

It has been suggested that holders of depositary receipts qualify as holders of other rights in the meaning of Art. 8 (7) SE-Regulation,[101] and that there

not yet been decided upon definitely. It is unclear whether the seat transfer would have to be cancelled if the decision were annulled in appeal. Art. 8 (16) SE-Regulation provides that, in respect of any cause of action arising prior to the transfer, the transferred SE shall be considered as having its registered office in the Member State where the SE was registered prior to the transfer, even if the SE is sued after the transfer. It is also unclear whether this provision applies to actions of minority shareholders.

[100] See also *Van Olffen* Ondernemingsrecht 2001, p. 194.

[101] *Van Olffen* Ondernemingsrecht 2001, p. 195.

could (thus) be a need for protection of their interests in connection with the transfer of seat of an SE. The Dutch legislative proposal does not make a reference to holders of depositary receipts in connection with the transfer of seat. Presumably, no special protection is deemed necessary. Nevertheless, a seat transfer may affect the rights of holders of depositary receipts, since other Member States (except for Belgium) do not know this legal instrument. Some of these rights would then disappear, in any event the rights contained in the Dutch Civil Code. A possible solution to protect the holders of depositary receipts would be to provide for a possibility to transform depositary receipts into shares at the request of the holder(s) within a certain period of time after publication of the transfer proposal.

8. Protection of employees

The SE-Regulation does not provide for explicit employee involvement in connection with the transfer of seat. It is, therefore, unclear whether a seat transfer would require a new employee involvement regime.[102] The "before-and-after" principle should, according to consideration 18 of the Preamble of the SE Directive, apply to "structural changes in an existing SE". A seat transfer may lead to a change in the structure of the company as the applicable Member State law changes (Art. 9 (1) lit. c) and because Member States options (for example in 39 (2) 2nd sentence SE-Regulation) may have been exercised differently. This could cause an indirect decrease or increase in the involvement of employees within the SE. In view of the "before-and-after principle" and of Art. 11 of the SE Directive, it has been argued that structural changes in an existing SE give the employees' representatives the right to re-negotiate the employee involvement agreement.[103] However, we take the view that under the system of the SE Directive, structural changes should be covered in the agreement concerning the involvement of employees.[104] To assume a (mandatory) right to re-negotiate in the event of each structural change would be to conflict with the contractual nature of the "negotiation-solution" in the Directive, and would furthermore lead to far-reaching inflexibility.[105] Nevertheless, in view of the controversial discussion on this topic, it seems advisable to include provisions concerning structural changes in the agreement between the SE and the employee's special negotiation group.

102 *Bellingwout* Ondernemingsrecht 2001, p. 357.

103 *Köstler* in: *Theisen/Wenz* (Eds.) Die Europäische Aktiengesellschaft, 303–337, p. 327.

104 *Wenz* in: *Theissen/Wenz* (Eds.) Die Europäische Aktiengesellschaft, 182–244, p. 215.

105 See *Heinze* Die Europäische Aktiengesellschaft, ZGR 2002, 66–95, p. 93.

9. Foreign SEs transferring into the Netherlands

If a foreign SE's registered office is transferred into the Netherlands, it has to be entered into the commercial register, together with the amended statutes (Art. 8 (10) SE-Regulation). Thus, according to national law, a notarial deed is required.[106] Whereas the formation of an NV requires a statement of no objection (see above), Art. 9 SE-Regulation prohibits the requirement of such a statement for the registration of a transferred SE.[107]

V. Involvement of employees

1. General

The Ministry of Social Affairs and Employment, responsible for the implementation of the SE Directive, has requested the advice of the *Sociaal-Economische Raad* (an advisory organ, consisting of employers' and employees' representatives and independent members) on a number of specific issues concerning the implementation.[108] A draft advice was published by the SER on the internet (www.ser.nl) in June 2003.[109] On 14 November 2003, a legislative proposal implementing the SE Directive has been introduced by the Dutch Government in Parliament, the Implementation Act concerning the SE Directive (referred to as "IAD").[110]

2. Negotiations

The starting point of the IAD is that, in the event of the formation of an SE, the competent organs of the participating companies and the special negotiating body shall endeavour to reach an agreement on the involvement of em-

[106] Cf. *Wenz* in: *Theissen/Wenz* (Eds.) Die Europäische Aktiengesellschaft, 182–244, p. 237.

[107] Notes p. 8.

[108] See www.ser.nl, Adviesaanvraag over de rol van de werknemers bij de Europese vennootschap, dated 15 November 2002 (hereafter the "Request for advice").

[109] SER Draft Advice as referred to above in fn. 50.

[110] Voorstel van wet tot uitvoering van richtlijn Nr. 2001/86/EG van de Raad van de Europese Unie van 8 oktober 2001 tot aanvulling van het statuut van de Europese vennootschap met betrekking tot de rol van de werknemers (Wet rol werknemers bij de Europese vennootschap), Tweede Kamer, vergaderjaar 2003–2004, 29 298, nrs. 1–5.

ployees (Art. 2: 5 IAD). Such an agreement must cover the issues mentioned in Art. 2: 12 (1) IAD concerning the information and consultation of employees and the composition of the body representative of the employees, unless the negotiating parties agree otherwise. Furthermore, the parties may make arrangements with respect to employee participation. In this respect, they may agree upon any form of employee participation during the negotiations, provided that the agreement address the topics mentioned in Art. 2: 12 (3) IAD.[111] If the parties would like to link their arrangements to the mandatory employee participation regime for "large" NVs (see below), it is likely that these will include a right to recommend and oppose the appointment of members of the supervisory organ (or, if applicable, of the administrative organ) to the general meeting of shareholders. It does not, however, seem possible to apply the system of "controlled co-optation", as contained in the large company regime, to SEs (see below), as this would conflict with Art. 40 (2) SE-Regulation.[112] In case of the establishment of an SE by means of transformation, the room for negotiation seems limited, since the agreement must then provide for at least the same level of all elements of employee protection as those previously existing within the company transforming into an SE (Art. 2: 12 (4) IAD). If the special negotiating body decides not to open negotiations, no arrangements on employee involvement are made (Art. 2: 7 (1) b IAD), unless an SE is established by means of transformation and employee participation exists in the company to be transformed (Art. 2: 8 (6) IAD).

3. Creation of the special negotiating body

Art. 3 SE Directive contains detailed provisions concerning the creation of a special negotiating body, leaving little room for deviating or supplementary national implementation rules. Nevertheless, the Netherlands has to determine

[111] According thereto, the arrangements concerning employee participation have to describe the nature of the employee participation, the number of members of the relevant company organ that the employees may appoint or recommend, the procedures according to which such members shall be appointed or recommend and the rights of the members thus appointed or recommended.

[112] The Notes p. 26 and the SER Draft Advice as referred to in fn. 50, p. 21, do, however, suggest that a voluntary application of the "large company regime" is possible. In our view, employee participation arrangements may only concern employee participation as defined in Art. 2 (k) SE Directive, i.e. (in the Dutch case) the right to recommend and oppose. The SE Directive does not seem to give the negotiating parties the right to deviate in the agreement from the responsibilities of the SE organs as laid down in the Regulation, e.g. by stipulating that the supervisory board may appoint its own members.

the method to be used for the election or appointment of the members of the special negotiating body who are to be elected or appointed in the Netherlands (Art. 3 (2) b SE Directive). Since a number of employee involvement issues are also dealt with in the European Works Council Directive (No. 94/45/EC of 22 September 1994), the Dutch Government proposes to closely link the implementation measures to the provisions of the implementation act of this Directive, the *Wet op de Europese ondernemingsraden* (WEOR).[113] Consequently, it is proposed to leave it up to the members of the works council and/or the employees whom they wish to appoint.[114] Under Art. 2: 4 (2) IAD, the members of the special negotiating body will be primarily appointed and/or their appointment will be withdrawn, by the works councils of the participating companies, subsidiaries and establishments.[115] Employees working at a participating company, subsidiary or establishment where no works council exists must be given the opportunity to render their advice on the persons to be appointed as members of the special negotiation group (Art. 2: 4 (7) IAD).[116] Only if no works council exists *at all* in the Netherlands, the joint employees of the participating companies, subsidiaries and establishments shall appoint the members of the special negotiating group (Art. 2: 4 (6) IAD).[117] In that case, a trade union whose members are employed at a participating company, subsidiary or establishment may submit a list of candidates, provided that it has consulted with its members employed at the company, subsidiary or establishment in question (Art. 2: 4 (6) 3rd sentence IAD).

On the basis of Art. 3 (7) SE Directive, Member States may limit the funding of experts, engaged by the special negotiation group. The Dutch Government proposes not to make use of this option and intends to align the imple-

[113] Wet van 23 januari 1997, Staatsblad 32. Cf. Request for advice, p. 2. See also *Timmerman* Ondernemingsrecht 2001, p. 199 and MvT bij Voorstel van Wet rol werknemers bij de Europese vennootschap (explanatory memorandum to IAD), Tweede Kamer, vergaderjaar 2003–2004, 29 298, nr. 3, p. 35

[114] Request for advice, p. 2. The SER agrees, Draft Advice as referred to in fn. 50, p. 39.

[115] See Request for advice, p. 2. The SER agrees, Draft Advice as referred to in fn. 50, p. 38. In respect of the proposed Art. 2: 4 IAD cf. MvT bij Voorstel van Wet rol werknemers bij de Europese vennootschap (explanatory memorandum to IAD), Tweede Kamer, vergaderjaar 2003–2004, 29 298, nr. 3, p. 35–37.

[116] It seems, however, from the wording of Art. 2: 4 (7) IAD that these employees do not have the right to vote for or against the persons to be appointed as members of the special negotiation group.

[117] Cf. MvT bij Voorstel van Wet rol werknemers bij de Europese vennootschap (explanatory memorandum to IAD), Tweede Kamer, vergaderjaar 2003–2004, 29 298, nr. 3, p. 36.

mentation to Art. 12 WEOR, stipulating that the costs reasonably necessary for the fulfilment of the task of the special negotiating body shall be borne by the participating companies. Expert fees shall be paid by these companies if they have been informed in good time of such expenditure (cf. Art. 2: 10 (3) IAD).[118]

4. Miscellaneous provisions

According to Art. 8 (2) SE Directive, the supervisory or administrative organ of an SE shall not be obliged to transmit information where its nature is such that, according to objective criteria, to do so would seriously harm the functioning of the SE and/or its subsidiaries and establishments or would be prejudicial to them (Art. 2: 6 (2) and 3: 7 (3) IAD). The Dutch Government has no intention of making such dispensation subject to prior administrative or judicial authorisation (Art. 8 (2) 2nd sentence SE Directive). Instead, the decision not to transmit information shall be subject to judicial review.[119] The special negotiation group, its members or the SE's works council will be able to appeal to the Enterprise Chamber of the Amsterdam Court of Appeal (Art. 1: 5 (2) IAD).

5. Standard rules

If no agreement is reached, or if the parties so agree, the standard rules apply under the conditions mentioned in Art. 7 SE Directive. Each Member State has to lay down such rules, which must satisfy the provisions in the Annex to the SE Directive. The Dutch standard rules, which are set out in Chapter 3 of the IAD, include provisions regarding the composition of the body representative of the employees (par. 2), information and consultation (par. 3) and employee participation (par. 4).

[118] Cf. MvT bij Voorstel van Wet rol werknemers bij de Europese vennootschap (explanatory memorandum to IAD), Tweede Kamer, vergaderjaar 2003–2004, 29 298, nr. 3, p. 42. The SER agrees, Draft Advice as referred to in fn. 50, p. 40.

[119] Request for advice, p. 3. The SER agrees, Draft Advice as referred to in fn. 50, p. 49.

a) Composition of the body representative of the employees

The standard rules concerning the composition of the body representative of the employees are described in detail in the Annex to the SE Directive. The Government intends to implement these aspects of the SE Directive by requiring every SE to create an SE works council (Art. 3: 3 (1) IAD). The composition of the SE works council shall be governed by the provisions concerning the special negotiation group (Art. 3: 4 in connection with 2: 3 IAD). It is also proposed to link the SE works council election procedure in the Netherlands to the rules governing the special negotiation group, Art. 3: 3 (3) and (4) in connection with Art. 2: 4 IAD.[120] Accordingly, the members of the SE works council representing employees in the Netherlands will in principle be elected by the (several) works council(s) existing in the SE's Dutch businesses, subsidiaries or establishments. If no works council exists at all in the Netherlands, the election shall be made by the joint employees working in the Netherlands. As opposed to the rules governing the membership of the special negotiation group, only employees of the SE and her subsidiaries and/or establishments may be elected to the SE works council (Art. 3: 3 (2) IAD).

b) Information and consultation

The standard rules concerning information and consultation are set out in paragraph 3 of chapter 3 IAD. Information and consultation must take place at such a time, in a manner and with such content which allows the SE works council (or other employees representatives) to undertake an in-depth assessment of the possible impact and, where appropriate, prepare consultations with the SE (Art. 3: 7 (1) IAD), or render its view to such measures which may be taken into account in the decision-making process within the SE (Art. 3: 7 (2) IAD).[121] The SE is not obliged to provide information to the extent this would seriously prejudice or harm the functioning of the SE or its subsidiaries or establishments and it may, if there are reasonable grounds, demand confidentiality with respect to information provided by it (Art. 3: 7 (3) IAD). The information and consultation rights are limited to questions concerning the SE itself and any of its subsidiaries or establishments situated in another Member State or which exceed the powers of the decision-making organs in a single Member State (Art. 3: 7 (4) IAD). Unless agreed otherwise, the SE is only obliged to pay for the expenses of only one expert per topic on the agenda to be consulted by

[120] See MvT bij Voorstel van Wet rol werknemers bij de Europese vennootschap (explanatory memorandum to IAD), Tweede Kamer, vergaderjaar 2003–2004, 29 298, nr. 3, p. 52. The SER agrees, Draft advice as referred to in fn. 50, p. 41.

the SE works council (Art. 3: 11 (2) IAD).[122] Meetings between the SE and the SE works council are chaired in turn by the management board of the SE and by the SE's works council, unless agreed otherwise (Art. 3: 10 (2) IAD).[123]

c) Participation

The third item to be covered in the Dutch standard rules is participation of employees in the SE. Here, a distinction must be made between SEs formed by way of transformation and SEs established in another way. The rules on participation apply only, in case of the formation of an SE by transformation, if national participation rules applied to the transforming company (Art. 3: 2 (1) IAD), or, in case of the formation of an SE by merger, if, before registration of the SE, one or more forms of participation applied in one or more participating companies covering at least 25% of the total number of employees in all the participating companies or, if, before registration of the SE, one or more forms of participation applied in one or more of the participating companies covering less than 25% of the total number of employees in all the participating companies and the special negotiating body so decides (Art. 3: 2 (2) IAD). In case of the formation of an SE by setting up a holding company or a subsidiary, this figure is raised to 50% (Art. 3: 2 (3) IAD). According to Art. 7 (3) SE Directive (the "opting out" clause), the Netherlands may provide that the standard rules in part 3 of the Annex shall not apply to the establishment of an SE by merger. The Dutch Government has no intention of doing so,[124] which is in line with the fact that Dutch law contains several forms of employee involvement. As Dutch company law already provides for employee participation as defined in Art. 2 (k) SE Directive in the "large company regime", we will set out some aspects of the current employee participation system for NVs prior to discussing the standard rules.

[121] Art. 3:7 (1) and (2) IAD are based upon Art. 2 i) and j) SE Directive, see MvT bij Voorstel van Wet rol werknemers bij de Europese vennootschap (explanatory memorandum to IAD), Tweede Kamer, vergaderjaar 2003–2004, 29 298, nr. 3, p. 52. The SER agrees, Draft advice as referred to in fn. 50, p. 56.

[122] Cf. Request for advice p. 3. The SER, however, advised not to limit the number of experts whose costs must be borne by the company. In its opinion, it suffices that the SE is informed in good time of the costs and that the costs are reasonably necessary for the fulfilment of the task of the representative body, see SER Draft Advice as referred to in fn. 50, p. 42.

[123] Cf. MvT bij Voorstel van Wet rol werknemers bij de Europese vennootschap (explanatory memorandum to IAD), Tweede Kamer, vergaderjaar 2003–2004, 29 298, nr. 3, p. 58. The SER agrees, Draft Advice as referred to in fn. 50, p. 43.

(1) Dutch employee participation system in the "large company regime"

If the large company regime applies, the appointment of members of the supervisory board is governed by the system of "controlled co-optation" (Art. 2: 158 BW). In this system, both the general meeting and the works council may propose candidates to the supervisory board. The supervisory board itself may then appoint new members, provided that the general meeting or the works council do not oppose a certain candidate on grounds of incompetence or lack of due composition of the board. When either the general meeting or the works council does oppose, the supervisory board must enter proceedings at the Enterprise Chamber of the Amsterdam Court of Appeal to enable the appointment.

This rather complicated system is expected to be replaced by a new (even more complicated) system, the legislative proposal of which is currently pending in Parliament.[125] In the proposed new appointment procedure, both the general meeting and the works council may still recommend candidates to the supervisory board. The supervisory board may then, in turn, propose candidates to the general meeting. For one third of the candidates, the supervisory board is obliged to follow the recommendations of the works council, unless it has objections against the recommended candidate(s) on grounds of incompetence or lack of due composition of the board. The supervisory board must then enter proceedings at the Enterprise Chamber to have the objections sustained. In that case, the works council must make a new recommendation. In accordance with the proposal of the supervisory board, the general meeting appoints the candidates. The proposal may be rejected by a resolution with two-thirds majority of the votes cast, representing at least one third of the issued capital. If the general meeting neither appoints nor rejects the candidate(s), the supervisory board may appoint the candidates.[126]

[124] See MvT bij Voorstel van Wet rol werknemers bij de Europese vennootschap (explanatory memorandum to IAD), Tweede Kamer, vergaderjaar 2003–2004, 29 298, nr. 3, p. 14. The SER agrees, Draft Advice as referred to in fn. 50, p. 45.

[125] Wijziging van boek 2 van het Burgerlijk Wetboek in verband met aanpassing van de structuurregeling, Tweede Kamer, vergaderjaar 2001–2002, 28 179. New discussions about the "large company regime" are to be expected early 2004.

[126] Contrary to the current legal regime, it is proposed that the new procedure will not be mandatory. The statutes of a company may prescribe an alternative procedure, provided that the supervisory board and the works council both agree.

(2) Participation in case of the establishment of an SE by transformation

In the case of an SE established by transformation, all prior existing aspects of employee participation shall continue to apply to the SE (Art. 3: 12 (1) IAD). In view thereof, two situations must be distinguished. On the one hand, if the transforming NV is subject to the large company regime, the employee participation regime as described above shall continue to apply. Accordingly, the representative body will have the right to recommend and oppose all candidates of the supervisory organ, analogous to the large company regime.[127] However, the system of "controlled co-optation" in which the supervisory board basically appoints its own members, shall not apply to SEs, as the general meeting has this power (Art. 40 (2) SE-Regulation). Presumably, the employees' representatives will thus be granted the right to propose candidates (directly) to the general meeting. The influence of employees may indirectly diminish if the statutes of the SE determine that the general meeting instead of the supervisory board is empowered to appoint the members of the management board (cf. the proposed Art. 11 (1) IAR).[128] On the other hand, a regular NV not qualifying as a "large company" is not subject to the large company regime and (therefore) does not have employee participation in the sense of Art. 2 (k) SE Directive. Thus, an SE established by transformation of a regular NV will not have employee participation either, unless so agreed. Therefore, a regular NV which is on the verge of fulfilling the criteria to be subject to the large company regime may use the transformation route to avoid that the large company regime becomes applicable to it. The Netherlands does not intend to adopt measures to prevent this (e.g. under Art. 11 SE Directive)[129]: on the contrary, Art. 3: 2 (1) IAD clearly provides that the standard rules concerning employee participation

[127] Cf. MvT bij Voorstel van Wet rol werknemers bij de Europese vennootschap (explanatory memorandum to IAD), Tweede Kamer, vergaderjaar 2003–2004, 29 298, nr. 3, p. 59.

[128] In that case, it is unclear whether it may be held that all aspects of employee participation continue, as is required in part 3 lit. (a) Annex to SE Directive and Art. 3: 12 (1) IAD. According to the Dutch Government, however, a diminishment of the powers of the company organ with respect to which the employees have participation rights does not constitute a violation of the before-and-after principle, see above in fn. 49.

[129] *Heinze* Die Europäische Aktiengesellschaft, ZGR 2002, p. 87, sees little practical relevance to this provision, as the Directive contains all appropriate provisions to prevent such misuse. The SER draws attention to the possibility of a corporate restructuring qualifying as misuse of the SE. It holds that such a restructuring may only qualify as misuse if the restructuring does not serve any legitimate purpose, Draft Advice as referred to in fn. 50, p. 31.

only apply *if* the large company regime applied to the transforming company prior to transformation.[130]

If a two-tier structured NV which is subject to the large company regime transforms into a one-tier SE, the aspects of employee participation stemming from the large company regime have to be applied to the one-tier structure. It would seem reasonable in this case to distinguish between executive and non-executive members of the administrative organ and to limit the employees' participation rights to non-executive members, in order to avoid a strengthening of employee influence on the company's current affairs.[131] However, the Dutch Government takes the view that the employees' rights of recommendation and opposition will in that case apply to *all* members of the administrative organ, i.e. without making a distinction between executives and non-executives.[132]

(3) Participation in other cases

The Netherlands also proposed standard rules in respect of the formation of an SE in other ways than by transformation, i.e., by way of merger, formation of a holding company or formation of a subsidiary. A distinction is made between the nature of the participation regime and the number of company organ members to which it applies. With respect to the *nature* of the participation regime, the Dutch standard rules provide that if more than one employee participation regime existed in the companies participating in the SE formation, the special negotiation group may determine which of these participation regimes shall apply to the SE (Art. 3: 2 (4) IAD). If such decision would lead to a decrease of the level of employee participation, it shall require a qualified majority of two thirds of the members of the special negotiation group, representing at least two thirds of the employees and stemming from at least two countries. This can only be determined after the form of employee participation has been chosen.[133]

[130] Cf. MvT bij Voorstel van Wet rol werknemers bij de Europese vennootschap (explanatory memorandum to IAD), Tweede Kamer, vergaderjaar 2003–2004, 29 298, nr. 3, p. 49.

[131] Cf. *Henssler* Unternehmerische Mitbestimmung in der Societas Europaea, in Festschrift für Peter Ulmer zum Geburtstag am 2. Januar 2003, 2003, 193–210, p. 203, 207. This proposal would make it necessary to determine the proportion of executives and non-executives, as this proportion would be relevant for the scope of the employees' participation rights.

[132] MvT bij Voorstel van Wet rol werknemers bij de Europese vennootschap (explanatory memorandum to IAD), Tweede Kamer, vergaderjaar 2003–2004, 29 298, nr. 3, p. 59.

[133] MvT bij Voorstel van Wet rol werknemers bij de Europese vennootschap (explanatory memorandum to IAD), Tweede Kamer, vergaderjaar 2003–2004, 29 298, nr. 3, p. 60.

If the special negotiation group does *not* select the applicable employee participation regime, the applicable regime will be the system of the (Dutch) large company regime described above, giving the employees representatives a right of recommendation and opposition with respect to members of the relevant company organ, *provided* that one or more companies forming the SE had been subject to the large company regime prior to the formation (first sentence, Art. 3: 2 (5) IAD). If, however, no participating company had been subject to the large company regime, the (foreign) employee participation regime rendering the employees the highest number of appointment or recommendation rights shall apply to the SE (second sentence, Art. 3: 2 (5) IAD). This is an entirely quantitative test: no distinction is made as to the nature of the foreign participation regimes that might apply.[134]

The *number* of members of the supervisory or administrative organ that shall be appointed or recommended by the employees depends on the form of participation regime that the special negotiation group elects or that applies in accordance with Art. 3: 2 (5) IAD.[135] The employees shall have participation rights in respect of the highest number of members with respect to which the same kind of participation rights could be exercised prior to the SE formation (Art. 3: 12 (2) IAD). For example, if two companies participating in the formation of an SE were subject to an employee participation system involving appointment rights and one participating company was subject to a recommendation system, and if the special negotiation group elects the appointment system for the SE, the highest number of appointment rights (not: recommendation rights) existing prior to formation shall apply to the SE.[136]

[134] MvT bij Voorstel van Wet rol werknemers bij de Europese vennootschap (explanatory memorandum to IAD), Tweede Kamer, vergaderjaar 2003–2004, 29 298, nr. 3, p. 51.

[135] By contrast, the SER proposed that the negotiating body's power to choose take precedence, cf. SER Draft Advice as referred to in fn. 50, p. 45, following *Winter* Nederlands Juristenblad 2002, p. 2038–2039.

[136] Consequently, if one of the participating companies is an NV subject to the large company regime, and the other is a German AG, subject to mandatory employee participation, it will not be possible to elect the German system of appointing the members, combined with the Dutch proportion, i.e. all members. Cf. *Timmerman* Ondernemingsrecht 2001, p. 201 and *Winter* Ondernemingsrecht 2001, p. 196. If, however, a German AG (having an appointment system involving 1/3 of the members of the supervisory board) and an Austrian AG (having an appointment system involving 50% of the members of the supervisory board) merge into an SE with registered office in the Netherlands, the employees shall have appointment rights with respect to 50% of the relevant company organ, cf. MvT bij Voorstel van Wet rol werknemers bij de Europese vennootschap (explanatory memorandum to IAD), Tweede Kamer, vergaderjaar 2003–2004, 29 298, nr. 3, p. 60.

6. National employee involvement

Existing rights regarding the involvement of employees (other than participation), according to national law, will, in the case of formation of an SE, continue to apply (Art. 13 (3) a SE Directive). This includes Member State legislation on employee information and consultation rights on a business level.[137] The WOR, which shall, as a result, be applicable to SEs and their subsidiaries registered in the Netherlands,[138] provides for rather far-reaching information and consultation rights for a business's works council. These rights include the right to request that a consultative meeting be held, where all the company's affairs may be discussed. At least twice a year the general course of business within the company is discussed. Moreover, the works council has a right of advice on a catalogue of important decisions which may affect the situation of the employees, e.g. merger or take-over decisions, the closing down or transfer of a business, a collective mass dismissal (Art. 25 WOR). The formation of an SE will in many cases qualify as a decision in respect of which the works council has a right of advice.[139] The works council must be able to give its advice at a time where it may have a real influence on the outcome of the decision (Art. 25 (2) WOR). If the advice is not sought or followed, the works council may challenge the decision at the Enterprise Chamber on the grounds that the entrepreneur could not reasonably have come to his decision, considering all the interests (Art. 26 WOR). Furthermore, the works council has a right of approval to – broadly stated – all matters relating to the working conditions in the enterprise (Art. 27 WOR), e.g. policies concerning working hours, holidays, payment, training, absence due to illness, etc. If the approval is refused, thc company must ask the magistrate's court (*kantonrechter*) for permission to implement the measure. Finally, the works council has a right of advice regarding the appointment of members of the management board (Art. 30 WOR). In this case, if the advice is not followed, the works council has no judicial remedy.[140]

[137] See *Buijs* Ondernemingsrecht 2001, p. 182, who argues that the influence of (national and European) works councils may increase as a result of the introduction of the SE. See further (in respect of German law): *Köstler* in: *Theissen/Wenz* (Eds.) Die Europäische Aktiengesellschaft, 303–337, p. 328.

[138] MvT bij Voorstel van Wet rol werknemers bij de Europese vennootschap (explanatory memorandum to IAD), Tweede Kamer, vergaderjaar 2003–2004, 29 298, nr. 3, p. 10.

[139] See *Buijs* Ondernemingsrecht 2001, p. 182.

[140] A degree of workers' influence is also derived from the fact that trade unions have the right to instigate an investigation procedure (see above).

VI. Conclusion

Under the SE-Regulation, Member States have the right to prepare implementation legalisation in order to regulate the SE in their territory. The Netherlands has already introduced a first draft for an implementation act (the IAR) into Parliament. The IAR appears to leave SEs a lot of flexibility to design their structure. However, in our view a number of issues in the IAR could be reconsidered or supplemented. This is especially the case with respect to the exercise of Member State's options in respect of the SE's board structure, the functioning of the administrative organ in the one-tier SE and the position of (minority) shareholders and creditors in connection with the transfer of seat and the SE merger. A legislative proposal for an implementation act with respect to the SE Directive has also been published (the IAD). The provisions of the IAD include detailed regulation of the involvement of employees in the SE, which are in many respects similar to the provisions of the European Works Council Act and which seem to grant substantial power to the Dutch works council(s) existing at companies involved in the formation of an SE. It is now up to Parliament to decide upon the proposals in order to make the Dutch SE company form effective as from 8 October 2004.

Poland

Krzysztof Oplustil / Anna Rachwał / Jacek Sokołowski

Bibliography: *Czerniawski, R.* Kodeks spółek handlowych. Przepisy o spółce akcyjnej, Warszawa 2001; *Doralt, P.* Die Europäische Aktiengesellschaft Societas Europaea, lecture at the Prof. W. Kastner's Symposium published in Internet: (http://recht.wu-wien.ac.at); *Heinze, M.* Die europäische Aktiengesellschaft, ZGR 1/2002, p. 66; *Herfs-Röttgen, E.* Arbeitnehmerbeteiligung in der Europäischen Aktiengesellschaft, Neue Zeitschrift für Arbeitsrecht (NZA) 8/2001, p. 429; *Hommelhoff, P.* Einige Bemerkungen zur Organisationsverfassung der Europäischen Aktiengesellschaft, Die Aktiengesellschaft (AG) 6/2001, p. 279; *Klyta, W.* Spółki kapitałowe w prawie prywatnym międzynarodowym, Kraków 2002; *Kruczalak* (ed.) Kodeks spółek handlowych. Komentarz, Warszawa 2002; *Ludwiczak, M.* Międzynarodowe prawo prywatne, Poznań 1996, p. 170; *Napierała, J.* Societas Europaea, Przegląd Prawa Handlowego (PPH) 11/2002, p. 30; *Neye, H.-W. / Teichmann, Ch.* Der Entwurf für das Ausführungsgesetz zur Europäischen Aktiengesellschaft, Die Aktiengesellschaft (AG) 4/2003, p. 169; *Oplustil, K.* Europejska Spółka Akcyjna. Teksty aktów prawnych z omówieniem, Warszawa 2002; *Oplustil, K.* Selected problems concerning formation of a holding SE, German Law Journal 2/2003, Internet Law Review, downloadable under http://www.germanlawjournal.com; *Oplustil, K. / Sokołowski, J.* Europejska Spółka Akcyjna – zadanie dla polskiego ustawodawcy. Okręt flagowy już płynie, „Rzeczpospolita" from 21.06.2002, supplement: "Law every day" ("yellow pages"); *Oplustil, K. / Rachwał, A.* Wprowadzenie Europejskiej Spółki Akcyjnej do prawa polskiego, Kwartalnik Prawa Prywatnego (KPP), 3/2003, p. 649; *Oplustil, K. / Rachwał, A.* Roszczenie wierzyciela o zabezpieczenie a instytucja odrębnego zarządu przy połączeniach spółek kapitałowych (Art. 496 § 2 i Art. 395 § 1 k.s.h.), PPH 1/2003, p. 49; *Pazdan, M.* Prawo prywatne międzynarodowe, Warszawa 1996, p. 83; *Pluskat, S.* Die Arbeitnehmerbeteiligung in der geplanten Europäischen AG, Deutsches Steuerrecht (DStR) 35/2001, p. 1490; *Poczobut, J.* Osoby prawne w polskim prawie prywatnym międzynarodowym. Projekt nowelizacji ustawy, KPP 3/2000, p. 545; *Rodzynkiewicz, M.* Łączenie się spółek. Komentarz, Warszawa 2002, p. 78 et seq.; *Rudolf, S.* (ed.) Nadzór właścicielski w spółkach prawa handlowego, Warszawa 1999; *Sokołowski, J.* Monistyczny system zarządu w Europejskiej Spółce Akcyjnej – wyzwanie dla polskiego ustawodawcy, Prawo Spółek (PrSp) 12/2003, p. 9; *Sołtysiński, S.* Prawo właściwe dla spółek prawa handlowego, Rejent 7–8/2001, p. 285; *Sołtysiński, S. / Szajkowski, A. / Szumański, A. / Szwaja, J.* Kodeks spółek handlowych, Warszawa 2002, vol. III; *Teichmann, Ch.* Vorschläge für das deutsche Ausführungsgesetz zur Europäischen Aktiengesellschaft, Zeitschrift für Wirtschaftsrecht (ZIP) 25–26/2002, p. 1109; *Teichmann, Ch.* Die Einführung der Europäischen Aktiengesellschaft. Grundlagen der Ergänzung des europäischen Statuts durch den deutschen Gesetzgeber, ZGR 2002, p. 383.

I. The Societas Europaea in relation to other limited companies in the Polish legal system

In the light of impending EU accession,[1] the Polish legislature is called upon to make provision for the opportunities contained in the Council Regulation on the Statute for the European Company (SE)[2]. However, merely to fulfil the obligations (i.e. the obligation to pass rules supplementing the SE-Regulation, e.g. Art. 64 para. 2 SE-Reg.) foreseen in the Regulation together with the necessary 'technical' provisions,[3] would not be desirable. The numerous opportunities provided by the European Regulation would allow, on the one hand, the secure positioning of the SE in the national legal environment, and, on the other hand, would provide a structure which would be more attractive from the point of view of national and foreign investors.[4] A further argument in favour of availing of the authorisations given by the Regulation, is the desirability of eliminating certain doubts that arise regarding the application of the Council Regulation within the Polish legal system. The optimum solution would therefore be the passing of a separate act introducing the European Company into Polish law, containing all the provisions implementing both the empowerments (authorisations) and delegations (obligations) arising from the SE-Regulation as well implementing the Directive (2001/86/WE) on the involvement of employees.[5]

The provisions adopted by the national lawmaker should be such as to enable the SE to be a company form as close as possible to the public limited liability company as it is regulated in Polish law.[6] Recital no. 5 to the SE-Reg. declares that Member States are obliged to ensure that the provisions applicable to European Companies do not result in discrimination because of unjustified

[1] After the referendum of 7–8 June 2003 was a success (77% of Poles voted for the accession of Poland in the EU) the last obstacle was removed and Poland will formally join the EU in may 2004.

[2] Cited below: SE-Reg.

[3] E.g. the adaptation of national provisions concerning the incorporation formalities.

[4] See *Napierała*, PPH p. 30, who postulates that Polish implementation of the SE should aim at encouraging the investors to choose Poland as the seat of future SE's. See also *Oplustil/Sokołowski*, "Rzeczpospolita" from 21.06.2002, supplement: "Law every day" ("yellow pages"); *Oplustil/Rachwal*, KPP 3/2003, p. 649 et seq.; *Oplustil* Europejska Spółka Akcyjna. Teksty aktów prawnych z omówieniem, Warszawa 2002, p. 33 et seq.

[5] As the German and Austrian legislators decided to do, cf. *Teichmann*, ZIP 25–26/2002, p. 1109 et seq.; *Neye/Teichmann*, AG 2003, p. 169 et seq.; *Doralt* Die Europäische Aktiengesellschaft "Societas Europaea", lecture at the Prof. W. Kastner's Symposium published in Internet: (http://recht.wu-wien.ac.at).

[6] So in the German doctrine *Teichmann* supra, ft. 5, p. 1110.

different treatment of SE's compared with national public limited liability companies. Practical arguments also speak in favour of adopting regulations parallel to the national public limited liability company law for the SE. Those dealing with the legal aspects of commercial activities, especially judges and legal advisors, as well as company executives, are familiar with the regulations of the Polish Commercial Companies Code of 2000 (CCC)[7]. Therefore, when the SE-Reg. empowers the national legislator to adopt special regulations with regard to the SE and adequate provisions already exist in CCC, the Polish legislator should incorporate them into the act introducing the SE.[8] However, this general rule does not exclude the possibility of adopting for the SE, solutions which differ from those in national company law, if it would be justified by the particular character of the European Company or if it would better facilitate the achievement of the aims of the European regulation.

II. General provisions

1. The founders

According to Art. 2 para. 1–4 SE-Reg., an SE may be formed only by companies with registered offices and head offices within the European Community, though not necessarily in the same Member State. The Council Regulation authorises national legislators to permit exceptions to this rule, under the conditions provided in Art. 2 para. 5 SE-Reg. A Member State may provide that a company, the head office of which is not in the Community may participate in the formation of an SE, provided that the company is formed under the law of a Member State, has its registered office in that Member State and has a real and continuous link with a Member State's economy.[9]

It must be mentioned that Polish Private International Law in principle follows the so-called real seat theory, according to which the law applicable to a commercial company (its *statut personae*) is determined by the real seat of its

[7] Ustawa z 15 września 2000 r. – Kodeks spółek handlowych (Act of 15 September 2000 – Commercial Companies Code), Dz. U. (Polish Law Journal) no. 94, pos. 1037 subsequently amended.

[8] This remark does not concern, however, the regulation of the CCC which would be applicable to SEs anyway as a result of the general reference of Art. 9 par 1 lit. c SE-Reg and need not, therefore,be repeated in the introducing act; cf. *Teichmann* supra, ft. 5, p. 1110.

[9] On this exception see also: *Neye/Teichmann* supra, ft. 5, p. 169, 170.

head office.[10] However, this fact should not deter the Polish legislator from making use of the cited empowerment. Firstly, Polish International Private Law is about to be amended and, after the important decisions of the European Court of Justice in the "Centros ltd." and "Überseering BV" cases,[11] there must be doubt as to whether the real seat theory will be sustained.[12] Secondly, regardless of future development of Polish Private International Law, pragmatic considerations also indicate that the authorities provided should be availed of. Enabling companies which comply with the conditions of Art. 2 para. 5 SE-Reg. to establish an SE with seat in Poland would make this country more attractive for investors from outside the EC and would also strengthen the position of Polish law in the competition of the company law systems.

The Polish legislator should allow companies with head offices outside the EC to participate in forming an SE in Poland, if they are incorporated according to the national law of one of the Member States (not necessarily Poland), have their registered office in that state and have "a real and continuous link with a Member State's economy" (not necessarily with the Polish economy).

2. Transfer of seat and the procedure to establish the identity of the incorporation seat and the real seat

a) *Protection of shareholders and creditors on the transfer of seat to another Member State*

Polish law does not allow the transfer of the seat of a public limited liability company abroad, while preserving its existence as a legal subject. According to the Art. 459 No. 2 CCC, the decision of the shareholders' meeting to transfer the seat, results in the liquidation of the company. Polish law therefore provides

[10] According to Art. 9 para. 2 Polish Private International Law Act (Ustawa z 12 listopada 1965 r. – Prawo prywatne międzynarodowe, Act of 12 November 1965 – Private International Law, Dz. U. no. 46, pos. 290 subsequently amended), the legal ability of a moral person is subject to the law of the country of its seat. In the Polish doctrine the standpoint prevails, that under the "seat" the head office of the company should be understood.
See Pazdan *Prawo prywatne międzynarodowe*, Warszawa 1996, p. 83, *Ludwiczak* Międzynarodowe prawo prywatne, Poznań 1996, p. 170, *Poczobut*, KPP 3/2000, p. 545, *Klyta* Spółki kapitałowe w prawie prywatnym międzynarodowym, Kraków 2002, p. 44.

[11] "Centros Ltd." (decision of 9.3.1999, C-212/97, ECR 1999, p. I-1459) i "Überseering B.V." (decision of 5.11.2002 – Rs C-208/00, publ. in Internet: http://curia.eu.int/en/actu/activities/act02/0229en.htm#ToC9).

[12] See *Poczobut* supra, ft. 10, p. 548 et. seq.

no legal protection for shareholders or creditors and holders of other rights in the transferring company. In contrast, a European Company incorporated in Poland would be allowed to transfer its seat to another Member State, according to the procedure foreseen in Art. 8 SE-Reg.

Transfer of the company's seat abroad results in a change of its personal statute, which determines also the law applicable to the rights and duties of the shareholders.[13] The opposition of the minority shareholders to an intended transfer is therefore justified, from their point of view, by the important fact that their rights and duties which are only fragmentarily regulated in the SE-Regulation itself, will, after the transfer, be determined by a different national law than before. This consideration speaks for introducing proper protection for the minority shareholders who oppose the transfer of seat, by means of the empowerment provided by Art. 8 para. 5 SE-Reg. From the purely pragmatic point of view, such protection would allow a minority shareholder who voted against the transfer of seat at the shareholders' meeting to exit from the company in return for compensation equivalent to the real value of his shares. This possibility would also prevent court challenges to the shareholders' resolution (Art. 422 CCC) and possible frustration of the resolution, in the event of a successful challenge.

The just solution would be to allow the shareholders opposing the transfer of seat to retreat from the company in return for the equivalent of their shares, estimated in relation to their market price or to their share in the company's assets. Art 416 § 4 CCC, according to which the validity of a shareholders' decision to essentially amend the objects of the company's activity is dependant on a purchase of the shares of the shareholders opposed to the resolution, could serve as an example of such a protective mechanism. Their shares should be acquired by other shareholders or third persons.[14] Introducing a similar procedure with regard to an SE planning to transfer its seat abroad seems legitimate, but with, however, an explicit permission for the SE itself to purchase the shares from the shareholders opposing the transfer of seat. For Polish SEs this would constitute a further admissible case of acquiring their own shares in the meaning of Art. 362 § 1 no. 7 CCC and would accelerate the procedure of seat transfer, as the board of the company would not have to look for a purchaser of the shares as it is required to do by Art. 416 CCC.[15] The shareholders' decision on the transfer of seat should be taken by means of public voting by name, in

[13] Cf. *Sołtysiński*, Rejent 7–8/2001, p. 285.

[14] Cf. *Oplustil* supra, ft. 4, p. 126.

[15] Cf. *Szumański* in *Sołtysiński/Szajkowski/Szumański/Szwaja*, vol. III, p. 928 (Art. 417 marginal number 21 et seq.).

order to identify the shareholders voting against the transfer and from whom the shares would be purchased afterwards (as in the case of a decision on alteration of the objects of the company's activity, Art. 416 § 3 CCC). Such a decision will also constitute an amendment of the SE statutes and therefore a majority of 3/4 will be required (Art. 415 § 1 CCC in relation to Art. 59 SE-Reg.). This means that a maximum number of its own shares to be purchased by an SE will not exceed 25%.[16] Further, in order to ensure that minority shareholders obtain a real equivalent of the value of their shares, the rules for the valuation of the shares, provided by Art. 417 § 1 sentence 1–3 CCC, should be incorporated into the SE introduction act. According to these rules, the purchase of shares is to be exercised at a price indicated by the average exchange rates on a regulated market during the three months preceding the resolution of the shareholders' meeting and if the shares are not quoted on a regulated market, the price is to be established by an auditor elected by the meeting or appointed by the Register Court. Should an SE decide not to purchase its own shares, the procedure analogous to that prescribed in Art. 417 § 1–3 CCC should take place: the shares of the opposing shareholders would be purchased by the other shareholders or third persons.

According to Art. 8 para. 8 SE-Reg., in order to complete the transfer of seat procedure, it is necessary that a 'certificate attesting to the completion of the acts and formalities to be accomplished before the transfer' has been issued by the competent authority in the state where the SE had its registered office hitherto. An indispensable condition for obtaining such a certificate would be for the SE to present evidence for the fact that the claims of minority shareholders opposing the transfer have been satisfied in the manner proposed above.

As Polish law does not allow domestic companies to transfer their seats to another state at all, there is no regulation concerning protection of creditors in case of such a transfer. However, it may be questionable whether special provisions for protection of creditors of the SE transferring its seat from Poland to another Member State, e.g. a right to security for their claims against the SE, are really demanded. Considering that an SE should *per definitionem* extend its activity to more than one Member State (cf. the rules of the formation of an SE, Art. 2 SE-Reg.), it could be expected from the SE's creditors that they take

[16] It should be underlined here that Art. 20 par. 1 lit. d of the Second Council Directive (77/91/EEC) empowers explicitly Member States to make an exception from the rules considering the purchase of own shares (limiting generally the number of own shares to be purchased to 10% of the registered share capital) formulated in Art. 19 of this Directive in case when the purchase of own shares occurs in execution of the provisions protecting minority shareholders (among others, in case of a merger and a transfer of seat).

into account the international character of the debtor's activities including the fact that it could transfer its seat as well as its assets between its branches and holding companies located in different states of the EC. Besides, according to Art. 8 para. 16 SE-Reg., an SE which has transferred its registered office from Poland shall be considered, in respect of any cause of action arising prior to the transfer, as having its registered office in Poland, even if the SE is sued after the transfer. Thus, the creditors will still have the possibility to sue the SE before the Polish court even after the completion of the transfer. Taking this into consideration, it should be expected that the Polish law will grant creditors of an SE transferring its seat abroad a right to demand security only in exceptional cases, i.e. if they will be capable to demonstrate that the transfer of seat will result in substantial deteriotation of the enforceability of their claims.

The Polish legislator is also expected to avail the empowerment of Art. 8 para. 14 SE-Reg. and to introduce a provision allowing a proper financial authority to oppose the transfer of seat if the SE is a financial institution as defined in Art. 4 § 1 No. 7 CCC.

b) Discrepancy between the real seat and the registered office of an SE

If the real seat and the registered offices of an SE happen to be located in two different Member States, Art. 64 SE-Reg. obliges the national legislators to introduce an adequate procedure for restoring legal conformity, i.e. that both head office and registered office are in the same state. The Polish legislator can refer hereby firstly to the procedure foreseen by the CCC to eliminate defects in articles of association due to non-compliance with legal provisions (Art. 327 CCC), secondly – to Art. 24–26 NJR Act. The competent authority to undertake actions to restore legal compliance with Art. 7 SE-Reg will be the Commercial Register with jurisdiction over the location of the registered head office of the SE (Art. 694^2 Polish Civil Procedure Act).

Penalties which could be imposed on an SE if it fails to remedy the situation which is in breach of Art. 7 SE-Reg. within a deadline set by the court, would be fines according to the rules laid down in the NJR Act (Art. 24 NJR Act), the appointment of a custodian for the SE (cf. Art. 26 NJR Act) and possibly a court order winding-up the SE and opening its liquidation. Taking into account the complexity of the acts that would be necessary to re-establish the unity of the registered office and head office, a period of adequate length should be set for their completion. To ensure conformity with Art. 64 SE-Reg., the possibility of appeal against the court's decision declaring non-compliance with Art. 7 SE-Reg. must be granted, and the appeal should suspend the running of the period set for eliminating the non-compliance.

c) Incorporation (registering the SE), competent authority according to Art. 68 para. 2 SE-Reg

(1) The proper register

European Companies formed in Poland will be incorporated by registration in the NJR, in the division 'Enterprises' Register'. As the SE-Regulation applies directly, Art. 12 para. 1 SE-Reg. should be treated as a sufficient legal basis for the registration of an SE in the NJR, which is a proper register according to Art. 3 of the First Directive.[17] For the sake of clarity and legal certainty, the Polish legislator should, however, specify the rules applicable to the incorporation of an SE in the NJR Act, as well as in ministerial decrees. The European Company should be explicitly added to the list of entrepreneurs in Art. 36 NJR Act which states all legal forms of companies (e.g. by adding point 7a: 'European Companies'). In addition, in Art. 38 NJR Act which lists data subject to registration, the words 'and European Companies' should be added. Official application forms required in the registration procedure should also mention the European Company; the appendix catalogue to the application forms should be amended, e.g. by adding the certificate of the competent authority required by Art. 25 para. 2 or Art. 8 para. 7 SE-Reg.

(2) The competent authority

According to Art. 68 par. 2 SE-Reg, Member States are obliged to designate the authorities competent to exercise the actions foreseen in the enumerated articles of the Regulation. The competent authority in all cases listed would, in Poland, be the Register Court competent locally in respect of the registered office of the SE. In the Polish legal system, the Register Court generally supervises all legal aspects of the activities of limited liability companies. It must be mentioned here that no authority will be designated in Poland as empowered to convene the general meeting at any time (Art. 54 para. 2 SE-Reg.), as the CCC grants no such competence with regard to limited liability companies to any authority.

[17] First Council Directive of 9 March 1968 on co-ordination of safeguards which, for the protection of the interests of members and others, are required by Member States of companies within the meaning of the second paragraph of Article 58 of the Treaty, with a view to making such safeguards equivalent throughout the Community (68/151/EEC).

III. Formation of an SE

1. Merger

a) Protection of minority shareholders

Mergers of limited liability companies are governed by Arts. 491–516 CCC, which are based on the regulations of the 3rd Company Law Directive.[18] Polish law, however, does not in fact contain any regulations designed to protect the shareholders of the merging companies who oppose the exchange ratio of the shares foreseen by the draft terms of merger. Moreover, the CCC excludes the possibility of having the merger decision challenged on the sole ground of objections to the exchange ratio (Art. 509 § 3 CCC), thus leaving the shareholders with only a claim for compensation against the members of the company's organs and merger auditors (Art. 512 and 513 in relation to Art. 509 § 3 sentence 2 CCC). In contrast to the provisions on transformation, shareholders cannot demand another share valuation by auditors, nor that a valuation be conducted by the court (cf. Art. 566 CCC). Except for the simplified merger within a group of companies, in which the acquiring company holds at least 90% but not all of the shares of the company being acquired (Art. 516 § 3 CCC), the code does not provide the shareholders opposing the merger with a right to have their shares bought and thus makes it impossible for them to leave the company.

Art. 24 par. 2 SE-Reg. opens the possibility of introducing adequate provisions for the benefit of minority shareholders in the case of the formation of an SE by means of cross-border merger. Taking into account, however, that Polish company law does not recognise a merger as a circumstance which justifies granting shareholders a possibility of retreating from the company in return for the equivalent of their share-value (cf. Art. 484 § 4 CCC), it does not seem legitimate to grant them this benefit in the case of a merger for the formation of an SE, under the condition that it is going to have its registered office in Poland. The position is different, however, in the case of a Polish public limited company acquired by a foreign company and is then transformed in this way into an SE or, in case of a merger leading to the formation of an SE, if the newly established SE should be incorporated abroad. From the point of view of Polish shareholders, such a situation is the same as the transfer of seat of 'their' company to a different Member State. Their rights and duties towards the company will afterwards be determined by the foreign law applicable to the SE

[18] Third Council Directive of 9 October 1978 based on Article 54 (3) (g) of the Treaty concerning mergers of public limited liability companies (78/855/EEC).

according to Art. 9 para. 1 lit. c ii) SE-Reg. This speaks clearly for granting them the same particular protection, as they should enjoy in case of the transfer of seat (cf. supra).

Nevertheless, it does not seem to be justified to provide any particular protection to minority shareholders in the acquiring company, which is to be transformed into an SE. Such a company does not loose its legal status in Poland and the shareholders' rights and duties continue to be governed by Polish law (apart from two minority rights governed directly by Art. 55 and 56 SE-Reg.). The argument that the transformation from a national public limited company into an SE leads to a change of legal regime (within which supranational European law is superior) and thus justifies the particular protection of the shareholders, is not convincing. It is rather doubtful whether the European Company is to be regarded as an entirely separate company form, different from the national public limited liability companies. Both Art. 10 SE-Reg. ensuring equal treatment for the SE and national public limited companies, and the wide scope of the references to the national law of public limited companies contained in the SE-Reg., indicate rather the opposite.[19]

The protection of minority shareholders should be granted by making the validity of a decision on merger dependant on the purchase of their shares – either by the company itself or by third persons, analogously to the solution proposed above with regard to the shareholders opposing the transfer of seat of a 'Polish SE' abroad, referring to Art. 416–417 CCC.[20] This purchase should be concluded before the certificate attesting the completion of all pre-merger acts and formalities (required by Art. 25 para. 2 SE-Reg.) is issued by the Commercial Register.

b) *Merger within an affiliated group*

Art. 516 CCC provides a simplified merger procedure within a group of companies. If an acquiring company is a non-listed company and already holds the shares in the target company, nominal value of which exceeds 90 % of the share capital, no merger resolution is needed, the draft terms of merger need not be scrutinised by auditors, and the management board need not prepare a merger

[19] For the same reason, it is rather doubtful, whether in case of the fomation of an SE by means of transformation of an already existing Polish public limited company (Art. 37 SE-Reg.), the rules of the CCC governing the transformation from the one company form into another (among them Art. 556 CCC, which provides for an exit right of the shareholders opposing the transformation) would be applicable according to the reference of Art. 15 SE-Reg.

[20] This solution has been also proposed by *Napierala* supra, ft. 4, p. 23.

report. Art. 31 para. 2 SE-Reg. provides for analogous simplification if the merger aims at the formation of an SE. According to Art. 31 para. 2 sentence 2 SE-Reg., the national legislator may declare these reliefs to be applicable to the situation when the acquiring company holds shares conferring at least 90% or more but not all of the voting rights, even if these shares do not represent more than 90% of the capital of the target company. Polish company law permits the granting of a voting privilege only in public limited companies which are not listed, and limits this privilege to a maximum of two votes per share (Art. 351 § 2 sentence 2 and Art. 352 sentence 1 CCC). With respect to mergers within groups of companies mentioned above, the legislator regarded the majority in share capital as crucial and not the majority of votes. Therefore, it does not seem justified to make use of this empowerment in regard to the formation of an SE by merger. This opinion is strengthened by the circumstance that the reliefs provided by Art. 31 SE-Reg. consist of diminution of the information duties towards the shareholders, performance of which gives the latter a proper background for taking a decision on remaining in the company or demanding a purchase of their shares.

2. Protection of shareholders and creditors by the formation of a holding SE

Polish law provides for the right of minority shareholders to "exit" the company only with regard to listed companies, in case of the taking control over it by another natural or legal person in the situation regulated in Art. 154 Securities Act.[21] Granting a particular protection to the minority shareholders on the grounds of empowerment of Art. 34 SE-Reg. could be justified by the cross-border character of the structural transformation of the companies participating in a holding SE-formation. In the case of a holding SE, for a shareholder who has not accepted the share exchange and at the same time has no opportunity to exit from the company for the reason that it is being taken over, the original basis of his decision to invest in shares of a company promoting the formation of a holding SE (which was either not a subsidiary company at all or was a subsidiary of a different company than the SE) changes.[22] Such a change could

[21] Ustawa z dnia 21 sierpnia 1997 r. – Prawo o publicznym obrocie papierami wartościowymi (Securities Act, further referred to as Sec. A.), uniform text in: Dz. U. (Polish Law Journal) from 2002 no. 49, pos. 447.
The situation mentioned is the one in which a person possessing shares or depository receipts granting a total of more then 50% votes on a general meeting is obliged to call the remaining shareholders to sell their shares for a price calculated according to Art. 155 Sec. A.

[22] It should be underlined, however, that the Council Regulation does not specify what

justify granting him the right to retreat from the company. However, unlike the merger into the SE, the company participating in the formation of a holding SE does not cease to exist and, consequently, the law determining the legal position of the shareholder does not change. The mere fact that the company will, as a result of a successful formation, be controlled by the SE with the seat outside Poland, seems not to be sufficient to justify an exit right of shareholders opposing this formation. Therefore, the Polish legislator will probably not introduce any special provisions on protection of the minority shareholders.

Apart from the above, Art. 34 SE-Reg. contains also an authorisation to adopt provisions protecting creditors and employees of the companies promoting the formation of a holding SE. Granting such a protection does not seem necessary. The fact that the companies participating in the formation of an SE will become subsidiaries to it does not directly endanger satisfaction of the claims of creditors, and therefore does not justify granting them particular rights. The same applies to the employees of the promoting companies. Firstly, they can influence the shape of their information, consultation and co-determination rights in the future SE within the formation procedure. Secondly, the formation of a holding SE does not directly affect either their individual contracts in the SE-subsidiary companies, nor the labour agreements in force in those companies.

3. Transforming an existing public limited company into an SE

Art. 37 para. 8 SE-Reg. permits the national legislator to subject the validity of a transformation of an existing company into SE to the permission of a statutory organ of the company in which co-determination of employees is foreseen. Co-determination is known to Polish company law only in the supervisory boards of companies created by means of commercialisation and privatisation of former state enterprises (see more below).[23] Polish law does not, however, know an institute of supervisory board permission for any structural changes of the

majority is required for the decision of shareholders meetings in each of the promoting companies to confirm the formation proposal (cf. Art. 32 par. 6 SE-Reg.). According to the view represented in the German legal doctrine the majority foreseen in the national law for the decision on merger must be observed, in accordance with Art. 7 of the 3rd Directive. cf. *Teichmann*, ZGR 2002, p. 383, 435. See also *Oplustil*, German Law Journal 2/2003, marginal number 17.

[23] Ustawa z dnia 30 sierpnia 1996 r. o komercjalizacji i prywatyzacji przedsiębiorstw państwowych (The Act of 30 August 1996 on the Commercialisation and Privatisation of state enterprises), Dz. U. (Polish Law Journal) from 2002 no. 171 pos. 1397.

company (its transformation), independently of whether employee representatives are co-opted to it or not. For this reason, it does not seem legitimate to make use of the empowerment mentioned above.

IV. Structure of the SE

1. The two-tier system

The two-tier system is the only admissible model of corporate governance in Polish law relating to public limited liability companies. According to Art. 368 CCC, the managing board manages the affairs of the company and represents it. According to Art. 381 CCC, in a public limited company a supervisory board is to be established which performs a continuous function of supervision of the company's activity. There is no need therefore for the Polish legislator to introduce a two-tier system for the SE. Moreover, the introduction of particular provisions on the two-tier system relating only to the SE seems not to be possible unless they are explicitly authorised by the SE-Reg. Adequate regulations of the CCC, governing the competencies and the functioning of management and supervisory board will be applicable to an SE incorporated in Poland, subject to the direct regulations of the Council Regulation (Art. 9 para. 1 lit c) ii) SE-Reg.).The two-tier system in force in Polish law will now be presented with particular reference to the empowerment and delegations contained in the SE-Reg.

The managing board of a public limited company incorporated in Poland can consist of one or more persons. Art. 368 § 2 CCC does not set either a minimum or maximum number of managing board members. No intervention by the legislator is desirable in respect to the SE, despite the empowerment of Art. 34 par. 4 sentence 2 SE-Reg. The number of managing board members should remain within the discretion of the SE founders.

Multi-persons managing boards take decisions on a collegial basis, which is expressed by Art. 371 § 1 CCC, which states that all members are obliged and entitled to participate in the joint management of the company's affairs unless otherwise provided in the statutes of the company. For the representation of the company, two members acting together are required, unless otherwise provided in the statutes (Art. 371, 373 CCC). The managing board members' authority to represent the company extends to all acts in or out of court and cannot be restricted with legal effect vis-à-vis third persons (Art. 372 CCC).

Despite the collegial principle, it is not impossible to introduce (in the statutes or – according to some authors – in the managing board regulations[24])

[24] *Czerniawski* Kodeks spółek handlowych. Przepisy o spółce akcyjnej, Warszawa 2001,

an internal division of the member's duties with regard to different fields of activity. In such a way, the scope of duties and rights could be differentiated between different managing board members within the management of the company's affairs. It also seems acceptable that within this internal division of competencies, the current affairs of the company (day-to-day management, in Polish terminology: matters not extending beyond the company's usual activities) can be entrusted to one member or to a group of members. It does not seem necessary therefore to introduce a managing director to the Polish two-tier system, as it is foreseen in the empowerment of Art. 39 para. 1 SE-Reg.

The members of a managing board are appointed by the supervisory board, unless otherwise provided in the statutes (Art. 368 § 4 sentence 1 CCC). The same rule will be applicable in relation to the SE (Art. 39 para. 2 SE-Reg.). The European legislator has empowered national legislators to grant this competence to the shareholders' meeting under the same conditions under which it is admissible to national limited liability companies. According to the Polish regulation cited above, it is admissible to foresee in the statutes of the company that the members of the managing board are appointed and dismissed by the general meeting. Moreover, according to Art. 368 § 4 sentence 2 CCC, the general meeting is mandatorily (i.e. contradictory provisions of the statutes are considered null and void) empowered to dismiss or suspend a member of the managing board at any time.[25]

In order to ensure that the general meetings of SEs incorporated in Poland have the same power, it is necessary to adopt adequate provisions in the national European Company Act. Otherwise, Art. 39 para. 2 sentence 1 SE-Reg. will apply directly, granting the exclusive competence of appointing and dismissing the members of the managing organ to the supervisory organ. Taking into account that the SE, as a legal form, should be as close to the national public limited company as possible, it is desirable to introduce a provision allowing the general meeting of the SE to appoint and dismiss (suspend) the members of the managing organ, as provided for in the rules of the CCC quoted.

Members of the managing board cannot at the same time be members of the supervisory board (Art. 387 § 1 CCC). Art. 39 para. 3 SE-Reg. permits the supervisory organ to delegate one of its members to perform the tasks of a

p. 371; this point of view seems to be supported by *Frąckowiak* in *Kruczalak* (ed.) Kodeks spółek handlowych. Komentarz, Warszawa 2002, p. 605 i 606. Contrary: *Szumański/Szajkowski* supra, ft. 15, p. 498 (Art. 368 marginal number 28), according to whom such a division of competencies can be subject only to the statutes of the company.

25 *Szumański/Szajkowski* supra, ft. 15, p. 509 (Art. 368 marginal number 56); *Frąckowiak* supra, s. 599.

member of the managing organ in the event of a vacancy. Functionally, this rule is close to Art. 383 § 1 CCC *in fine*, which permits such a delegation if a member of the managing board is temporally incapable of performing his tasks. The newest amendment of the CCC introduced a three months' limitation on this delegation. The same limitation will most probably be introduced for the SE with seat in Poland. Moreover, the supervisory organ member will be obliged to undertake adequate actions immediately in order to change the composition of the managing organ in case the incapacity of one of its members becomes permanent (which seems to include the death of a member).[26]

Based on Art. 385 § 1 CCC, it would be legitimate to set a minimum number of three members of a supervisory organ of an SE. Otherwise the number of supervisory organ members will be subject only to the provision in the statutes.

According to the supervisory model introduced in the CCC, the supervisory board is a collegial organ, i.e. the competence to perform the supervisory tasks is vested in board as a whole and not in its members individually (cf. Art. 390 § 1 CCC).[27] The board can, however, empower some of its members to perform a certain supervisory action or delegate them to perform such actions independently within a prescribed scope (Art. 390 § 3 CCC). The Polish legislator has left open the possibility of deviating from the collegial principle at the supervisory board's discretion. With the objective of more efficient supervision in the SE, the Polish legislator should make use of the empowerment of Art. 41 par. 3 SE-Reg. and introduce a deviating regulation. The authority to demand a report on the management of the company's affairs could be granted individually to each supervisory board member. The report itself, however, should be presented to the whole board. The managing board could reject the demand of an individual supervisory board member but would be obliged to comply, if a further member supported the demand.[28]

2. The one-tier system

Although Art. 43 para. 4 SE-Reg. formally provides for an authority for the Member States to regulate the one-tier system in relation to the SEs, it is to be assumed that the Polish legislator will be obliged to adopt a regulation comple-

26 *Szwaja*, supra ft. 15 p. 630 (Art. 383, marginal number 15).

27 See *Szwaja* supra, ft. 15, p. 622 (Art. 382, marginal number 14).

28 Such a regulation is contained in the German Stock Exchange Act (§ 9 sec. 3 *Aktiengesetz*). cf. Hüffer *Aktiengesetz. Kommentar*, 5th Ed., München 2002, p. 435.

mentary to the scant regulation of the one-tier system (Art. 43–45 SE-Reg.).[29] Such an obligation is justified in the light of Art. 68 para. 1 SE-Reg. according to which the Member States shall make such provision as is appropriate to ensure the effective application of this Regulation. With regard to the fact, that the Polish law of public limited company (similarly to the German *Aktiengesetz*) does not principally allow the regulations of statutes deferring from the statutory model (Art. 304 para. 3 CCC), the possibility given to the European companies in Art. 38 lit. b) SE-Reg. to choose between the two-tier and one-tier system would be practically thwarted, if the Polish legislator does not take the proper legislative measures to supplement the scant regulation of the SE-Reg. regarding the one-tier system.[30] The latter does not include provision for such important questions (subject to the provisions of the CCC with regard to the two-tier system) as:

- the functional division between managing competencies *sensu stricto* and supervising competencies within the administrative organ[31] as well as powers of all bodies (committees) constituted within it and the frequency of the organ's meetings,
- the rules of representation of the company in the one-tier system,
- the liability of the members of the administrative organ,
- the remuneration rules,
- the rules for deciding on disputed questions and for the representation of the company in case of conflict of interest between the company and a member of the administrative organ,
- the admissibility of cumulative voting during the election of administrative organ members (cf. Art. 385 § 3–9 CCC with regard to the election of supervisory board members),
- limitation on competitive activities of the organ members,
- the rules for dismissing of members of the organ.

When adopting provisions with regard to the questions mentioned above, the Polish legislator should refer to the CCC-rules applicable to the two-tier model, insofar as the legal nature of the one-tier system would not be affected thereby. The specific character of the board-model should be stressed, especially in regard to management and representation rules. One of the possible solutions

[29] Cf. with regard to the German law which knows also only two-tier system, *Hommelhoff*, AG 6/2001, p. 284.

[30] *Oplustil/Rachwał*, KPP 3/2003, p. 672 et seq.; *Sokołowski*, PrSP 12/2003, p. 9.

[31] Cf. Recital 14 to the Council Regulation, according to which it is desirable that the scopes of responsibility of those responsible for management and those responsible for supervision were clearly defined.

would be to permit a concentration of both of these powers in the hands of one person (as is the case in French law), to be elected by the administrative organ, the role of which would therefore be reduced to acceptance of the company's development strategy and supervision of its execution. For this solution to be realised, a functional division of powers between the administrative organ members must be provided in the regulation of the one-tier system for the SE, which would include the managing director and his position. It is highly recommended that a minimum number of members of the administrative organ be specified in order to facilitate the normative separation of managing and supervisory duties, guaranteeing that non-executive members would prevail in the board's composition. The French regulation of Art. L225-17 *Code de commerce* (amended version after 2001) sets the minimum number of the administrative organ members at 3. At the same time, it would be reasonable to allow 'small SEs', the shares of which are not listed on a stock exchange, to compose their boards freely. It would be more appropriate for the needs of shareholders of such a company, especially if it is a 100% subsidiary within an affiliated group, to be able to entrust the tasks of the administrative organ to one person (e.g. a member of the managing board of the holding company), while employing an outsider to manage its affairs.[32] In order to fulfil the postulate of Recital 14 to the SE-Reg. it is necessary, however, to exclude the admissibility of a one-person administrative organ which at the same time manages the company, as it does not provide a 'proper definition' of management and supervision responsibilities.

3. Transactions requiring authorisation by the supervisory organ or an express decision of the whole administrative organ

Polish law does not oblige companies to list the categories of transactions in their statutes which require authorisations of the supervisory board to be concluded. Art. 384 § 1 CCC foresees only that the necessity of such an authorisation can be introduced in the statutes. Statutes of an SE, however, must always provide a catalogue of transactions for which authorisation of the supervisory organ or an express decision of the whole administrative organ is required (Art. 48 para. 2 SE-Reg.). The second sentence of this provision permits enlargement of the scope of competencies of the supervisory organ by granting it the right to itself specify such transactions. As current Polish law does not know

[32] See sec. 19 par 1 and sec. 24 of the draft of German Act Introducing the SE. See also the convincing remarks of *Neye/Teichmann* supra, ft. 5, p. 169, 176.

such empowerment of the supervisory board,[33] it is to be assumed that its position within the SE is sufficiently assured by the provision of Art. 48 para. 1 sentence 1 SE-Reg. providing a duty to list the transactions requiring authorisation of the supervisory or whole administrative organ.

It is worth considering, however, if it would not be desirable to adapt, for the one-tier SE, a catalogue of transactions requiring an express decision by the administrative organ. Based on the project of the 5th Directive on the structure of the public limited company,[34] such a catalogue would include transactions of substantial importance for the company's business which go far beyond day-to-day management (e.g. selling essential components of the company's business or concluding a contract of dependence of the company). The Polish legislator should also prescribe that for all transactions for which the CCC provides a requirement of supervisory board authorisation (e.g. situations foreseen in Art. 15 § 2, 446 § 2, 447 § 1 CCC), an express decision by the administrative organ should be required.

4. General meeting

a) Minority rights

Arts. 55 and 56 SE-Reg. govern so called minority rights, also known to Polish company law (Art. 400 CCC). The rights in question consist of the power to request the convening of a general meeting and certain matters to be included in the agenda of the forthcoming meeting. As Polish law requires exactly the same percentage of participation in the share capital (10 %) for this right to be exercised, it is not possible to introduce a divergent regulation (introducing a lower percentage) for the European Company.

b) Amendment of the statutes

Polish law requires a 3/4 majority for the shareholders' decision on the amendment of the statutes (Art. 415 § 1 CCC),[35] which means that the same majority

[33] Contrast German law, in which sec. 111 par. 4 sentence 2 German Stock Corporation Act (*Aktiengesetz*) provides that the statutes or supervisory board itself can appoint categories of transactions valid only with authorisation of the supervisory board.

[34] Amended proposal of 20 November 1991 for a Fifth Council Directive concerning the structure of public limited companies and the powers and obligations of their organs, COM (91) 372, OJ C 321, of 12.12.1991, p. 9 et seq.

[35] The difference between the vote cast according to CCC and vote cast according to SE-Reg is to be noted. At the general meeting of an SE, a decision is taken if there are more

will be required according to Art. 59 para. 1 SE-Reg. for the amendment of the statutes of an SE incorporated in Poland. According to the provision of Art. 59 para. 2 SE-Reg., a Member State may provide that where at least half of an SE's subscribed capital is represented, a simple majority of the votes referred to in paragraph 1 shall suffice. Such a rule is reserved in Polish law only for the amendment of the company statutes in connection with the amortisation of its shares. Polish law provides also that the general meeting can decide on the dissolution of the company only with an absolute majority of votes, if the loss disclosed in the company's balance sheet exceeds the sum of its reserve capital and one third of its subscribed capital (Art. 397 CCC). These provisions in Polish law which deviate from the principle of a qualified majority required for the amendment of the statutes, will be applicable also to SEs incorporated in Poland according to Art. 9 para. 1 lit. c) ii) SE-Reg. Taking this into account it does not seem desirable, that the Polish legislator should make use of the empowerment contained in Art. 59 para. 2 SE-Reg.

Neither is it desirable that the managing or administrative organ should be able to amend the SE-statutes if this is necessary to harmonise the statutes with the agreement on the involvement of the employees (according to Council Directive 2001/86/WE). Making use of the empowerment of Art. 12 para. 4 SE-Reg. in order to grant such a competence to the managing or administrative organ, would mean too much restriction of the rights of shareholders as the economical proprietors of the company. Amendment of the statutes and, in particular, of the right to set up the institutional framework of management and supervision in the company statutes, belong to the principal competencies of the shareholders' meeting in Polish company law.

V. Implementation of the Directive on the involvement of employees

1. Polish regulations in force governing the involvement of employees

a) Information and consultation rights of the employees

The involvement of the employees in the enterprise's management is defined as one of the principles of Polish labour law (Art. 18^2 Labour Code[36]). Never-

votes pro than contra of the valid votes (cf. according to Art. 58 SE-Reg. abstentions do not count as votes cast); whereas in a Polish public limited company the votes pro must prevail over the votes contra and the abstentions as the latter count as votes cast (cf. Art. 415 in relation to Art. 4 par. 1 pkt 9 and 10 CCC).

[36] Ustawa z dnia 26 czerwca 1974 r. – Kodeks pracy (Act of 26 June 1974 – Labour Code), uniform text in: Dz. U. (Polish Law Journal) from 1998, no. 21, pos. 94 subsequently amended.

theless, Polish legislation neither knows any general rules on informing or consulting employees of limited liability companies nor does it provide co-determination in the form known to other European countries and proposed in the Directive on the involvement of employees. It is trade unions which take part in the enterprises' management in Poland. Trade unions' organisations have rather broad competencies, which are rooted in Art. 59 of the Polish Constitution. These include negotiation with the employer, especially in order to solve collective conflicts, conclusion of collective labour agreements and other agreements, as well as negotiations on the agreement on the rules of collective dismissals.[37] The Labour Code also foresees that an employer co-operates with the unions' organisation in an enterprise in all matters resulting from individual labour contracts.

The Act of 5 April 2002 on European works councils and methods of informing and consulting the employees in enterprises and groups of enterprises of communitarian dimension,[38] has adapted the provisions of Polish law to the requirements of Council Directive 94/45/WE of 22 September 1994 on the European works council. This act will come into force at the moment of Poland's accession into the European Union.

b) Co-determination

Co-determination exists solely in limited liability companies established as a result of commercialisation (transformation of state enterprises into commercial companies, in which the State holds all the shares, in accordance with the Commercialisation and Privatisation Act, hereafter: the CPA).[39] According to

[37] See Art. 2, Art. 4 ustawy z dnia 28 grudnia 1989 r. o szczególnych zasadach rozwiązywania z pracownikami stosunków pracy z przyczyn dotyczących zakładu pracy (Act of 28 December 1989 on the particular rules governing the dismissal of the employees for reasons related to the enterprise (redundancy, uniform text in: Dz. U. from 1994, no. 1, pos. 1 subsequently amended).

[38] Ustawa z dnia 5 kwietnia 2002 r. o europejskich radach zakładowych oraz sposobach informowania pracowników i konsultacji z pracownikami w przedsiębiorstwach i grupach przedsiębiorstw o zasięgu wspólnotowym, publ. in: Dz. U. (Polish Law Journal) from 2002, no. 62, pos. 556.

[39] Ustawa z dnia 30 sierpnia 1996 r. o komercjalizacji i prywatyzacji przedsiębiorstw państwowych (The Act of 30 August 1996 on the Commercialisation and Privatisation of state enterprises), Dz. U. (Polish Law Journal) from 2002 no. 171 pos. 1397.
For questions arising on the supervision in so called employees' companies created according to Art. 37, 38 of the former Privatisation Act of 13 July 1990 (Dz.U. no. 51, pos. 298, subsequently amended) see: *Ogrodowczyk* Specyfika nadzoru właścicielskiego w spółkach pracowniczych in *Rudolf* (ed.) Nadzór właścicielski w spółkach prawa handlowego, Warszawa 1999, p. 210.

Art. 12 CPA, as long as the State Treasury remains the sole shareholder in a public limited company [40] created by means of commercialisation, the employees are empowered to elect 2/5ths of the supervisory board members. The members of the supervisory board elected by the employees have the same rights and duties as the other members. The employee representatives on the supervisory board can be dismissed if 15 % of the total of the employees bring forward a written motion on this subject. The statutes can provide that the right of the employees to elect members to the supervisory board can be changed but not before the Treasury has sold at least 50 % of the shares of the transformed company and without changes to the right to elect a part of the members of the supervisory board according to Art. 14 para. 1 CPA, depending on the total number of its members (from 2 up to 4). In companies created by means of commercialisation and also after alienation of 50 % of the shares by the Treasury, the employees elect thereto one member of the managing board, if the average number of employees of the company exceeds 500 (Art. 16 CPA).[41]

2. Implementation of the rules of the Directive in detail[42]

a) Creation of a special negotiating body (Art. 3 para. 2 lit b of the Directive)

The Act on European works councils, mentioned above, is the only Polish law provision which grants a procedure for appointing employees' representatives. The conduct of the election to the special negotiating body has been generally entrusted to the enterprises' union organisations. Only if no such organisation is present in an enterprise shall the alternative procedures apply. Because of the fact that the Directive on involvement of the employees in an SE in certain aspects copies the solution of the Directive on European works councils and also because of the fact that, for the first time in Polish law, the appointment of the employees' representatives to the body which is to represent them in negotiations with their employer, has been regulated (in the Act on European works councils), it seems rational to unify the procedures for appointing the members of the negotiating body, whether it is going to negotiate the rights of employees in the enterprise or group of enterprises or in an SE.

[40] According to Art. 11 par. 2 CPA in private limited liability companies created by means of commercialisation, no supervisory board is required.

[41] See also *Rudolf* Przedstawicielstwo pracownicze w radach nadzorczych spółek, in Rudolf (ed.) Nadzór właścicielski w spółkach prawa handlowego, Warszawa 1999, p. 178.

[42] Only the provisions of the Directive, which give national legislators certain discretion as to its implementation, are analysed below.

b) *Composition of a negotiating body (Art. 3 para. 2 lit b sentence 4 of the Directive)*

Considering the particular role of trade unions in Polish labour law, the unions' representatives should be allowed to enter the negotiating body even if they are not employees of the engaged companies. They cannot be, however, the sole members of the body, the employees of the engaged companies must also be represented.[43]

c) *Financing the activities of the negotiating body (Art. 3 para. 7 of the Directive)*

The Directive offers a certain freedom in regard to the methods of funding of the negotiating body by the companies participating in the creation of an SE, in particular, it permits limitation on the expenses related to experts' activities. Such rule is foreseen also by Art. 15 of the Polish Act on European works councils, which restricts the obligatory expenses of the employer's company to one expert and leaves possible funding of more experts to the disposition of management and the negotiating body, if they agree upon it. Funding rules can have a stimulating impact on the activities of the negotiating body. It is desirable therefore to adapt a similar solution in the Act introducing the rules of the SE-Directive to Polish law.

d) *The option of Art. 7 para. 3 of the Directive (Art. 12 para. 3 SE-Reg.)*

The Polish legislator should not make use of the option foreseen in Art. 7 par. 3 of the Directive. It is business practice that should demonstrate whether co-determination rules prove themselves to be widely accepted or whether national companies which are subject to them will rarely participate in SE-formations. Co-determination is the most important element of the competition of legal systems with regard to employees' involvement. If the presence of certain forms of co-determination in national law imposes the necessity of solving this question in agreement and at the same time model rules foresee that in case no agreement is reached, the broadest rights of the employees are to be maintained, the fact that companies incorporated in the states foreseeing such broad rights of the employees would not be chosen as partners for SE-formation may

[43] Cf. however, critical remarks of *Heinze*, ZGR 1/2002, p. 94, according to whom the participation of trade unions' representatives in the negotiating body will give an unjustified advantage to the employees' side in the negotiations with the representatives of the companies founding an SE.

convince these states to review their co-determination rules.[44] Poland, especially if it does not make use of the option, will present an interesting case here: both the companies subject to co-determination (companies created by means of commercialisation) and the companies free of any form of co-determination (created on the sole ground of CCC provisions) will be able to participate in the formation of an SE.

[44] Cf. from the German point of view: *Herfs-Röttgen*, NZA 8/2001, p. 429, *Pluskat*, DStR 35/2001, p. 1490, *Heinze* supra, ft. 46, p. 94.

Portugal

Rui Pinto Duarte

Literature on SE published in Portugal: *Campos, Rui Falcão de* A Sociedade Anónima Europeia: Projectos e Perspectivas, Revista de Direito e de Estudos Sociais, 1989, XXXI, 1/2, p. 255 et seq.; *Correia, Aires* O Direito das Sociedades na Comunidade Económica Europeia, Boletim do Ministério da Justiça, nº 190, 1969, p. 120 et seq.; *Correia, Luís Brito* Direito Europeu das Sociedades, Temas de Direito Comunitário, Lisboa, Ordem dos Advogados, 1983; *Pocar, Fausto* Le Statut de la Société Européenne: une Étape Importante dans l'Évolution du Droit Communautaire, Estudos em Homenagem à Professora Doutora Isabel de Magalhães Collaço, Coimbra, Livraria Almedina, 2002, vol. I; *Quadros, Fausto de* Direito Europeu das Sociedades, Estruturas Jurídicas da Empresa, Lisboa, AAFDL, 1989; *Xavier, Humberto F.* Le Statut du Comissaire aux Comptes dans la Société Anonyme Européenne, Documentação e Direito Comparado, nº 2, 1980.

I. Introduction

Council Regulation (EC) No. 2157/2001 of 8 October 2001 (hereinafter "the Regulation") does not aim to be self-sufficient. On the contrary, it states that European Companies (hereinafter "SE") shall be governed by the laws of Member States and by their statutes.

With regard to the laws of Member States, the Regulation provides for the application to the SE of both rules specifically adopted for the SE and rules generally applicable to common[1] public limited-liability companies.[2]

Council Directive 2001/86/EC of 8 October 2001 (hereinafter "the Directive") states also that the laws of Member States applicable to common public limited-liability companies shall, to a certain extent[3], be applicable to the SE, with regard to the "involvement of employees".

[1] The text states the position as at *31 October 2003.* Developments after that date could not be taken into account.

[2] Throughout this text I sometimes qualify the expression "public limited-liability companies" with the word "common" to emphasise that I am making reference to companies incorporated under common national laws and not to SE.

[3] In my opinion, the border line between the two groups of rules as well as references made by the Regulation to each of them is not totally clear. As an example of such lack of clarity I point out the words "subject to the additional requirements imposed by the Member State to which the company concerned is subject" used in article 21.

So far,* it is not known what measures the Portuguese Government intends to take for the implementation of the Regulation and for the transposition of the Directive. How the options provided in the Regulation and the Directive for national laws will be used by Portuguese Law is entirely unpredictable.

In the absence of this knowledge, the purpose of this text is to describe the more relevant aspects of Portuguese law on common public limited-liability companies that shall in any case be applicable to the SE, by force of the Regulation and of the Directive.

II. General information on Portuguese company law

The main Portuguese statute on companies is the "Código das Sociedades Comerciais" (approved in 1986 and amended several times since).[4] The code is complemented by other laws, including a code on commercial registration.

Portuguese commercial companies are subject to *Typengesetzlichkeit*[5], the following types being admitted:

- *sociedades em nome colectivo* – which correspond to the French, Spanish and Italian types with similar names,
- *sociedades por quotas* – which correspond to the German and Austrian *GmbH*, to the French *société a responsabilité limitée* and to the Spanish and Italian types with names similar to the latter,
- *sociedades em comandita simples* – which correspond to the French, Spanish and Italian types with similar names,
- *sociedades em comandita por acções* – which correspond to the French, Spanish and Italian types with similar names,
- *sociedades anónimas* – which correspond to the French and Spanish types with similar names, to the Italian *società per azioni* and to the German and Austrian *Aktiengesellschaften*, and, less exactly, to the UK public company limited by shares.

Of course, the main rules relevant for SE are those on the *sociedades anónimas*.

* The main exception is the participation of employees in company bodies.

[4] Hereinafter "CSC 1986".

[5] I have recourse to this German word to express the idea that companies have to adopt one of the types specified by law.

III. The organs of the *sociedades anónimas*

Using the language adopted by the Regulation, one can say (although not very precisely, as will be evident later) that since CSC 1986 is in force, Portuguese rules on the *sociedades anónimas* admit both the one-tier system and the two-tier system.[6] Until then, only the one-tier system was admitted and perhaps therefore the large majority of Portuguese *sociedades anónimas* still adopts this system.

The names of the organs in the two-tier system are *conselho geral* and *direcção* (the members of the latter being called *directores*), which correspond to the German *Aufsichtsrat* and *Vorstand.*

The administrative organ of the Portuguese traditional system is called *conselho de administração* (the members of this being called *administradores*).

One must underline, however, that the expressions one-tier system and two-tier system are not entirely appropriate to Portuguese law, because, in the so-called one-tier system, there may also be two organs. Indeed in this system, besides the administrative organ there may be (and often is) a so-called *conselho fiscal*[7] – charged with the control of the management activity. The main differences between the *conselho fiscal* and the *conselho geral* of the two-tier system are:

- the *conselho geral* elects the *directores*, while *administradores* are elected by the general meeting (not by the *conselho fiscal*);
- the *conselho geral* approves the annual accounts, while the *conselho fiscal* only gives an opinion on them, their approval falling within the competence of the general meeting;
- the statutes of the company may ascribe to the *conselho geral* powers to intervene in some management matters, for example, prohibiting *directores* from acting in such matters without the consent of the *conselho geral*, while no similar powers may be given to the *conselho fiscal.*[8]

Finally in these general remarks, one must note that Portuguese law admits that the organ charged with the management of the *sociedade anónima* (both in the one-tier system and in the two-tier system) be composed of a sole member. However, such possibility is only open to companies with share capital not exceeding 200,000 Euro.

[6] The relevant aspects of the organic structure of the *sociedades anónimas* result from articles 390 to 446 of CSC 1986. The possibility of choice between the two systems is clearly stated in article 278.

[7] Very similar to the Italian *collegio sindacale.*

[8] As the law says nothing about this possibility, one could argue that the statutes may

IV. Some specific aspects of Portuguese law on *sociedades anónimas* relevant for the Regulation purposes

1. Capital, shares and other securities

Article 5 of the Regulation states that the capital of an SE, its maintenance and changes thereto together with its shares, bonds and other similar securities shall be governed by the provisions applicable to a public limited-liability company with a registered office in the Member State in which the SE is registered.

With regard to capital, its maintenance and changes thereto, Portuguese Law complies with the second directive on companies and therefore no further remarks seem necessary.[9]

Regarding representation of shares, bonds and other securities, Portuguese law admits either paper documents or registrations in an account. Both may be registered or bearer shares.[10]

2. Publication of documents and particulars

Article 13 of the Regulation states that the publication of the documents and particulars concerning an SE which must be publicised under the Regulation shall be effected in the manner laid down in the laws of the Member State in which the SE has its registered office in accordance with Directive 68/15/EEC.

With regard to the Portuguese implementation of this Directive, the following should be noted:

- the registration of companies is made with the Commercial Registries which are spread throughout the country;
- besides publication in the official gazette, documents issued by public limited-liability companies must also be published in an ordinary newspaper.[11]

also give such powers to the *conselho fiscal*; in my opinion, however, that would violate mandatory rules.

[9] Main relevant rules result from articles 31 to 35 and 87 to 96 of CSC 1986.

[10] Main rules on representation of shares are contained in articles 46 to 54 of "Código dos Valores Mobiliários" (Securities Code, approved in 1999) – and not in CSC 1986.

[11] Article 167, n° 2, of CSC 1986.

3. Formation of companies

Article 15 of the Regulation states that, subject to the rules contained therein, the formation of an SE shall be governed by the law applicable to public limited-liability companies in the Member State in which the SE establishes its registered office.

The formation of the *sociedades anónimas* is ruled by CSC 1986,[12] by the code on commercial registration, as well as by the rules on the so-called *Registo Nacional de Pessoas Colectivas*, which is the State department charged, among other responsibilities, with the control of companies' names.

The main rules on formation of companies relevant for SE purposes seem to be:

- the adoption of the company's name must be previously authorised by the *Registo Nacional de Pessoas Colectivas*;
- the document by which the company is formed must be prepared by a notary.

4. Legal entities may be members of the SE's organs

Article 47, nº 1, of the Regulation states that the statutes of the SE may permit legal entities to be members of its organs, provided that the law applicable to public limited-liability companies in the Member State in which the registered office of the SE is located, does not provide otherwise. Moreover, the same article states that such a legal entity shall designate a natural person to exercise its functions on the organ in question.

According to Portuguese law, legal entities may be elected to the *conselho de administração* and to the *conselho geral*, but such entities must designate a natural person to exercise the functions in question, and the persons so designated "exercise their functions in their own name".[13] The members of the *conselho fiscal* must be individuals, with two exceptions: legal firms and chartered public accountants firms.[14] Members of the *direcção* may never be legal entities.[15]

[12] Main rules are contained in articles 7 to 19 of CSC 1986.

[13] This rule (contained in articles 390 and 434 of CSC 1986), raises some doubts, *inter alia, as to whether*: i) the elected legal entity may remove the designated natural person; or, ii) if the natural person ceases to exercise the office, the elected legal entity may designate another person (or if a new election must take place).

[14] The main rules are contained in article 414 of CSC 1986.

[15] The main rules are contained in article 425 of CSC 1986.

5. Competence of the general meeting

Article 52 of the Regulation states that the general meeting of an SE shall decide on matters for which: i) it is given sole responsibility by the Regulation or by the implementing legislation of the Member State in which the SE's registered office is situated; ii) it is given responsibility by the law of the Member State in which the SE's registered office is situated; iii) it is given responsibility by its own statutes, in accordance with the law of the Member State in which the SE's registered office is situated.

According to Portuguese Law, the main responsibilities of the general meeting of *sociedades anónimas* are:

- to amend the statutes of the company;
- to decide on the allocation of results;
- if the company adopts the one-tier system, to approve the annual accounts;
- to make an annual assessment of the management of the company;
- if the company adopts the one-tier system, to elect and dismiss the *administradores;*
- if the company adopts the two-tier system, to elect and dismiss the members of the *conselho geral.*[16]

It is very important is to underline that the general meeting may not take decisions on management issues unless the management organ requests it to do so.[17]

6. Organisation and conduct of general meetings

Article 53 of the Regulation states that the organisation and conduct of general meetings together with voting procedures shall be governed by the law applicable to public limited-liability companies in the Member State in which the registered office of the SE is situated – without prejudice to the rules of the Regulation.

The main remark in this field is that, under Portuguese law, the general meeting (*assembleia geral*) of *sociedades anónimas* has a kind of permanent sub-organ, called the *mesa da assembleia geral*, composed of at least a chairperson and a secretary. Convening and conducting meetings fall within the competence of the chairperson. It is also the chairperson who, together with the secretary, drafts and signs the minutes of the meetings.[18]

[16] The main rules are contained in articles 435 and 455 of CSC 1986.

[17] Article 373, nº 3, of CSC 1986.

[18] The main rules are contained in articles 374 to 388 of CSC 1986.

7. Decisions on the amendment of statutes

Article 59 of the Regulation states that the amendment of the statutes of an SE requires a decision by the general meeting taken by a majority which may not be less than two thirds of the votes cast, unless the law applicable to public limited-liability companies in the Member State in which the registered office of the SE is situated, requires or permits a larger majority.

The main rules of Portuguese law on ordinary *sociedades anónimas* are the following:

- the amendment of statutes falls within the competence of the general meeting;[19]
- the decisions on the amendment of statutes require two thirds of the votes cast;
- in principle, the general meeting may only decide on the amendment of statutes if the votes of the shareholders participating in the meeting correspond to at least one third of the total votes; such requirement, however, is not applicable if the general meeting is convened for a second time for the same purpose.[20]

8. Liability of the members of the organs

Article 51 of the Regulation states that members of the management, supervisory and administrative organs of the SE shall be liable for loss or damage sustained by the SE following any breach of their obligations in accordance with the provisions applicable to public limited-liability companies in the Member State in which the registered office of the SE is situated.

The main Portuguese rules on the liability of *administradores* and *directores* to the company are the following:

- liability depends on intention or negligence; the burden of proof (of the non-existence of intention or negligence) falls on the *administradores* and *directores* involved;
- there is no liability in case the relevant act has been performed in accordance with a resolution of the general meeting;

[19] However, CSC 1986 (article 456) admits that the statutes ascribe to the management organ authority (concurrent to the one of the general meeting) to increase the share capital by contributions in cash, provided that such authority is limited in terms of amount and time.

[20] The main rules are contained in articles 374 to 388 of CSC 1986.

- the *administradores* and *directores* involved are jointly liable;
- proceedings to enforce such liability may be started by the company, upon a resolution of the general meeting, or (for the benefit of the company) by any shareholders owning 5% or more of the share capital.[21]

It must be underlined that Portuguese authors discuss the extent to which the law imposes a general duty of good management on *administradores* and *directores*.[22]

Members of the organs charged with the control of management and chartered public accountants charged with the mandatory auditing, are liable jointly with *administradores* and *directores* whenever loss or damage sustained by the company would not have occurred if they had fulfilled their duties[23].

9. Annual accounts

Article 61 states that with regard to annual accounts, the accompanying annual report, their auditing and publication, the SE shall be governed by the rules applicable to public limited-liability companies under the law of the Member State in which its registered office is situated.
Portuguese law conforms to the fourth, seventh and eighth Directives on companies and therefore no special observation seems necessary.[24]

10. Merger

According to articles 2 and 17 to 31 of the Regulation, one of the possible procedures for the formation of an SE is the merger of two or more common public limited-liability companies (provided that at least two of them are governed by the law of different Member States).

[21] The main rules are contained in articles 71 to 80 of CSC 1986.

[22] See, among others, *Luís Brito Correia* Os Administradores de Sociedades Anónimas, Almedina, 1993, p. 596 et seq., *António Menezes Cordeiro* Da Responsabilidade Civil dos Administradores das Sociedades Comerciais, Lex, 1997, p. 524 et seq., *Pedro Caetano Nunes* Responsabilidade Civil dos Administradores perante os Accionistas, Almedina, 2001, p. 100 and 101, and *Maria Elisabete Gomes Ramos* Responsabilidade Civil dos Administradores e Directores de Sociedades Anónimas perante os Credores Sociais, Coimbra Editora, 2002, p. 110 et seq.

[23] The main rules are contained in articles 81 and 82 of CSC 1986.

[24] Some of such rules are contained in CSC 1986 but others have been transposed by acts laying down accounting rules.

Article 18 of the Regulation provides for the application to a certain extent to each of the merging companies of the provisions of the law of the Member State to which it is subject.

Moreover articles 24 and 25 of the Regulation provide for the application of the laws of the Member States governing each of the merging companies with regard to: (i) the protection of the creditors, the holders of bonds and the holders of securities, other than shares, which carry special rights; (ii) the control of the legality of the merger.

Portuguese law complies with the third directive on companies. Nevertheless, considering the degree of freedom given to the Member States by such directive, it seems useful to make two notes on Portuguese rules on merger of companies.[25]

Firstly, with regard to the protection of creditors and holders of securities, Portuguese law gives to each of the creditors and to each category[26] of holders of common bonds or of convertible bonds or of bonds with warrants, the right to oppose the merger by means of judicial proceedings. Such opposition may be removed, *inter alia*, by depositing the amounts due to the opposing persons.[27]

Secondly, Portuguese law does not give to minority shareholders of merging public limited-liability companies the right to exit. Article 105 of CSC 1986 governs the exit of members of companies that vote against a merger, but presupposes that such right results from another legal rule or from the statutes of the company. There is no such rule with regard to public limited-liability companies.[28]

11. Merger by acquisition

Article 31, n° 1, states that where a merger by acquisition is carried out by a company which holds all the shares and other securities conferring the right to vote at the general meeting of the acquired company, some of the general

[25] For further information, see *Raul Ventura* Fusão, Cisão, Transformação de Sociedades, Almedina, 1990, p. 138 et seq.

[26] Acting pursuant to a decision taken in a general meeting of holders of such bonds.

[27] Articles 107 to 110 of CSC 1986.

[28] With regard to "sociedades por quotas", article 240 of CSC 1986 ascribes a right to exit to the "shareholder" (using this word in a broad sense equivalent to the German "Gesellschafter") that votes against some types of resolutions of the general meeting which do not expressly include merger but to which a merger may correspond (such as an increase of capital to be subscribed by third parties and the transfer to another country of the registered office).

requirements and general consequences of a merger do not apply, but adds that national law governing each merging company in accordance with article 24 of Directive 78/855/EEC (the above mentioned third directive on companies) shall nevertheless apply.

Such Article 24 of Directive 78/855/EEC is transposed into Portuguese law by Article 116 of CSC 1986, which exempts this kind of merger from the rules concerning the share-exchange ratio, the reports by the acquired companies' organs and independent experts. Moreover, the same Article 116 states that mergers by acquisition may take place without resolutions of the general meetings of the merging companies under some conditions that correspond to those allowed by article 25 of Directive 78/855/EEC.

V. The "involvement of employees" in Portuguese law

The Portuguese Constitution[29] states that the employees are entitled to establish councils for protecting their interests and for intervening in the life of the enterprises. Moreover, the Portuguese Constitution ascribes certain rights to such councils, including a right to information, a right to consultation and a right to management control. No right to appoint members to the organs of the enterprises is contemplated except with regard to State-controlled entities.

Such constitutional rules are detailed by an infra-constitutional act.[30] This law makes reference to the possibility of employees appointing members to the organs of private companies (i.e., non State-controlled entities), leaving some flexibility to private autonomy. No case of such use is known to me – which of course means that, in Portugal, there is no tradition of involvement of employees in companies' life on a consensus basis.

[29] Article 54.

[30] Lei 46/79, dated September 12th.

Spain

José María Muñoz-Paredes

Literature on SE published in Spain (since 2001; for earlier see *Esteban, Quijano y Sagasti*): *Aguiló Piña* La sociedad anónima europea: constitución, órganos y otros aspectos, Revista de Derecho Mercantil, 2002, 1795; *Esteban Velasco, G* El compromiso de Niza: por fin la Sociedad Europea, in Revista de Derecho de Sociedades, issue 16, 2001, 141; idem Participación de los trabajadores en la sociedad europea. ¿Más cerca de un compromiso político?, Derecho de Sociedades. Libro Homenaje al prof. Sánchez Calero, Madrid, 2002, vol. II, 1677; *Garcimartín Alférez, F. J.* El Reglamento de la Sociedad Europea: una primera lectura, Gaceta jurídica de la Unión Europea, issue 217, 2002, 7; *Quijano González* La sociedad anónima europea, Derecho de Sociedades. Libro Homenaje al prof. Sánchez Calero, cit., vol. IV, 4285; *Sagasti Aurrekoetxea* La constitución de la «Societas Europaea», Revista de Derecho de Sociedades, issue 19, 2002, 115.

I. Antecedents: legislative work in progress and current Spanish law

In mid-November 2002, the Spanish Ministry of Justice presented to the public a Preliminary Draft of Company Law Code[1] (PDC) elaborated by a group of experts[2], previously named by this Ministry in 1994. This was an ambitious project with two aims: to unify in one single legal text (of almost 700 articles) all of Spanish Company Law, nowadays dispersed in special laws and in some, though presently few, articles of our Commercial Code; and to modernize it. The necessary regulation to complete the SE-Regulation is inserted within this PDC.

As this is a unitary law for all companies, the PDC contains a general part (Book I), containing norms that are applicable to all companies, and a special part (Book II) containing the distinctive norms for each of the different types of company, followed by other specific norms (Book III) for listed companies. Annual accounts (Book IV), company transformation, merger, division, dissolu-

[1] Published by the Ministry of Justice itself under the title "Propuesta de Código de Sociedades Mercantiles", Madrid, 2002 (Isbn 84-7787-879-X).

[2] Special proposal of the General Commission of Codification of the Ministry of Justice formed by Profs. Drs. Fernando Sánchez Calero, Alberto Bercovitz Rodríguez-Cano and Ángel Rojo Fernández-Río. Approved by the Commercial Law Section of the General Commission of Codification on 16th May 2002.

tion and liquidation (Books V and VI) and groups of companies (Book VII) are likewise regulated. Finally, Book VIII, is precisely the one devoted to "European Companies with a registered office in Spain". It consists of 25 articles (643 to 667) and is divided into three parts.

The first deals with the registration of European companies with a registered office in Spain as well as with the transfer of seat. The second part of the proposal is focused on the formation procedures of European Companies. And the last and most important part is mainly devoted to the structure of the company. In particular, it focuses largely on the two-tier system of management.

It should be made clear that the PDC is no more than a proposal elaborated by a group of experts. At the time of writing this report, it is totally uncertain whether it will be approved – or even debated – in Parliament. Already in its act of presentation, one of the intervening Ministers qualified it as a "document to be debated", which does not indicate that it will be dealt with within a short period of time. What is more, since the provisions concerning SE's are integrated within this PDC, they are not likely to be approved separately as such, since they refer in several points to other precepts of the PDC, especially as regards the protection of minorities. If the draft is not dealt with, and it is necessary to pass a separate Law on SE's, then the current Preliminary Draft will have to be modified in order to incorporate these norms.

The actual form of large companies in Spain, as in so many other states, is the "Sociedad Anónima" (Public Limited Liability Company, hereafter SA). It is regulated by the "Ley de Sociedades Anónimas" (Public Limited-Liability Company Law) of 1989 (hereafter LSA), adapted, of course, to the Community Directives on the matter and which, if the PDC should be passed, would be repealed. Its regulation and practical implementation logically present certain peculiarities with respect to the effects of introducing the SE, which we will see as our exposition develops.

SE's with a registered office in Spain would therefore be governed by the SE-Regulation and by the PDC. Their formation and other acts would be registered in the Commercial Register corresponding to its registered office, and if these should need to be publicised, the norms of the SA would apply.

Let us now go on to present the fundamental contents of Book VIII of the PDC.

II. Formation of a European Company

1. Companies that may participate in the formation of an SE

The PDC has opted within the framework of Art. 2. 5 of the SE-Regulation to allow companies "the head office of which is not in the Community .../... provided that company is formed under the law of a Member State, has its registered office in that Member State and has a real and continuous link with a Member State's economy" to participate in the formation of an SE.

Availing of this option, granted by the SE-Regulation, is logical if we bear in mind the LSA norms regarding the nationality and registered office of SA's. The Registered Office is always understood as being the one that figures in the statutes and, thus, in the Commercial Register, and in this regard, Art. 6 of the LSA states that "The company shall establish its registered office within Spanish territory in the place in which its effective centre of administration and management is to be found, or in which its main establishment or business is situated".[3]

Art. 5 LSA likewise states, on the one hand, that "all the SA's that have their registered offices on Spanish territory will be Spanish and will be governed by the LSA, wherever they may have been formed", and on the other hand, that "the SA's whose main establishment or business is situated in its territory must have their registered offices in Spain".

From all the aforementioned, it may be concluded that Spanish SA's:

- must have their registered offices in Spain, and
- hence must have either their main establishments or businesses or their head offices in spain.

It is therefore possible for Spanish SA's to exist (which are governed by the LSA and have their registered offices in Spain), as a result of their main establishments or businesses being here, but who have their Head Office outside of Spain or outside of the Community. Such companies, which are not allowed, in principle, by Art. 2 SE-Regulation to participate in the formation of an SE[4] could do so in conformity with the PDC. Moreover, this measure may favour companies from other countries and, as such, is one of the few provisions of the PDC that may make the choice of Spain more attractive as the seat of an SE.

[3] Though Art. 6.2 then goes on to state that "in the case of discordance between the registered office and that which would conform to the above section, third parties may consider either of these as the registered office". Articles 54 and 55 of the PDC provide similarly in this regard.

[4] In so far as it is compulsory for their Head Offices and their Registered Offices to be in Community territory.

2. Formation by merger

a) Protection of shareholders

The PDC contains two provisions aimed at protecting the shareholders of Spanish companies that intend to participate in the formation of an SE by merger.

(1) The right of veto of the Government

The first, which drew the attention of the representatives of other Member States in the meeting that gave rise to this publication,[5] is that, making use of the possibility conferred by Art. 19 SE-Regulation, it provides the Government, at the proposal of the Ministry of Justice, with the right to oppose the participation of a Spanish company in the formation by merger of an SE in another Member State (Art. 647 PDC).

This right exists only when the SE is to be formed in another Member State and must be exercised before the certificate "to which Art. 8 SE-Regulation[6] refers" is issued, as provided for in Art. 19 SE-Regulation.

Art. 647 PDC likewise includes the provision, in accordance with Art. 19 SE-Regulation, that the veto may be legally appealed, but says no more: it neither states who is entitled to avail of this appeal, nor what may be the grounds for contesting the said veto. Logically, any interested party whatsoever must be allowed to contest the veto: the participating companies and also their shareholders and administrative organs. Apart from the formal grounds, there remains only the discussion whether the "reasons of public interest" invoked by the Government really exist; a state of affairs that is not easily controllable by the Courts.

(2) Right of minority shareholders to leave the company

The second protective measure is aimed specifically at minorities. Art. 649 PDC grants shareholders of Spanish companies that vote against the merger that implies the formation of an SE with its registered office in another Member State, the right, provided for in a general manner for all companies in Art. 145

[5] Heidelberg, 11–12 November 2002.

[6] Art. 19 SE-Regulation states "before the issue of the certificate referred to in Article 25 (2)". The reference of the PDC to Art. 8 (the certificate in the case of transfer of seat) must be an error.

PDC,[7] to leave the company on receipt of cash compensation corresponding to the "real value" of their shares. The "real value" of the shares would be established by the company's auditor (or if the company does not have an auditor, one named by the Commercial Register), if agreement between the shareholder and the company is not reached. This system of appraisal, provided for in similar terms in Art. 147.2 LSA, and which is also applied in other cases, has functioned quite well in practice, although unsatisfactory cases, due to a lack of independence on the part of the auditor,[8] are also known.

The same right to leave the company on receipt of cash compensation for their shares is granted to the shareholders of a merger by acquisition of a Spanish company by an SE *whose registered office is located in another Member State.*

All these rights, both the Government veto, as well as that of shareholders to leave the company, arise, as we have seen, solely in the case that the registered office of the SE is to be located in a Member State other than Spain. Although the SE-Regulation allowed the establishment of both rights for all cases of mergers (Articles 19 and 24.2), the PDC considers that such measures are not required when the registered office of the SE is located in Spain, which, in my opinion, seems appropriate.

b) Competences of the Commercial Register

The PDC entrusts the Commercial Register with the following functions in the merger process:

a) The naming, in case of a joint application of the participating companies, of independent experts to draw up the joint report referred to in Art. 22 SE-Regulation (Art. 648 PDC). It does not state, however, which of the Commercial Registers (there are, roughly speaking, one per provincial capital) will be competent.

b) The issuing of the certificate referred to in Art. 25.2 SE-Regulation attesting conclusively to the completion of the pre-merger acts and formalities (Art. 650 PDC). This certificate provides solely for "the Spanish SA that merges in the course of the formation of an SE which will have its registered office in another Member State", which seems to exclude the need for a certificate when the SE has its registered office in Spain. This exclusion is not provided

[7] Under current law, the possibility of leaving the company is provided for in Art. 149 LSA, which refers to the moving of the registered office abroad.

[8] See *Muñoz Planas* Derecho de adquisición preferente: Alcance de la oferta de venta y valor real de las acciones, in: Estudios Jurídicos en Homenaje al Prof. Aurelio Menéndez, Madrid, 1996, 2125ff.

for in the SE-Regulation and places the legality of this provision in doubt, although it may be explained by the fact that:

c) the Commercial Register of the registered office of the SE resulting from the merger must scrutinise the legality of the merger, as regards the part of the procedure concerning the completion of the merger and the formation of the SE, and the existence of the certificates from the competent authorities of the foreign companies participating in the merger.

3. Formation of a holding SE

a) Publicising the formation draft terms

Art. 652 PDC establishes that the administrative organ of Spanish companies participating in the formation of a holding SE have to deposit the draft terms of the formation alluded to in Art. 32.2 SE-Regulation in the Commercial Register of its registered office, and that said deposit is to be announced in the *Boletín Oficial del Registro Mercantil* (BORM), which is the official gazette for publicising the acts inscribed in Spanish Commercial Registers. The period of one month referred to in Art. 32.3 SE-Regulation is calculated from the date of said publication.

b) Protection of shareholders

Making use of the possibility granted it by Art. 34 SE-Regulation, Art. 654 PDC states that the norms of protection of minorities provided for in the PDC for the integration of a company in a holding are applicable to the shareholders of Spanish promoting companies that oppose the formation of a holding SE. Said norms have no equivalent under current Spanish Law and are contained in Art. 599 PDC. According to this precept, if the company is not listed, the shareholders may leave the company within a period of two years,[9] receiving in compensation the real value of their shares, as referred to *supra sub* II. 1. b), though deducting what they would have received in the form of dividends since said date.[10]

[9] Which in this case would be calculated, in my opinion, from the formation of the holding SE.

[10] What is not so clear now is whether Art. 600 PDC, which would permit the SE-holding (if it had its registered office in Spain) to acquire the shares of the minority shareholders without the need for these to give their consent if it possesses 90% of the subsidiary and 75% of the voting rights, would also be applicable.

c) Competences of the Commercial Register

As in the case of formation by merger, the independent experts provided for in Art. 32.4 SE-Regulation are named by the Commercial Register of the registered office of each of the Spanish promoting companies.

4. Formation of a subsidiary SE

The PDC contains no specific provisions for the formation of a Subsidiary-SE, which is likewise not subject in our current law to special norms.

5. Conversion of an existing SA into an SE

a) Conversion draft terms

The PDC (Art. 655) does not establish any novelty with respect to the conversion draft terms referred to in Art. 37.4 SE-Regulation, except for providing for its deposit in the Commercial Register and the publication of this act in the BORM.[11] The operation is subject to the general norms regulating the conversion of SA's. These[12] oblige the administrative organ to place the following documents at the disposal of the shareholders, at the same time as obliging it to call a General Meeting that must approve said conversion:

- a report from the administrative organ justifying the conversion
- the company balance sheet
- a report from the auditor on the balance sheet, if the company is subject to auditing
- the Draft Statutes of the company to be formed

b) Competences of the Commercial Register

The independent expert or experts that are to issue the certificate referred to in Art. 37.6 are to be named by the Commercial Register of the registered office of the company.

[11] Art. 655, when speaking of publication, makes reference to Art. 10 SE-Regulation, instead of Art. 13, which must be a misprint.

[12] Art. 507 PDC. For current law, Articles 144, 224 and 227 LSA.

III. Structure of the SE

Only a one-tier system of administration exists under current Spanish Law, and it is not possible today to opt for the two-tier system in any class of company, not even in those listed. The approval of the PDC would not alter the existing situation, since it solely contemplates the two-tier system for an SE. However, the underlying differences between the Spanish one-tier system and the two-tier system are not very relevant, as we shall see.

1. One-tier system

If an SE, whose registered office is located in Spain, opted for the one-tier system, the applicable norms would be those that regulate the one-tier system in the SA's. The PDC refers directly to the rules for public limited companies and contains no specific norm for SE's. It is therefore worth outlining the one-tier system in Spanish law and practice.

The Spanish LSA provides that management is conferred on a single organ that may consist of a single person, two or more people with sole or joint powers, or a Board of Administration. This is the option chosen by all large and listed companies.

The Board of Administration is the holder of all the management powers and represents the company. All members have the same rights and duties and are subject to the same liability. The members of the Board of Administration may be natural persons or legal entities. In the latter case, they must designate a natural person to exercise this function. They are appointed by the General Meeting for a maximum period of five years, and can be removed at any time. There is no provision regarding the participation of employees in the administrative organ.

The LSA grants a great deal of freedom to the statutes and to the Board to organise its functioning. It provides merely that meetings are to be called by the President, that the presence of one half plus one of its members is required and that resolutions be adopted by absolute majority of the members present. The regulation proposed in the PDC goes into more detail, above all for listed companies; however, its exposition exceeds the object of this report.

Of course, the Board may delegate its powers, except that of presenting the accounts at the General Meeting and those powers which the General Meeting in turn delegates to it. To take the delegation resolution, the vote in favour of two thirds of its members is necessary. This delegation can be to one or several managing directors, who have individual powers, or on committees. In practice, all large companies have one or more managing directors and an executive committee.

If we now examine what actually happens in practice, we find that full delegation of powers breaches the equality between the Board members and so, in large companies, two classes of directors can be differentiated: executive directors, who actually run the company and have access to all the information; and passive or non-executive directors, who are not involved in the management of the company and only know what is reported to them at the Board Meetings. Many of these are what is known as "show or trophy" administrators: prestigious individuals who give the company a name but who are not specifically qualified for the office.

We may therefore state that, in practice, the administration of public limited companies is similar to the two-tier system: there is a management organ, the executive directors, and above these an organ that, in theory, supervises their work: the Board.

Nevertheless, there are two substantial differences with respect to the two-tier system, just as it is regulated, for example, in the German Aktiengesetz. The first and most basic difference is that Spanish law does not attribute a right to information to the Administration Board, nor to the directors individually, regarding the acts of its delegates, nor does it impose on these the obligation to periodically inform them, as provided for the SE by Article 41 of the Regulation. The second difference is that both types of directors are subject to the same system of liability. As regards this point, the law is also based on the fact that all the directors are equal. This causes the position of non-executive directors to be particularly risky. These differences will disappear if the PDC becomes law, because the rules that will regulate SA's state that the non-executive directors shall supervise the work of their executive counterparts and give them an individual and very extensive right to information. On the other hand, the Board cannot delegate the company's main policy.

2. Two-tier system

Having examined the one-tier system, let us now look at how the Spanish legislature aims to apply the SE two-tier system in accordance with art. 39.5 SE-Regulation.

a) Organisation and appointment of the management organ

The PDC establishes (Art. 660) that management may consist of:

- a single person,
- various people with joint or individual powers,
- or a Management Board consisting of a minimum of 3 and a maximum of 7 members.

All of these may be natural persons or legal entities. Their appointment falls on the Supervisory Board, which will have to write a contract for each of the directors expressly stipulating the amount and form of their remuneration. Regarding the possibility, considered in Article 39.3 of the SE-Regulation, that a member of the Supervisory Board provisionally occupies a vacancy on the Management organ, the PDC limits the duration of this substitution to a maximum period of one year.

The Management organ assumes the management and representation of the company for all the acts involved in the company's objects. Such powers cannot be limited regarding third parties and hence the prohibition of the registration in the Commercial Register of the enumeration of its powers, even if this appears in the statutes.

When a Management Board exists, Art. 660.2 indicates that its organisation, internal procedures and passing of resolutions are to be governed by the statutes and, if there is no such provision in the statutes, by the norms established for the Board of Administration of SA's.

b) Supervisory organ

The organisation, calling of meetings, etc. of the Supervisory Board are governed (art. 662.1 PDC) by the same norms established for the Board of Administration of SA's. Their members are appointed and removed by the General Meeting, and there is no provision concerning their number.

The PDC has established two peculiarities for this organ. The first one consists in attributing to the Chairman of the Supervisory Board the representation of this organ in the relations with the Management Organ. The second is that the Supervisory Board may establish that certain management decisions require its previous authorisation. Nevertheless, the company cannot rely against other persons on the lack of authorisation.

Also taking into account the norms established for the Board of Administration, which, as already mentioned, are applicable to the Supervisory Board, each member is entitled to require the management organ to provide information of any kind which is needed to exercise supervision. The Supervisory Board may also request that the members of the management organ attend its meetings, though without voting rights.

c) Liability

The problem of the liability of the members of both organs is solved by simply referring to public limited company legislation, establishing that these are liable in the same way as the directors of a public limited company with a one-tier system, in the field of their respective functions.

According to the PDC[13] (Articles 121 and 128), the administrative organ must carry out its responsibilities "with the diligence of an orderly employer and of a loyal representative" and, if it should fail to do so, it is answerable to the company, to the shareholders and to the company's creditors for the damage it causes. Said responsibility is collective in the case of resolutions of the Board of Administration, unless the members prove that they did not participate in its adoption and were ignorant of its existence, or having knowledge of it, did everything possible to prevent the harm, or at least expressly opposed the agreement.

d) Challenging resolutions

Finally, the PDC recognises (art. 665), as in the case of SA's, the challenging of the resolutions of the Management Board and the Supervisory Board. Such litigation may be brought by the members of the respective Boards or shareholders with at least 5% of the corporate capital. They have to initiate the litigation within a month of their knowledge of the resolution, provided that the adoption of the resolution took place less than one year ago.

3. General meeting

The norms concerning the structure of an SE are completed by two provisions relative to the General Meeting.

The first affects the calling of the meeting in the two-tier system. According to Art. 666 PDC, the General Meeting is to be called by the Management Organ, but it may also be called by the Supervisory Organ, when the latter considers it convenient for the interests of the company. It says nothing about who is to chair the meeting in either case, which is obviously not resolved by the norms on SA's. The Management Organ is, moreover, obliged to call the meeting when requested by shareholders who hold 5% of the SE's subscribed capital, instead of the 10% required in Art. 55 SE-Regulation, by application of the current norms for SA's. In this case, the meeting is to be held within the two months following the request. Currently, this period in only one month in the LSA.

The meeting may likewise be called by the judge having jurisdiction over the location of the registered office on request of any shareholder if it has not met in the first six months of the financial year, or if, having been requested by

[13] Which hardly varies with respect to the LSA.

shareholders who hold 5% of the capital, it was not called. The LSA provides likewise for SA's (and SE's) with the one-tier system.

The second, which is common to both the one- and two-tier systems, concerns the provision of Art. 56 that "one or more shareholders who together hold at least 10% of an SE's subscribed capital may request that one or more additional items be put on the agenda of any general meeting". Under current Spanish law (LSA), this possibility is not expressly contemplated, solely in relation to the request for a meeting. However, Art. 83.2 PDC provides for it for all companies, and the same would be applicable to SE's (Art. 667 PDC). According to Art. 83.2 PDC, the shareholders who hold at least 5% of the capital may request the addition of other items within the five days following the publication of the agenda. The addenda will have to be likewise published twenty days prior to the date of the Meeting, which would otherwise be null and void.

IV. Transfer of seat

The transfer of seat to another Member State is regulated in Art. 645 PDC, which establishes the following norms.

1. The right of veto of the Government

Once again, the PDC makes use of the possibility of the Government, or also, in this case, the national financial supervisory authority, to oppose the transfer of an SE for reasons of public interest, when said transfer implies a change in the applicable legislation (which will always occur when transferring to another Member State). The veto is liable to review by a judicial authority, but the PDC specifies no more as regards this judicial procedure.

2. Protection of minority shareholders

The shareholders who vote against the transfer of seat to another Member State may leave the company under the same conditions as we saw in the formation by merger of an SE in another Member State.

3. Protection of creditors

The PDC also grants the creditors of an SE whose credit exists prior to the publication of the transfer proposal, the right to oppose said transfer. This right is conferred, in a general manner for all companies, in Articles 520.2 and 535.2 PDC. If they should oppose the transfer, the company would have to offer sufficient guarantee of said credits before being able to effect the transfer of seat. An equivalent provision is not contemplated under current Spanish law.

4. Competences of the Commercial Register

As in the above cases, the certificate referred to in Art. 8.8 SE-Regulation is issued by the Commercial Register of the registered office.

V. Involvement of employees

There exist to date no publisised preliminary drafts to introduce Directive 2001/86 in Spain. Book VIII of the PDC limits itself to completing the SE-Regulation and touches on no aspect relative to the involvement of employees.

Spain's position as regards the introduction of the Directive is difficult to anticipate. In order to evaluate this, we have only two definite facts at our disposal. The first is that at the present time "co-determination" does not exist in Spain, nor does any other form of participation of employees in the administration organs of the company, though it did exist in the past. This was established by Law 41/1962, of 21st July, but was repealed in 1980 owing to its evident failure.[14] The second is the posture that the Spanish Government held in the

[14] That Law, which followed the German Mitbestimmung model, was enacted in the peak of Franco's regime, a time when no political freedoms nor trade unions rights were recognised, aimed more than nothing to keep up appearances towards foreign countries. That is evidenced by the fact that it was not until three years after its enactment that the rules to put it into practice were approved (Decreto of July the 15th, 1965). It was reluctantly received both by the employers and employees, and deserved also a lot of academic criticism (vid. *J. Garrigues* Hacia un nuevo Derecho mercantil, Madrid, 1971, p. 295–331, the lecture of *J. A. Garrigues Walker* in the vol. La participación de los trabajadores en los consejos de administración, Madrid, 1965 and more deeply, among others, *Almansa Pastor* La participación del trabajador en la administración de la empresa, Madrid, 1965). Clandestine trade unions leaders were early aware of its futility and therefore they showed no interest in maintaining it when, once democracy was reached, it was decided to change the labour law. The Estatuto de los Trabajadores of 1980 replaced the co-determination system by another one in which employees' representatives ("delegados de personal" and "Comité de empresa") just have information and consultation rights.

final phases of negotiations on SE's, which forced the inclusion of Item 3 in Art. 7. This would allow us to hazard the opinion that perhaps Spain excludes the application of the standard rules of Art. 7.2 b (one or more forms of participation were applied in one or more of the participating companies covering less than 25 % of the total number of employees in all the participating companies and if the special negotiating body so decides), but which nonetheless shows the posture of the Spanish Government concerning co-determination.

Sweden

Paulina Dejmek

References cited in the article: *Dejmek* Nya trender i Europeisk bolagsrätt – inte bara gyllene aktier och Europabolag, Europarättslig Tidskrift no 4/2002, p. 709 et seq.; *Dejmek* Genomförandet av Europabolaget i nationell rätt – lättare sagt än gjort? Europarättslig Tidskrift no 4/2003, p. 726 et seq.; *Goulet* Europabolaget, Europarättslig Tidskrift no 3/2001, p. 299 et seq.; *Nielsen* Medarbejderindflydelse i SE-selskaber, Nordisk Tidsskrift for selskabsret no 2/2002, p. 240 et seq.; *Werlauff* SE – the Law of the European Company, Copenhagen 2003

I. Introduction

The SE-Regulation and the supplementing Directive regarding involvement of employees in the SE enter into force on October 8th, 2004[1]. They will oblige the European Union Member States and the three EFTA States, Norway, Iceland and Liechtenstein, which are parties to the European Economic Area Agreement, to adopt the necessary legislative measures to ensure that the SE will be a workable company form. It is common ground that Community Regulations may not be subjected to national implementing measures.[2] However, the SE-Regulation contains several provisions that require – or allow – Member States to adopt certain measures. In addition, Article 68 of the SE-Regulation explicitly states an obligation for Member States to make the provisions necessary to ensure the effective application of the SE-Regulation. To this end, legislative preparations were initiated by the Swedish Ministry of Justice in the autumn of 2002. A Draft Act on the European Company (hereinafter referred to as the Draft Act) and the explanatory memorandum thereto (hereinafter referred to as the Memorandum), were published in January 2003.[3] The following overview

[1] Regulation 2157/2001/EC on the Statute for a European Company and Directive 2001/86/EC supplementing the Statute for a European Company with regard to the involvement of employees.

[2] Cf. to that effect, e.g. Case 39/72 *Commission v Italy* [1973] ECR 101, Case 50/76 *Amsterdam Bulb BV v Produktschap voor Siergewassen* [1977] ECR 137.

[3] Ds 2003: 15, Europabolag. The Memorandum, which includes the Draft Act, is accessible on-line from the website of the Swedish Ministry of Justice, http://justitie.regeringen.se.

is based on the Draft Act and the Memorandum, which may, however, be subjected to changes before the final adoption by the Swedish parliament.[4] The Ministry of Justice intends to submit a proposal to the parliament in spring 2004.

In addition to the Draft Act, the Ministry of Justice proposes amendments to several legislative acts concerning the financial sector.[5] It follows from recital 26 of the SE-Regulation that harmonised legislation and national law, regulating the activities of financial institutions, shall apply fully to an SE. As a logical consequence hereof, the implications of the SE-Regulation for financial institutions have been duly considered in the Memorandum and changes to the relevant legislation have been proposed to the extent considered necessary. As will be further substantiated below, the Draft Act contains only 27 provisions, the aim being to keep the SE-Regulation self-perpetuating and reduce the need to introduce new legislation to a minimum. However, concerning financial institution SEs, a special regime has been considered necessary in some situations.

It seems fair to claim that the SE has so far generated limited interest among practitioners in Sweden.[6] There may be different reasons for this, one probably being the fact that Sweden joined the European Union as recently as in 1995. On the Community level, the SE has been discussed for decades and has appeared quite extensively in the legal discussion and in the literature. However, the idea of a common European company form and its potential advantages for national and cross border business activities are probably less evident to Swedish enterprises. Furthermore, Sweden is a comparatively small financial market with a limited number of bigger companies involved in cross-border activities to an extent justifying the interest to participate in the formation of an SE at the initial stage.

As for the companies currently established outside Sweden, Sweden does not enjoy an international reputation of being an exceptionally investor friendly

Tax issues related to the European Company are under examination by the Ministry of Finance.

4 According to common Swedish practice, the legislative proposal has been subjected to a hearing procedure. Around 40 public and private organisations and bodies have submitted comments to the Ministry of Justice.

5 The proposed amendments concern *inter alia* the Banking Act (1987: 617), the Act on Securities Funds (1990: 1114), the Act on Investment Services Activities (1991: 981), the Act on Stock exchange and clearing activities (1992: 543). Swedish legislation and preparatory legislative work are accessible from the web page of the Swedish parliament, www.riksdagen.se.

6 Cf. to that effect, the Memorandum, at 89. It shall, however, be noted that the Swedish banking group, Nordea AB, in a press release dated 19 June 2003, announced its intention to restructure the group into a European Company.

state, offering a particularly competitive business environment. Labour law is complex and employment costs relatively high. All these circumstances might be discouraging elements for potential SE-founders, who would consider registering a future SE in Sweden. This said, it shall be emphasised that corporate tax is relatively low in Sweden, approximately 28 %.[7] Moreover, the formation of a company is relatively simple.

Generally seen, it can be concluded that states that wish to attract future SEs would be well advised to adopt clear, concise and business friendly national legislation complementing the SE-Regulation.

II. The formation of an SE

1. General

An SE can be founded by four different means, all presupposing that at least two, already existing public limited companies of different nationalities participate in the formation. The means of formation are the following: i) merger ii) formation of a holding SE, iii) formation of a joint subsidiary or iiii) transformation of an existing public limited liability company, provided that this company has had a subsidiary company governed by the law of another Member State for at least two years. An SE created in one of the mentioned ways may establish its own SE-subsidiaries. Whereas the SE-Regulation contains detailed rules on the formation procedure with regard to merger, transformation and the formation of a holding, it is worth noting that Articles 35 and 36 of the SE-Regulation provide only limited guidance as far as the formation of a subsidiary-SE is concerned. It can be suspected that this relatively simple and practical way to form an SE will appear attractive. Suffice it to note that the only legal frames for this means of formation are found in Article 2(3) of the SE-Regulation, laying down the basic criteria on the companies thus jointly establishing an SE-subsidiary.[8]

Article 15 of the SE-Regulation contains the general rule stating that the formation of an SE shall – unless otherwise provided by the SE-Regulation – be governed by the law applicable to public limited liability companies in the State

[7] Cf. Communication from the European Commission, Towards an Internal Market without Tax Obstacles COM (2001) 582 final.

[8] As pointed out by *Werlauff*, p. 65 the use of the notion subsidiary can be considered to be misleading. The SE-subsidiary will be the subsidiary of one of its founding companies only, or of neither of them, in case none of the founding companies hold a majority of the shares.

where the SE will establish its registered office. In this context, it shall be mentioned that the concept of notary involvement in the formation of a limited liability company is unknown in Swedish company law. Consequently, the formation of SEs according to Swedish law will not involve a notary.

The rules of the SE-Regulation governing the formation and functioning of the SE are a clear indication of the intention to provide rules that suit the needs and interests of large, public limited liability companies in the first place. However, it must be stressed that the formation of an SE in the form of a holding or by the establishment of a subsidiary is open not only to public limited liability companies, but also to private limited liability companies. The forms of association thus covered are listed in Annex II of the SE-Regulation. In this context, it may be noted that Swedish company law – similar to Finland, but in contrast to that of Norway and Denmark – still operates with one single form of company with limited liability. The relevant provisions are contained in the Companies Act (Aktiebolagslagen (1975: 1385), hereinafter ABL). However, in connection with the Swedish access to the European Union in 1995, the limited liability companies were divided into public companies with a share capital of at least 500,000 SEK,[9] the shares of which might be admitted to trading on a regular market, and private limited liability companies with a minimum share capital of 100,000 SEK[10]. As far as the formation of an SE through a subsidiary is concerned, the SE-Regulation contains a direct reference to Article 48 EC. This provision covers all kinds of commercial/profit making companies and firms, provided that they are formed in accordance with the laws of a Member State and have their registered offices, central administrations or principal places of business within the Community. In practical terms, co-operative companies can be assumed to be one form of association, that may show interest in the participation in the establishment of an SE-subsidiary.[11]

As far as the participation of a financial institution in the creation of an SE through a merger is concerned, the Memorandum proposes that the supervisory authority (*Finansinspektionen*) should be allowed to oppose the merger, thus making use of the option provided by Article 19 of the SE-Regulation. As will be further elaborated below, the same possibility is introduced with regard to a financial institution SE's intended transfer of its registered office. Although the special interests in relation to financial institutions must be acknowledged,

[9] Approx. 57,000 €.

[10] Approx. 11,000 €.

[11] Co-operatives may, however, also make use of the recently adopted statute on a European Co-operation (Council Regulation (EC) No 1435/2003 of 22 July 2003 on the Statute for a European Cooperative Society (SCE)).

the reason for introducing a possibility for the supervisory authority to oppose a merger is less evident than in the case of a transfer of the head office. This will hopefully be acknowledged by the supervisory authority in its future decisions with regard to financial institutions' participation in the formation of an SE through merger.

2. No Swedish crowns in the SE ...

Since Sweden does not participate in the third phase of the European Monetary Union (EMU),[12] attention shall be drawn to Article 67 (1) of the SE-Regulation. This provision allows Member States, to which the third phase of the monetary union does not yet apply, to allow SEs with registered offices within their territories to state their share capital and prepare their annual accounts in the national currency. Sweden does not intend to use this option. Thus, all SEs with a registered office in Sweden will be obliged to use Euro as the currency for the share capital as well as in the annual accounts. As correctly pointed out in the Memorandum, the use of the Euro as currency is presumably the most natural and logical choice for companies interested in establishing an SE.[13]

3. Participation of companies with their head offices outside the Community

According to Article 2 (5) of the SE-Regulation, Member States may under certain circumstances allow companies with their head offices outside the Community, to participate in the formation of an SE. The option thus provided for the Member States must be seen in light of the fact that some Member States apply the seat theory, according to which a corporation is subject to the laws of the country in which it has its de facto head office, whereas other Member States apply the incorporation theory, pursuant to which a company is governed by the laws of the country in which it is incorporated, regardless of any subsequent transfer of the head office.[14] Sweden follows the latter principle. In order to register, the statutes must state an address of the administrative board in Sweden.[15] However, nothing prevents the company from having its head

[12] Which has been confirmed by public referendum in September 2003.

[13] Cf. the Memorandum, at 88.

[14] Cf. e.g. *Neville/Engsig Sörensen* Corporate Migration in the EU, Colombia Journal of European Law, vol. 6 2000, at 183ff.

[15] Section 2-4 ABL.

office or its core business in another State.[16] Consequently, it is proposed in the Memorandum to allow companies with their head offices in a state outside the Community to participate in the formation of a "Swedish" SE, provided that the requirements of Article 2 (5) of the SE-Regulation are fulfilled, i.e. that the company must be formed under the law of a Member State, have its statutory seat in that state and maintain a real and continuous link with a Member State's economy.[17] As mentioned above, Article 2 (3) of the SE-Regulation allows association forms other than public limited liability companies to participate in the formation of a subsidiary SE. Consequently, the Draft Act states that co-operatives with their head office outside the Community may also participate in the formation of an SE.[18]

The Memorandum consequently also takes financial institutions into account. As far as the requirement concerning the location of the head office in relation to the statutory seat is concerned, it is recalled that the obligation for a financial institution to have its head office and registered office in the same State is contained in several Directives in the financial sector.[19] Thus, the option of allowing corporations with their head offices outside the EEA to participate in the formation of an SE, will not apply to the formation of financial institution SEs.

4. The location of the registered office

Article 7 of the SE-Regulation concerns a related issue, notably the location of the registered office of an SE. The SE-Regulation adheres to the real seat theory by stating that the registered office must be located in the same Member State as the SE's head office. Furthermore, a Member State may require that the head office and registered office are located in the same place. As a logical consequence of the fact that Sweden follows the incorporation theory, this option will not be exercised.[20] In case an SE infringes the criteria of having its

[16] Cf. *Skog* Kan aktiebolag emigrera? Balans no 7–8/1997, at 20ff.

[17] It shall be noted that the economic link can be to an EEA-State other than the incorporation state.

[18] Section 5 of the Draft Act.

[19] Cf. e.g. Article 6 (2) of the Banking Directive 2000/12/EG, Article 3 (2) of the Investment Services Directive 93/22/EC, Article 3 (2) of the Directive on Undertakings for collective investment in transferable securities (UCITS) 85/611/EEC, as amended.

[20] In this context, cf. Article 69 (a) of the SE-Regulation, pursuant to which the Commission shall within five years after the entry into force of the Regulation present a report analysing in particular the location of the SE's head office and registered office.

head office and registered office in the same state, the Registration Authority, i.e. the Swedish Patent and Registration Office (*Patent- och Registreringsverket*), shall issue a statement to this end and require the SE concerned to rectify the situation. In case of non-compliance, the Registration Authority shall order the liquidation of the SE.[21] The obligation for Member States to prescribe appropriate measures in case the registered office is located in another state than the head office follows from Article 64 of the SE-Regulation. In this context, it shall be emphasised that European case law has clearly developed since the date of adoption of the SE-Regulation. Hence, in Case C-208/00 *Überseering*, the Court of Justice of the European Communities implicitly accepted the fact that a company had its head office and registered seat in different Member States.[22] Hence, it may be argued that case law has overruled Article 7 of the SE-Regulation, before the latter has even entered into force.[23]

5. Minority protection

The SE-Regulation provides options for the Member States to introduce special minority protection rules in case of the formation of an SE through merger or holding.[24] In the Memorandum, the Ministry refrains from proposing the introduction of any particular minority protection rules in case of the formation of an SE through a merger or holding procedure.[25] This approach must be seen in light of the fact that Swedish national company law, in contrast to e.g. Finnish and Danish law, does not foresee any particular minority protection rules, either in case of a merger of two national companies or by the formation of a holding. In the Memorandum, the idea of introducing some kind of sell out right for the minority shareholders who oppose the formation of an SE, is considered. However, it is eventually concluded that a certain degree of minority protection is granted already, due to the fact that a merger decision, according to Swedish company law, requires the approval of 2/3[rds] of the shareholders present at the shareholders' meeting, provided that these shareholders represent 2/3[rds] of the capital thus represented at that meeting.[26] Moreover, it is pointed

[21] Section 26 of the Draft Act.

[22] Case C-208/00 *Überseering*, ECR [2002] I-9919. For a Swedish comment on this case, cf. *Nelson* Überseeringdomen utgör ingen ändring av EG-domstolens praxis, Nordisk Tidsskrift for selskabsret no 4/2002, p. 417 et seq.

[23] Cf. *Dejmek* Genomförandet av Europabolaget i nationell rätt – lättare sagt än gjort?

[24] Cf. Articles 24 (2) and 34 respectively of the SE-Regulation.

[25] The Memorandum, at 50 and 54 respectively.

[26] Cf. Section 14-11 ABL. Swedish company law generally seen stipulates voting criteria

out in the Memorandum that the shareholders would, generally, not be worse off and consequently more worthy of protection in a merger procedure or holding procedure resulting in the formation of an SE, than in the corresponding procedures involving national companies.[27]

In the context of minority shareholder protection, any shareholder may, according to national law, challenge the decision of the shareholders' meeting in which the draft terms of merger were approved, within six months. However, it shall be noted that only procedural mistakes or the fact that the decision is contrary to ABL, the Act on the Annual Accounts[28] or the company's statutes may be invoked.[29] Where the court decides that the merger decision was illegal, the merger is reversed, regardless of whether the acquired company has already ceased to exist. It shall be emphasised that a shareholder may not challenge a decision due to the fact that he is dissatisfied with the share exchange ratio. Given this regime under national law, attention is drawn to Article 30 of the SE-Regulation, pursuant to which a merger may not be declared null and void once the SE has been registered.

As far as the formation of an SE-holding is concerned, the SE-Regulation does not provide any special majority rules with regard to the decision of the general meeting. However, it follows from Article 32 (2) of the SE-Regulation that the management or administrative organs of the companies which promote such an operation shall draw up draft terms for the formation of the holding, including, *inter alia,* the minimum proportion of the shares in each of the companies promoting the operation which the shareholders must contribute to the formation of the holding SE. That proportion shall be shares conferring more than 50 % of the permanent voting rights. Thus, in practical terms, shareholders representing at least 50 % of the votes must agree to contribute their shares. From the Swedish point of view, no special measures have been considered necessary in this regard, since the shareholders are free to decide whether they will contribute shares to the holding or not. Consequently, no particular minority protection provisions are proposed.[30]

With regard to the transformation from a national company to an SE, the SE-Regulation provides a possibility to introduce a requirement of a majority

both with regard to the required majority of shareholders and their proportion of the represented share capital. This is due to the fact that different classes of shares are allowed – and very common – in Swedish limited liability companies.

[27] However, several hearing instances have expressed the view that the Swedish legislator should introduce minority protection rules.

[28] Act no 1995: 1554.

[29] Cf. Sections 14-30 and 9-40 ABL.

[30] The Memorandum, at 54.

stricter than 2/3rds of the voting shares at the shareholders' meeting. This possibility is discussed – but rejected – in the Memorandum. It is concluded that it would be inappropriate to grant a limited number of shareholders the possibility to veto the creation of an SE, in this case.[31]

III. Transfer of the registered office

1. General

One of the repeatedly emphasised advantages of the SE-Regulation is the possibility open to an SE to transfer its registered office without any requirements of liquidation and subsequent new incorporation under the laws of the recipient state. As far as this transfer is concerned, the SE-Regulation provides possibilities to adopt certain protective measures with regard to minority shareholders and creditors. Moreover, Member States may allow its competent authorities to object to the transfer of the registered office, on grounds of public interest. Following the approach outlined above in relation to the formation of an SE, it is emphasised in the Memorandum that certain protective measures already follow from the SE-Regulation. It can be noted that the provisions regulating the transfer of seat are clearly inspired by the provisions of the Merger Directive,[32] long since familiar to all Member States. Thus, the management or administrative organ shall draw up a transfer proposal stating the details of the transfer, and a report, explaining the legal and economic aspects and implications of the transfer. That proposal shall be published and made available to the shareholders and creditors at least one month before the decision on the merger. In the light of these provisions, the Memorandum concludes that no particular minority protection rules are necessary. Moreover, it is pointed out that one main reason for selecting an SE as a business form will probably be the possibility to transfer the registered office. This should be evident to shareholders participating in the formation of an SE or acquiring its shares at a later stage.[33]

As far as the majority required for the transfer decision is concerned, reference is made to Article 59 of the SE-Regulation, according to which the statutes of an SE may be amended by a majority which may not be less than two

[31] The Memorandum, at 56.

[32] Council Directive 78/855/EEC concerning mergers of public limited liability companies.

[33] The Memorandum, at 31.

thirds of the votes cast, unless the law applicable to public limited liability companies in the Member State in which the registered office is situated, requires a larger vote. The Memorandum does not mention the issue. Thus, it can be concluded that the transfer of the registered office out of Sweden would normally require two thirds of the votes cast, representing two thirds of the represented capital, as provided in Section 9-30 ABL.

2. Creditor protection

As far as the protection of creditors in case of a transfer of the registered office is concerned, the regime provided for in the case of national mergers shall be applied to SEs, i.e. the management organ of the SE must apply to the Registration Authority for a transfer authorisation. The Registration Authority will then notify the known creditors of the company, who may object to the transfer within a certain time limit set by the Registration Authority. If they do so, the Registration Authority must submit the case to the competent civil court. The Court may approve the transfer only after the objecting creditors have received full payment for claims dating prior to the date of objection set by the Registration Authority, or have been granted a satisfactory security.[34] It may be noted that the Draft Act does not require the creditors to provide any evidence as to their potential deteriorated position due to the transfer of the registered office.

National law on mergers allows exceptions from the obligation to inform the creditors under certain circumstances.[35] One of the most significant examples is related to employees' salary claims. Since these claims are guaranteed by the State, the employees do not have to be informed of the merger in their capacities as creditors. It shall be noted that this protection is the consequence of a Community Directive[36]. It can, thus be presupposed that similar legislation exists in all EU States. However, the Memorandum nevertheless concludes that this exemption shall not apply to the transfer of an SE. This implies that the Swedish salary guarantee system shall continue to apply to employees of the SE who work in Sweden, even after the transfer of the registered office.[37] In other words, employees of an SE will always be covered by the Swedish salary guarantee system, provided that their regular place of work is Sweden. This applies regardless of where the SE has its registered office and its head office.

[34] Cf. Section 13-15 of the Draft Act.

[35] Section 14-13 paragraph 2 ABL

[36] Cf. Council Directive 80/987/EEC on the approximation of the laws of the Member States relating to the protection of employees in the event of the insolvency of their employer.

[37] The Memorandum, at 35.

3. Special rules with regard to financial institution SEs

A different regime is provided in case a financial institution SE intends to transfer its registered office. In this case, the Financial Supervisory Authority (*Finansinspektionen*) must be informed. No creditors need to be notified. By contrast, the supervisory authority shall assess the suitability of the transfer in light of the financial situation of the company and the legitimate interests of its investors, customers and other creditors. As far as the possibility for the authorities to oppose a transfer on grounds of public interest is concerned, i.e. Article 8 (14) of the SE-Regulation, such a possibility will only be introduced in case of a financial institution SE. It can be noted that the Draft Act does not provide any guidelines with respect to the public interest criterion. Thus, it appears suitable to refer to the public interests acknowledged as legitimate interests by the Court of Justice of the European Communities. In this context, the Memorandum mentions e.g. efficient tax supervision, the prevention of money laundering and tax evasion. Moreover, media diversity, consumer protection and the good reputation of financial institutions might, according to the Memorandum, be invoked in order to restrict the free movement of capital.[38]

Without taking a position on these statements, it shall be pointed out that the Court has repeatedly interpreted possible justification grounds strictly. According to the Court's case-law, national measures liable to hinder or make less attractive the exercise of fundamental freedoms guaranteed by the Treaty must fulfil four conditions: they must be applied in a non-discriminatory manner; they must be justified by imperative requirements in the general interest; they must be suitable for securing the attainment of the objective which they pursue; and they must be in accordance with the principle of proportionality, i.e. they may not go beyond what is necessary in order to attain it.[39] As far as the justification ground related to the public interest is concerned, suffice it to recall that the general financial interests of a Member State cannot constitute

[38] The Memorandum, at 48. It is unclear why the Memorandum refers to free movement of capital, since the freedom of establishment appears to be the freedom affected in the first place. However, the issue can be considered to be of minor relevance, since the Court shows a clear tendency to apply the same reasoning with regard to all freedoms.

[39] Cf. to that effect with regard to the freedom of establishment, e.g. Case C-167/01 *Inspire Art*, not yet reported, paragraph 133, Case C-212/97 *Centros* [1999] ECR I-1459, paragraph 34, Case C-19/92 *Kraus* v *Land Baden-Württemberg* [1993] ECR I-1663, paragraph 32, Case C-55/94 *Gebhard* v *Consiglio dell'Ordine degli Avvocati e Procuratori di Milano* [1995] ECR I-4165, paragraph 37. With regard to free movement of capital, cf. Joined Cases C-163/94, C-165/94 and C-250/94 *Sanz de Lera and Others*, paragraphs 23, Case C-54/99 *Eglise de Scientologie* [2000] ECR I-1335, paragraph 18, Case C-483/99 *Commission v France* [2002] ECR I-4781, paragraph 45.

adequate justification for a restriction of a fundamental freedom. It is settled case-law that economic grounds can never serve as justification for obstacles to the fundamental freedoms.[40] In this context, it shall furthermore be emphasised that national administrative authorities must, in their decision making, be bound by objective criteria that might be subject to review and leave as little discriminatory powers as possible to the authorities.[41] These requirements should be of relevance also in the context of Article 8 paragraph 14 of the SE-Regulation.

IV. The structure of the SE

1. National law

An extensively discussed feature of the SE-Regulation is the obligation on the Member States to ensure that an SE should be able to choose between a one-tier and a two-tier management system.[42] Under current company law, Sweden has a one-tier system with a unitary board. As mentioned above, both private and public limited liability companies are governed by ABL. However, a certain flexibility is allowed as far as the organisation of private companies is concerned.[43]

The highest body of a Swedish limited liability company is the general meeting.[44] In the public limited liability company, the general meeting must appoint the majority of the members of the administrative board (employees' representatives not included).[45] A public limited liability company must have at least three board members, the mandate of whom may not exceed 4 years. The administrative board is responsible for the organisation and the management of the company. In addition, it has supervisory functions. Thus, the administrative board of a Swedish company combines, to a certain extent, the functions that

40 Cf. in particular, Case C-367/98 *Commission v Portugal* [2002] ECR I-4731, paragraph 52.

41 Cf. for this kind of reasoning, *inter alia*, Case C-205/99 *Analir* [2001] I-1271, paragraph 38, Case C-503/99 *Commission v Belgium* [2002] ECR I-4809, paragraph 52, Case C-483/99 *Commission v France* [2002] ECR I-4781, paragraphs 51–53.

42 *Werlauff*'s suggestion (p. 73) that Member States may restrict the choice of SEs registered within its territory is probably not to be followed.

43 For example, a managing director is mandatory in public limited liability companies only.

44 The general meeting is regulated in Chapter 9 ABL.

45 The administrative board and the managing director are dealt with in Chapter 8 ABL.

are allocated to the management organ on the one hand and the supervisory organ on the other hand in the two-tier system. Moreover, it shall be noted that the auditor is considered a separate company body under Swedish company law. The auditor reports directly to the general meeting and can be held liable to the company or the individual shareholders for damage caused due to negligence. The general meeting, acting by simple majority, may dismiss a board member at any time.

The day-to-day management is, by law, delegated to the managing director, who is appointed by the board by majority decision. A public limited liability company must have a managing director. The tasks of the managing director are specified in a written working order from the administrative board. Within the scope of the day-to-day management, the managing director represents the company in relation to third parties. The managing director may – and this is usually the case – be a member of the management board. However, in public limited liability companies, he may not be chairman of the board. It is important to point out that although ABL provides a certain flexibility as far as the management and division of tasks are concerned, and nowadays it is very common to establish special committees with special assignments – the board can never delegate its overriding management and supervisory function. This responsibility remains with the board. The administrative board and the managing directors are liable for damage caused to the company or its creditors through negligent behaviour. In addition, they may be held liable to the shareholders, in case the damage caused to the shareholders is due to a breach of ABL, the Act on the Annual Accounts or the company's statutes.[46]

Article 47 of the SE-Regulation provides the possibility of allowing legal persons to become board members. Such an option is unknown to Swedish company law and will not be introduced with regard to the SE. In order to ensure equal treatment of national limited liability companies and SEs with the registered office in Sweden, it is proposed to add a paragraph to Section 8-9 ABL, clarifying that legal persons cannot be appointed as board members.

2. The one-tier system SE

The Memorandum takes as its starting point that the administrative organ of the one tier system SE can be considered equivalent to the administrative board of a Swedish public limited liability company, thus rendering additional legislation redundant. From a technical point of view, this is expressed by a general

[46] Section 15-1 ABL.

reference clause, stating that unless otherwise provided in the SE-Regulation, all provisions in ABL or in other legislative acts referring to the management board or its members shall apply accordingly to the administrative organ of the SE.[47]

3. The two-tier system SE

In case an SE with its registered seat in Sweden would opt for a dualistic system with a two-tier board, the issue would be more problematic. In that case, the management organ shall be considered equivalent to the Swedish administrative board. Consequently, the Draft Act contains a reference clause in order to ensure that all Swedish legislation concerning the administrative board and its members will apply to the management organ. The management organ shall be appointed and removed by the supervisory organ. Article 39 paragraph 2 of the SE-Regulation provides an optional right for Member States to decide that the members of the management organ be appointed and removed by the shareholders' meeting. However, this possibility has not been made use of in the Draft Act.

In the context of the two-tier system SE, the Swedish legislator has found certain inspiration in the Finnish Companies Act. Finnish law provides the optional possibility for the general meeting of public limited liability companies to appoint a supervisory board in addition to the management organ. The supervisory organ thus appointed shall supervise the management organ and the managing director and shall *inter alia* submit an opinion concerning the annual account and the auditor's report to the annual general meeting.[48] The Draft Act states a similar duty for the supervisory organ of a two-tier SE with its registered seat in Sweden. The management organ will in these companies be appointed by the supervisory organ.

As rightly acknowledged in the Memorandum, a mere reference to the provisions concerning the Swedish administrative board would be inappropriate with regard to the supervisory organ in the two tier-system SE, since this concept is unknown in Swedish law. Article 19 of the SE-Regulation entitles Member States to adopt appropriate measures in relation to SEs where no provision is made for a two-tier system. To solve the problem of lack of default rules, the Draft Act lists a number of provisions of the ABL concerning the administrative board and its members, which shall apply accordingly to the supervisory

[47] Section 19 of the Draft Act.

[48] Cf. Section 8-11 of the Finnish Companies Act no. 734/1998.

organ.[49] This applies, for example, to provisions on the required impartiality of board members, assignments in other companies, duty to inform the general meeting and, in particular, as far as the liability against the company and the shareholders is concerned. The Swedish legislator has refrained from extending the powers of the supervisory organ to include more far reaching influence on the company management, despite the mentioned legal reference technique with regard to the functions of the supervisory organ. The possibility to grant the supervisory organ a right to decide on for example the change of the company's main scope of activities is discussed – and rejected – in the Memorandum.[50] Thus, the general overriding management functions will remain with the management organ, in the two-tier system SE as well.

The liability of board members is of particular interest, since the members of the Swedish administrative board can, as has been mentioned, be held personally liable not only to the company itself and its creditors, but also to the shareholders. In the two-tier SE, the members of the supervisory organ may be held responsible under the same conditions. Practice will show whether the liability of the members of the supervisory organ will be invoked more often than the liability of the members of the management organ.

4. The general meeting

Articles 52–60 of the SE-Regulation regulate the tasks of the General Meeting. Notwithstanding the lack of secondary legislation regarding shareholders as a collegiate body, this is an area in which the European legal orders appear fairly similar. Consequently, most of the provisions in the SE-Regulation are already contained in ABL. The Draft Act provides only two provisions concerning the general meeting. Section 24 of the Draft Act reflects a provision in national company law, section 9–11 ABL, and states that all shareholders are entitled to require that certain points are added to the agenda of the annual general meeting, regardless of the size of their holdings. As far as the convening of extraordinary general meetings is concerned, ABL provides, as does the SE-Regulation, such a right for shareholders holding at least 10% of the shares of the company. Section 25 of the Draft Act states the duty for the administrative board to convene a general meeting in certain circumstances.

Article 58 of the SE-Regulation concerns the calculation of votes. The votes cast shall not include votes attaching to shares in respect of which the share-

[49] Section 17 of the Draft Act.

[50] Cf. the Memorandum, at 63.

holder has not taken part in the vote, or has abstained, or has returned a blank or damaged ballot paper. In this context, it can be noted that ABL states percentages of votes required, not only relating to the number of votes cast, but also to the ratio of the capital thus represented at the general meeting. In order to establish whether the majority requirement has been met, blank votes shall also be taken into account.[51]

5. The managing director

Articles 39 paragraph 1 and 43 paragraph 1 of the SE-Regulation deal with the managing director. A managing director may be appointed, regardless of the management system chosen. From the Swedish point of view, these provisions are of particular interest. According to national company law, public limited liability companies must have a managing director, who is responsible for the day-to-day management of the company. Not surprisingly, the Draft Act obliges all SEs with a registered office in Sweden, to appoint a managing director, regardless of whether the SE has opted for the one-tier or the two-tier system. In case of a dualistic SE, the managing director will be appointed by the supervisory organ. In the monist SE, he shall be appointed by the administrative board.[52] In addition, the Draft Act contains a general reference to the provisions concerning the managing director in ABL.

In case of a one-tier SE, the managing director will, as is the case under ABL, report to the administrative board. In the two-tier SE, the managing director will be under a reporting duty to both the management organ and the supervisory organ. The managing director shall, in the first case, be under the supervision of the administrative board. In case of a two-tier SE, the managing director will be supervised by both the management organ and the supervisory organ.

V. The participation of employees in the SE

1. General

One of the most problematic points during the negotiations concerning the SE-Regulation was undoubtedly the participation of the employees. Member States with strict and far reaching rules on participation of employees feared that

[51] Cf. *Johansson* Bolagsstämma, Stockholm 1990, p. 464.

[52] Section 21 of the Draft Act.

companies would, by the formation of an SE, "merge out of" national employee participation rules[53] or transfer the registered office at a later stage, in order to circumvent employee participation in the management. Due to the complexity of the issue, it was decided, early in the legislative procedure, to separate the company law issues in the SE-Regulation from the employee involvement, by the adoption of a separate directive on employee involvement. However, the negotiations proved difficult, in particular due to the fact that the systems of employee involvement differ widely between the member states. Thus, legislative progress was severely blocked for several years.

The Directive on European Works Council of 1994[54] has brought about some harmonisation in the field. However, that Directive grants the employees information and consultation rights only and moreover, is only applicable to "Community scale" undertakings, i.e. undertakings with at least 1.000 employees within the Member States and at least 150 employees in each of at least two Member States.[55] Nevertheless, it is clear that the Directive on European Works Council has been a very useful tool when drafting the Directive on the employee involvement in the SE (hereinafter the SE-Directive). This is clearly shown in the provisions regarding the establishment of the special negotiating body.[56] This body shall consist of representatives of the involved parties, i.e. the employees of the participating companies and concerned subsidiaries or establishments.

The decisive link between the SE-Regulation and the complementing Directive on employee involvement is expressed in Article 12 of the SE-Regulation, according to which an SE may not be registered unless an agreement on arrangements for the employees has been reached, or a decision has been made under Article 3 paragraph 6 of the SE-Directive, i.e. a decision made by the special negotiating body to terminate the procedure to conclude the voluntary agreement referred to in Article 4, or the negotiation period under Article 5 (i.e., in general, six months) of the SE-Directive has expired without any agreement being reached. This implies that the SE may be registered even though the

[53] It can be noted that this possibility exists, notably if the home state of the continuing SE has no participation rules corresponding to part 3 of the Annex and if a participation agreement is not reached in accordance with the negotiation procedure. cf. *Werlauff* The SE Company – A New Common European Company from 8 October 2004 [2003] European Business Law Review (ELBR), p. 85 (100).

[54] Council Directive 94/45/EC on the establishment of a European Works Council or a procedure in Community-scale undertakings and Community-scale groups of undertakings for the purposes of informing and consulting employees.

[55] Cf. Article 2 of Directive 94/45.

[56] Cf. Article 3 of the SE-Directive.

negotiations have terminated or the time limit has expired. In these cases, the provisions of the SE-Directive will apply, i.e. the standard rules as laid down by the legislation of the Member State in which the registered office of the SE is to be situated.[57]

The wording and structure of the SE-Directive is regrettably complicated and places a particularly heavy burden on the national legislators, who have to transform the rules of the Directive to clear and comprehensible national law.[58] Since an SE may only be registered provided that the employee representation issue has been solved, the potential success of the SE is indispensably linked to the appropriate implementation of the rules on employee participation. In practical terms, it can be expected that most companies interested in forming an SE will aim at reaching an amicable solution with the representatives of the employees involved, before even entering into negotiations concerning the formation of the company as such.

In the Swedish legislative process, it was decided to separate the implementation of the SE-Directive into national law from the drafting of the legislative measures necessary to supplement the SE-Regulation. A Report on the implementation of the SE-Directive, including the Draft Act on the involvement of employees in the SE, was published in June 2003[59] (hereinafter referred to as the Draft Act on employee involvement). The Draft Act contains 62 provisions. Some of these provisions will be highlighted in the following.

2. National law

National rules on employee participation are to be found mainly in the Act on Co-determination on the working place[60] and in the Act on Right to representation at the Board for employees in the private sector.[61] Only the latter concerns employee involvement directly on the company's management organ. According to the Act on Right to representation at the Board, employees are

[57] Cf. Article 7 (1) of Directive 2001/86.

[58] The great complexity of the rules has been acknowledged by the European Commission. Hence, a Working Group of experts from the EU Member States was established with the view of finding common solutions. The work of this Working Group has been considered in the Swedish legislative work.

[59] Cf. SOU 2003: 64. The Report contains an English summary and can be downloaded from the homepage of the Swedish Ministry of Commerce, http://www.naring.regeringen.se/propositioner_mm/sou/2003/index.htm

[60] Cf. SFS 1976: 580.

[61] Act no SFS 1987: 1245.

entitled to be represented by two members and two deputy members at the administrative board, provided that the company has had at least 25 employees during the previous year. If the company has more than 1.000 employees, the employees are entitled to three board members and three deputy board members. However, the employee representatives can never outvote the ordinary board members. In case of a group of companies, the number of employees in the whole group shall be taken into account. This implies that there will always be employee representatives on the board of the parent company, even if this is organised as a holding company and has as such less than 25 employees.

The Swedish system is closely linked to the tradition of labour unions. The employee representation is not mandatory, but depending on whether a local labour union, which has concluded a collective agreement with the company, exercises its right to appoint board members. Correspondingly, if the company has no agreements with any labour union at all, there is no right of employee representation. Moreover, it should be underlined that the employee representatives are not selected by the employees themselves, but by the local labour unions. Contrasting to the situation in several other EU States, the employee representatives do not have to be employed in the relevant company. If several labour unions are represented, the labour unions should agree on how the representatives should be selected. If no agreement is reached, the union representing at least 80 % of the employees will appoint all the representatives. However, if another union represents at least 5 %, this union will be entitled to appoint one of the deputy members. In terms of the degree of participation rights thus granted to the employees, it is important to note that the employee board members have the same duties and obligations as all other board members. In particular, they can be held liable for damages caused to shareholders, to the company and the creditors to the same extent as the ordinary board members.

3. Main features of the SE-Directive – allocation of seats in the special negotiating body

Under current Swedish law, there are no rules that would satisfy the requirements of the SE-Directive with regard to those future SEs that will have their registered offices in Sweden. Hence, legislative action was considered as necessary.[62]

[62] Cf. the Report, at 73. It may be noted that the Act on Right to representation at the Board for employees in the private sector will not be applicable to European Companies.

As indicated above, one of the decisive features of the SE-Directive is the establishment and composition of the special negotiating body, on which all entities participating in the creation of the SE shall be represented. Hence, unsurprisingly, a considerable part of the Report revolves around the procedures of the special negotiating body and, in particular, the allocation of seats in this organ. The composition of the special negotiation body is of particular relevance in case the SE is established through a merger, since a merger implies that one or several of the participating companies will cease to exist as a separate legal entity after completion of the merger. Considering the main aims of the SE-Directive, it is of particular importance to safeguard the rights of the employees of these "disappearing" companies.

The SE-Directive's rules on allocation of seats in the special negotiating body may be divided into three levels. The first step is the geographical allocation of seats among the Member States that are involved in the creation of the SE. As a second step, every State must distribute the seats which have been allocated to it, in case there is more than one establishment involved within that States' territory. After completion of this distribution of seats among the establishments within the State, employee representatives shall be assigned to each single seat. Whereas, for obvious reasons, the first step must be regulated through harmonised legislation (cf. Article 3 paragraph 2 a (i) of the SE-Directive), the second and third steps will be matters of national law, regardless where the SE will have its registered office. Hence, the allocation of seats within Sweden and the appointment of employee representatives for Swedish entities shall be regulated in Swedish law.

With regard to the first step, Article 3 paragraph 2 a (i) of the SE-Directive is reflected in Section 8 of the Draft Act on employee involvement. Hence, as a general rule, the employees shall be given one permanent place on the negotiation body for every ten per cent or fraction of the number of employees employed by the participating companies and concerned subsidiaries or establishments in all the EEA States taken together. If the SE is established by way of merger, the employees shall be rewarded extra seats, if this is necessary to ensure representation of the employees in the participating companies which cease to exist.

As far as the allocation within Sweden is concerned, it is proposed to give the participating companies priority over the concerned subsidiaries and establishments. Hence, participating companies will get their seats first. Afterwards, the seats shall be allocated in descending order, following the number of employees in the different entities. As a starting point, every entity shall receive one seat.[63]

[63] Sections 11-14 of the Draft Act on employee involvement.

As to the third step in the allocation process, it can be observed that the proposed regime for appointment of representatives for the different entities involved follows closely the Swedish tradition of labour unions and their involvement in the appointment of employee representatives. The system of the Draft Act on employee involvement mirrors the guiding principles of the Act on Right to representation at the Board for employees in the private sector.[64] Hence, the employee representatives shall be appointed by those local labour unions, which have entered into collective agreements with the involved companies (or concerned subsidiaries or establishments, as the case may be). In case only one person shall be selected, he shall be selected by the largest labour union that is represented. When several persons are to be selected, reference is made to the appointment procedure foreseen in the Act on Right to Representation on the Board. The local labour organisations may agree on a different arrangement.[65] In case the employer has not entered into any collective agreements at all, the representative in the special negotiating delegation shall be selected by the labour union which has the largest number of members in the involved entities. This rule may be deviated from, provided that the local labour organisations agree to do so.[66]

Section 10 of the Draft Act on employee involvement concerns structural changes and changes in the number of employees during the negotiation process, before any final agreement on the employee involvement has been reached. This issue is not mentioned in the SE-Directive. However, taking into account the time necessary to establish the negotiation delegation and the time that might pass before any agreement has been reached, this matter may well prove to be of practical relevance. In order to avoid unnecessary complications, it is proposed in the Report that a renewed calculation and distribution of seats should be undertaken only in case the changes affect the geographical allocation of seats among the states.[67] Hence, internal changes within the participating Swedish entities shall not trigger any re-opening of the allocation procedure.

4. An equivalent level of employee involvement ...

Sections 21 et seq. of the Draft Act on employee involvement state the majority rules required for the decisions taken by the special negotiation delegation. Generally seen, simple majority is sufficient. However, qualified majority is

[64] Act no SFS 1987: 1245.

[65] Section 15 of the Draft Act on employee involvement.

[66] Section 15 paragraph 3 of the Draft Act on employee involvement.

[67] Section 10 of the Draft Act on employee involvement.

foreseen, in case the parties agree to introduce a lower level of employee involvement. There is, however, one important exception to this rule. In case the SE is established by way of transformation, it follows directly from the SE-Directive that the representatives are precluded from reaching an agreement on a lesser degree of involvement than existed in the company before the transformation to an SE. This matter is likely to create practical problems. The SE-Directive neither appraises different levels of employee involvement, nor are the different systems of the Member States compared in the Directive. Considering the aims behind the Swedish rules on employee involvement, i.e. to give employee representatives direct influence on the management of the company by granting them rights and duties equal to those of the ordinary members of the management board, the question arises how this level of involvement shall be maintained in, e.g. a Swedish one-tier company which is transformed into an SE with a two-tier structure. As rightly pointed out in the Report, the Court of Justice is the only forum which will, eventually, be competent to decide whether two different systems of employee involvement can be considered to be equivalent.[68]

5. Transparency and confidentiality

From the Swedish perspective, rules on transparency and confidentiality are of particular interest. Article 8 paragraph 2 of the SE-Directive obliges Member States to provide, in specific cases and under the conditions and limits laid down by national legislation, that the supervisory or administrative organ of an SE or of a participating company established in its territory is not obliged to transmit information where its nature is such that, according to objective criteria, it would seriously harm the functioning of the SE (or, as the case may be, the participating company or its subsidiaries and establishments), or would be prejudicial to them. Member States may make such dispensation subject to prior administrative or judicial authorisation. Confidentiality rules of this kind are not uncommon in Community legislation, but are, generally seen, difficult to conceive with the Swedish tradition of transparency and openness. This principle is considered to be of particular importance in the context of employee involvement. Hence, the Draft Act does not provide any provision corresponding to Article 8 paragraph 2 of the SE-Directive. Having due regard to the Member States' implementation obligations, it may be disputed whether this is

[68] Cf. the Report, at 109.

acceptable. In the current context, suffice it to note that this omission from the side of the Swedish legislator is unlikely to create major practical problems.[69]

6. Prevention of misuse and enforcement measures

Article 11 of the SE-Directive requires Member States to introduce appropriate measures with a view to preventing the misuse of an SE for the purpose of depriving employees of their involvement rights. Section 59 of the Draft Act on employee involvement reflects this rule. Moreover, a special presumption rule is found in Section 59 paragraph 2 of the Draft Act on employee involvement. Hence, if the SE implements a change within one year after registration, and it appears that the required employee involvement would have been more extensive, would this change have been undertaken prior to registration, it shall be presumed that the change was made to the end of depriving employees of their rights of involvement, unless otherwise proved by the company. It can be assumed that this will, generally seen, be a hard burden of proof to fulfil for the SE. As far as sanctions are concerned (cf. Article 12 of the SE-Directive), the Draft Act on employee involvement suggests damages in the event of non-compliance with its rules and in case of a breach of an agreement concluded pursuant to that act. If no special negotiation body and/or representative body has been established, the company or the entity to which the breach can be attributed, will be liable towards the involved labour unions.[70] The labour court shall be the competent court, as far as any disputes related to the application of the Act on employee involvement are concerned.

[69] Cf. the Report, at 148. As pointed out in the Report, the Directive on European Works Council contains a corresponding provision (Article 8 paragraph 2). Similar to the present situation, it was decided not to transpose that provision into Swedish law.

[70] Section 60 of the Draft Act on employee involvement.

United Kingdom

Mike Edbury

I. General background to company law regulation in the United Kingdom

It is important to stress at the outset that there is no single body of company law that applies throughout the United Kingdom. The principal legal provisions related to limited companies within Great Britain (England, Wales and Scotland) are presently contained in the Companies Act 1985 (as amended) together with the Insolvency Act 1986, dealing with company insolvency, and the Company Directors Disqualification Act 1986 which sets out procedures under which persons may be disqualified from acting as directors of limited companies where they have been found guilty of misconduct. The law related to England and Wales contained within these Acts is the same, but there are important differences in relation to the manner in which these Acts apply in relation to Scotland, particularly in the field of insolvency.

Northern Ireland has its own separate company legislation, although currently this is closely aligned with the provisions applicable in England and Wales.

In all of the jurisdictions within the United Kingdom, there are the following four types of limited company vehicle available:

- public companies limited by shares,
- public companies limited by guarantee,
- private companies limited by shares and
- private limited companies limited by guarantee.

There has been extensive review of the company law framework within the United Kingdom in recent years. In particular, the independent review of company law sponsored by the Department of Trade and Industry which reported finally in July 2001 and the Government White Paper published in 2002 in response to that Report. The Government aims to move forward with reform of company law as soon as practicable. There has also been recent fundamental review of issues related to corporate governance, for instance the Higgs Review of the role of non-executive directors and the Co-ordinating Group on Auditing and Accountancy, both of which reported finally in January 2003. Additionally, a new Bill, The Companies (Audit, Investigations and Community Enterprise) Bill, is now being considered by the UK Parliament. The Bill has the twin aims of improving confidence in financial markets and also promoting social enterprise.

II. Plans for implementation of the European Company Statute in Great Britain

The Department of Trade and Industry published a consultation document in October 2003, "Implementation of the European Company Statute: The European Public Limited-Liability Company Regulations 2004", setting out its plans for implementation of the European Company Statute Regulation ("the Statute") and the Directive supplementing the Statute with regard to the involvement of employees ("the Directive") by the Statute's entry into force date of 8 October 2004. The proposed implementing provisions will apply throughout Great Britain, although there will be a need to make separate provision for implementation in Northern Ireland where the Department for Enterprise, Trade and Industry will be undertaking separate consultation on application of the European Company Statute (ECS). The implementing provisions in Northern Ireland are not further discussed in this paper.

The Consultation Document proposes that the ECS should be implemented by means of a single set of regulations made under section 2(2) of the European Communities Act 1972 which deals with both company law and employee involvement issues. A draft of the proposed regulations ("the Regulations") is contained in the Consultation Document. Tax issues which may arise from implementation of the Statute remain under consideration. It is intended that these will be separately consulted upon should it be concluded that it is necessary to make changes to tax law.

The Consultation Document was open for public consultation until 9 January 2004 and, clearly, the final implementing provisions will need to reflect issues raised during the course of that consultation, the responses to which are now being considered.

III. Implementation of company law provisions

As the Statute is free standing and has direct effect in Great Britain, there is, of course, limited scope for "implementation" of the Statute. It is, therefore, intended to confine implementing legislation of the company law provisions to four matters:

a) Essential measures necessary to ensure the effective application of the Statute (for instance, in relation to the formalities of registering a European Company ["SE"] at Companies House);

b) Provisions in the Statute which require Member States to enact measures (eg to deal with breach of the Statute where the head office and registered office of an SE are no longer in the same Member State);
c) Exercise of the Member State "options" under the Statute which it has been decided to apply (such as, the right for the Member State to prevent a merger or transfer proposal on public interest grounds); and
d) Provisions of sanctions and penalties for contravention of the Statute (eg for misuse of the term SE).

In this paper, it is not intended to discuss at length the provisions of the Statute itself nor the proposed detailed implementing provisions in Great Britain. Instead, the focus is on some of the areas where the Statute will introduce novel concepts or where its provisions appear anomalous or to run contrary to existing law in relation to public companies in Great Britain.

1. Means of creating a European Company and registration

The Statute lays down four principal means by which an SE may be formed. All of these involve essentially two or more commercial bodies, at least two of which must be resident in a different Member State. The four main mechanisms for forming an SE are as follows:

- cross-border merger of two or more PLC's,
- formation of an SE as a holding company,
- formation of an SE as a subsidiary and
- transformation of an existing public limited company.

An SE may also be formed as a subsidiary of another SE.

Formation of holding companies and subsidiaries is presently possible under company law in Great Britain and commonplace in business practice. The transformation of a public limited company to an SE has parallels with the current procedure under the law in Great Britain for a private limited company to transform itself from, or to, a public limited company.

The formation of an SE by cross-merger is, perhaps, the most novel concept in terms of the law in Great Britain as, whilst there are a number of devices utilised by British companies to facilitate cross-border corporate restructuring, this is the first occasion a specific legal framework designed to permit this will be in place. The facility for companies, other than SEs, to take part in cross-border mergers within the EU is, of course, currently subject to consideration at the EU level following publication by the Commission of the 10th Company Law (Cross-border Mergers) Directive on 18 November 2003.

2. Legal personality and share capital of an SE

The Statute provides that the share capital of an SE must be at least EUR 120,000 and also that it is possible for there to be a single member SE (where the SE is a wholly owned subsidiary of another SE). Presently, public limited companies in Great Britain are required to have a minimum capital of £ 50,000. As the UK is currently outside of the third phase of economic and monetary union (EMU), it is proposed that the Regulations exercise the Member State option to provide that the capital of the SE may be expressed in sterling (as may the accounts of an SE registered in Great Britain), although such capital must, of course, be at least equivalent to EUR 120,000, which is rather more than £ 50,000. Additionally, the current requirement under the Companies Act 1985 for a public limited company to have at least two members will be overridden in the case of single member SE subsidiaries. Private GB companies may have only one member.

3. Registered office and head office of an SE

The Statute provides that the head office of an SE must be in the same Member State as the registered office (the EU Commission is required to provide a report on the appropriateness of this within 5 years of the Statute coming into force). The issue of the linkage of locality of the head office to that of the registered office of a company has been subject to considerable recent examination in the "Centros" line of cases in the European Court of Justice. GB applies the "incorporation doctrine" approach on this matter and the head office of a GB registered public limited company need not be in GB (nor, indeed, within the EU). This will represent an important difference for SEs.

4. Transfer of an SE to another Member State

It is currently only possible for a public company in Great Britain to transfer its registered office to another Member State by means of a Private Act of Parliament and, in practice, there are few such transfers. The Company Law Review recommended that a legislative procedure should be put in place to allow companies in Great Britain to transfer their registered office both within the British jurisdiction (ie from England and Wales to, or from, Scotland) or to another Member State. However, the White Paper published in July 2002 in response to the Company Law Review indicated that the Government were not minded to proceed with the latter recommendation due to certain concerns, principally the scope for loss of tax revennes.

In line with Member State options under the Statute, it is proposed to put in place a number of safeguards to protect shareholders, creditors and others in the event of an SE deciding to migrate to another Member State, these include:

- Transfer proposals will have to be noted on letters, invoices and orders for goods issued by the SE whilst the transfer is under consideration;
- A statement of solvency will be required from any transferring SE; and
- A right to oppose transfer applications on "public interest" grounds will be provided.
  (The Consultation document states that "public interest" considerations would probably include wrongdoing by the SE that might involve fraud and tax evasion. In practice, the power to oppose transfer would generally be exercised by the Secretary of State for Trade and Industry who would, however, be able to consider representations from others, such as the tax authorities and the police, who had an interest).

As with cross-border mergers, the issue of company "migration" for companies other than SEs will be subject to further consideration at the EU level as part of the EU Action Plan on Company Law and Corporate Governance which proposes that the Fourteenth Company Law (Migration) Directive proposal be brought forward as a priority measure.

5. Supervisory and management organs of an SE (one and two tier-system)

One of the key innovations of the Statute was the provision which enables all SEs to choose through the mechanism of their "statutes" (Memorandum and Articles of Association in Great Britain) either a one-tier or two tier board structure. The extension of the choice as to one or two tier board structures to all companies (not just SEs) is proposed as a medium term priority under the EU Action Plan on Company Law and Corporate Governance.

Traditionally, Great Britain is viewed as being within the "one tier" board school of corporate governance. However, as the Consultation Document points out, there is nothing in law at present to prevent PLCs incorporated in Great Britain from adopting a structure under their articles under which the powers granted to the directors are divided between two tiers of directors, one exercising management functions and the other exercising a supervisory role in relation to those functions. In other words, there is nothing preventing GB PLCs from currently adopting a two-tier structure.

It is, therefore, proposed to seek to preserve present flexibilities for SEs by avoiding prescriptive legal intervention in the implementing legislation. Accordingly, it is not intended to invoke the Member State options provided by the

Statute to make specific legislative provision in relation to one or two tier board structures. In this way, considerable latitude will be left to Statutes of the SE to define these matters and the governance structure.

6. Winding up, liquidation, insolvency and cessation of payments

In Great Britain, the Insolvency Act 1986 governs the regulation of insolvency proceedings in respect of public limited companies and will apply to SEs. This means that a variety of insolvency procedures will be available to SEs, including court ordered winding up and voluntary liquidation and so-called "rescue procedures" (company voluntary arrangements and administration) for SEs in financial difficulties to enter into binding agreements with their creditors. The Consultation Document also notes that, in all insolvency cases, the EC Insolvency Regulation will apply due to the transnational nature of the SE.

7. Sanctions

To facilitate operation of the Statute by putting in place proper safeguards for members, creditors and other third parties, it is proposed to create specific new offences in relation to SEs (for instance, in relation to misuse of the designation SE). Generally, however, the existing sanctions under the Companies Act 1985 applicable to public limited companies will apply to SEs in those areas not dealt with in the Statute. The Consultation Document also says that the Company Directors Disqualification Act 1986 will probably apply to SEs, so that misconduct in relation to the running or insolvency of an SE could result in a person being banned from being a director of a company.

IV. Employee involvement provisions

1. Background

The UK was represented on a Working Group, made up of experts from each Member State, which met regularly in Brussels over an 18 month period to June 2003 to discuss the various provisions and the practicalities of transposing the employee involvement Directive into national law. The Group sought to coordinate implementation where appropriate and achieve agreement on provisions which required similar transposition in all countries.

As with the company law issues, the implementation of the employee involvement Directive which accompanies the Statute will be implemented separately in Great Britain and in Northern Ireland. (It is intended that, as in GB, that should be one Statutory Instrument implementing both the Statute and the Directive in the Province.) However, where the Directive refers to Member States, such as when calculating the location of employee representatives per Member State, provisions will be applied to the United Kingdom as a whole. The basic position is that the law in Great Britain will apply to the establishment of employee involvement arrangements and ongoing employee involvement arrangements once the SE is registered in Great Britain. In such cases, the law of other Member States will also apply on certain matters, for instance the rules relating to the process by which the Special Negotiating Body representatives are to be appointed and protections for employees' representatives where the employees or their representatives are situated outside the UK.

2. Confidential information

Where the competent organ of a participating company or of the SE entrusts information to people who are, or were, members of a special negotiating body, information entrusted to such persons in confidence in certain circumstances, must not be disclosed to a third party. The employer may bring an action in the civil courts for breach of such provisions. The employer need not disclose information where to do so would, according to objective criteria, seriously harm the functioning of the undertaking or be prejudicial to it.

3. Negotiation of the employee involvement agreement

The present intention, as outlined in the Consultation Document is that the Regulations will provide for appointment of members of a Special Negotiating Body by a combination of election by ballot and appointment by any existing employee representative body. Where employees of participating companies are situated in both Great Britain and Northern Ireland, ballots related to election of representatives must be held on a UK basis as the allocation of delegates to Special Negotiating Bodies is by reference to the number of employees per Member State. Detailed arrangements are also set out relating to the holding of ballots. These are closely modelled on existing legislation implementing the European Works Council Directive in Great Britain.

The parties (the competent organs of the participating companies and the Special Negotiating Body) are under a duty to negotiate in a spirit of cooperation with a view to reaching an employee involvement agreement. It is not presently intended to exercise the Member State option to specify the conditions under which employee involvement arrangements must be renegotiated. Instead, a voluntary approach is preferred, leaving negotiated agreements as a matter between the management of participating companies and employees.

As a general rule, the parties have considerable latitude to negotiate the contents of any employee involvement agreement. The Regulations specify what should be in an agreement (for instance, information with regards to the representative body and the means by which it will inform and consult employees and procedures for any employee participation arrangements), but this does not prejudice the freedom of the parties.

4. Compliance and enforcement

The Central Arbitration Committee in Great Britain will play a central role in dealing with alleged breaches of the employee involvement aspects of the Regulations. For instance, the following issues may be referred to it:

- complaints that the competent organ of a participating company has failed to provide information or provided false or incomplete information in relation to the creation of a Special Negotiating Body;
- a request for a declaration that a Special Negotiating Body has not been established at all or properly;
- requests by persons in possession of information provided in confidence for a declaration as to whether it was reasonable for the employer to impose such a confidentiality restriction;
- complaints as to employers justification for withholding confidential information;
- complaints as to possible defectiveness of decisions made by Special Negotiating Bodies;
- complaints that the ballot arrangements for appointment of a member of a Special Negotiating Body have not been properly carried out;
- complaints related to non-compliance with the employee involvement agreement or the standard employee involvement provisions (including a complaint that the competent organ of the SE had failed to establish the agreed or required procedure at all, or that they had failed to inform and consult in accordance with the arrangements); and
- complaints that an SE is being misused for the purpose of depriving employees of their rights, or withholding those rights.

Where a complaint against the competent organ of a participating company or the SE is upheld, the complainant may apply to the Employment Appeal Tribunal in Great Britain for a penalty (maximum of £ 75,000 to be payable to the Secretary of State) to be imposed on the company.

5. Protection for members of the Special Negotiating Body

The Regulations set out a number of measures designed to protect employees and their representatives when pursuing their rights under the legislation. In particular:

- rights to reasonable time off and remuneration for employees who are members of the Special Negotiating Body; and
- employee protections from unfair dismissal or detriment by an employer when acting as a representative of employees under the legislation or seeking to enjoy rights conferred by the legislation.

6. Registration

In order to register the SE, an employee involvement declaration must be completed, indicating the employee involvement arrangements that are to apply. This requirement does not, however, apply to an SE formed by merger, where the Court will consider whether the employee involvement arrangements are satisfactory, or to an SE migrating to Great Britain from another Member State, as it will be assumed that such SEs will have already satisfied the requirements of the employee involvement Directive.

V. Costs and benefits

The Consultation Document states that the ECS offers potential benefits to companies in Great Britain by creating a framework for cross-border mergers with companies from other Member States where at present there are no harmonised rules in the EU governing cross-border mergers.

The Consultation Document contains a draft Regulatory Impact Assessment ("RIA") which aims to analyse the proposed costs and benefits of the European Company Statute. This notes that the European Company Statute is, of course, a purely voluntary additional corporate vehicle available to businesses across the EU and, presumably, will only, therefore, be adopted by those companies which perceive there is a real benefit from incorporating under the European Company Statute model. The RIA also observes that the impact of the European Company Statute will apply across all business sectors since any company may form or convert to an SE, subject to the provisions of the Statute.

The RIA asks whether there are issues of equity and fairness that arise out of, firstly, the restricted application of the Statute (only PLCs may merge to form an SE or transform to an SE) and, secondly, the minimum capital requirement of EUR 120,000. However, this is set in the context of possible future plans to move forward at the European Union level with a new form of European Private Company (in the EU Action Plan on Company Law and Corporate Governance, a feasibility study into such a vehicle is included as a short term priority).

The principal potential benefits from introduction of the European Company Statute that are identified by the RIA are as follows:

- The creation of a new framework within which companies will be able to engage in cross-border activities with companies from other Member States;
- A more consensual approach to cross-border restructuring within the EU for those companies wishing to take over, or form a joint venture with, another company in another Member State through the formation of a joint holding company or joint subsidiary in the form of an SE;
- Presentational advantages, for those companies trading in a number of Member States simultaneously, in adopting a more obviously European corporate identity through incorporation under the SE name and form; and
- Greater alignment of the interests of companies and employees through the flexible options allowed on employee involvement models.

The potential costs identified by the RIA are:

- The setting up of employee involvement structures (although it is clearly expected that only those companies who see real benefits in the SE will adopt such a structure and these also have to be viewed in the light of potential benefits from enhanced employee involvement models); and
- Possible costs involved in investigating the possibility of conversion to, or formation of, an SE, but ultimately deciding against such conversion/formation (such costs were stated to include initial consideration of such an option by a senior manager, further consideration by the board and ultimately legal advice on possible conversion).

More specifically, the costs of the employee involvement structures would include those of:

- Establishing a Special Negotiating Body of employee representatives of merging companies;

- Costs of balloting to elect the members of the Special Negotiating Body;
- Costs of meetings of the Special Negotiating Body; and
- Additional costs of employee participation on the board (such as time taken by employees representatives).

List of publications or documents refered to in the paper on UK implementation of the European Company Statute:

1. Company Law Review – In March 1998, the Department of Trade and Industry (DTI) launched a three year fundamental review of core company law led by an independent Steering Group. The Steering Group consulted widely, issuing 9 consultation documents, and presented its final Report on 26 July 2001. The Review Documents and other related material are available on the DTI website: http://www.dti.gov.uk/cld/review.htm.
2. The Government responded to the Company Law Review by means of a White Paper ("Modernising Company Law") presented to Parliament in July 2002. This paper is also available on the DTI website: http://www.dti.gov.uk/cld/review.htm.
3. Derek Higgs was appointed in March 2002 to lead a short independent review of the role and effectiveness of non-executive directors in the UK. The final report of the review ("Review of the Role and Effectiveness of Non-Executive Directors") is available on the DTI website: www.dti.gov.uk/cld/non_exec_review.
4. The Government set up a Co-ordinating Group of Audit and Accounting Issues to examine issues arising in the wake of ENRON to ensure that the effectiveness of UK systems of financial reporting and audit regulation was reviewed thoroughly by the appropriate regulators. The Group presented its Final Report to Ministers in January 2003. This is available on the DTI website: http://www.dti.gov.uk/cld/post_enron.htm.
5. The Consultation Document on implementation of the European Company Statute is available on the DTI website: http://www2.dti.gov.uk/cld/condocs.htm.
6. The EU Commission proposal for a cross-border mergers Directive ("Directive of the European Parliament and of the Council on cross-border mergers of companies with share capital") is available on the Europa website: http://europa.eu.int/comm/internal_market/en/company/company/mergers/mergers_en.htm.
7. The EU Commission published a communication to the Council and the European Parliament ("Modernising Company Law and Corporate Governance in the European Union – A Plan to Move Forward") on 21 May 2003.

The Action Plan consists of 24 proposed EU measures, both legislative and non-legislative, to be undertaken over approximately the next 10 years. The Action Plan is available on the Europa website: http://europa.eu.int/comm/internal_market/en/company/company/modern/index.htm.

8. Further details about the Companies (Audit, Investigations and Community Enterprise) Bill are available on the DTI website: http://www.dti.gov.uk/cld/companies_audit_etc_bill/index.htm.

ANNEX I

Employee Participation in Company Organs of Public Limited-Liability Companies

	Management System		Sector		employee representation in company organ
	One-tier	Two-tier	Public	Private	
Austria		×	including groups		1/3 of the members of the supervisory board
Belgium	×		state-owned railway company		1/3 of the members out of 21
Czech Republic		×	50 or more employees		1/3 of the members of the supervisory board
Denmark	× +managing director		More than 35 employees		1/2 of the members, at least 2 members
Finland	× +managing director		150 or more empl. in Finland		According to agreement, otherwise 1/4 of members, but not more than 4 altogether
France	×	(×) optional	in two-tier system	in two-tier system	2 or 4 members of works council with advisory voting right, right to express an opinion which shall be taken into account
			more than 200 empl.	if statutes provide for	2 members if 200–1000 empl., 1/3 of members if +1000 employees
					maximum 4 members (5 in listed company) or 1/4 of members
Germany		×	at least 500 employees		1/3 of members of the supervisory board if 500–2000 employees
			including groups		1/2 of members of the supervisory board if more than 2000 employees, president (usually appointed by shareholders) with casting vote
					1/2 of members of the supervisory board in mine-iron and steel industry if +1000 employees and attached groups; human resource manager by employee agreement
Greece	×		×		1/3 of members

Hungary		×	More than 200 employees		1/3 of the members of the supervisory board
Ireland	×		×		1/3 of members
Italy	×	(×) optional	Only Alitalia		3 members
Luxembourg	×		if at least 25% of shares state-owned	more than 1000 employees	1/3 of members
Netherlands		×	At least 100 employees Capital at least 13 million euro		veto right on appointment of supervisory board and executive committee joint meetings of works council and supervisory board
Poland		×	commercial companies created in result of privatisation of state-owned enterprises; employee participation is obligatory as long as the state holds at least 50% of shares		2/5 of members of the supervisory board 1 member of the management board if more than 500 employees
Portugal	×		×		conditions provided for that have never been applied
Spain	×		+1000 employees		choice between joint committees and 1 member per trade union (with 25% of union representatives and works council members) in B. of Directors
Sweden	× + managing director		at least 25 employees at level of the group		minority 2 members (and 2 alternates); 3 members (and 3 alternates) If more than 1000 employees in Sweden

ANNEX II

10.11.2001 Official Journal of the European Communities L 294/1

COUNCIL REGULATION (EC) NO 2157/2001
of 8 october 2001
on the Statute for a European Company (SE)

THE COUNCIL OF THE EUROPEAN UNION,
Having regard to the Treaty establishing the European Community, and in particular Article 308 thereof,
Having regard to the proposal from the Commission[1],
Having regard to the Opinion of the European Parliament[2],
Having regard to the Opinion of the Economic and Social Committee[3],

Whereas:

(1) The completion of the internal market and the improvement it brings about in the economic and social situation throughout the Community mean not only that barriers to trade must be removed, but also that the structures of production must be adapted to the Community dimension. For that purpose it is essential that companies the business of which is not limited to satisfying purely local needs should be able to plan and carry out the reorganisation of their business on a Community scale.

(2) Such reorganisation presupposes that existing companies from different Member States are given the option of combining their potential by means of mergers. Such operations can be carried out only with due regard to the rules of competition laid down in the Treaty.

(3) Restructuring and cooperation operations involving companies from different Member States give rise to legal and psychological difficulties and tax problems. The approximation of Member States' company law by means of Directives based on Article 44 of the Treaty can overcome some

[1] OJ C 263, 16.10.1989, p. 41 and OJ C 176, 8.7.1991, p. 1.

[2] Opinion of 4 September 2001.

[3] OJ C 124, 21.5.1990, p. 34.

of those difficulties. Such approximation does not, however, release companies governed by different legal systems from the obligation to choose a form of company governed by a particular national law.

(4) The legal framework within which business must be carried on in the Community is still based largely on national laws and therefore no longer corresponds to the economic framework within which it must develop if the objectives set out in Article 18 of the Treaty are to be achieved. That situation forms a considerable obstacle to the creation of groups of companies from different Member States.

(5) Member States are obliged to ensure that the provisions applicable to European companies under this Regulation do not result either in discrimination arising out of unjustified different treatment of European Companies compared with public limited-liability companies or in disproportionate restrictions on the formation of a European Company or on the transfer of its registered office.

(6) It is essential to ensure as far as possible that the economic unit and the legal unit of business in the Community coincide. For that purpose, provision should be made for the creation, side by side with companies governed by a particular national law, of companies formed and carrying on business under the law created by a Community Regulation directly applicable in all Member States.

(7) The provisions of such a Regulation will permit the creation and management of companies with a European dimension, free from the obstacles arising from the disparity and the limited territorial application of national company law.

(8) The Statute for a European public limited-liability Company (hereafter referred to as "SE") is among the measures to be adopted by the Council before 1992 listed in the Commission's White Paper on completing the internal market, approved by the European Council that met in Milan in June 1985. The European Council that met in Brussels in 1987 expressed the wish to see such a Statute created swiftly.

(9) Since the Commission's submission in 1970 of a proposal for a Regulation on the Statute for a European public limited-liability Company, amended in 1975, work on the approximation of national company law has made substantial progress, so that on those points where the functioning of an SE does not need uniform Community rules reference may be made to the law governing public limited-liability companies in the Member State where it has its registered office.

(10) Without prejudice to any economic needs that may arise in the future, if the essential objective of legal rules governing SEs is to be attained, it must be possible at least to create such a company as a means both of

enabling companies from different Member States to merge or to create a holding company and of enabling companies and other legal persons carrying on economic activities and governed by the laws of different Member States to form joint subsidiaries.

(11) In the same context it should be possible for a public limited-liability company with a registered office and head office within the Community to transform itself into an SE without going into liquidation, provided it has a subsidiary in a Member State other than that of its registered office.

(12) National provisions applying to public limited-liability companies that offer their securities to the public and to securities transactions should also apply where an SE is formed by means of an offer of securities to the public and to SEs wishing to utilise such financial instruments.

(13) The SE itself must take the form of a company with share capital, that being the form most suited, in terms of both financing and management, to the needs of a company carrying on business on a European scale. In order to ensure that such companies are of reasonable size, a minimum amount of capital should be set so that they have sufficient assets without making it difficult for small and medium-sized undertakings to form SEs.

(14) An SE must be efficiently managed and properly supervised. It must be borne in mind that there are at present in the Community two different systems for the administration of public limited-liability companies. Although an SE should be allowed to choose between the two systems, the respective responsibilities of those responsible for management and those responsible for supervision should be clearly defined.

(15) Under the rules and general principles of private international law, where one undertaking controls another governed by a different legal system, its ensuing rights and obligations as regards the protection of minority shareholders and third parties are governed by the law governing the controlled undertaking, without prejudice to the obligations imposed on the controlling undertaking by its own law, for example the requirement to prepare consolidated accounts.

(16) Without prejudice to the consequences of any subsequent coordination of the laws of the Member States, specific rules for SEs are not at present required in this field. The rules and general principles of private international law should therefore be applied both where an SE exercises control and where it is the controlled company.

(17) The rule thus applicable where an SE is controlled by another undertaking should be specified, and for this purpose reference should be made to the law governing public limited-liability companies in the State in which the SE has its registered office.

(18) Each Member State must be required to apply the sanctions applicable to public limited-liability companies governed by its law in respect of infringements of this Regulation.

(19) The rules on the involvement of employees in the European Company are laid down in Directive 2001/86/EC[4], and those provisions thus form an indissociable complement to this Regulation and must be applied concomitantly.

(20) This Regulation does not cover other areas of law such as taxation, competition, intellectual property or insolvency. The provisions of the Member States' law and of Community law are therefore applicable in the above areas and in other areas not covered by this Regulation.

(21) Directive 2001/86/EC is designed to ensure that employees have a right of involvement in issues and decisions affecting the life of their SE. Other social and labour legislation questions, in particular the right of employees to information and consultation as regulated in the Member States, are governed by the national provisions applicable, under the same conditions, to public limited-liability companies.

(22) The entry into force of this Regulation must be deferred so that each Member State may incorporate into its national law the provisions of Directive 2001/86/EC and set up in advance the necessary machinery for the formation and operation of SEs with registered offices within its territory, so that the Regulation and the Directive may be applied concomitantly.

(23) A company the head office of which is not in the Community should be allowed to participate in the formation of an SE provided that company is formed under the law of a Member State, has its registered office in that Member State and has a real and continuous link with a Member State's economy according to the principles established in the 1962 General Programme for the abolition of restrictions on freedom of establishment. Such a link exists in particular if a company has an establishment in that Member State and conducts operations therefrom.

(24) The SE should be enabled to transfer its registered office to another Member State. Adequate protection of the interests of minority shareholders who oppose the transfer, of creditors and of holders of other rights should be proportionate. Such transfer should not affect the rights originating before the transfer.

(25) This Regulation is without prejudice to any provision which may be inserted in the 1968 Brussels Convention or in any text adopted by Member

[4] See p. 22 of this Official Journal.

States or by the Council to replace such Convention, relating to the rules of jurisdiction applicable in the case of transfer of the registered offices of a public limited-liability company from one Member State to another.

(26) Activities by financial institutions are regulated by specific directives and the national law implementing those directives and additional national rules regulating those activities apply in full to an SE.

(27) In view of the specific Community character of an SE, the "real seat" arrangement adopted by this Regulation in respect of SEs is without prejudice to Member States' laws and does not pre-empt any choices to be made for other Community texts on company law.

(28) The Treaty does not provide, for the adoption of this Regulation, powers of action other than those of Article 308 thereof.

(29) Since the objectives of the intended action, as outlined above, cannot be adequately attained by the Member States in as much as a European public limited-liability company is being established at European level and can therefore, because of the scale and impact of such company, be better attained at Community level, the Community may take measures in accordance with the principle of subsidiarity enshrined in Article 5 of the Treaty. In accordance with the principle of proportionality as set out in the said Article, this Regulation does not go beyond what is necessary to attain these objectives,

HAS ADOPTED THIS REGULATION:

TITLE I

GENERAL PROVISIONS

Article 1

1. A company may be set up within the territory of the Community in the form of a European public limited-liability company (Societas Europaea or SE) on the conditions and in the manner laid down in this Regulation.
2. The capital of an SE shall be divided into shares. No shareholder shall be liable for more than the amount he has subscribed.
3. An SE shall have legal personality.
4. Employee involvement in an SE shall be governed by the provisions of Directive 2001/86/EC.

Article 2

1. Public limited-liability companies such as referred to in Annex I, formed under the law of a Member State, with registered offices and head offices within the Community may form an SE by means of a merger provided that at least two of them are governed by the law of different Member States.
2. Public and private limited-liability companies such as referred to in Annex II, formed under the law of a Member State, with registered offices and head offices within the Community may promote the formation of a holding SE provided that each of at least two of them:
   (a) is governed by the law of a different Member State, or
   (b) has for at least two years had a subsidiary company governed by the law of another Member State or an establishment situated in another Member State.
3. Companies and firms within the meaning of the second paragraph of Article 48 of the Treaty and other legal bodies governed by public or private law, formed under the law of a Member State, with registered offices and head offices within the Community may form a subsidiary SE by subscribing for its shares, provided that each of at least two of them:
   (a) is governed by the law of a different Member State, or
   (b) has for at least two years had a subsidiary company governed by the law of another Member State or an establishment situated in another Member State.
4. A public limited-liability company, formed under the law of a Member State, which has its registered office and head office within the Community may be transformed into an SE if for at least two years it has had a subsidiary company governed by the law of another Member State.
5. A Member State may provide that a company the head office of which is not in the Community may participate in the formation of an SE provided that company is formed under the law of a Member State, has its registered office in that Member State and has a real and continuous link with a Member State's economy.

Article 3

1. For the purposes of Article 2 (1), (2) and (3), an SE shall be regarded as a public limited-liability company governed by the law of the Member State in which it has its registered office.
2. An SE may itself set up one or more subsidiaries in the form of SEs. The provisions of the law of the Member State in which a subsidiary SE has its registered office that require a public limited-liability company to have more than one shareholder shall not apply in the case of the subsidiary SE. The

provisions of national law implementing the Twelfth Council Company Law Directive (89/667/EEC) of 21 December 1989 on single-member private limited-liability companies[5] shall apply to SEs "mutatis mutandis".

Article 4

1. The capital of an SE shall be expressed in euros.
2. The subscribed capital shall not be less than EUR 120 000.
3. The laws of a Member State requiring a greater subscribed capital for companies carrying on certain types of activity shall apply to SEs with registered offices in that Member State.

Article 5

Subject to Article 4 (1) and (2), the capital of an SE, its maintenance and changes thereto, together with its shares, bonds and other similar securities shall be governed by the provisions which would apply to a public limited-liability company with a registered office in the Member State in which the SE is registered.

Article 6

For the purposes of this Regulation, "the statutes of the SE" shall mean both the instrument of incorporation and, where they are the subject of a separate document, the statutes of the SE.

Article 7

The registered office of an SE shall be located within the Community, in the same Member State as its head office. A Member State may in addition impose on SEs registered in its territory the obligation of locating their head office and their registered office in the same place.

Article 8

1. The registered office of an SE may be transferred to another Member State in accordance with paragraphs 2 to 13. Such a transfer shall not result in the winding up of the SE or in the creation of a new legal person.
2. The management or administrative organ shall draw up a transfer proposal and publicise it in accordance with Article 13, without prejudice to any additional forms of publication provided for by the Member State of the

[5] OJ L 395, 30. 12. 1989, p. 40. Directive as last amended by the 1994 Act of Accession.

registered office. That proposal shall state the current name, registered office and number of the SE and shall cover:

(a) the proposed registered office of the SE;
(b) the proposed statutes of the SE including, where appropriate, its new name;
(c) any implication the transfer may have on employees' involvement;
(d) the proposed transfer timetable;
(e) any rights provided for the protection of shareholders and/or creditors.

3. The management or administrative organ shall draw up a report explaining and justifying the legal and economic aspects of the transfer and explaining the implications of the transfer for shareholders, creditors and employees.
4. An SE's shareholders and creditors shall be entitled, at least one month before the general meeting called upon to decide on the transfer, to examine at the SE's registered office the transfer proposal and the report drawn up pursuant to paragraph 3 and, on request, to obtain copies of those documents free of charge.
5. A Member State may, in the case of SEs registered within its territory, adopt provisions designed to ensure appropriate protection for minority shareholders who oppose a transfer.
6. No decision to transfer may be taken for two months after publication of the proposal. Such a decision shall be taken as laid down in Article 59.
7. Before the competent authority issues the certificate mentioned in paragraph 5, the SE shall satisfy it that, in respect of any liabilities arising prior to the publication of the transfer proposal, the interests of creditors and holders of other rights in respect of the SE (including those of public bodies) have been adequately protected in accordance with requirements laid down by the Member State where the SE has its registered office prior to the transfer.

   A Member State may extend the application of the first subparagraph to liabilities that arise (or may arise) prior to the transfer.

   The first and second subparagraphs shall be without prejudice to the application to SEs of the national legislation of Member States concerning the satisfaction or securing of payments to public bodies.
8. In the Member State in which an SE has its registered office the court, notary or other competent authority shall issue a certificate attesting to the completion of the acts and formalities to be accomplished before the transfer.
9. The new registration may not be effected until the certificate referred to in paragraph 8 has been submitted, and evidence produced that the formalities required for registration in the country of the new registered office have been completed.

10. The transfer of an SE's registered office and the consequent amendment of its statutes shall take effect on the date on which the SE is registered, in accordance with Article 12, in the register for its new registered office.
11. When the SE's new registration has been effected, the registry for its new registration shall notify the registry for its old registration. Deletion of the old registration shall be effected on receipt of that notification, but not before.
12. The new registration and the deletion of the old registration shall be publicised in the Member States concerned in accordance with Article 13.
13. On publication of an SE's new registration, the new registered office may be relied on as against third parties. However, as long as the deletion of the SE's registration from the register for its previous registered office has not been publicised, third parties may continue to rely on the previous registered office unless the SE proves that such third parties were aware of the new registered office.
14. The laws of a Member State may provide that, as regards SEs registered in that Member State, the transfer of a registered office which would result in a change of the law applicable shall not take effect if any of that Member State's competent authorities opposes it within the two-month period referred to in paragraph 6. Such opposition may be based only on grounds of public interest.

    Where an SE is supervised by a national financial supervisory authority according to Community directives the right to oppose the change of registered office applies to this authority as well.

    Review by a judicial authority shall be possible.
15. An SE may not transfer its registered office if proceedings for winding up, liquidation, insolvency or suspension of payments or other similar proceedings have been brought against it.
16. An SE which has transferred its registered office to another Member State shall be considered, in respect of any cause of action arising prior to the transfer as determined in paragraph 10, as having its registered office in the Member States where the SE was registered prior to the transfer, even if the SE is sued after the transfer.

Article 9

1. An SE shall be governed:
   (a) by this Regulation,
   (b) where expressly authorised by this Regulation, by the provisions of its statutes
   or

(c) in the case of matters not regulated by this Regulation or, where matters are partly regulated by it, of those aspects not covered by it, by:
   (i) the provisions of laws adopted by Member States in implementation of Community measures relating specifically to SEs;
   (ii) the provisions of Member States' laws which would apply to a public limited-liability company formed in accordance with the law of the Member State in which the SE has its registered office;
   (iii) the provisions of its statutes, in the same way as for a public limited-liability company formed in accordance with the law of the Member State in which the SE has its registered office.

2. The provisions of laws adopted by Member States specifically for the SE must be in accordance with Directives applicable to public limited-liability companies referred to in Annex I.
3. If the nature of the business carried out by an SE is regulated by specific provisions of national laws, those laws shall apply in full to the SE.

Article 10

Subject to this Regulation, an SE shall be treated in every Member State as if it were a public limited-liability company formed in accordance with the law of the Member State in which it has its registered office.

Article 11

1. The name of an SE shall be preceded or followed by the acronym "SE".
2. Only SEs may include the acronym "SE" in their name.
3. Nevertheless, companies, firms and other legal entities registered in a Member State before the date of entry into force of this Regulation in the names of which the acronym "SE" appears shall not be required to alter their names.

Article 12

1. Every SE shall be registered in the Member State in which it has its registered office in a register designated by the law of that Member State in accordance with Article 3 of the First Council Directive (68/151/EEC) of 9 March 1968 on coordination of safeguards which, for the protection of the interests of members and others, are required by Member States of companies within the meaning of the second paragraph of Article 58 of the Treaty, with a view to making such safeguards equivalent throughout the Community[6].

[6] OJ L 65, 14. 3. 1968, p. 8. Directive as last amended by the 1994 Act of Accession.

2. An SE may not be registered unless an agreement on arrangements for employee involvement pursuant to Article 4 of Directive 2001/86/EC has been concluded, or a decision pursuant to Article 3 (6) of the Directive has been taken, or the period for negotiations pursuant to Article 5 of the Directive has expired without an agreement having been concluded.
3. In order for an SE to be registered in a Member State which has made use of the option referred to in Article 7 (3) of Directive 2001/86/EC, either an agreement pursuant to Article 4 of the Directive must have been concluded on the arrangements for employee involvement, including participation, or none of the participating companies must have been governed by participation rules prior to the registration of the SE.
4. The statutes of the SE must not conflict at any time with the arrangements for employee involvement which have been so determined. Where new such arrangements determined pursuant to the Directive conflict with the existing statutes, the statutes shall to the extent necessary be amended.

   In this case, a Member State may provide that the management organ or the administrative organ of the SE shall be entitled to proceed to amend the statutes without any further decision from the general shareholders meeting.

Article 13

Publication of the documents and particulars concerning an SE which must be publicised under this Regulation shall be effected in the manner laid down in the laws of the Member State in which the SE has its registered office in accordance with Directive 68/151/EEC.

Article 14

1. Notice of an SE's registration and of the deletion of such a registration shall be published for information purposes in the Official Journal of the European Communities after publication in accordance with Article 13. That notice shall state the name, number, date and place of registration of the SE, the date and place of publication and the title of publication, the registered office of the SE and its sector of activity.
2. Where the registered office of an SE is transferred in accordance with Article 8, notice shall be published giving the information provided for in paragraph 1, together with that relating to the new registration.
3. The particulars referred to in paragraph 1 shall be forwarded to the Official Publications Office of the European Communities within one month of the publication referred to in Article 13.

TITLE II

FORMATION

SECTION 1

General

Article 15

1. Subject to this Regulation, the formation of an SE shall be governed by the law applicable to public limited-liability companies in the State in which the SE establishes its registered office.
2. The registration of an SE shall be publicised in accordance with Article 13.

Article 16

1. An SE shall acquire legal personality on the date on which it is registered in the register referred to in Article 12.
2. If acts have been performed in an SE's name before its registration in accordance with Article 12 and the SE does not assume the obligations arising out of such acts after its registration, the natural persons, companies, firms or other legal entities which performed those acts shall be jointly and severally liable therefor, without limit, in the absence of agreement to the contrary.

SECTION 2

Formation by merger

Article 17

1. An SE may be formed by means of a merger in accordance with Article 2 (1).
2. Such a merger may be carried out in accordance with:
   (a) the procedure for merger by acquisition laid down in Article 3 (1) of the Third Council Directive (78/855/EEC) of 9 October 1978 based on Article 54(3)(g) of the Treaty concerning mergers of public limited-liability companies [7] or

[7] OJ L 295, 20. 10. 1978, p. 36. Directive as last amended by the 1994 Act of Accession.

(b) the procedure for merger by the formation of a new company laid down in Article 4 (1) of the said Directive.

In the case of a merger by acquisition, the acquiring company shall take the form of an SE when the merger takes place. In the case of a merger by the formation of a new company, the SE shall be the newly formed company.

Article 18

For matters not covered by this section or, where a matter is partly covered by it, for aspects not covered by it, each company involved in the formation of an SE by merger shall be governed by the provisions of the law of the Member State to which it is subject that apply to mergers of public limited-liability companies in accordance with Directive 78/855/EEC.

Article 19

The laws of a Member State may provide that a company governed by the law of that Member State may not take part in the formation of an SE by merger if any of that Member State's competent authorities opposes it before the issue of the certificate referred to in Article 25 (2).

Such opposition may be based only on grounds of public interest. Review by a judicial authority shall be possible.

Article 20

1. The management or administrative organs of merging companies shall draw up draft terms of merger. The draft terms of merger shall include the following particulars:
   (a) the name and registered office of each of the merging companies together with those proposed for the SE;
   (b) the share-exchange ratio and the amount of any compensation;
   (c) the terms for the allotment of shares in the SE;
   (d) the date from which the holding of shares in the SE will entitle the holders to share in profits and any special conditions affecting that entitlement;
   (e) the date from which the transactions of the merging companies will be treated for accounting purposes as being those of the SE;
   (f) the rights conferred by the SE on the holders of shares to which special rights are attached and on the holders of securities other than shares, or the measures proposed concerning them;
   (g) any special advantage granted to the experts who examine the draft terms of merger or to members of the administrative, management, supervisory or controlling organs of the merging companies;

(h) the statutes of the SE;
(i) information on the procedures by which arrangements for employee involvement are determined pursuant to Directive 2001/86/EC.

2. The merging companies may include further items in the draft terms of merger.

Article 21

For each of the merging companies and subject to the additional requirements imposed by the Member State to which the company concerned is subject, the following particulars shall be published in the national gazette of that Member State:

(a) the type, name and registered office of every merging company;
(b) the register in which the documents referred to in Article 3 (2) of Directive 68/151/EEC are filed in respect of each merging company, and the number of the entry in that register;
(c) an indication of the arrangements made in accordance with Article 24 for the exercise of the rights of the creditors of the company in question and the address at which complete information on those arrangements may be obtained free of charge;
(d) an indication of the arrangements made in accordance with Article 24 for the exercise of the rights of minority shareholders of the company in question and the address at which complete information on those arrangements may be obtained free of charge;
(e) the name and registered office proposed for the SE.

Article 22

As an alternative to experts operating on behalf of each of the merging companies, one or more independent experts as defined in Article 10 of Directive 78/855/EEC, appointed for those purposes at the joint request of the companies by a judicial or administrative authority in the Member State of one of the merging companies or of the proposed SE, may examine the draft terms of merger and draw up a single report to all the shareholders.

The experts shall have the right to request from each of the merging companies any information they consider necessary to enable them to complete their function.

Article 23

1. The general meeting of each of the merging companies shall approve the draft terms of merger.

2. Employee involvement in the SE shall be decided pursuant to Directive 2001/86/EC. The general meetings of each of the merging companies may reserve the right to make registration of the SE conditional upon its express ratification of the arrangements so decided.

Article 24

1. The law of the Member State governing each merging company shall apply as in the case of a merger of public limited-liability companies, taking into account the cross-border nature of the merger, with regard to the protection of the interests of:
   (a) creditors of the merging companies;
   (b) holders of bonds of the merging companies;
   (c) holders of securities, other than shares, which carry special rights in the merging companies.
2. A Member State may, in the case of the merging companies governed by its law, adopt provisions designed to ensure appropriate protection for minority shareholders who have opposed the merger.

Article 25

1. The legality of a merger shall be scrutinised, as regards the part of the procedure concerning each merging company, in accordance with the law on mergers of public limited-liability companies of the Member State to which the merging company is subject.
2. In each Member State concerned the court, notary or other competent authority shall issue a certificate conclusively attesting to the completion of the pre-merger acts and formalities.
3. If the law of a Member State to which a merging company is subject provides for a procedure to scrutinise and amend the share-exchange ratio, or a procedure to compensate minority shareholders, without preventing the registration of the merger, such procedures shall only apply if the other merging companies situated in Member States which do not provide for such procedure explicitly accept, when approving the draft terms of the merger in accordance with Article 23 (1), the possibility for the shareholders of that merging company to have recourse to such procedure. In such cases, the court, notary or other competent authorities may issue the certificate referred to in paragraph 2 even if such a procedure has been commenced. The certificate must, however, indicate that the procedure is pending. The decision in the procedure shall be binding on the acquiring company and all its shareholders.

Article 26

1. The legality of a merger shall be scrutinised, as regards the part of the procedure concerning the completion of the merger and the formation of the SE, by the court, notary or other authority competent in the Member State of the proposed registered office of the SE to scrutinise that aspect of the legality of mergers of public limited-liability companies.
2. To that end each merging company shall submit to the competent authority the certificate referred to in Article 25 (2) within six months of its issue together with a copy of the draft terms of merger approved by that company.
3. The authority referred to in paragraph 1 shall in particular ensure that the merging companies have approved draft terms of merger in the same terms and that arrangements for employee involvement have been determined pursuant to Directive 2001/86/EC.
4. That authority shall also satisfy itself that the SE has been formed in accordance with the requirements of the law of the Member State in which it has its registered office in accordance with Article 15.

Article 27

1. A merger and the simultaneous formation of an SE shall take effect on the date on which the SE is registered in accordance with Article 12.
2. The SE may not be registered until the formalities provided for in Articles 25 and 26 have been completed.

Article 28

For each of the merging companies the completion of the merger shall be publicised as laid down by the law of each Member State in accordance with Article 3 of Directive 68/151/EEC.

Article 29

1. A merger carried out as laid down in Article 17 (2) (a) shall have the following consequences ipso jure and simultaneously:
   (a) all the assets and liabilities of each company being acquired are transferred to the acquiring company;
   (b) the shareholders of the company being acquired become shareholders of the acquiring company;
   (c) the company being acquired ceases to exist;
   (d) the acquiring company adopts the form of an SE.

2. A merger carried out as laid down in the second indent of Article 17 (2) (b) shall have the following consequences ipso jure and simultaneously:
   (a) all the assets and liabilities of the merging companies are transferred to the SE;
   (b) the shareholders of the merging companies become shareholders of the SE;
   (c) the merging companies cease to exist.
3. Where, in the case of a merger of public limited-liability companies, the law of a Member State requires the completion of any special formalities before the transfer of certain assets, rights and obligations by the merging companies becomes effective against third parties, those formalities shall apply and shall be carried out either by the merging companies or by the SE following its registration.
4. The rights and obligations of the participating companies on terms and conditions of employment arising from national law, practice and individual employment contracts or employment relationships and existing at the date of the registration shall, by reason of such registration be transferred to the SE upon its registration.

Article 30

A merger as provided for in Article 2 (1) may not be declared null and void once the SE has been registered.

The absence of scrutiny of the legality of the merger pursuant to Articles 25 and 26 may be included among the grounds for the winding-up of the SE.

Article 31

1. Where a merger within the meaning of the first indent of Article 17 (2) is carried out by a company which holds all the shares and other securities conferring the right to vote at general meetings of another company, neither Article 20 (1) (b), (c) and (d), Article 29 (1) (b) nor Article 22 shall apply. National law governing each merging company and mergers of public limited-liability companies in accordance with Article 24 of Directive 78/855/EEC shall nevertheless apply.
2. Where a merger by acquisition is carried out by a company which holds 90 % or more but not all of the shares and other securities conferring the right to vote at general meetings of another company, reports by the management or administrative body, reports by an independent expert or experts and the documents necessary for scrutiny shall be required only to the extent that the national law governing either the acquiring company or the company being acquired so requires.

Member States may, however, provide that this paragraph may apply where a company holds shares conferring 90% or more but not all of the voting rights.

SECTION 3

Formation of a holding SE

Article 32

1. A holding SE may be formed in accordance with Article 2 (2).
   A company promoting the formation of a holding SE in accordance with Article 2 (2) shall continue to exist.
2. The management or administrative organs of the companies which promote such an operation shall draw up, in the same terms, draft terms for the formation of the holding SE. The draft terms shall include a report explaining and justifying the legal and economic aspects of the formation and indicating the implications for the shareholders and for the employees of the adoption of the form of a holding SE. The draft terms shall also set out the particulars provided for in Article 20 (1) (a), (b), (c), (f), (g), (h) and (i) and shall fix the minimum proportion of the shares in each of the companies promoting the operation which the shareholders must contribute to the formation of the holding SE. That proportion shall be shares conferring more than 50% of the permanent voting rights.
3. For each of the companies promoting the operation, the draft terms for the formation of the holding SE shall be publicised in the manner laid down in each Member State's national law in accordance with Article 3 of Directive 68/151/EEC at least one month before the date of the general meeting called to decide thereon.
4. One or more experts independent of the companies promoting the operation, appointed or approved by a judicial or administrative authority in the Member State to which each company is subject in accordance with national provisions adopted in implementation of Directive 78/855/EEC, shall examine the draft terms of formation drawn up in accordance with paragraph 2 and draw up a written report for the shareholders of each company. By agreement between the companies promoting the operation, a single written report may be drawn up for the shareholders of all the companies by one or more independent experts, appointed or approved by a judicial or administrative authority in the Member State to which one of the companies promoting the operation or the proposed SE is subject in accordance with national provisions adopted in implementation of Directive 78/855/EEC.

5. The report shall indicate any particular difficulties of valuation and state whether the proposed share-exchange ratio is fair and reasonable, indicating the methods used to arrive at it and whether such methods are adequate in the case in question.
6. The general meeting of each company promoting the operation shall approve the draft terms of formation of the holding SE.

   Employee involvement in the holding SE shall be decided pursuant to Directive 2001/86/EC. The general meetings of each company promoting the operation may reserve the right to make registration of the holding SE conditional upon its express ratification of the arrangements so decided.
7. These provisions shall apply mutatis mutandis to private limited-liability companies.

Article 33

1. The shareholders of the companies promoting such an operation shall have a period of three months in which to inform the promoting companies whether they intend to contribute their shares to the formation of the holding SE. That period shall begin on the date upon which the terms for the formation of the holding SE have been finally determined in accordance with Article 32.
2. The holding SE shall be formed only if, within the period referred to in paragraph 1, the shareholders of the companies promoting the operation have assigned the minimum proportion of shares in each company in accordance with the draft terms of formation and if all the other conditions are fulfilled.
3. If the conditions for the formation of the holding SE are all fulfilled in accordance with paragraph 2, that fact shall, in respect of each of the promoting companies, be publicised in the manner laid down in the national law governing each of those companies adopted in implementation of Article 3 of Directive 68/151/EEC.

   Shareholders of the companies promoting the operation who have not indicated whether they intend to make their shares available to the promoting companies for the purpose of forming the holding SE within the period referred to in paragraph 1 shall have a further month in which to do so.
4. Shareholders who have contributed their securities to the formation of the SE shall receive shares in the holding SE.
5. The holding SE may not be registered until it is shown that the formalities referred to in Article 32 have been completed and that the conditions referred to in paragraph 2 have been fulfilled.

Article 34

A Member State may, in the case of companies promoting such an operation, adopt provisions designed to ensure protection for minority shareholders who oppose the operation, creditors and employees.

SECTION 4

Formation of a subsidiary SE

Article 35

An SE may be formed in accordance with Article 2 (3).

Article 36

Companies, firms and other legal entities participating in such an operation shall be subject to the provisions governing their participation in the formation of a subsidiary in the form of a public limited-liability company under national law.

SECTION 5

Conversion of an existing public-liability company into an SE

Article 37

1. An SE may be formed in accordance with Article 2 (4).
2. Without prejudice to Article 11 the conversion of a public limited-liability company into an SE shall not result in the winding up of the company or in the creation of a new legal person.
3. The registered office may not be transferred from one Member State to another pursuant to Article 8 at the same time as the conversion is effected.
4. The management or administrative organ of the company in question shall draw up draft terms of conversion and a report explaining and justifying the legal and economic aspects of the conversion and indicating the implications for the shareholders and for the employees of the adoption of the form of an SE.
5. The draft terms of conversion shall be publicised in the manner laid down in each Member State's law in accordance with Article 3 of Directive 68/151/EEC at least one month before the general meeting called upon to decide thereon.

6. Before the general meeting referred to in paragraph 7 one or more independent experts appointed or approved, in accordance with the national provisions adopted in implementation of Article 10 of Directive 78/855/EEC, by a judicial or administrative authority in the Member State to which the company being converted into an SE is subject shall certify in compliance with Directive (EEC) 77/91[8] mutatis mutandis that the company has net assets at least equivalent to its capital plus those reserves which must not be distributed under the law or the Statutes.
7. The general meeting of the company in question shall approve the draft terms of conversion together with the statutes of the SE. The decision of the general meeting shall be passed as laid down in the provisions of national law adopted in implementation of Article 7 of Directive 78/855/EEC.
8. Member States may condition a conversion to a favourable vote of a qualified majority or unanimity in the organ of the company to be converted within which employee participation is organised.
9. The rights and obligations of the company to be converted on terms and conditions of employment arising from national law, practice and individual employment contracts or employment relationships and existing at the date of the registration shall, by reason of such registration be transferred to the SE.

TITLE III

STRUCTURE OF THE SE

Article 38

Under the conditions laid down by this Regulation an SE shall comprise:
(a) a general meeting of shareholders and
(b) either a supervisory organ and a management organ (two-tier system) or an administrative organ (one-tier system) depending on the form adopted in the statutes.

[8] Second Council Directive 77/91/EEC of 13 December 1976 on coordination of safeguards which, for the protection of the interests of members and others, are required by Member States of companies within the meaning of the second paragraph of Article 58 of the Treaty, in respect of the formation of public limited liability companies and the maintenance and alteration of their capital, with a view to making such safeguards equivalent (OJ L 26, 31. 1. 1977, p. 1). Directive as last amended by the 1994 Act of Accession.

SECTION 1

Two-tier system

Article 39

1. The management organ shall be responsible for managing the SE. A Member State may provide that a managing director or managing directors shall be responsible for the current management under the same conditions as for public limited-liability companies that have registered offices within that Member State's territory.
2. The member or members of the management organ shall be appointed and removed by the supervisory organ.

   A Member State may, however, require or permit the statutes to provide that the member or members of the management organ shall be appointed and removed by the general meeting under the same conditions as for public limited-liability companies that have registered offices within its territory.
3. No person may at the same time be a member of both the management organ and the supervisory organ of the same SE. The supervisory organ may, however, nominate one of its members to act as a member of the management organ in the event of a vacancy. During such a period the functions of the person concerned as a member of the supervisory organ shall be suspended. A Member State may impose a time-limit on such a period.
4. The number of members of the management organ or the rules for determining it shall be laid down in the SE's statutes. A Member State may, however, fix a minimum and/or a maximum number.
5. Where no provision is made for a two-tier system in relation to public limited-liability companies with registered offices within its territory, a Member State may adopt the appropriate measures in relation to SEs.

Article 40

1. The supervisory organ shall supervise the work of the management organ. It may not itself exercise the power to manage the SE.
2. The members of the supervisory organ shall be appointed by the general meeting. The members of the first supervisory organ may, however, be appointed by the statutes. This shall apply without prejudice to Article 47 (4) or to any employee participation arrangements determined pursuant to the Directive 2001/86/EC.
3. The number of members of the supervisory organ or the rules for determining it shall be laid down in the statutes. A Member State may, however, stipulate the number of members of the supervisory organ for SEs registered within its territory or a minimum and/or a maximum number.

Article 41

1. The management organ shall report to the supervisory organ at least once every three months on the progress and foreseeable development of the SE's business.
2. In addition to the regular information referred to in paragraph 1, the management organ shall promptly pass the supervisory organ any information on events likely to have an appreciable effect on the SE.
3. The supervisory organ may require the management organ to provide information of any kind which it needs to exercise supervision in accordance with Article 40 (1). A Member State may provide that each member of the supervisory organ also be entitled to this facility.
4. The supervisory organ may undertake or arrange for any investigations necessary for the performance of its duties.
5. Each member of the supervisory organ shall be entitled to examine all information submitted to it.

Article 42

The supervisory organ shall elect a chairman from among its members. If half of the members are appointed by employees, only a member appointed by the general meeting of shareholders may be elected chairman.

SECTION 2

The one-tier system

Article 43

1. The administrative organ shall manage the SE. A Member State may provide that a managing director or managing directors shall be responsible for the day-to-day management under the same conditions as for public limited-liability companies that have registered offices within that Member State's territory.
2. The number of members of the administrative organ or the rules for determining it shall be laid down in the SE's statutes. A Member State may, however, set a minimum and, where necessary, a maximum number of members.

   The administrative organ shall, however, consist of at least three members where employee participation is regulated in accordance with Directive 2001/86/EC.

3. The member or members of the administrative organ shall be appointed by the general meeting. The members of the first administrative organ may, however, be appointed by the statutes. This shall apply without prejudice to Article 47 (4) or to any employee participation arrangements determined pursuant to Directive 2001/86/EC.
4. Where no provision is made for a one-tier system in relation to public limited-liability companies with registered offices within its territory, a Member State may adopt the appropriate measures in relation to SEs.

Article 44

1. The administrative organ shall meet at least once every three months at intervals laid down by the statutes to discuss the progress and foreseeable development of the SE's business.
2. Each member of the administrative organ shall be entitled to examine all information submitted to it.

Article 45

The administrative organ shall elect a chairman from among its members. If half of the members are appointed by employees, only a member appointed by the general meeting of shareholders may be elected chairman.

SECTION 3

Rules common to the one-tier and two-tier systems

Article 46

1. Members of company organs shall be appointed for a period laid down in the statutes not exceeding six years.
2. Subject to any restrictions laid down in the statutes, members may be re-appointed once or more than once for the period determined in accordance with paragraph 1.

Article 47

1. An SE's statutes may permit a company or other legal entity to be a member of one of its organs, provided that the law applicable to public limited-liability companies in the Member State in which the SE's registered office is situated does not provide otherwise.

   That company or other legal entity shall designate a natural person to exercise its functions on the organ in question.

2. No person may be a member of any SE organ or a representative of a member within the meaning of paragraph 1 who:
   (a) is disqualified, under the law of the Member State in which the SE's registered office is situated, from serving on the corresponding organ of a public limited-liability company governed by the law of that Member State, or
   (b) is disqualified from serving on the corresponding organ of a public limited-liability company governed by the law of a Member State owing to a judicial or administrative decision delivered in a Member State.
3. An SE's statutes may, in accordance with the law applicable to public limited-liability companies in the Member State in which the SE's registered office is situated, lay down special conditions of eligibility for members representing the shareholders.
4. This Regulation shall not affect national law permitting a minority of shareholders or other persons or authorities to appoint some of the members of a company organ.

Article 48

1. An SE's statutes shall list the categories of transactions which require authorisation of the management organ by the supervisory organ in the two-tier system or an express decision by the administrative organ in the one-tier system.

   A Member State may, however, provide that in the two-tier system the supervisory organ may itself make certain categories of transactions subject to authorisation.
2. A Member State may determine the categories of transactions which must at least be indicated in the statutes of SEs registered within its territory.

Article 49

The members of an SE's organs shall be under a duty, even after they have ceased to hold office, not to divulge any information which they have concerning the SE the disclosure of which might be prejudicial to the company's interests, except where such disclosure is required or permitted under national law provisions applicable to public limited-liability companies or is in the public interest.

Article 50

1. Unless otherwise provided by this Regulation or the statutes, the internal rules relating to quorums and decision-taking in SE organs shall be as follows:

(a) quorum: at least half of the members must be present or represented;
(b) decision taking: a majority of the members present or represented.

2. Where there is no relevant provision in the statutes, the chairman of each organ shall have a casting vote in the event of a tie. There shall be no provision to the contrary in the statutes, however, where half of the supervisory organ consists of employees' representatives.
3. Where employee participation is provided for in accordance with Directive 2001/86/EC, a Member State may provide that the supervisory organ's quorum and decision-making shall, by way of derogation from the provisions referred to in paragraphs 1 and 2, be subject to the rules applicable, under the same conditions, to public limited-liability companies governed by the law of the Member State concerned.

Article 51

Members of an SE's management, supervisory and administrative organs shall be liable, in accordance with the provisions applicable to public limited-liability companies in the Member State in which the SE's registered office is situated, for loss or damage sustained by the SE following any breach on their part of the legal, statutory or other obligations inherent in their duties.

SECTION 4

General meeting

Article 52

The general meeting shall decide on matters for which it is given sole responsibility by:

(a) this Regulation or
(b) the legislation of the Member State in which the SE's registered office is situated adopted in implementation of Directive 2001/86/EC.

Furthermore, the general meeting shall decide on matters for which responsibility is given to the general meeting of a public limited-liability company governed by the law of the Member State in which the SE's registered office is situated, either by the law of that Member State or by the SE's statutes in accordance with that law.

Article 53

Without prejudice to the rules laid down in this section, the organisation and conduct of general meetings together with voting procedures shall be governed by the law applicable to public limited-liability companies in the Member State in which the SE's registered office is situated.

Article 54

1. An SE shall hold a general meeting at least once each calendar year, within six months of the end of its financial year, unless the law of the Member State in which the SE's registered office is situated applicable to public limited-liability companies carrying on the same type of activity as the SE provides for more frequent meetings. A Member State may, however, provide that the first general meeting may be held at any time in the eighteen months following an SE's incorporation.
2. General meetings may be convened at any time by the management organ, the administrative organ, the supervisory organ or any other organ or competent authority in accordance with the national law applicable to public limited-liability companies in the Member State in which the SE's registered office is situated.

Article 55

1. One or more shareholders who together hold at least 10% of an SE's subscribed capital may request the SE to convene a general meeting and draw up the agenda therefore; the SE's statutes or national legislation may provide for a smaller proportion under the same conditions as those applicable to public limited-liability companies.
2. The request that a general meeting be convened shall state the items to be put on the agenda.
3. If, following a request made under paragraph 1, a general meeting is not held in due time and, in any event, within two months, the competent judicial or administrative authority within the jurisdiction of which the SE's registered office is situated may order that a general meeting be convened within a given period or authorise either the shareholders who have requested it or their representatives to convene a general meeting. This shall be without prejudice to any national provisions which allow the shareholders themselves to convene general meetings.

Article 56

One or more shareholders who together hold at least 10% of an SE's subscribed capital may request that one or more additional items be put on the agenda of any general meeting. The procedures and time limits applicable to such requests shall be laid down by the national law of the Member State in which the SE's registered office is situated or, failing that, by the SE's statutes. The above proportion may be reduced by the statutes or by the law of the Member State in which the SE's registered office is situated under the same conditions as are applicable to public limited-liability companies.

Article 57

Save where this Regulation or, failing that, the law applicable to public limited-liability companies in the Member State in which an SE's registered office is situated requires a larger majority, the general meeting's decisions shall be taken by a majority of the votes validly cast.

Article 58

The votes cast shall not include votes attaching to shares in respect of which the shareholder has not taken part in the vote or has abstained or has returned a blank or spoilt ballot paper.

Article 59

1. Amendment of an SE's statutes shall require a decision by the general meeting taken by a majority which may not be less than two-thirds of the votes cast, unless the law applicable to public limited-liability companies in the Member State in which an SE's registered office is situated requires or permits a larger majority.
2. A Member State may, however, provide that where at least half of an SE's subscribed capital is represented, a simple majority of the votes referred to in paragraph 1 shall suffice.
3. Amendments to an SE's statutes shall be publicised in accordance with Article 13.

Article 60

1. Where an SE has two or more classes of shares, every decision by the general meeting shall be subject to a separate vote by each class of shareholders whose class rights are affected thereby.
2. Where a decision by the general meeting requires the majority of votes specified in Article 59 (1) or (2), that majority shall also be required for the separate vote by each class of shareholders whose class rights are affected by the decision.

TITLE IV

ANNUAL ACCOUNTS AND CONSOLIDATED ACCOUNTS

Article 61

Subject to Article 62 an SE shall be governed by the rules applicable to public limited-liability companies under the law of the Member State in which its registered office is situated as regards the preparation of its annual and, where appropriate, consolidated accounts including the accompanying annual report and the auditing and publication of those accounts.

Article 62

1. An SE which is a credit or financial institution shall be governed by the rules laid down in the national law of the Member State in which its registered office is situated in implementation of Directive 2000/12/EC of the European Parliament and of the Council of 20 March 2000 relating to the taking up and pursuit of the business of credit institutions [9] as regards the preparation of its annual and, where appropriate, consolidated accounts, including the accompanying annual report and the auditing and publication of those accounts.
2. An SE which is an insurance undertaking shall be governed by the rules laid down in the national law of the Member State in which its registered office is situated in implementation of Council Directive 91/674/EEC of 19 December 1991 on the annual accounts and consolidated accounts of insurance undertakings [10] as regards the preparation of its annual and, where appropriate, consolidated accounts including the accompanying annual report and the auditing and publication of those accounts.

TITLE V

WINDING UP, LIQUIDATION, INSOLVENCY AND CESSATION OF PAYMENTS

Article 63

As regards winding up, liquidation, insolvency, cessation of payments and similar procedures, an SE shall be governed by the legal provisions which would apply to a public limited-liability company formed in accordance with the law

[9] OJ L 126, 26. 5. 2000, p. 1.

[10] OJ L 374, 31. 12. 1991, p. 7.

of the Member State in which its registered office is situated, including provisions relating to decision-making by the general meeting.

Article 64

1. When an SE no longer complies with the requirement laid down in Article 7, the Member State in which the SE's registered office is situated shall take appropriate measures to oblige the SE to regularise its position within a specified period either:
   (a) by re-establishing its head office in the Member State in which its registered office is situated or
   (b) by transferring the registered office by means of the procedure laid down in Article 8.
2. The Member State in which the SE's registered office is situated shall put in place the measures necessary to ensure that an SE which fails to regularise its position in accordance with paragraph (1) is liquidated.
3. The Member State in which the SE's registered office is situated shall set up a judicial remedy with regard to any established infringement of Article 7. That remedy shall have a suspensory effect on the procedures laid down in paragraphs 1 and 2.
4. Where it is established on the initiative of either the authorities or any interested party that an SE has its head office within the territory of a Member State in breach of Article 7, the authorities of that Member State shall immediately inform the Member State in which the SE's registered office is situated.

Article 65

Without prejudice to provisions of national law requiring additional publication, the initiation and termination of winding up, liquidation, insolvency or suspension of payment procedures and any decision to continue operating shall be publicised in accordance with Article 13.

Article 66

1. An SE may be converted into a public limited-liability company governed by the law of the Member State in which its registered office is situated. No decision on conversion may be taken before two years have elapsed since its registration or before the first two sets of annual accounts have been approved.
2. The conversion of an SE into a public limited-liability company shall not result in the winding up of the company or in the creation of a new legal person.

3. The management or administrative organ of the SE shall draw up draft terms of conversion and a report explaining and justifying the legal and economic aspects of the conversion and indicating the implications of the adoption of the public limited-liability company for the shareholders and for the employees.
4. The draft terms of conversion shall be publicised in the manner laid down in each Member State's law in accordance with Article 3 of Directive 68/151/EEC at least one month before the general meeting called to decide thereon.
5. Before the general meeting referred to in paragraph 6, one or more independent experts appointed or approved, in accordance with the national provisions adopted in implementation of Article 10 of Directive 78/855/EEC, by a judicial or administrative authority in the Member State to which the SE being converted into a public limited-liability company is subject shall certify that the company has assets at least equivalent to its capital.
6. The general meeting of the SE shall approve the draft terms of conversion together with the statutes of the public limited-liability company. The decision of the general meeting shall be passed as laid down in the provisions of national law adopted in implementation of Article 7 of Directive 78/855/EEC.

TITLE VI

ADDITIONAL AND TRANSITIONAL PROVISIONS

Article 67

1. If and so long as the third phase of EMU does not apply to it each Member State may make SEs with registered offices within its territory subject to the same provisions as apply to public limited-liability companies covered by its legislation as regards the expression of their capital. An SE may, in any case, express its capital in euro as well. In that event the national currency/euro conversion rate shall be that for the last day of the month preceding that of the formation of the SE.
2. If and so long as the third phase of EMU does not apply to the Member State in which an SE has its registered office, the SE may, however, prepare and publish its annual and, where appropriate, consolidated accounts in euros. The Member State may require that the SE's annual and, where appropriate, consolidated accounts be prepared and published in [the] national currency under the same conditions as those laid down for public limited-liability companies governed by the law of that Member State. This shall not prejudge the additional possibility for an SE of publishing its annual and,

where appropriate, consolidated accounts in euros in accordance with Council Directive 90/604/EEC of 8 November 1990 amending Directive 78/60/EEC on annual accounts and Directive 83/349/EEC on consolidated accounts as concerns the exemptions for small and medium-sized companies and the publication of accounts in ecus [11].

TITLE VII

FINAL PROVISIONS

Article 68

1. The Member States shall make such provision as is appropriate to ensure the effective application of this Regulation.
2. Each Member State shall designate the competent authorities within the meaning of Articles 8, 25, 26, 54, 55 and 64. It shall inform the Commission and the other Member States accordingly.

Article 69

Five years at the latest after the entry into force of this Regulation, the Commission shall forward to the Council and the European Parliament a report on the application of the Regulation and proposals for amendments, where appropriate. The report shall, in particular, analyse the appropriateness of:

(a) allowing the location of an SE's head office and registered office in different Member States;

(b) broadening the concept of merger in Article 17 (2) in order to admit also other types of merger than those defined in Articles 3 (1) and 4 (1) of Directive 78/855/EEC;

(c) revising the jurisdiction clause in Article 8 (12) in the light of any provision which may have been inserted in the 1968 Brussels Convention or in any text adopted by Member States or by the Council to replace such Convention;

(d) allowing provisions in the statutes of an SE adopted by a Member State in execution of authorisations given to the Member States by this Regulation or laws adopted to ensure the effective application of this Regulation in respect to the SE which deviate from or are complementary to these laws, even when such provisions would not be authorised in the

[11] OJ L 317, 16. 11. 1990, p. 57.

statutes of a public limited-liability company having its registered office in the Member State.

Article 70

This Regulation shall enter into force on 8 october 2004.

This Regulation shall be binding in its entirety and directly applicable in all Member States.

Done at Luxembourg, 8 october 2001

Annex I to the Council Regulation (EC) No 2157/2001 of 8 october 2001 on the Statute for a European Company (SE)

PUBLIC LIMITED-LIABILITY COMPANIES REFERRED TO IN ARTICLE 2 (1)

BELGIUM: la société anonyme/de naamloze vennootschap

DENMARK: aktieselskaber

GERMANY: die Aktiengesellschaft

GREECE: ανώνυμη εταιρία

SPAIN: la sociedad anónima

FRANCE: la société anonyme

IRELAND: public companies limited by shares

public companies limited by guarantee having a share capital

ITALY: società per azioni

LUXEMBOURG: la société anonyme

NETHERLANDS: de naamloze vennootschap

AUSTRIA: die Aktiengesellschaft

PORTUGAL: a sociedade anónima de responsabilidade limitada

FINLAND: julkinen osakeyhtiö/publikt aktiebolag

SWEDEN: publikt aktiebolag

UNITED KINGDOM: public companies limited by shares

public companies limited by guarantee having a share capital

Annex II to the Council Regulation (EC) No 2157/2001 of 8 october 2001 on the Statute for a European Company (SE)

PUBLIC AND PRIVATE LIMITED-LIABILITY COMPANIES REFERRED TO IN ARTICLE 2 (2)

BELGIUM: la société anonyme/de naamloze vennootschap, la société privée à responsabilité limitée/besloten vennootschap met beperkte aansprakelijkheid

DENMARK: aktieselskaber, anpartselskaber

GERMANY: die Aktiengesellschaft, die Gesellschaft mit beschränkter Haftung

GREECE: ανώνυμη εταιρία, εταιρία περιορισμένης ευθύνης

SPAIN: la sociedad anónima, la sociedad de responsabilidad limitada

FRANCE: la société anonyme, la société à responsabilité limitée

IRELAND: public companies limited by shares, public companies limited by guarantee having a share capital, private companies limited by shares, private companies limited by guarantee having a share capital

ITALY: società per azioni, società a responsabilità limitata

LUXEMBOURG: la société anonyme, la société à responsabilité limitée

NETHERLANDS: de naamloze vennootschap, de besloten vennootschap met beperkte aansprakelijkheid

AUSTRIA: die Aktiengesellschaft, die Gesellschaft mit beschränkter Haftung

PORTUGAL: a sociedade anónima de responsabilidade limitada, a sociedade por quotas de responsabilidade limitada

FINLAND: osakeyhtiö, aktiebolag

SWEDEN: aktiebolag

UNITED KINGDOM: public companies limited by shares, public companies limited by guarantee having a share capital, private companies limited by shares, private companies limited by guarantee having a share capital

ANNEX III

L 294/22 Official Journal of the European Communities 10.11.2001

COUNCIL DIRECTIVE 2001/86/EC
of 8 october 2001
supplementing the Statute for a European Company
with regard to the involvement of employees

THE COUNCIL OF THE EUROPEAN UNION,

Having regard to the Treaty establishing the European Community, and in particular Article 308 thereof,
Having regard to the amended proposal from the Commission[1],
Having regard to the Opinion of the European Parliament[2],
Having regard to the Opinion of the Economic and Social Committee[3],

Whereas:

(1) In order to attain the objectives of the Treaty, Council Regulation (EC) No 2157/2001[4] establishes a Statute for a European Company (SE).

(2) That Regulation aims at creating a uniform legal framework within which companies from different Member States should be able to plan and carry out the reorganisation of their business on a Community scale.

(3) In order to promote the social objectives of the Community, special provisions have to be set, notably in the field of employee involvement, aimed at ensuring that the establishment of an SE does not entail the disappearance or reduction of practices of employee involvement existing within the companies participating in the establishment of an SE. This objective should be pursued through the establishment of a set of rules in this field, supplementing the provisions of the Regulation.

[1] OJ C 138, 29. 5. 1991, p. 8.

[2] OJ C 342, 20. 12. 1993, p. 15.

[3] OJ C 124, 21. 5. 1990, p. 34.

[4] See page 1 of this edition of the Official Journal.

(4) Since the objectives of the proposed action, as outlined above, cannot be sufficiently achieved by the Member States, in that the object is to establish a set of rules on employee involvement applicable to the SE, and can therefore, by reason of the scale and impact of the proposed action, be better achieved at Community level, the Community may adopt measures, in accordance with the principle of subsidiarity as set out in Article 5 of the Treaty. In accordance with the principle of proportionality, as set out in that Article, this Directive does not go beyond what is necessary to achieve these objectives.

(5) The great diversity of rules and practices existing in the Member States as regards the manner in which employees' representatives are involved in decision-making within companies makes it inadvisable to set up a single European model of employee involvement applicable to the SE.

(6) Information and consultation procedures at transnational level should nevertheless be ensured in all cases of creation of an SE.

(7) If and when participation rights exist within one or more companies establishing an SE, they should be preserved through their transfer to the SE, once established, unless the parties decide otherwise.

(8) The concrete procedures of employee transnational information and consultation, as well as, if applicable, participation, to apply to each SE should be defined primarily by means of an agreement between the parties concerned or, in the absence thereof, through the application of a set of subsidiary rules.

(9) Member States should still have the option of not applying the standard rules relating to participation in the case of a merger, given the diversity of national systems for employee involvement. Existing systems and practices of participation where appropriate at the level of participating companies must in that case be maintained by adapting registration rules.

(10) The voting rules within the special body representing the employees for negotiation purposes, in particular when concluding agreements providing for a level of participation lower than the one existing within one or more of the participating companies, should be proportionate to the risk of disappearance or reduction of existing systems and practices of participation. That risk is greater in the case of an SE established by way of transformation or merger than by way of creating a holding company or a common subsidiary.

(11) In the absence of an agreement subsequent to the negotiation between employees' representatives and the competent organs of the participating companies, provision should be made for certain standard requirements to apply to the SE, once it is established. These standard requirements should ensure effective practices of transnational information and consultation of

employees, as well as their participation in the relevant organs of the SE if and when such participation existed before its establishment within the participating companies.

(12) Provision should be made for the employees' representatives acting within the framework of the Directive to enjoy, when exercising their functions, protection and guarantees which are similar to those provided to employees' representatives by the legislation and/or practice of the country of employment. They should not be subject to any discrimination as a result of the lawful exercise of their activities and should enjoy adequate protection as regard dismissal and other sanctions.

(13) The confidentiality of sensitive information should be preserved even after the expiry of the employees' representatives terms of office and provision should be made to allow the competent organ of the SE to withhold information which would seriously harm, if subject to public disclosure, the functioning of the SE.

(14) Where an SE and its subsidiaries and establishments are subject to Council Directive 94/45/EC of 22 September 1994 on the establishment of a European Works Council or a procedure in Community-scale undertakings and Community-scale groups of undertakings for the purposes of informing and consulting employees,[5] the provisions of that Directive and the provision transposing it into national legislation should not apply to it nor to its subsidiaries and establishments, unless the special negotiating body decides not to open negotiations or to terminate negotiations already opened.

(15) This Directive should not affect other existing rights regarding involvement and need not affect other existing representation structures, provided for by Community and national laws and practices.

(16) Member States should take appropriate measures in the event of failure to comply with the obligations laid down in this Directive.

(17) The Treaty has not provided the necessary powers for the Community to adopt the proposed Directive, other than those provided for in Article 308.

(18) It is a fundamental principle and stated aim of this Directive to secure employees' acquired rights as regards involvement in company decisions. Employee rights in force before the establishment of SEs should provide the basis for employee rights of involvement in the SE (the "before and after" principle). Consequently, that approach should apply not only to the initial establishment of an SE but also to structural changes in an existing SE and to the companies affected by structural change processes.

[5] OJ L 254, 30.9.1994, p. 64. Directive as last amended by Directive 97/74/EC (OJ L 10, 16.1.1998, p. 22).

(19) Member States should be able to provide that representatives of trade unions may be members of a special negotiating body regardless of whether they are employees of a company participating in the establishment of an SE. Member States should in this context in particular be able to introduce this right in cases where trade union representatives have the right to be members of, and to vote in, supervisory or administrative company organs in accordance with national legislation.

(20) In several Member States, employee involvement and other areas of industrial relations are based on both national legislation and practice which in this context is understood also to cover collective agreements at various national, sectoral and/or company levels,

HAS ADOPTED THIS DIRECTIVE:

SECTION I

GENERAL

Article 1

Objective

1. This Directive governs the involvement of employees in the affairs of European public limited-liability companies (*Societas Europaea*, hereinafter referred to as "SE"), as referred to in Regulation (EC) No 2157/2001.
2. To this end, arrangements for the involvement of employees shall be established in every SE in accordance with the negotiating procedure referred to in Articles 3 to 6 or, under the circumstances specified in Article 7, in accordance with the Annex.

Article 2

Definitions

For the purposes of this Directive:

(a) "SE" means any company established in accordance with Regulation (EC) No 2157/2001;

(b) "Participating companies" means the companies directly participating in the establishing of an SE;

(c) "Subsidiary" of a company means an undertaking over which that company exercises a dominant influence defined in accordance with Article 3 (2) to (7) of Directive 94/45/EC;

(d) "Concerned subsidiary or establishment" means a subsidiary or establishment of a participating company which is proposed to become a subsidiary or establishment of the SE upon its formation;

(e) "Employees' representatives" means the employees' representatives provided for by national law and/or practice;

(f) "Representative body" means the body representative of the employees set up by the agreements referred to in Article 4 or in accordance with the provisions of the Annex, with the purpose of informing and consulting the employees of an SE and its subsidiaries and establishments situated in the Community and, where applicable, of exercising participation rights in relation to the SE;

(g) "Special negotiating body" means the body established in accordance with Article 3 to negotiate with the competent body of the participating companies regarding the establishment of arrangements for the involvement of employees within the SE;

(h) "Involvement of employees" means any mechanism, including information, consultation and participation, through which employees' representatives may exercise an influence on decisions to be taken within the company;

(i) "Information" means the informing of the body representative of the employees and/or employees' representatives by the competent organ of the SE on questions which concern the SE itself and any of its subsidiaries or establishments situated in another Member State or which exceed the powers of the decision-making organs in a single Member State at a time, in a manner and with a content which allows the employees' representatives to undertake an in-depth assessment of the possible impact and, where appropriate, prepare consultations with the competent organ of the SE;

(j) "Consultation" means the establishment of dialogue and exchange of views between the body representative of the employees and/or the employees' representatives and the competent organ of the SE, at a time, in a manner and with a content which allows the employees' representatives, on the basis of information provided, to express an opinion on measures envisaged by the competent organ which may be taken into account in the decision-making process within the SE;

(k) "Participation" means the influence of the body representative of the employees and/or the employees' representatives in the affairs of a company by way of:
- the right to elect or appoint some of the members of the company's supervisory or administrative organ; or
- the right to recommend and/or oppose the appointment of some or all of the members of the company's supervisory or administrative organ.

SECTION II

NEGOTIATING PROCEDURE

Article 3

Creation of a special negotiating body

1. Where the management or administrative organs of the participating companies draw up a plan for the establishment of an SE, they shall as soon as possible after publishing the draft terms of merger or creating a holding company or after agreeing a plan to form a subsidiary or to transform into an SE, take the necessary steps, including providing information about the identity of the participating companies, concerned subsidiaries or establishments, and the number of their employees, to start negotiations with the representatives of the companies' employees on arrangements for the involvement of employees in the SE.
2. For this purpose, a special negotiating body representative of the employees of the participating companies and concerned subsidiaries or establishments shall be created in accordance with the following provisions:
   (a) in electing or appointing members of the special negotiating body, it must be ensured:
      (i) that these members are elected or appointed in proportion to the number of employees employed in each Member State by the participating companies and concerned subsidiaries or establishments, by allocating in respect of a Member State one seat per each portion of employees employed in that Member State which equals 10%, or a fraction thereof, of the number of employees employed by the participating companies and concerned subsidiaries or establishments in all the Member States taken together;
      (ii) that in the case of an SE formed by way of merger, there are such further additional members from each Member State as may be necessary in order to ensure that the special negotiating body includes at least one member representing each participating company which is registered and has employees in that Member State and which it is proposed will cease to exist as a separate legal entity following the registration of the SE, insofar as:
         - the number of such additional members does not exceed 20% of the number of members designated by virtue of point (i); and
         - the composition of the special negotiating body does not entail a double representation of the employees concerned.

If the number of such companies is higher than the number of additional seats available pursuant to the first subparagraph, these additional seats shall be allocated to companies in different Member States by decreasing order of the number of employees they employ.

(b) Member States shall determine the method to be used for the election or appointment of the members of the special negotiating body who are to be elected or appointed in their territories. They shall take the necessary measures to ensure that, as far as possible, such members shall include at least one member representing each participating company which has employees in the Member State concerned. Such measures must not increase the overall number of members.

Member States may provide that such members may include representatives of trade unions whether or not they are employees of a participating company or concerned subsidiary or establishment.

Without prejudice to national legislation and/or practice laying down thresholds for the establishing of a representative body, Member States shall provide that employees in undertakings or establishments in which there are no employees' representatives through no fault of their own have the right to elect or appoint members of the special negotiating body.

3. The special negotiating body and the competent organs of the participating companies shall determine, by written agreement, arrangements for the involvement of employees within the SE.
To this end, the competent organs of the participating companies shall inform the special negotiating body of the plan and the actual process of establishing the SE, up to its registration.

4. Subject to paragraph 6, the special negotiating body shall take decisions by an absolute majority of its members, provided that such a majority also represents an absolute majority of the employees. Each member shall have one vote. However, should the result of the negotiations lead to a reduction of participation rights, the majority required for a decision to approve such an agreement shall be the votes of two thirds of the members of the special negotiating body representing at least two thirds of the employees, including the votes of members representing employees employed in at least two Member States,
   - in the case of an SE to be established by way of merger, if participation covers at least 25% of the overall number of employees of the participating companies, or
   - in the case of an SE to be established by way of creating a holding company or forming a subsidiary, if participation covers at least 50% of the overall number of employees of the participating companies.

Reduction of participation rights means a proportion of members of the organs of the SE within the meaning of Article 2 (k), which is lower than the highest proportion existing within the participating companies.

5. For the purpose of the negotiations, the special negotiating body may request experts of its choice, for example representatives of appropriate Community level trade union organisations, to assist it with its work. Such experts may be present at negotiation meetings in an advisory capacity at the request of the special negotiating body, where appropriate to promote coherence and consistency at Community level. The special negotiating body may decide to inform the representatives of appropriate external organisations, including trade unions, of the start of the negotiations.

6. The special negotiating body may decide by the majority set out below not to open negotiations or to terminate negotiations already opened, and to rely on the rules on information and consultation of employees in force in the Member States where the SE has employees. Such a decision shall stop the procedure to conclude the agreement referred to in Article 4. Where such a decision has been taken, none of the provisions of the Annex shall apply.

   The majority required to decide not to open or to terminate negotiations shall be the votes of two thirds of the members representing at least two thirds of the employees, including the votes of members representing employees employed in at least two Member States.

   In the case of an SE established by way of transformation, this paragraph shall not apply if there is participation in the company to be transformed.

   The special negotiating body shall be reconvened on the written request of at least 10% of the employees of the SE, its subsidiaries and establishments, or their representatives, at the earliest two years after the abovementioned decision, unless the parties agree to negotiations being reopened sooner. If the special negotiating body decides to reopen negotiations with the management but no agreement is reached as a result of those negotiations, none of the provisions of the Annex shall apply.

7. Any expenses relating to the functioning of the special negotiating body and, in general, to negotiations shall be borne by the participating companies so as to enable the special negotiating body to carry out its task in an appropriate manner.

   In compliance with this principle, Member States may lay down budgetary rules regarding the operation of the special negotiating body. They may in particular limit the funding to cover one expert only.

Article 4

Content of the agreement

1. The competent organs of the participating companies and the special negotiating body shall negotiate in a spirit of cooperation with a view to reaching an agreement on arrangements for the involvement of the employees within the SE.
2. Without prejudice to the autonomy of the parties, and subject to paragraph 4, the agreement referred to in paragraph 1 between the competent organs of the participating companies and the special negotiating body shall specify:
   (a) the scope of the agreement;
   (b) the composition, number of members and allocation of seats on the representative body which will be the discussion partner of the competent organ of the SE in connection with arrangements for the information and consultation of the employees of the SE and its subsidiaries and establishments;
   (c) the functions and the procedure for the information and consultation of the representative body;
   (d) the frequency of meetings of the representative body;
   (e) the financial and material resources to be allocated to the representative body;
   (f) if, during negotiations, the parties decide to establish one or more information and consultation procedures instead of a representative body, the arrangements for implementing those procedures;
   (g) if during negotiations the parties decide to establish arrangements for participation, the substance of those arrangements including (if applicable) the number of members in the SE's administrative or supervisory body which the employees will be entitled to elect, appoint, recommend or oppose, the procedures as to how these members may be elected, appointed, recommended or opposed by the employees, and their rights;
   (h) the date of entry into force of the agreement and its duration, cases where the agreement should be renegotiated and the procedure for its renegotiation.
3. The agreement shall not, unless provision is made otherwise therein, be subject to the standard rules referred to in the Annex.
4. Without prejudice to Article 13 (3) (a), in the case of an SE established by means of transformation, the agreement shall provide for at least the same level of all elements of employee involvement as the ones existing within the company to be transformed into an SE.

Article 5

Duration of negotiations

1. Negotiations shall commence as soon as the special negotiating body is established and may continue for six months thereafter.
2. The parties may decide, by joint agreement, to extend negotiations beyond the period referred to in paragraph 1, up to a total of one year from the establishment of the special negotiating body.

Article 6

Legislation applicable to the negotiation procedure

Except where otherwise provided in this Directive, the legislation applicable to the negotiation procedure provided for in Articles 3 to 5 shall be the legislation of the Member State in which the registered office of the SE is to be situated.

Article 7

Standard rules

1. In order to achieve the objective described in Article 1, Member States shall, without prejudice to paragraph 3 below, lay down standard rules on employee involvement which must satisfy the provisions set out in the Annex.

   The standard rules as laid down by the legislation of the Member State in which the registered office of the SE is to be situated shall apply from the date of the registration of the SE where either:
   (a) the parties so agree; or
   (b) by the deadline laid down in Article 5, no agreement has been concluded, and:
      - the competent organ of each of the participating companies decides to accept the application of the standard rules in relation to the SE and so to continue with its registration of the SE; and
      - the special negotiating body has not taken the decision provided in Article 3 (6).
2. Moreover, the standard rules fixed by the national legislation of the Member State of registration in accordance with part 3 of the Annex shall apply only:
   (a) in the case of an SE established by transformation, if the rules of a Member State relating to employee participation in the administrative or supervisory body applied to a company transformed into an SE;
   (b) in the case of an SE established by merger:
      - if, before registration of the SE, one or more forms of participation applied in one or more of the participating companies covering at

least 25% of the total number of employees in all the participating companies; or
- if, before registration of the SE, one or more forms of participation applied in one or more of the participating companies covering less than 25% of the total number of employees in all the participating companies and if the special negotiating body so decides;

(c) in the case of an SE established by setting up a holding company or establishing a subsidiary:
- if, before registration of the SE, one or more forms of participation applied in one or more of the participating companies covering at least 50% of the total number of employees in all the participating companies; or
- if, before registration of the SE, one or more forms of participation applied in one or more of the participating companies covering less than 50% of the total number of employees in all the participating companies and if the special negotiating body so decides.

If there was more than one form of participation within the various participating companies, the special negotiating body shall decide which of those forms must be established in the SE. Member States may fix the rules which are applicable in the absence of any decision on the matter for an SE registered in If there was more than one form of participation within the various participating companies, the special their territory. The special negotiating body shall inform the competent organs of the participating companies of any decisions taken pursuant to this paragraph.

3. Member States may provide that the reference provisions in part 3 of the Annex shall not apply in the case provided for in point (b) of paragraph 2.

SECTION III

MISCELLANEOUS PROVISIONS

Article 8

Reservation and confidentiality

1. Member States shall provide that members of the special negotiating body or the representative body, and experts who assist them, are not authorised to reveal any information which as been given to them in confidence.

The same shall apply to employees' representatives in the context of an information and consultation procedure.

This obligation shall continue to apply, wherever the persons referred to may be, even after the expiry of their terms of office.

2. Each Member State shall provide, in specific cases and under the conditions and limits laid down by national legislation, that the supervisory or administrative organ of an SE or of a participating company established in its territory is not obliged to transmit information where its nature is such that, according to objective criteria, to do so would seriously harm the functioning of the SE (or, as the case may be, the participating company) or its subsidiaries and establishments or would be prejudicial to them.

   A Member State may make such dispensation subject to prior administrative or judicial authorisation.
3. Each Member State may lay down particular provisions for SEs in its territory which pursue directly and essentially the aim of ideological guidance with respect to information and the expression of opinions, on condition that, on the date of adoption of this Directive, such provisions already exist in the national legislation.
4. In applying paragraphs 1, 2 and 3, Member States shall make provision for administrative or judicial appeal procedures which the employees' representatives may initiate when the supervisory or administrative organ of an SE or participating company demands confidentiality or does not give information.

   Such procedures may include arrangements designed to protect the confidentiality of the information in question.

Article 9

Operation of the representative body and procedure for the information and consultation of employees

The competent organ of the SE and the representative body shall work together in a spirit of cooperation with due regard for their reciprocal rights and obligations.

The same shall apply to cooperation between the supervisory or administrative organ of the SE and the employees' representatives in conjunction with a procedure for the information and consultation of employees.

Article 10

Protection of employees' representatives

The members of the special negotiating body, the members of the representative body, any employees' representatives exercising functions under the information and consultation procedure and any employees' representatives in the supervisory or administrative organ of an SE who are employees of the SE, its subsidiaries or establishments or of a participating company shall, in the exercise of their functions, enjoy the same protection and guarantees provided for employees' representatives by the national legislation and/or practice in force in their country of employment.

This shall apply in particular to attendance at meetings of the special negotiating body or representative body, any other meeting under the agreement referred to in Article 4 (2) (f) or any meeting of the administrative or supervisory organ, and to the payment of wages for members employed by a participating company or the SE or its subsidiaries or establishments during a period of absence necessary for the performance of their duties.

Article 11

Misuse of procedures

Member States shall take appropriate measures in conformity with Community law with a view to preventing the misuse of an SE for the purpose of depriving employees of rights to employee involvement or withholding such rights.

Article 12

Compliance with this Directive

1. Each Member State shall ensure that the management of establishments of an SE and the supervisory or administrative organs of subsidiaries and of participating companies which are situated within its territory and the employees' representatives or, as the case may be, the employees themselves abide by the obligations laid down by this Directive, regardless of whether or not the SE has its registered office within its territory.
2. Member States shall provide for appropriate measures in the event of failure to comply with this Directive; in particular they shall ensure that administrative or legal procedures are available to enable the obligations deriving from this Directive to be enforced.

Article 13

Link between this Directive and other provisions

1. Where an SE is a Community-scale undertaking or a controlling undertaking of a Community-scale group of undertakings within the meaning of Directive 94/45/EC or of Directive 97/74/EC[6] extending the said Directive

[6] OJ L 10, 16. 1. 1998, p. 22.

to the United Kingdom, the provisions of these Directives and the provisions transposing them into national legislation shall not apply to them or to their subsidiaries.

However, where the special negotiating body decides in accordance with Article 3 (6) not to open negotiations or to terminate negotiations already opened, Directive 94/45/EC or Directive 97/74/EC and the provisions transposing them into national legislation shall apply.

2. Provisions on the participation of employees in company bodies provided for by national legislation and/or practice, other than those implementing this Directive, shall not apply to companies established in accordance with Regulation (EC) No 2157/2001 and covered by this Directive.
3. This Directive shall not prejudice:
   (a) the existing rights to involvement of employees provided for by national legislation and/or practice in the Member States as enjoyed by employees of the SE and its subsidiaries and establishments, other than participation in the bodies of the SE;
   (b) the provisions on participation in the bodies laid down by national legislation and/or practice applicable to the subsidiaries of the SE.
4. In order to preserve the rights referred to in paragraph 3, Member States may take the necessary measures to guarantee that the structures of employee representation in participating companies which will cease to exist as separate legal entities are maintained after the registration of the SE.

Article 14

Final provisions

1. Member States shall adopt the laws, regulations and administrative provisions necessary to comply with this Directive no later than 8 october 2004, or shall ensure by that date at the latest that management and labour introduce the required provisions by way of agreement, the Member States being obliged to take all necessary steps enabling them at all times to guarantee the results imposed by this Directive. They shall forthwith inform the Commission thereof.
2. When Member States adopt these measures, they shall contain a reference to this Directive or shall be accompanied by such reference on the occasion of their official publication. The methods of making such reference shall be laid down by the Member States.

Article 15

Review by the Commission

Not later than 8 october 2007, the Commission shall, in consultation with the Member States and with management and labour at Community level, review the procedures for applying this Directive, with a view to proposing suitable amendments to the Council where necessary.

Article 16

Entry into force

This Directive shall enter into force on the date of its publication in the Official Journal of the European Communities.

Article 16

Addressees

This Directive is addressed to the Member States.

Done at Luxembourg, 8 october 2001

ANNEX

STANDARD RULES

(referred to in Article 7)

Part 1: Composition of the body representative of the employees

In order to achieve the objective described in Article 1, and in the cases referred to in Article 7, a representative body shall be set up in accordance with the following rules:

(a) The representative body shall be composed of employees of the SE and its subsidiaries and establishments elected or appointed from their number by the employees' representatives or, in the absence thereof, by the entire body of employees.

(b) The election or appointment of members of the representative body shall be carried out in accordance with national legislation and/or practice.

Member States shall lay down rules to ensure that the number of members of, and allocation of seats on, the representative body shall be adapted to take account of changes occurring within the SE and its subsidiaries and establishments.

(c) Where its size so warrants, the representative body shall elect a select committee from among its members, comprising at most three members.
(d) The representative body shall adopt its rules of procedure.
(e) The members of the representative body are elected or appointed in proportion to the number of employees employed in each Member State by the participating companies and concerned subsidiaries or establishments, by allocating in respect of a Member State one seat per each portion of employees employed in that Member State which equals 10%, or a fraction thereof, of the number of employees employed by the participating companies and concerned subsidiaries or establishments in all the Member States taken together.
(f) The competent organ of the SE shall be informed of the composition of the representative body.
(g) Four years after the representative body is established, it shall examine whether to open negotiations for the conclusion of the agreement referred to in Articles 4 and 7 or to continue to apply the standard rules adopted in accordance with this Annex.

Articles 3 (4) to (7) and 4 to 6 shall apply, mutatis mutandis, if a decision has been taken to negotiate an agreement according to Article 4, in which case the term "special negotiating body" shall be replaced by 'representative body'. Where, by the deadline by which the negotiations come to an end, no agreement has been concluded, the arrangements initially adopted in accordance with the standard rules shall continue to apply.

Part 2: Standard rules for information and consultation

The competence and powers of the representative body set up in an SE shall be governed by the following rules:

(a) The competence of the representative body shall be limited to questions which concern the SE itself and any of its subsidiaries or establishments situated in another Member State or which exceed the powers of the decision-making organs in a single Member State.
(b) Without prejudice to meetings held pursuant to point (c), the representative body shall have the right to be informed and consulted and, for that purpose, to meet with the competent organ of the SE at least once a year, on the basis of regular reports drawn up by the competent organ, on the pro-

gress of the business of the SE and its prospects. The local managements shall be informed accordingly.

The competent organ of the SE shall provide the representative body with the agenda for meetings of the administrative, or, where appropriate, the management and supervisory organ, and with copies of all documents submitted to the general meeting of its shareholders.

The meeting shall relate in particular to the structure, economic and financial situation, the probable development of the business and of production and sales, the situation and probable trend of employment, investments, and substantial changes concerning organisation, introduction of new working methods or production processes, transfers of production, mergers, cut-backs or closures of undertakings, establishments or important parts thereof, and collective redundancies.

(c) Where there are exceptional circumstances affecting the employees' interests to a considerable extent, particularly in the event of relocations, transfers, the closure of establishments or undertakings or collective redundancies, the representative body shall have the right to be informed. The representative body or, where it so decides, in particular for reasons of urgency, the select committee, shall have the right to meet at its request, the competent organ of the SE or any more appropriate level of management within the SE having its own powers of decision, so as to be informed and consulted on measures significantly affecting employees' interests.

Where the competent organ decides not to act in accordance with the opinion expressed by the representative body, this body shall have the right to a further meeting with the competent organ of the SE with a view to seeking agreement.

In the case of a meeting organised with the select committee, those members of the representative body who represent employees who are directly concerned by the measures in question shall also have the right to participate.

The meetings referred to above shall not affect the prerogatives of the competent organ.

(d) Member States may lay down rules on the chairing of information and consultation meetings.

Before any meeting with the competent organ of the SE, the representative body or the select committee, where necessary enlarged in accordance with the third subparagraph of paragraph (c), shall be entitled to meet without the representatives of the competent organ being present.

(e) Without prejudice to Article 8, the members of the representative body shall inform the representatives of the employees of the SE and of its subsidiaries and establishments of the content and outcome of the information and consultation procedures.

(f) The representative body or the select committee may be assisted by experts of its choice.
(g) Insofar as this is necessary for the fulfilment of their tasks, the members of the representative body shall be entitled to time off for training without loss of wages.
(h) The costs of the representative body shall be borne by the SE, which shall provide the body's members with the financial and material resources needed to enable them to perform their duties in an appropriate manner.

In particular, the SE shall, unless otherwise agreed, bear the cost of organising meetings and providing interpretation facilities and the accommodation and travelling expenses of members of the representative body and the select committee.

In compliance with these principles, the Member States may lay down budgetary rules regarding the operation of the representative body. They may in particular limit funding to cover one expert only.

Part 3: Standard rules for participation

Employee participation in an SE shall be governed by the following provisions:
(a) In the case of an SE established by transformation, if the rules of a Member State relating to employee participation in the administrative or supervisory body applied before registration, all aspects of employee participation shall continue to apply to the SE. Point (b) shall apply mutatis mutandis to that end.
(b) In other cases of the establishing of an SE, the employees of the SE, its subsidiaries and establishments and/or their representative body shall have the right to elect, appoint, recommend or oppose the appointment of a number of members of the administrative or supervisory body of the SE equal to the highest proportion in force in the participating companies concerned before registration of the SE.

If none of the participating companies was governed by participation rules before registration of the SE, the latter shall not be required to establish provisions for employee participation.

The representative body shall decide on the allocation of seats within the administrative or supervisory body among the members representing the employees from the various Member States or on the way in which the SE's employees may recommend or oppose the appointment of the members of these bodies according to the proportion of the SE's employees in each Member State. If the employees of one or more Member States are not covered by this proportional criterion, the representative body shall appoint a member from one of those Member States, in particular the Member State of the SE's registered office where that is appropriate. Each Member State may determine the allocation of the seats it is given within the administrative or supervisory body.

Every member of the administrative body or, where appropriate, the supervisory body of the SE who has been elected, appointed or recommended by the representative body or, depending on the circumstances, by the employees shall be a full member with the same rights and obligations as the members representing the shareholders, including right to vote.

ANNEX IV

Key elements of national implementation measures *

Austria

A. Status of implementation (p. 1)

Drafts for the implementation of the regulation and the directive have been presented at the beginning of february 2004.

B. Formation of the SE

Companies participating in the formation (option of Art. 2 para. 5 Reg.): The option will most likely not be exercised. (p. 2)

I. Merger (p. 15)

Minority Protection: In *general company law* shareholders with a minimum stock of 1% or 70.000 Euro may demand the compensation if the share-exchange ratio does not reflect the value of the shares. For the *formation of an SE* it has been proposed an exit right for the shareholders of the Austrian company if the merger is for the shareholders at the same time a transfer of seat to another member-state.
Opposition by public authority on grounds of public interest (Art. 19 Reg.): Probably no provision.

II. Holding SE (p. 21)

Formalities: Probably some special provisions.
Minority protection: There will probably be no special provision dealing with the protection of objecting minorities.

III. Conversion (p. 15)

Probably some special – rather technical – provisions.

* The following page indications refer to the articles in the main part of the book.

C. Management structure (p. 4, 8)

Two-tier system: Common system in Austria. *Supervisory organ* consisting of at least 3 members – maximum size according to the amount of the share capital.
One-tier system: Not regulated in domestic company law, it will most likely be introduced only for the SE.
Rules common to both systems: The option of Art. 48 para. 2 Reg. will probably be exercised. Legal entities are not allowed to be members of organs.

D. General meeting (p. 9)

Request to convene a general meeting (Art. 55 para. 1 Reg.): Under domestic law: Minority of 5 % of the subscribed capiatal.
Request to put additional items on the agenda of any general meeting (Art. 56 Reg.): Under domestic law: Minority of 5 % of the subscribed capital.
Option of Article 59 para. 2 Reg.: The option will probably not be exercised.

E. Seat of the SE and transfer of Seat (p. 11)

Obligation of locating head office of the SE and its registered office in the same place (Art. 7 second sentence Reg.): The option will probably not be exercised.
Opposition by public authority on grounds of public interest (Art. 8 para. 14 Reg.): Probably no provision.
Protection of minority shareholders (Art. 8 para. 5): Unconditional exit right in return for cash compensation has been proposed.
Protection of creditors (Art. 8 para. 7 Reg.): The option of Art. 8 para. 7, subpara. 2 Reg. will probably be exercised.

F. Involvement of employees (p. 10)

Under domestic law employees have right to appoint 1/3 of the supervisory board

Belgium

A. Status of implementation (p. 24)

No draft yet; expert working group (initiative taken by ministry of justice) studies the necessary implementation measures, report expected by the beginning of the year 2004. Parliament has given the authority to the King to take the necessary steps to implement the regulation.

B. Formation of the SE (p. 25)

Companies participating in the formation (option of Art. 2 para. 5 Reg.): The option will probably be exercised.

I. Merger (p. 28)

Minority protection: In *General company law* a qualified majority of votes is provided for; no exit right. With regard to the *formation of an SE* there will probably be no exit rights.
Opposition by public authority on grounds of public interest (Art. 19 Reg.): Most likely no provision.

II. Holding SE (p. 30)

Formalities: Probably no specific provisions. Publication according to general company law.
Minority protection: Probably no specific provisions.

III. Conversion (p. 30)

Probably no specific provisions.

C. Management structure (p. 31)

Two-tier system: Not regulated in domestic company law. It will most likely be introduced for the SE.
One-tier system: Common system in Belgium. From September 1st, 2002 Belgian companies may opt for modified one-tier board structure with a board of directors and a management board.
Option of Art. 43 para. 1, second sentence Reg. will probably be exercised.
Rules common to both systems: Legal entities may be members of organs; natural person who represents a legal entity must be an employee, board member or shareholder of the entity he represents.

D. General meeting (p. 37)

Request to convene a general meeting (Art. 55 para. 1 Reg.): No specific provisions (under domestic law minority of 20% of the subscribed capital is required).
Request to put additional items on the agenda of any general meeting (Art. 56 Reg.): No special provisions (under domestic law minority of 20% of the subscribed capital is required).
Option of Article 59 para. 2 Reg.: The option will probably not be exercised.

E. Seat of the SE and transfer of seat (p. 38)

Obligation of locating head office of the SE and its registered office in the same Place (Art. 7 second sentence Reg.): The option will probably not be exercised.

Opposition by public authority on grounds of public interest (Art. 8 para. 14 Reg.): The granting of the opposition right is not unlikely.
Protection of minority shareholders (Art. 8 para. 5): It has been proposed in the legal doctrine to provide for the majority of 80% of votes to approve the transfer.
Protection of creditors (Art. 8 para. 7 Reg.): Probably protective measures similar to the ones in case of a capital reduction or a merger.

F. **Involvement of employees** (p. 43)

Under general company law there is no system of co-determination; work council is a consultative body representing employees.

Czech Republic

A. **Status of implementation** (p. 48)

Draft

B. **Formation of the SE** (p. 49)

Companies participating in the formation (option of Art. 2 para. 5 Reg.): The option will probably be exercised.

I. **Merger** (p. 51)

Minority protection: Under *General company law* minority shareholders receive cash compensation in case of inappropriate share-exchange ratio. The successor company should be bound to buy out its shares issued in exchange for the shares of the merging companies from shareholders specified by the law, if the quality of the shares in the successor company is in a specified way lower than the quality of the shares in the original companies (e.g. listed shares exchanged for unlisted etc.). For the *formation of an SE* these national provisions should be applicable accordingly.
Opposition by public authority on grounds of public interest (Art. 19 Reg.): The option will probably be exercised.

II. **Holding SE** (p. 55)

Formalities: Probably no special provisions.
Minority Protection: Reference to the same means of protection as in the case of the establishment by a merger (see above). However, the solution might be re-considered for reasons of suboptimal applicability; other solutions are being discussed.

III. Conversion

Probably no special provisions.

C. Management structure (p. 60)

Two-tier system: Common system in Czech Republic. With regard to the *management organ* the option of Art. 39 para. 2 subpara. 2 Reg. will most likely be exercised. With regard to the *supervisory organ* the option of Art. 41 para. 3, second sentence Reg. will most likely be exercised.
One-tier system: Not regulated in domestic company law, it will be introduced for the SE: Administrative organ to be composed of between three and eighteen natural persons. The management functions are entrusted with the chairman of the administrative board, if he also acts as a general manager, or a general manager, who is not member of the administrative board. Upon the initiative of the general manager the administrative board may appoint delegate managers to assist the general manager.
Rules common to both systems: The option of Art. 48 para. 2 Reg. will probably not be exercised.

D. General meeting (p. 64)

Request to convene a general meeting (Art. 55 para. 1 Reg.): The right will be given to minority representing 5 % of subscribed capital not exeeding 100 million CZK (approx. 3,2 million €) and in other cases to minority representing 3 % of subscribed capital.
Request to put additional items in the agenda of any general meeting (Art. 56 Reg.): See previous point.
Option of Article 59 para. 2 Reg.: The option will probably not be exercised.

E. Seat of the SE and transfer of seat (p. 60)

Obligation of locating head office of the SE and its registered office at the same place (Art. 7 second sentence Reg.): The option will probably be exercised.
Opposition by public authority on grounds of public interest (Art. 8 para. 14 Reg.): The option will probably be exercised.
Protection of minority shareholders (Art. 8 para. 5 Reg.): National provisions concerning the protection of shareholders opposing merger should be applicable accordingly (see above).
Protection of creditors (Art. 8 para. 7 Reg.): National provisions concerning the protection of creditors in case of merger should be applicable accordingly.

F. **Involvement of employees** (p. 64)

Management or administrative organ should be obliged to amend the statutes of the SE without any further decision from the general meeting, if any of its provisions conflict with arrangements for employee involvement (option provided for in Art. 12 para. 4, second subpara. Reg.). Under domestic law employees have right to appoint 1/3 of the supervisory board in public companies employing at least 50 employees.

Denmark

A. **Status of implementation** (p. 72)

Official draft for an SE Act introduced before the Parliament on January 28th 2004 (L 142, available at: www.folketinget.dk).

B. **Formation of the SE** (p. 73)

Companies participating in the formation (option of Art. 2 para. 5 Reg.): The option is exercised.

I. **Merger** (p. 74)

Minority protection: Under *General company law* there are no specific provisions. If an SE is formed by merger, shareholders who have opposed the merger may require the company to buy their shares (Draft, Aricle 5).
Opposition by public authority on grounds of public interest (Art. 19 Reg.): Probably no provision.

II. **Holding SE** (p. 74)

Formalities: No specific provisions.
Minority Protection: No specific provisions.

III. **Conversion** (p. 74)

No specific provisions.

C. **Management structure** (p. 74)

Two-tier system: Not regulated in general company law. Special regulation will be introduced for the SE (Draft, Article 8–10).
One-tier system: The Danish (Scandinavian) management system is considered to be a one-tier system with regard to the SE-Reg. In a Danish PLC at

least one managing director and three members of the supervisory board must be appointed.

D. General meeting (p. 75)

Request to convene a general meeting (Art. 55 para. 1 Reg.): Under domestic law: minority of 10 % of the subscribed capital.
Request to put additional items in the agenda of any general meeting (Art. 56 Reg.): Under domestic law: any shareholder; the same provision will be introduced for the SE.
Option of Art. 59 para. 2 Reg.: The option is not exercised.

E. Seat of the SE and transfer of seat (p. 74)

Obligation of locating head office of the SE and its registered office at the same place (Art. 7 second sentence Reg.): Head office must be located at the same place as the registered office of the SE (Draft, Article 3).
Opposition by public authority on grounds of public interest (Art. 8 para. 14 Reg.): Not exercised.
Protection of minority shareholders (Art. 8 para. 5): Shareholders who have opposed the transfer of seat may require that the SE buy their shares (Draft, Article 6 para. 1).
Protection of creditors (Art. 8 para. 7 Reg.): No specific provisions.

F. Involvement of employees (p. 76)

Under domestic law two or more members of the board ma be appointed by the employees in companies with at least 35 employees.

France

A. Status of implementation (p. 77)

Several expert groups, one of them chaired by Senators *Branger* and *Hyest* (referred to as "proposal Branger"), another chaired by Senator *Marini* (referred to as "proposal Marini").

B. Formation of the SE (p. 87)

Proposal Marini contains provisions with regard to publication of the formation plan, issuance of certificate attesting the completion of the pre-merger acts and formalities, registration of the new SE. Proposal Branger in favour of allowing companies the head office of which is not in the Community to participate in the formation of an SE (option of Art. 2 para. 5).

Minority protection: Application of national law should be sufficient, according to proposal Branger, who, however, provides for possibility of having an expert opinion in case of irregularities in the case of the formation of a holding. Proposal Branger requires majority of extraordinary general meeting for resolving on transformation to an SE.

C. **Management structure** (p. 99)

National law allows the choice between one-tier and two-tier system. Therefore few rules needed for implementation of the SE. Proposal Branger fixes maximum number of supervisory organ at 18 and regulates the adoption of categories of transactions which require prior authorisation by supervisory organ or express decision by administrative organ.

D. **General meeting** (p. 102)

According to both proposals, *first general meeting* may be held at any time in the 18 months following the SE's incorporation.

E. **Statutes of an SE** (p. 85)

Interpretation of the regulation by proposal Marini in a way allowing to reduce the scope of the regulation and to offer contractual freedom to SEs which are not listed. Thereby the statutes of an SE which is *not listed* might contain the following provisions: requirement of prior approval by the company to transfer of shares; requirement of shareholder to sell his shares; obligation of shareholders to notify change of control to the company. Proposal Branger provides for simplified procedure of calling a general meeting in case the statutes are in conflict with the arrangements for employee involvement.

F. **Transfer of seat** (p. 103)

Proposal Branger against making use of option of Art. 7 to have head office and registered office in the same place. According to the proposal Marini, *creditors* may oppose the transfer. Opposition may lead to a court order; as long as company does not comply with the court order, it may not invoke the transfer against the creditor. Creditor opposition, however, does not prevent the transfer. Proposal Branger pleads for additional disclosure, in particular notification of BODACC.

G. **Involvement of Employees** (p. 104)

Proposal Branger on implementation of Directive, whereas proposal Marini does not cover the Directive.

Germany

A. Status of implementation

Draft on the company law implementation, no draft yet on employee involvement

B. Formation of the SE (p. 110)

Companies participating in the formation (option of Art. 2 para. 5 Reg.): The option will most likely not be exercised.

I. Merger (p. 111)

Minority Protection: Under *General company law* minority shareholders have an exit right in return for cash compensation if legal form changes in result of the merger. In addition they have the right to challenge the share-exchange ratio in a special court procedure which is not blocking the accomplishment of the merger. For the *formation of SE* the draft proposes the same procedure for challenging the share-exchange ratio as well as an exit right in return for cash compensation; current discussion is in favor of exit right restricted to cases where the future SE has its seat outside Germany.
Opposition by public authority on grounds of public interest (Art. 19 Reg.): Most likely no provision.

II. Holding SE (p. 115)

Formalities: No specific provision; publication according to general company law.
Minority Protection: Draft proposes same procedure for challenging the share-exchange ratio as in case of the merger as well as exit right in return for cash compensation; current discussion is in favor of exit right restricted to cases where future SE has its seat outside Germany or to have even no exit right at all.

III. Conversion

No specific provision; publication according to general company law.

C. Management structure (p. 118)

Two-tier system: Common system in Germany. With regard to the management organ, at least two members must be appointed in a SE if subscribed capital exceeds 3 Millions €. In event of vacancy members of the supervisory organ may act as member of the management organ for a maximum

period of one year. With regard to the *supervisory organ*, at least three members must be appointed. The number of members must be divisible through three. The option of Art. 41 para. 3 second sentence Reg. will be exercised.
One-tier system: No provisions in general company law. It will be introduced for the SE with an administrative organ consisting of one or more persons as well as one or more managing directors to be appointed by the administrative organ from within or/and outside the organ.
Rules common to both systems: The option of Art. 48 para. 1 subpara. 2 Reg. will be exercised.

D. **General meeting** (p. 127)

Request to convene a general meeting (Art. 55 para. 1 Reg.): The right will be given to the minority representing 5% of the subscribed capital.
Request to put additional items on the agenda of any general meeting (Art. 56 Reg.): The right will be given to the minority representing 5% of the subscribed capital.
Option of Article 59 para. 2 Reg.: The option will not be exercised.

E. **Seat of the SE and transfer of seat** (p. 127)

Obligation of locating head office of the SE and its registered office in the same Place (Art. 7 second sentence Reg.): The option will be exercised.
Opposition by public authority on grounds of public interest (Art. 8 para. 14 Reg.): The option will not be exercised.
Protection of minority shareholders (Art. 8 para. 5): Exit right in return for cash compensation.
Protection of creditors (Art. 8 para. 7 Reg.): Right to demand security provided that they can credibly establish that the satisfaction of their claims is endangered by the transfer, the transfer itself, however, is not regarded as being dangerous to creditors.

F. **Involvement of employees** (p. 129)

Under domestic law: Representation of employees in supervisory board if the company has at least 500 employees. It is expected that the same rule will apply to administrative organ in monistic system of SE.

Greece

A. Status of implementation

No draft yet.

B. Formation (p. 133)

Companies participating in the formation (option of Art. 2 para. 5 Reg.): The option will probably not be exercised.

I. Merger (p. 134)

Minority protection: In *general company law* an unfair exchange ratio may cause the nullity of the merger. For the *formation of SE* an exit right or right to review the exchange ratio are the possible measures to be introduced.

II. Holding SE (p. 135)

Minority protection: Exit right or right to review the exchange ratio are the possible measures.

III. Conversion (p. 135)

Probably no special provisions.

C. Management structure (p. 135)

Two-tier system: Not known in *general company law*; may be introduced for the SE.
One-tier system: Common system in Greece; board of directors consisting of at least three members, appointed and removed *ad nutum* by the general meeting; empowered by the statues, the board can entrust certain of its functions to a managing director.
Rules common to both systems: Legal entities may be members of the board; general diligence rule of liability.

D. General meeting (p. 136)

Request to convene a general meeting (Art. 55 para 1 Reg.): Under domestic law: Minority of 5 % of the subscribed capital.
Request to put additional items on the agenda of any general meeting (Art. 56 Reg): Under domestic law: Minority of 5 % of the subscribed capital.

E. Involvement of employees (p. 138)

Domestic law does not provide for mandatory co-determination.

Hungary

A. Status of implementation

No draft yet.

B. Formation of the SE (p. 140)

I. Merger (p. 140)

Minority protection (p. 150): *General company law* provides for the right to exit in return for the cash compensation calculated in the statutory determined way. For the *formation of the SE* the option of Art. 24 para. 2 will probably not be exercised; exit right according to general company law.
Opposition by public authority on grounds of public interest (Art. 19 Reg.): Probably no provision.

II. Holding SE (p. 147)

Minority protection (p. 150): An exit right for the shareholders of the company with seat in Hungary according to general company law has been proposed.

III. Conversion (p. 149)

Probably no special provisions.

C. Management structure (p. 152)

Two-tier system: Common system in Hungary. For the *management organ* the option of Art. 39 para. 2 subpara. 2 reg. will probably be exercised. For the *supervisory organ* it is proposed to exercise the option of Art. 40 para. 3 second sentence.
One-tier system: Not regulated in domestic company law; it will probably be introduced for the SE.
Rules common to both systems: Legal entities are not allowed to be members of organs.

D. General meeting (p. 150)

Request to convene a general meeting (Art. 55 para 1 Reg.): Under domestic law: Minority of 10 % of the subscribed capital minority representing 5 % of the subscribed capital, if neither of the shareholders of a public company has more than 10 % of the votes or it is excluded by the provisions of the statutes to have more than 10 % of the votes.

Request to put additional items on the agenda of any general meeting (Art. 56 Reg): Under domestic law: Minority of 10% of the subscribed capital minority representing 5% of the subscribed capital, if neither of the shareholders of a public company has more than 10% of the votes or it is excluded by the provisions of the statutes to have more than 10% of the votes.
Option of Art. 59 para. 2 Reg. (simple majority of votes for amendment of an SE's statutes): The option will probably not be exercised.

E. Seat of the SE and transfer of seat

Protection of minority shareholders (Art. 8 para. 5 Reg.): An exit right for the shareholders of the company with seat in Hungary according to general company law has been proposed (p. 151).
Protection of creditors (Art. 8 para. 7 Reg.): A right to demand security according to general company law has been proposed (p. 151).

F. Involvement of employees (p. 155)

Under *domestic law* employees have right to appoint 1/3 of the supervisory board in companies with more than 200 employees.

Ireland

A. Status of implementation

No draft yet.

B. Formation of the SE (p. 160)

Minority protection in case of merger: In *general company law* a merger occurring by means of the S. 260 reconstruction does not bind dissenting shareholders. A buy-out usually results. The Minister has a power under Mergers, Takeovers and Monopolies (Control) Act 1978 to make a prohibition order on quite broad grounds including the likely effect on shareholders.

C. Management structure (p. 162)

Two-tier system: Not regulated in domestic company law.
One-tier system: Common system in Ireland.
Rules common to both systems: Legal entities are not allowed to be board members.

D. General meeting

Request to convene a general meeting (Art. 55 para. 1 Reg.): Under domestic law: Members holding not less than 10% of the paid up share capital with voting rights may compel the holding of a general meeting.
Request to put additional items in the agenda of any general meeting (Art. 56 Reg.): Under domestic law: Subject to the differing notice requirements for different species of resolutions, the request of the holders of 10% of the paid up share capital with voting rights for a general meeting may logically be met by the addition of the relevant matter(s) to the agenda of an already planned meeting.

E. Seat of the SE and transfer of seat (p. 163)

Obligation of locating head office of the SE and its registered office at the same place (Art. 7 second sentence Reg.): The option will most likely not be exercised.
Protection of minority shareholders (Art. 8 para. 5): Under domestic law: General minority petition procedure.
Protection of creditors (Art. 8 para. 7 Reg.): Special provisions will probably be introduced.

F. Involvement of employees (p. 165)

Under domestic law co-determination is mandatory in state-owned commercial companies. Apart from this, employees have no co-determination rights.

Italy

A. Status of implementation

No draft yet.

B. Formation of the SE (p. 173)

Companies participating in the formation (option of Art. 2 para. 5 Reg.): The option will probably be exercised.

I. Merger (p. 177)

Minority protection: General company law provides for an exit right of shareholders not approving the merger, following the general principle provided in the case of mergers implying a conversion.

III. Holding SE (p. 180)

Probably no additional formalities.
Minority protection: exit right for the minority shareholders on the assumption that the Italien company enters a group controlled by the SE.

IV. Conversion (p. 181)

Probably no special provisions. Exit right of minority shareholders as provided by general company law.

C. Management structure (p. 182)

Two-tier system: Under domestic law coming in force in 2004 the system may be chosen by all companies. *Management Organ:* The option of Art. 39 para. 2 subpara.2 Reg. will most likely be exercised. The structure of the SE where both the members of the management organ and of the supervisory organ are elected by the general meeting is similar to the traditional structure of the S.p.A. *Supervisory organ:* The option of Art. 41 para. 3, second sentence Reg. will probably be exercised as the same regulation is provided for in the Italian law.
One-tier system: Under domestic law: companies may choose between "traditional" one-tier system (with board of directors and board of statutory auditors) and one-tier system in its strict sense (board of directors with executive and not executive directors).
Rules common to both systems: The option of Art. 48 para. 2 Reg. will probably not be exercised.

D. General Meeting (p. 184)

Request to convene a general meeting (Art. 55 para. 1 Reg.): Probably the option will not be exercised because general company law provides the percentage of 10% as in the Reg.
Request to put additional items on the agenda of any general meeting (Art. 56 Reg.): Nothing provided for in general company law. Terms and procedures will be probably remitted to the statutes.
Option of Art. 59 para. 2 Reg. (simple majority of votes for amendments of an SE's statutes): The option will probably be exercised because the general company law provides quorums lower than the quroms provided in para. 2.

E. Seat of the SE and Transfer of Seat (p. 193)

Obligation of locating head office of the SE and its registered office in the same place (Art. 7 second sentence Reg.): Probably no specific provisions.

Opposition by public authority on grounds of public interest (Art. 8 para. 14 Reg.): The option will probably be exercised.
Protection of minority shareholders (Art. 8 para. 5): National provisions ensuring exit rights for shareholders opposing a transfer abroad should be applicable.
Protection of creditors (Art. 8 para. 7 Reg.): National provisions do not protect private crediters in case of transfer of seat.

F. **Involvement of employees** (p. 197)

Domestic law: no co-determination is provided for.

The Netherlands

A. **Status of implementation** (p. 200)

Legislative proposals concerning the Regulation and the Directive introduced in Parliament (November 2003).

B. **Formation of the SE** (p. 201)

Companies participating in the formation (option of Art. 2 para. 5 Reg.): The option will most likely be exercised.

I. **Merger** (p. 203)

Minority protection: No particular rules in *general company law*. For the *formation of the SE* no particular minority protection rules are proposed.
Opposition by public authority on grounds of public interest (Art. 19 Reg.): A right of opposition by the Minister of Justice is proposed.

II. **Holding** (p. 209)

Formalities: It is proposed that the draft terms and the auditor's report are to be filed at the commercial register at least one month prior to the general meeting resolving on the formation of a holding SE and that the filing be announced in a national newspaper.
No particular *minority protection rules* are proposed.

III. **Conversion** (p. 213)

It is proposed that the draft terms of conversion including the report of the management organ are to be filed at the commercial register and that the filing is to be announced in a national newspaper.

C. Management structure

Two-tier system: Common system in the Netherlands; mandatory for "large companies". For the *management organ* it is proposed to exercise the authorisation of art. 39 para. 2, second sentence Reg.. Consequently, the general meeting may appoint members of the management organ if the statutes so determine. Otherwise: appointment by the supervisory organ. It is proposed not to exercise the option of art. 48 para. 2 Reg. (list of categories of transactions which require the approval of the supervisory organ).

One-tier system: In *domestic law* available only for small companies and international holding companies (management organ without supervisory organ). The proposed Implementation Act contains scanty provisions on this subject, which concern the minimum number of members (three) and the requirement that all "non-executives" be natural persons.

Rules common to both systems: It is proposed to allow legal entities to be members of the management organ or executive members (but not non-executive members) of the administrative organ.

D. General meeting

Request to convene a general meeting (Art. 55 para. 1 Reg.): Under *domestic law*: minority of 10 % of the subscribed capital.

Request to put additional items on the agenda of any general meeting (Art. 56 Reg.): Currently no provisions under domestic law (but it is proposed to introduce a right to put items on the agenda for a minority holding at least 1% of subscribed capital or shares having a value of at least 50 million Euro).

Option of Article 59 para. 2 Reg. (simple majority of votes for amendment of an SE's statutes): It is proposed that the option be exercised.

E. Seat of the SE and transfer of seat (p. 227)

Obligation of locating head office of the SE and its registered office in the same place (Art. 7 second sentence Reg.): The option will most likely not be exercised.

Opposition by public authority on grounds of public interest (Art. 8 para. 14 Reg.): It is proposed that the Minister of Justice will have the right to oppose the transfer on grounds of public interest within two months after publication of the transfer.

Protection of minority shareholders (Art. 8 para. 5): No specific provisions were proposed.

Protection of creditors (Art. 8 para. 7 Reg.): It is proposed that creditors of the SE may oppose the transfer of seat within a period of two months after publication of the transfer proposal. The SE has to give any opposing creditor security or other guarantees to meet its liabilities, on penalty of validating the opposition, unless the creditor already has received sufficient guarantee or the financial position of the SE offers sufficient security that the SE will be able to meet its liabilities.

F. **Involvement of employees** (p. 234)

Domestic law provides for co-determination in "large companies" ("large company regime"). The proposed Dutch standard rules leave the choice of the applicable employee participation regime to the special negotiation group in the event of the formation of an SE by way of merger, formation of a holding SE or of a subsidiary. If no decision is taken, a system giving the employees representatives a right of recommendation and opposition with respect to members of the relevant company organ shall apply, *provided* that one or more companies forming the SE had been subject to the large company regime prior to the formation. If, however, no participating company had been subject to the large company regime, the (foreign) employee participation regime rendering the employees the highest number of appointment or recommendation rights shall apply to the SE.

Poland

A. **Status of implementation** (p. 247)

No draft yet.

B. **Formation of the SE** (p. 254)

Companies participating in the formation (option of Art. 2 para. 5 Reg.): The option of Art. 2 para. 5 Reg will probably be exercised.

I. **Merger** (p. 254)

Minority protection: In *general company law* no particular minority protection rules are provided for. The challenge of the merger decision only for the reason of an alleged unfair share exchange ratio is not possible. For the *formation of the SE* an exit right for the shareholders of the Polish company will probably be introduced if the SE shall have its seat in other member state.
Opposition by public authority on grounds of public interest (Art. 19 Reg.): Probably a right to oppose if a Polish financial institution participates in the merger and an SE shall have its seat outside Poland.

II. **Holding SE** (p. 256)

Probably no additional formalities and no minority and creditors protection rules.

III. **Conversion** (p. 257)

Probably no special provisions.

C. **Management structure** (p. 258)

Two-tier system: Common system in Poland. The option of Art. 39 para. 2 subpara. 2 Reg. (appointment and removal of management organ' members also by the general meeting) will probably be exercised. The option of Art. 41 para. 3 second sentence Reg. will probably be exercised in a limited way.
One-tier system: Not regulated in domestic company law, it will probably be introduced for the SE.
Rules common to both systems: Legal entities are not allowed to be members of organs.

D. **General meeting** (p. 263)

Request to convene a general meeting (Art. 55 para. 1 Reg.): Under *domestic law:* Minority of 10 % of the subscribed capital.
Request to put additional items on the agenda of any general meeting (Art. 56 Reg.): Under *domestic law*: Minority of 10 % of the subscribed capital.
Option of Article 59 para. 2 Reg. (simple majority of votes for amendment of an SE's statutes): The option will probably not be exercised.

E. **Seat of the SE and transfer of seat** (p. 249)

Obligation of locating head office of the SE and its registered office in the same place (Art. 7 second sentence Reg.): The option will probably not be exercised.
Opposition by public authority on the grounds of public interest (Art. 8 para. 14 Reg.): Probably a right to oppose if the SE is a financial institution.
Protection of minority shareholders (Art. 8 para. 5): It has been proposed an exit right in return for cash compensation for shareholders who voted against the transfer of seat.
Protection of creditors (Art. 8 para. 7 Reg.): Probably no special provisions.

F. **Involvement of employees** (p. 264)

Under domestic law there is no mandatory co-determination except state-owned commercial companies.

Portugal

A. Status of implementation (p. 269)

No draft yet.

B. Formation of the SE (p. 273, 276)
Merger

Minority Protection: In *general company law:* An exit right only if provided for by another legal rule or by the statutes of the company.
Creditor Protection: In *general company law:* Right to oppose the merger; may be removed by depositing the amounts due to the opposing persons.

C. Management structure (p. 271, 275)

Two-tier system: May be chosen by a company according to domestic law; rare in practice.
One-tier system: Common system in Portugal.
Rules common to both systems: Legal entities may be elected members of management and administrative organ, although they must designate individuals for those positions.

D. General meeting (p. 274)

Request to convene a general meeting (Art. 55 para. 1 Reg.): Under *domestic law*: Minority of 5% of the subscribed capital.
Request to put additional items on the agenda of any general meeting (Art. 56 Reg.): Under *domestic law*: Minority of 5% of the subscribed capital.

E. Involvement of employees (p. 278)

Under *domestic law* co-determination is mandatory in state-owned companies and left to private autonomy in the others.

Spain

A. Status of implementation (p. 279)

Draft.

B. Formation of the SE (p. 281)

Companies participating in the formation (option of Art. 2 para. 5 Reg.): The option will most likely be exercised.

I. **Merger** (p. 282)

Minority protection: No special provisions in *general company law*. For the *formation of SE* an exit right in return for cash compensation has been proposed if the SE should have its registered office outside Spain.
Opposition by public authority on grounds of public interest (Art. 19 Reg.): A right of opposition by the government if SE`s registered office should be outside Spain.

II. **Holding SE** (p. 284)

Formalities: Publication of draft terms in the Official Journal.
Minority protection: Shareholders of non-listed promoting companies who oppose the formation of the holding SE will probably have an exit right in return for cash compensation. The right may be exercised within a period of two years.

III. **Conversion** (p. 285)

Publication of draft terms.

C. **Management structure** (p. 286)

Two-tier system: Not regulated in domestic company law. It will most likely be introduced for the SE. No special provisions concerning the number of member of *management* and *supervisory organ* of the SE are provided for. In event of vacancy members of the supervisory organ of the SE may act as member of its management organ for a maximum period of one year. The option of Art. 48 para. 1 subpara. 2 Reg. will probably be exercised.
One-tier system: Common system in Spain.
Rules common to both systems: Legal entities may be members of organs. It should be introduced the possibility to challenge resolutions of the management organ and supervisory organ by organ members or shareholders with at least 5 % of the subscribed capital. General diligence rule of liability.

D. **General meeting** (p. 289)

Request to convene a general meeting (Art. 55 para. 1 Reg.): The right will most likely be given to the minority representing 5 % of the subscribed capital.
Request to put additional items on the agenda of any general meeting (Art. 56 Reg.): The right will most likely be given to the minority representing 5 % of the subscribed capital.

Option of Article 59 para. 2 Reg. (simple majority of votes for amendment of an SE's statutes): The option will probably not be exercised.

E. Seat of the SE and transfer of seat (p. 290)

Obligation of locating head office of the SE and its registered office in the same place (Art. 7 second sentence Reg.): The option will probably not be exercised.
Opposition by public authority on grounds of public interest (Art. 8 para. 14 Reg.): Right of opposition by the government or the financial supervisory authority.
Protection of minority shareholders (Art. 8 para. 5): Exit right in return for cash compensation will probably be introduced.
Protection of creditors (Art. 8 para. 7 Reg.): Creditors may oppose the transfer but opposition can be put aside if company grants sufficient guarantee.

E. Involvement of employees (p. 291)

Not yet included in the draft. Under general *company law* there are no rules on co-determination.

Sweden

A. Status of implementation (p. 293)

Memorandum (published January 2003)

B. Formation of the SE (p. 295)

Companies participating in the formation (option of Art. 2 para. 5 Reg.): The option will most likely be exercised.

I. Merger (p. 296, 299)

Minority protection: In *general company law* no particular rules are provided for. Also for the *formation of the SE* no particular minority protection rules have been proposed.
Opposition by public authority on grounds of public interest (Art. 19 Reg.): The supervisory authority (*Finanzinspektionen*) should be allowed to oppose the merger, if a Swedish financial institution participates in the merger.

II. Holding SE (p. 295, 299)

Probably no additional formalities and no minority and creditors protection rules.

IV. Conversion (p. 295)

No specific provisions.

C. Management structure (p. 304)

Two-tier system: Not regulated in domestic company law. It will most likely be introduced for the SE. All Swedish legislation concerning the administrative board and its members should apply to the *management organ* of the SE. The management organ shall be appointed and removed by the supervisory organ.
Option of Art. 39 para. 2 SE-Reg. (appointment and removal of management organ' members also by the general meeting) will not be exercised.
The draft lists a number of provisions of the domestic law concerning the administrative board and its members, which shall apply accordingly to the *supervisory organ* of the SE.
One-tier system: Common system in Sweden. Option of Art. 43 para. 1, second sentence Reg. (responsibility of a managing director for the day-to-day management) will be exercised.
Rules common to both systems: Legal entities may not be members of organs.

D. General meeting (p. 307)

Request to convene a general meeting (Art. 55 para. 1 Reg.): No specific provisions.
Request to put additional items on the agenda of any general meeting (Art. 56 Reg.): No specific provisions.
Option of Article 59 para. 2 Reg. (simple majority of votes for amendment of an SE's statutes): The option will not be exercised.

E. Seat of the SE and transfer of seat (p. 301)

Obligation of locating head office of the SE and its registered office in the same place (Art. 7 second sentence Reg.): The option will not be exercised.
Opposition by public authority on the grounds of public interest (Art. 8 para. 14 Reg.): The supervisory authority (*Finanzinspektionen*) should be allowed to oppose the transfer if the SE is a financial institution.
Protection of minority shareholders (Art. 8 para. 5): No specific provisions.
Protection of creditors (Art. 8 para. 7 Reg.): Creditors who object the transfer are to be paid or granted satisfactory security. No evidence as to their potential deteriorated position due to the transfer of the seat of the SE is necessary.

F. Involvement of employees (p. 308)

Not yet included in the memorandum. *National law* provides for co-determination – employee representatives in the administrative organ are to be appointed by the local labour unions.

United Kingdom

A. Status of implementation (p. 317)

Official draft.

B. Formation of the SE (p. 318)

Companies participating in the formation (option of Art. 2 para. 5 Reg.): The option should not be exercised.

II. Merger

Minority protection: No special rules are proposed.
Opposition by public authority on grounds of public interest (Art. 19 Reg.): Secretary of State for Trade and Industry may oppose the merger on public interest grounds.

II. Holding SE

Probably no special provisions.

III. Conversion

Probably no special provisions.

C. Management structure (p. 320)

Two-tier system: Possible under domestic law although there are no specific provisions relating to it; very rare in practice. For the SE only few provisions should be introduced:
- the management organ and the supervisory organ should each have a minimum of one member
- the statutes may permit the member or members of the management organ to be appointed and removed by the general meeting.

One-tier system: Common system in Great Britain. For the SE only one provision concerning the minimum number of the members of the administrative organ (two).
Rules common to both systems: Legal entities may be members of the board.

D. General meeting

Option of Art. 54 para. 1 Reg. (the first general meeting may be held at any time in the eighteen months following an SE's incorporation) should be exercised.

E. Seat of the SE and transfer of seat (p. 319)

Obligation of locating head office of the SE and its registered office in the same place (Art. 7 second sentence Reg.): The option will not be exercised.
Additional publication requirements (Art. 8 para. 2 Reg.):
- notification of shareholders and creditors, at least one month ahead of the general meeting, of the opportunity of examining, and obtaining free of charge, the transfer proposal and report;
- requirements of notification of the transfer proposal on letters, documents, invoices, etc. that the SE issues subsequent to the publication of the proposal

Opposition by public authority on the grounds of public interest (Art. 8 para. 14 Reg.): Secretary of State for Trade and Industry may oppose the transfer on public interest grounds.
Protection of minority shareholders (Art. 8 para. 5): No provisions.
Protection of creditors (Art. 8 para. 7 Reg.): The option of Art. 8 para. 7 subara 2 (extension of protection to liabilities incurred before transfer) should be exercised.

F. Involvement of employees (p. 321)

Domestic law does not provide for mandatory co-determination. Detailed regulation for the SE:
Appointment of a Special Negotiating Body: Combination of election by ballot and appointment by any existing employee representative body.
Option of Art. 7 para. 3 Directive (Exclusion of the application of the Part 3 of the Annex if, in case of the merger to the SE, participation rules applied only on 25% of the employees of the participating companies): The option will not be exercised.
Standard rules on employee involvement: "Copy out" approach to Part 3 of the Annex of the Directive.
Compliance and Enforcement: Complaints about alleged breaches of the employee involvement rights by the competent organ of a participating company or the SE may be brought to the Central Arbitration Committee. If a complaint is upheld, the complainant may apply to the Employment Appeal Tribunal in Great Britain for a penalty to be imposed on the company.

Option of Art. 14 para. 2 Reg. (authorisation of the management or administrative organ of an SE to amend statutes where in conflict with employees involvement arrangements): The option should be exercised.

www.ingramcontent.com/pod-product-compliance
Lightning Source LLC
Chambersburg PA
CBHW071329230926
51849CB00002B/348
9783899490961